THE RELATION BETWEEN

THE HOLY SCRIPTURES

AND SOME PARTS OF

GEOLOGICAL SCIENCE.

There is a knowledge which creates doubts that nothing but a larger knowledge can satisfy; and he who stops in the difficulty will be perplexed and uncomfortable for life.

Mr. Sharon Turner.

Philadelphia:
Deacon & Peterson, Printers, 66 South Third Street.

Alpha Nu society

7 — 66

THE RELATION

BETWEEN

THE HOLY SCRIPTURES

AND SOME PARTS OF

GEOLOGICAL SCIENCE.

BY

JOHN PYE SMITH, D.D. LL.D. F.R.S. & F.G.S.

DIVINITY TUTOR IN THE PROTESTANT DISSENTING COLLEGE AT HOMERTON; MEMBER OF THE PHILOLOGICAL, ETHNOLOGICAL, MICROSCOPICAL, AND PALÆONTOLOGICAL SOCIETIES; AND HONORARY MEMBER OF THE NATURAL HISTORY SOCIETY OF DEVON AND CORNWALL, AND OF THE WASHINGTON U. S. NATIONAL INSTITUTE FOR THE PROMOTION OF SCIENCE.

FROM THE FOURTH LONDON EDITION, GREATLY ENLARGED.

Οὐθὲν ἀνθρώπῳ λαβεῖν μεῖζον, οὐ χαρίσασθαι Θεῷ σεμνότερον, ἀληθείας.

PLUTARCH. *de Is. et Osir.*

"Than TRUTH, no greater blessing can man receive, or God bestow."

PHILADELPHIA:
ROBERT E. PETERSON,
NORTH-WEST CORNER OF FIFTH AND ARCH STREETS.
....
1850.

GEOLOGY, in the magnitude and sublimity of the objects which it treats, undoubtedly ranks, in the scale of the sciences, next to Astronomy.

SIR JOHN F. W. HERSCHEL.

The conclusions of GEOLOGY have lent, in fact, a new evidence to revealed religion. They have broken the arms of the sceptic; and, when we ponder over the great events which they proclaim, the mighty revolutions which they indicate, the wrecks of successive creations which they display, and the immeasurable cycles of their chronology, the era of man shrinks into contracted dimensions; his proudest and most ancient dynasties wear the aspect of upstart and ephemeral groups; the fabrics of human power, the gorgeous temple, the monumental bronze, the regal pyramid, sink into insignificance beside the mighty sarcophagi of the brutes that perish.

QUARTERLY REVIEW, vol. lxx. p. 57.

PREFACE.

The following Lectures were prepared and delivered, by the appointment of the Committee of the Congregational Lecture, under some peculiarity of circumstances. The appointment was unexpected, and the notice unavoidably short. Several parts, therefore, and those referring to subjects of the greatest importance, were treated in a manner too brief, and, indeed, extemporaneously: but to the kind and attentive audience the promise was given that, if the publication should take place, the author would supply those deficiencies. This he has endeavoured to do partly by filling up the portions which, in the delivery, were but sketched, and partly by adding Notes, both on the immediate pages, and in a Supplementary Appendix.

The reader will perceive that numerous citations are introduced. For this no apology is requisite: and, indeed, so richly interesting are the most of those passages, that it would have been a wrong to the subject and to the reader to have withheld them. Another circumstance proves their importance, and even necessity. The facts which are the basis of geological reasonings can be known to the majority even of well-educated persons, only by testimony; as, in the greater number of instances, they are to the author himself. To bring forwards, therefore, the statements of the most competent authorities, in their own words, is due to the right position of the subject and to the satisfaction of the reader. Should it be objected, that some of those citations contain reasonings and opinions, besides statements of fact; the reply is, that they are the reasonings and opinions of men who thoroughly understood the grounds upon which they are built; and that, therefore, the inferences which such men have seen to be just, are entitled to stand in the next line of authority to their testimony as eye-witnesses and labourers in the great field. It involves no disrespect to the multitude of pious and intelligent persons, to say that they cannot form an independent opinion upon many subjects in Natural Philosophy. It is no dishonour to accept the conclusions of NEWTON and his followers, though we confess ourselves unable to read the *Principia*.

FOURTH EDITION.

As the requirement for the publication of these Lectures arose from their having been delivered to an audience, at the Congregational Library, I have not thought myself at liberty to add or omit or change any part, paragraph, or sentence, except in some two or three instances, not considerable, and of which in the passages an intimation is given. But in the Appended Notes, I have felt no restraint. They have been increased in each of the subsequent editions, with the view of placing my readers, as much as is for me possible, in the advancing positions of geological knowledge. The amount of this accumulation is now not small: for I have felt it my duty to verify the encomium with which, on the publication of the third edition, I was honoured by the REV. DR. WHEWELL, the Master of Trinity College, Cambridge. He then wrote these words: "I perceive you have given it the interest which belonged to the former editions, of making your readers acquainted with the most recent geological discussions. On this account, it cannot fail to be a general favourite."

Of those Notes peculiar to this edition, I have to regret the not having, in due time, adopted a uniform mode of designation. Some of them have a date, or imply a reference to time; others are included in brackets; and to others, the words *Fourth Edition* are prefixed.

I should feel it not becoming to relate the expressions of approbation with which this book has been favoured by eminent men of science, in our own country and in the North American States; or, what is a more exalted gratification, the testimonies of usefulness in relation to its religious element. But it would be a failing to the great cause for which I plead, if I did not avail myself of a communication which, to well-informed persons, will have the appropriate interest in a very high degree. It is a part of a letter with which Sir John Herschel honoured me in the summer of 1843.

"—— Abstractedly, one might have thought that such wild and 'vehement denunciations' as those you cite from * * * * and others, were hardly worth very seriously handling. Yet, in effect, I am disposed to regard it as doing good service not only to science but to religion and moral feeling, to put down, as you have done, with a strong (though not a cruel) hand, that sort of barking and yelping. There cannot be two truths in contradiction to one another: and a man must have a mind fitted neither for scientific nor for religious truth, whose religion can be disturbed by geology, or whose geology can be distorted from its character of an inductive science, by a determination to accommodate its results to preconceived interpretations of the Mosaic cosmogony.

"I should hope that, on this painful and troublesome point, your work will prove *final*, and put an end, once and for ever, to the sort of outcry in question; or at least so far crush it, that this and the next generation may be allowed to pursue their geological researches in peace."

It is my duty to add that these citations from private letters are thus made public, with the kind assent of the writers.

J. P. S.

HOMERTON COLLEGE,
February 5, 1848.

CONTENTS.

LECTURE I. Page 1.

Psalm cxi. 2. *The works of the Lord are great, sought out of all them that have pleasure therein.*

Object, design, utility, and importance of geological science. Requisites and method of the study. Harmony of all science with the announcements of Revelation. Truth. Evidence. The world. The Supreme Being. Accountableness. Authority of Scripture. Necessity of ascertaining its genuine sense. Danger of presumption. Citations from Christian Philosophers.

LECTURE II. Page 25.

Deuteronomy xxxiii. 13, 15, 16. *Blessed of the Lord be his land; for the precious things of heaven, for the dew, and for the deep that coucheth beneath,——and for the chief things of the ancient mountains, and for the precious things of the lasting hills, and for the precious things of the earth and the fulness thereof.*

Change in the material universe, constant, but according to law. A series of Propositions, describing the most general facts relating to the crust of the earth. Internal condition. Pyrogenous rocks. Stratified formations. Remains of creatures which once had life. Their distinct periods, and areas. Separate creations. Uniformity of sequence.

LECTURE III. Page 52.

Romans xi. 36. *Of* Him, *and through* Him, *and to* Him, *are all things: to whom be glory for ever.*

Recital of opinions which are by many assumed to be asserted or implied in the Scriptures, but which are contrary to geological doctrines. I. The recent creation of the world. II. A previous universal chaos over the earth. III. The creation of the heavenly bodies after that of the earth. IV. The derivation of all vegetables and animals from one centre of creation. V. That the inferior animals were not subject to death till the fall of man.

LECTURE IV. Page 69.

GENESIS VI. 17. *And behold I, even I, do bring a flood of waters upon the earth, to destroy all flesh wherein is the breath of life from under heaven: and every thing that is in the earth shall die.*

Continuation of apparent discrepancies between geological doctrines and the testimony of Scripture, as generally understood. VI. Concerning the deluge. The reason for that judicial infliction, in the righteous government of God. The testimony of history and tradition. Common ascription of geological phænomena to the Deluge erroneous.

LECTURE V. Page 84.

2 PETER II. 5. *God spared not the old world,—bringing the flood upon the world of the ungodly.*

Continuation. More accurate and discriminating inquiry. Investigation of the masses of rolled stony fragments which have been attributed to the diluvial action. Those masses found to be of different character and age. Effect of the investigation upon the convictions of the most eminent geologists. Evidence from phænomena in Auvergne and Languedoc. The quantity of water requisite for a deluge geographically universal. The effect of such an addition to the bulk of the earth. The reception of animals in the ark. Estimated number of the animal creation. Other difficulties.

LECTURE VI.

PART I. Page 114.

1 THESSALONIANS V. 21. *Prove all things: hold fast that which is good.*

Examinations of various methods which have been proposed for the removal of the difficulties and alleged contradiction, between Geology and the Scriptures. I. Denial of any difficulty, by shutting the eyes to the evidence of geological facts, and representing the inquiry as impious.

PART II. Page 134.

II. Sacrificing the Mosaic records, as unintelligible, or as being the language of mythic poetry. III. Regarding the Mosaic six days as designed to represent indefinite periods. IV. Attributing stratification and other geological phænomena to the interval between the Adamic creation and the Deluge, and the action of the diluvial waters.

PART III. Page 149.

Examination continued of the Diluvial Theory.

LECTURE VII.

Part I. Page 162.

Psalm xii. 6. *The words of the Lord are pure words; as silver tried in a furnace of earth, purified seven times.*

The certain and infallible truth of all that is taught in the Holy Scriptures, when taken in its own genuine sense. Our duty to elicit that sense. Induction and examination of the forms of language used in Scripture to convey to man a knowledge of the nature and perfection of God. The gracious condescension and benefit of this method, for the religious instruction of mankind. This character of the scriptural style displayed in the descriptions of natural objects. General rule of interpretation hence derived. Prejudices of former interpreters, both Romanist and Protestant. Galileo. Milton. Superior advantages of the Christian dispensation.

Part II. Page 184.

Application of the principle established, to the interpretation of the narrative concerning the Creation. The independent position of the first sentence. Astral creation. The subsequent description refers to a limited region of the earth. The series of operations. The human creation. Death, before the fall of man.——The same principle applied to the fact of the Deluge, which is shown to have been universal as to the extent of the human population, but not geographically universal.—Concluding vindication of the principle and its applications, as irrefutable, and absolutely necessary for maintaining the honour of the word of God.

LECTURE VIII. Page 214.

Ecclesiastes xii. 13. *Let us hear the conclusion of the whole matter: Fear God, and keep his commandments: for this is the whole of man.*

Religion the perfection of our nature. The duty of scientific studies, especially in a course of education. Exhortations to personal efforts for improvement. Peculiar claims of Botany and Geology. The proper accompaniments of scientific pursuits. Advantage to the comforts of life. Moral uses. Responsibility to the just and holy God. Interest and urgency of these considerations. The rational claims and attractions of religion.

SUPPLEMENTARY NOTES.

A, *referred to at pages* 7 *and* 200. PAGE

DISSERTATION on the Laws of Organized Natures involving the Necessity of Death; and on Geological studies in general . 239

B, *referred to at page* 11.

On the Evidence derived from Astronomy to the Extent and Antiquity of the Universe 252

B b, *referred to at page* 32.

On the Thickness of the Solid Crust of the Earth . . 258

C, *referred to at page* 41.

On the Number of Species in the earlier Fossiliferous Rocks 261

D, (*page* 47,) *referring to the series of Propositions, page* 26 *to* 50.

Synoptic Table of the Stratified Formations 263

E, *referred to at page* 49.

DISSERTATION on the Varieties of the Human Species . . 270

F, *referred to at pages* 55 *and* 159.

DISSERTATION on the Evidence of a very high Antiquity of the Earth 284

G, *referred to at pages* 67 *and* 244.

On the Fossil Animalcules 318

G g, *referring to page* 85. PAGE.

On the Pebbles 326

H, *referred to at page* 91.

On Ancient Glaciers, and their Effects 327

I, *referred to at page* 102.

Mr. Hartley's Account of Christian Piety in the Puy de Dome 332

K, *referred to at page* 106.

On the Volcanic District of Auvergne 334

L, *referred to at pages* 112 *and* 202.

On the Longevity of Trees 336

M, *referred to at page* 152.

On Dr. George Young's Scriptural Geology; and on the Coal Formations 344

N, *referred to at page* 158.

On the Comparison of the Egyptian and the Mosaic Cosmogonies 352

O, *referred to at page* 158.

On some Passages in Mr. Lyell's Principles of Geology . 357

P, *referred to at page* 183.

Sentiments of the elder Rosenmüller, Bishop Bird Sumner, and Dean Conybeare, on the initial portion of the Book of Genesis 360

Q, *referred to at page* 185.

Professors Wiseman and Hitchcock, on the reference of the Mosaic Records to Geological Truths 363

R, *referred to at pages* 188 *and* 196.

Dissertation on the Solution of Difficulties with respect to the Mosaic Narrative, in reply to Observations by Professor Baden Powell 365

S, *referred to at pages* 189 *and* 192.

On the Duty of these Investigations; and in Vindication of Dean Buckland 382

T, *referring to page* 207. PAGE.

On Mount Ararat 387

U, *referred to at page* 234.

The Geological Society vindicated from Misrepresentation . 388

ADDENDA.

Quotations from Lamarck and Herder, on the meaning and use of the term *Nature*.—Professor Agassiz on the Series of Animal Creatures through the Strata 392

Lord Bacon's Prayer for the right use of Science, and its practical connexion with Revealed Religion 394

INDEX 395

ON THE RELATION

BETWEEN

THE HOLY SCRIPTURES

AND SOME PARTS OF

GEOLOGICAL SCIENCE.

LECTURE I.

Psalm cxi. 2. *The works of the Lord are great, sought out of all them that have pleasure therein.*

Geology does so seek out the works of the Most High. It has claims upon the regard of all cultivated and pious minds. It leads us to study that which God has made our earthly abode, in its present state, filled with monuments of past conditions, and presages, I venture to think, of the future. It leads us into some acquaintance with a magnificent part of the counsel of Jehovah's will, according to which He worketh all things; the machine of dependent beings and subordinate causes, by which the Supreme Cause accomplishes his purposes of wisdom and righteousness. We see those causes to be the same in their nature, and similar in their mode of operation now, as in countless ages past; though differing through a wide range in the intensity of their action and the form of their results.

Rain, rills, and rivers, aided by the electric and chemical and mechanical agency of the atmosphere, are continually wearing away the solid earth, transporting it into the estuaries of the sea, and committing it to the currents which spread it out upon the ocean-bed. There the spoils of the land are added to the defunct shells and skeletons of marine life, the astonishing amount of the works of men, and the millions of human skeletons which, through more than fifty centuries, have been swallowed up in the watery deep. At the time which inviolable justice has fixed, "the sea shall give up her dead." Can it be thought improbable that the operations which are now in progress, in the dark abyss, and at its greatest depths, are subservient to the righteous proceedings of that day, the finishing of the mystery of God as to this one portion of his ways;—the termination of man's existence as an animal-species upon earth, but his resurrection to an immortal life, a new sphere of being, the possession of a more exquisite organization, which, in a manner inconceivable to our present faculties, will be incomparably more effective for the highest purposes of mind than that which we now possess?—We trace the monuments of change to early and still earlier conditions, carrying us back to the grand simplicity of elementary creation; and we are permitted to contemplate the all-surrounding proofs that our globe only waits the will of the Almighty Being, to develop its mechanical, electrical, and chemical forces; and, if that will have so ordained, "the heavens," the atmospheric constitution, "shall pass away with a great noise, and the elements shall melt with fervent heat; the earth also and the works that are therein shall be burned up." (2 Pet. iii. 10.)

The design of geological studies is to acquire a satisfactory knowledge of the substances (airs, water, earth, stones, and metals,) which, in different combinations and arrangements, form the accessible parts of the planet assigned by the Almighty Creator for our present dwelling-place; and of the changes through which they have passed and are passing; with a view to the enlargement of human knowledge, the promotion of our present happiness, and the celebration of HIS perfections "of whom, and through whom, and to whom are all things."

It is obvious that this is an attractive field of investigation, promising not only to be productive of intellectual pleasure, but to bring many and great benefits to the arts of usefulness and comfort in life, and to furnish interesting discoveries of the power, wisdom, and goodness of HIM who exists independently and by necessity of nature, possessed of all perfections, the designing cause and active sustainer of all other beings, and to whom it is equally our duty and our happiness to render the highest veneration and love and homage.

It is not less obvious, that this study cannot be undertaken, with any reasonable hope of success, without the aid of some other branches of natural science. Indeed, to so high a point have the pursuits of Natural History and Natural Philosophy been raised in our day, that it is no longer possible for one department to be cultivated, with the hope of success and so as to avoid the danger of falling into egregious mistakes, without some acquaintance with the others. This fact has been both proved and elucidated, with equal force of reasoning and elegance of manner, by a lady of extraordinary attainments, in her work entitled The Connexion of the Physical Sciences.

The substances which compose the external part of our earth, and which present themselves sometimes in a simple state, but generally in various forms of composition, must be ascertained by their external appearance; and such knowledge is the science of the Mineralogist. But their inward nature, and the states of union in which we find them, must also be known; together with the principles or laws, as they are usually called, which regulate those states of union, preventing or separating some, favouring and effectuating others: and this cannot be without chemical knowledge. In the production of geological formations and their subsequent changes of position, the common law of gravitation and other regular modes of attraction and repulsion, [including the wonderful agencies of Universal Electro-Magnetism,] have performed and are always performing an important part: the investigation of those modes of action cannot be attempted, with the least hope of success, but by the application of mathematical Dynamics. The larger number of the earthy and stony masses which we have to study contain, in immense multitudes, the skeletons, the coverings, whether adherent integuments or such as supply the place of habitations, and various other remains of animals; and the substance, or mineral matter moulded upon the substance, of vegetable species, trunk, stems, leaves, and fruits: it is therefore indispensable to the right understanding of geological facts, that a competent knowledge should be obtained of Zoology and Comparative Anatomy, and of Botany according to a Natural System.* It must

* "It is now admitted on all hands, that no man can be qualified to enter any of the highest walks of science, who is acquainted with only one branch of natural knowledge; and the mutual dependence of them all is now so positively demonstrated, that the philosopher of our days can no longer be allowed to remain satisfied with those inquiries

further be remarked, that the best books and the richest cabinets are not sufficient to convey complete ideas; but to closet-study must be added personal inspection of the face of a country, of sea-cliffs and beaches, of mountain-sides, rocky precipices, land-slips, and ravines; besides every kind of artificial excavation; and this labour, in travelling and exploring, must be carried to an extent greater than can be expected from most individuals, though there are eminent men who have personally achieved wonders in this respect. There are Geologists, who have devoted severe and self-denying toil, exposure to great perils, and vast expense, through the best years of life, to this object; and with a noble disinterestedness, they communicate the results of their untiring exertions. Those results are, by themselves and other qualified persons, brought together, scrutinized, compared, connected; and then, by publication, exposed to the renewed criticism of the scientific world: so that, in the issue, ample knowledge has been obtained, and that knowledge resting upon rigorously examined evidence, of the geological conditions of Europe generally; of large districts in North and South America, India and Central and Western Asia; and of some portions of Africa, Australia, and the Isles of the Pacific Ocean.

It may not unreasonably be alleged, that few persons are qualified to this extent. To this objection we reply:

1. Though they may be few, compared with the general population of any country, yet, if we take the aggregate of persons possessed of the qualifications required, in an eminent degree, we shall find them to rise to a very high amount, in Europe and the European settlements throughout the earth. Here might be mentioned a long line of illustrious names, both British and foreign, whom it would be a delight to honour; but I deny myself the pleasure of so doing, because though the catalogue of those whose names instantly rise in an admiring and grateful memory would be very considerable, many of high and probably equal merit would be omitted, and thus no little injustice would be inflicted.*

which belong exclusively to any single branch, but must extend his investigations over the whole range of sciences, and illuminate his path by the varied combinations of them all." Prof. Buckland's *Vindiciæ Geologicæ;* his Inaugural Lecture, 1819; p. 10.

* I venture to adapt to this topic the words of Leclerc. "Whoever attempts this study, should well understand what a task he undertakes, and by what laws he must be governed: or else he will be a most infelicitous critic [geologist]; and, instead of reaping that high honour which men of real erudition [and science] have obtained from this

2. It is no extravagance to affirm that the distinguished men to whom I allude, and who have given us the details of their travels and labours, are entitled personally to the fullest credit of their testimony upon the facts and scenery which they describe. Yet, if any person, moved, I doubt not, by honourable and even religious principles, should allow a painful suspicion still to lurk in his mind, let him consider that the individual veracity of persons of the finest talents and the greatest advantages of education, and whose integrity is unquestionable, is not our only guarantee; but that the number of explorers and observers is great, that they belong to different nations and parties, and are subject to be influenced by various interests and prepossessions, so that the correction of any involuntary mistake is sure and speedy; but, if superficial observation, or negligent statement, or designed misrepresentation, were to occur, the detection would be prompt and the penalty severe, in a public forfeiture of character and confidence. From some measure of knowledge and some care in observation, I feel myself bound in duty to profess my thorough persuasion, that the firmest reliance may be placed on the reports and descriptions for which we are indebted to the most distinguished geologists of our time.

3. All the natural sciences ramify into each other, in so extensive a manner, that their points of contact shew themselves perpetually. This fact not only brings to view the necessity of the combination of these parts of knowledge, but it creates an ardent desire for practically effecting it; it opens numerous avenues into the domain of other sciences; it suggests methods of proceeding for making the desired acquirements; and, while we feel ourselves obliged to submit to the necessity of being but imperfectly acquainted with many parts of the field, we are preserved (if we maintain a becoming moral discipline) from the vanity and pedan-

art, he will become contemptible and ridiculous. I think I hear my reader asking me, Whether I myself look for any portion of this honour?——I will only venture to say, that I do not PROFESS this arduous and hazardous study, though I highly honour those who do profess it, and have long read their writings with great pleasure, from which perhaps some tinge——may have adhered to me." From a larger quotation out of his *Ars Critica*, in Pye Smith's Scripture Testimony to the Messiah, vol. iii. p. 25, third ed. Yet, if any should suspect me of being captivated by novelty, and ensnared by a precipitate disposition, I take leave to say that these are not to me the studies of yesterday, and that I have professed and taught the leading sentiments of this volume, within my own circle of connexions, for at least five and thirty years. 1839.

try of half-knowledge, we are enabled to apprehend *with accuracy* what we do learn; and we gain safe positions from which, when the opportunity may occur, we can make further advances.

4. Any person of good mental faculties and liberal education, if he will take the pains of attention and some self-cultivation, may acquire an ability to draw satisfactory inferences from the facts recited and the reasonings propounded in the best geological works; or at least to exercise an unpresuming judgment whether the conclusions are sound which others have drawn.

But it cannot be denied, and ought not to be suppressed, that a different view of the whole matter is taken by many estimable persons. The objects of geological investigation, especially in the department of organic remains, are in the highest degree attractive: casual allusions and fragments of information float plentifully in the atmosphere of social intercourse, so that none but the incurious can fail to hear something; and the periodical papers of the day have occasionally paragraphs of wonder, upon real or alleged geological discoveries; which frequently indeed turn out to be the echoes of ignorance. Hence, the assumption is easily made, that the circuit of this kind of knowledge may be filled up by any young and ardent mind, with a small degree of trouble and a little easy reading; without laying in even a moderate share of the prerequisites. Above all, it is incumbent upon us to be aware, that a vague idea has obtained circulation, that certain geological doctrines are at variance with the Holy Scriptures. This notion works with pernicious effect. The *semblance* of discrepancy is indeed undeniable; but I profess my conviction that it is nothing but a semblance, and that, like many other difficulties on all important subjects which have tried the intellect of man, it vanishes before careful and sincere examination. The naked fact, however, the mere appearance, is eagerly laid hold of by some irreligious men, and is made an excuse for dismissing from their minds any serious regard to the LAW and GOSPEL of GOD, and any rational investigation of the Evidences of Revelation; for they are very willing to assume that Christianity is either a mass of obsolete prejudices, or a theory so labouring under heavy suspicion as to have but slender claims upon a philosopher's attention. In the opposite extreme, many excellent persons, devout and practical Christians, knowing that "the word of our God shall stand for ever," feel no desire to become acquainted with the real merits of the question; and sit down with a persuasion, that geological theories are visionary plausibilities, each having its day of fashion, then being exploded in favour of some other vagary, which in its turn gives way, and all falling under the description of false "philosophy and vain deceit, according to the tradition of men, the rudiments of the world;—the oppositions of science falsely so called;—perverse disputings of men of corrupt minds, destitute of the truth,—reprobate concerning the faith." (Col. ii. 8; 1 Tim. vi. 5; 2 Tim. iii. 8.)*

That such a state of opinion is injurious to the cause of Christianity, can admit of no doubt. It is a fearful thing to array science and religion against each other; for, however unnatural and unjust this antagonist position certainly is, the fact of its existence is pregnant with evil on both sides. Men who have well studied the questions at issue, and who *know* the evidence of those geological facts to which such strong exception is taken, cannot by any possibility be brought to renounce their convic-

*A clergyman whose piety and integrity, as manifested in his book, attract my sincere respect, notwithstanding egregious defects of candour and justice in his animadversions, has expressed the opinions of many other good men, in the following words. "J. P. S.——— deprecates the idea of any person entering upon Geological questions, who does not possess considerable acquaintance with the principles of Chemistry, Electricity, Mineralogy, Zoology, Conchology, Comparative Anatomy, and even of 'the sublimest mathematics.' It will be readily conceded that, to prosecute the study of Geology advantageously, some insight into most of the natural sciences is necessary. But, when this assertion is intended to deter men of good common sense from giving their opinion upon Geology in its connexion with the Scriptures, the position may be safely questioned. It would be just as reasonable to maintain, that a minute acquaintance with the principles of Surgery and Morbid Anatomy was requisite, before a man was qualified to say whether a leg of mutton was tainted, and ought to be sent from the table; or that an honest countryman was unfit to sit in the jury-box, because he was ignorant of the English Law-Reports, or Coke upon Lyttleton. In the controversy between Geologists and the Sacred Scriptures, nothing more is required but an acquaintance with the common laws of evidence, and a knowledge of the distinction between Divine and human testimony." (*Reflections on Geology, suggested by the perusal of Dr. Buckland's Bridgewater Treatise; with Remarks on a letter by J. P. S. on the Study of Geology;* by the Rev. J. Mellor Brown, B. A. &c. p. 52.) This Letter will be reprinted in the Appendix; (1) so that the reader may see whether Mr. Brown has not, undesignedly I am willing to believe, exaggerated the description of prerequisites to Geological study. It is hardly needful to remind him that comparisons are not arguments; and that, when they are intended to be illustrations, they ought to be just. Upon his first comparison I make no remark, for its propriety is equal to its elegance: but, to invest his second with any semblance of analogy, he ought to have made his "honest countryman" very ill informed upon the facts connected with the cause which he was called to try, yet imagining himself to know all about it, and determined to shut his ears against the evidence.

(1) Supplementary Note A; on the Laws of Organized Natures, involving the necessity of Death; and on Geological Studies in general.

tions.* Were they treated as Galileo was, were they, like him, unwilling to be the martyrs of conscience, were they to profess a change of sentiment which they could not feel; they would act the part of hypocrites. The nature of the impression which is actually made upon such minds, may be judged of from the language of a mathematician and philosopher of the highest order, distinguished by the originality and independence of his mind, and whose sincerity, as a professed friend of Christianity, it would be most unjust to call into question.

"What then have those accomplished who have restricted the Mosaic account of the Creation to that diminutive period, which is as it were but a span in the duration of the earth's existence; and who have imprudently rejected the testimony of the senses, when opposed to their philological criticisms?——The very argument which Protestants have opposed to the doctrine of transubstantiation, would, if their view of the case were correct, be equally irresistible against the book of Genesis. But let us consider what would be the conclusion of any reasonable being in a parallel case. Let us imagine a manuscript written three thousand years ago, and professing to be a revelation from the Deity, in which it was stated that the colour of the paper of the very book now in the reader's hands is *black*, and that the colour of the ink in the characters which he is now reading is *white*. With that reasonable doubt of his own individual faculties which would become the inquirer into the truth of a statement said to be derived from so high an origin, he would ask of all those around him, whether to their senses the paper appeared to be *black* and the ink to be *white*. If he found the senses of other individuals agree with his own, then he would undoubtedly pronounce the alleged revelation a forgery, and those who propounded it to be either deceived

* *Fourth ed.*—The labours of the most distinguished men, in Geology and Natural History universally, are constantly bringing confirmations. "In no instance [of the results obtained by modern Geological investigations,] have general conclusions been shaken by subsequent observations.——Whatever alterations and minute adjustments may take place, the great fundamental principles of the science, and the grand subdivisions already introduced into its history, will not be upset, but will be *extended* and *confirmed* by future inquiry." Prof. SEDGWICK, at the Brit. Assoc. Camb., 1845. At the same time and place, "Dr. BUCKLAND wished to correct a false impression, not uncommon among novices, who hear only debates and conflicts on disputable points in Geology,—that there is *nothing certain* in the conclusions of that science; and he wished it to be understood, that, from the moment when Organic Remains were appealed to, as the true ground of comparison between the rocks of different ages and different countries, there had been *no difference of opinion* amongst Geologists upon the broad principles of their science." See the very accurate reports of that meeting, in the *Athenæum* for June 21 and 28, and July 5, 1845.

or deceivers. He would rightly impute the attempted deceit to moral turpitude, to gross ignorance, or to interested motives, in the supporters of it; but he certainly would not commit the impiety of supposing the Deity to have wrought a miraculous change upon the senses of our whole species, and then to demand their belief in a fact directly opposed to those senses; thus throwing doubt upon every conclusion of reason in regard to external objects; and, amongst others, upon the very evidence by which the authenticity of that very questionable manuscript was itself supported, and even upon the fact of its existence when before their eyes."*

Should any of those who honour me with their attention, be not at all, or only as the result of cursory reading, acquainted with geological science, they are intreated to consider the case before them very seriously. Here is a mind of high order, versed in philosophical knowledge, whose acquirements in the exact sciences, their highest branches, and their most astonishing applications, are acknowledged with admiration through the world; who has deeply studied the nature and rules of evidence; and who is not an enemy, but an avowed friend to Revealed Religion: he marches up to the front of the imagined discrepance,—and we see the strength of his conviction. He is indeed satisfied, for himself, that Geology and Revelation are not at variance; and his method of resolving the difficulty will be mentioned in a future lecture. But, we may ask in the mean time, What is the conclusion which the uninstructed observer ought in fairness to draw? Can he satisfy himself with the assertion, that the most eminent geologists are, in general, secret or open infidels; that their doctrines upon the constitution and antiquity of the earth are fond fancies, changeable as the wind, or irreligious hypotheses of men "ever learning, but never able to come to the knowledge of the truth;" and that he runs no risk of being mistaken, or of becoming the instrument of moral injury to others, perhaps his own children, by making it an article of religion to maintain that all dependent nature came from the creative power of the Supreme Being, only about six thousand years ago? Will he say that all solicitude upon the question may be safely dismissed, and that he gains firm footing for his faith on this subject by reposing upon an *interpretation* of the Mosaic records, which though extensively received has been

* Mr. Babbage's *Ninth Bridgewater Treatise*, pp. 68—70

seriously doubted of by sound expositors in ancient and in modern times, and by some absolutely disallowed:—yea, independently of geological knowledge?

An inquiry thus opens before us which cannot but appear, to every reflecting person, to be of the first importance. "RELIGION is the highest style of man." But religion, the internal and practical principle of all piety, virtue, and morality, rests upon *Theology*. And what is theology, but the *knowledge* of that which is in itself *true* and in its relations to us infinitely *important*, concerning the SUPREME BEING, his perfections and works and purposes, the duty which we owe to him, and the hopes which we are permitted to entertain of the greatest blessings by his bestowment? That knowledge it is our duty to obtain, from all the sources and by all the means that he has put into our power. His works are the first of those means, in the order of human apprehension. In them much of (τὸ γνωστὸν τοῦ Θεοῦ) "that which can be known of God is manifested:—his invisible perfections are contemplated from the creation of the world, being understood by his works, his eternal power and godhead." Can any declaration be more clear and full, than this of the inspired apostle?

We have then the most satisfactory proofs, that this all-perfect Being has not only given us mental faculties, by which we are capable of making ever progressive improvement in the study of the dependent universe of which we are a part, and in which so bright rays shine forth of his "eternal power and godhead;" but that he has further dignified our present condition of existence, by the *communication of positive information* concerning our relations to himself and to each other, and the results of those relations in the eternal state to which we are hastening.

Christianity rests upon the explicit acknowledgment of a succession of such communications, commencing with the earliest epoch of the human history, and growing in comprehension and clearness, till the series is completed in the doctrine of Jesus "the Saviour of the world." Of these communications we have written monuments, proved to be genuine and authentic; presenting the truths, laws, promises, warnings, and threatenings, of the Divine Government; and containing the history of the persons and the circumstances connected with those successive revelations. The earlier of those records are far more ancient than any other monuments in alphabetical writing known to exist; and the most early of them affirm the fact of both the universal creation of the world, and the preparation and adaptation of that part of it which was designed to be the habitation of man.

But there are two sciences, Astronomy and Geology, which bring us into an acquaintance with facts of amazing grandeur and interest, concerning the Extent and the Antiquity of the created Universe. The knowledge which each communicates rests upon its own appropriate evidence; in the one case, the evidence of sense obtained by innumerable observations made and compared by the most competent men, and confirmed by rigorous mathematical processes;* and, in the other, the evidence of sense also, and the testimony of a host of accomplished observers, and, though not to the same perfect extent as Astronomy, yet in a degree which objectors little imagine, receiving support from mathematical applications.

Are then the discoveries and deductions of those sciences consistent, or are they not, with the declarations of primeval divine revelation?

We cannot but expect such consistency. Our Creator has given us faculties suited to the perception and the right appreciation of it. Cases indeed are conceivable, and they do occur, in which difficulties appear, because we see only detached portions of the truth, and the intervening parts of our field of view are covered with an obscurity which we cannot dispel. Yet such cases are not those of contradictory propositions, in which the affirming of one destroys that of the other. But unhappily this is the predicament of the subject which we have to consider, as it is too commonly understood. If from the discoveries of Astronomy and Geology we infer that the created universe, including our own globe, has existed through an unknown but unspeakably long period of time past; and IF, from the records of revelation, we *draw the conclusion* that the work of creation, or at least so far as respects our planet, took place not quite six thousand years ago; it is evident that the two positions cannot both stand: one destroys the other. One of them must be an error; both may be wrong; only one can be right.

Our first care must be to ascertain the true state of the facts on each side. Are the propositions respectively drawn from their

* Supplementary Note B; on the Evidence from Astronomy.

premises, by sound reasoning? Have we guarded sufficiently against all causes of error? Are the facts in nature satisfactorily proved? And is our interpretation of the Scriptures legitimate? Doubts and renewed investigation of the latter question imply no precarious issue with respect to the great designs of revelation. "The foundation of God standeth sure." The great principles of faith and obedience, hope and happiness; the doctrines, warnings, and promises of the gospel; shine forth in the most clear and satisfying manner; and their certainty is not diminished by philological inquiry into the interpretation of words, or by discussing the relations to history and antiquities, and other collateral bearings of the Scriptures. For example; the recent discoveries in the monuments of Egypt* have cast much light upon the history and the phraseology of the Old Testament, by bringing to our knowledge facts and usages which were before imperfectly or not at all known: but these accessions of knowledge, and the more correct interpretation of particular passages which we hence obtain, take nothing from us in any other respect, but add materially to the proofs and the right understanding of the whole system of revelation. The more firmly we stand upon the rock of evidence, the more completely we possess "the assurance of faith."

TRUTH, therefore, is our object: Truth, in religion, in morals, and in natural science. The more completely we attain it, if we faithfully apply it to its proper purposes, the more we shall bring happiness to ourselves and our fellow-creatures, and reverential honour to our God.

All men admit and act upon the value of Truth. Even those who practically disregard its obligations, pay to Truth an implicit homage; for they plainly manifest that it is only wicked selfishness which leads them to violate it.

Truth in sentiment is the agreement of our conceptions or belief, with the real nature and circumstances of the things which are the objects of those conceptions: and *conventional Truth* is the agreement of the signs by which we express our conceptions, with the conceptions themselves.

That our conceptions may be thus in accordance with the reality of things, is to be secured by the due consideration of Evidence:

* Now, in 1847, we add, of Nineveh, and the ancient Assyrian empire.

and we believe that God, the Fountain of all truth and goodness, has furnished us with *means* for the obtaining of evidence, *sufficient* for a rational satisfaction, upon all objects which it concerns us to know.

All Truth must be consistent. Let the objects contemplated be never so different in their nature, and remote from each other, in their position, or aspect, or other connexions of their occurrence; the facts concerning them cannot but be in mutual agreement; for to say that one fact is contradictory to another, is to utter a manifest absurdity. But our conception of a fact may fail of being in accordance with the reality: from the variety of causes which, we are aware, are the sources of frequent error among mortals, and of which the chief are, the not being possessed of adequate means for acquiring the knowledge requisite as the basis of our deductions; or the want of giving due attention to the means which we do possess for acquiring the necessary data; or a want of correct habitude of mind in drawing our conclusions. If we have done our best and fail, we have not forfeited moral truth; we are sincere, though mistaken: but, if we have not done our best, we cannot be blameless. For the consequences of our indifference, or negligence, or prejudice, we must be responsible to the divine tribunal; and that responsibility will be according to the nature of the object proposed for investigation, its circumstances of greater or less importance to the well-being of mankind, our obligations to possess accurate knowledge, and our profession to communicate it.

The criterion of truth is *Evidence:* and, though evidence is formed of different materials in different departments, the effect of real evidence, upon a mind sincerely desirous of knowing the truth, will be satisfactory, however different the kind or form of the materials which constitute it.

In Physical Science, the evidence of truth is obtained by drawing inferences from the observation of facts made known by our senses; and confirmed in many cases, and those the most important, by the application of Mathematics, which indeed derive their certainty from reducing all propositions to the plainest evidence of sense.

Truth, in matters of history, and in all that relates to the good or evil conduct of rational beings, their relation to social systems and to law, their dispositions and motives, their dependence upon the Supreme Sovereign, their obligations to HIM, and their expectations from him; can be attained only by what is usually called Moral Evidence. This kind of evidence arises from our consciousness of the manner in which we ourselves feel and act in given circumstances; and our observation of the manner in which other men act under similar conditions. We hence deduce conclusions: these are confirmed by universal experience: we feel a perfect confidence, that, whenever the conditions are similar, the results will be similar also: and we call the principles or causes of such uniformity in voluntary action, Laws of Mind.

Thus we come at last to find, that clear cases of Moral Evidence produce an assent and satisfaction not less complete than is our confidence in the Evidence of our Senses. We arrive at a conviction, that the same wisdom and rectitude of the omnipotent and infinitely good Being, which established the Laws of Matter, have also established laws of Mind; and that to refuse our belief, where sufficient moral evidence has been laid before us, is not less unreasonable than it would be to doubt the dictates of our senses or the results of mathematical proof.

It is however a fact that even moral truth may derive important aid from a judicious application of mathematical methods of investigation. The progress made, within the last sixty years, in the most refined branches of Analytics, has contributed its measure of auxiliary support to the resolution of questions which have a relation to the evidences of religion; by the doctrine of chances. The probabilities for and against the occurrence of a supposed fact, or the credibility of witnesses warranting the belief of a miracle, have been reduced to equations and satisfactorily worked out. The late Bishop of Peterborough (Dr. Herbert Marsh) in his Letters to Archdeacon Travis, nearly fifty years ago, employed this method on a question of criticism; and Mr. Babbage, in his Ninth Bridgewater Treatise, has applied it to the refutation of Hume's endeavour to set up an argument against miracles wrought in favour of religion.*

* *Sec. ed.* A scientific friend has written to me upon this passage; "You appear to give Mr. Babbage the credit of replying to Hume on Miracles, on the numerical plan. Are you not aware that Dr. Chalmers previously did the same? See the third volume of his Works. I heard him deliver the matter there published, in 1830—31."

Certainly I was not aware of this circumstance. The publication referred to is a collection of all the works of Dr. Chalmers, which began to be published, I believe, about four years ago, and is not yet completed. The third volume commences with *The Miraculous and Internal Evidences of the Christian Revelation;* and is entirely

These considerations should deepen our conviction of the duty of dealing faithfully with evidence. Those who have temporary purposes to answer, and selfish interests to promote, may, if they be regardless of moral obligation, permit their predilections to infect their judgment, and to trample down their sincerity. But christian principles will not allow us to do so. "Whatsoever things are true, whatsoever are (σεμνὰ) fair, whatsoever just, whatsoever pure, whatsoever amiable, whatsoever (εὔφημα) deserve honourable mention,"—it is our duty and our happiness to seek, and when acquired to profess. Let us exert our utmost diligence to obtain true premises; let our attention be vigilant, that we may rightly understand them; let us watch carefully every step of our deductions, that they trespass not the limit of correct reasoning; but let us not be stopped in our course, nor desist from pursuing the straight line, because objections meet us which are drawn from other departments of human knowledge. Our duty is to bid those objections to stand aside for a time. In the pursuit of our present line of inquiry, it is more than barely possible that new light may arise; or another point of view may be reached, which will have the effect of exterminating the difficulty. Should this not be the result, our work then will be to trace the derivation of the difficulty from its own source; and to follow out the separate course of investigation by its own principles.* Thus we may find a deliverance from our perplexity in the most effectual manner, by ascertaining that it had no foundation in its own class of knowledge: or the pressure of the difficulty may

a different work from the *Evidence and Authority*, &c. which was published in 1814. In this more recent and comprehensive work, the distinguished Professor applies the mathematical doctrine of Chances to the illustration of our belief in the constancy of natural phenomena, and to the dissection and refutation of the objection made by Hume and La Place against the credibility of the scripture miracles. I am greatly obliged to my correspondent for giving me the opportunity of mentioning this fact. But it does not diminish the merit of Mr. Babbage. He indeed refers to Dr. Chalmers, but it is to another part of his Works, namely, vol. i. p. 129. Yet it appears almost certain that the numeral of the volume is a mistake of the printer, and that vol. iii. was meant; and then we have the very passage to which I presume that my friend alludes. Mr. Babbage gives his formulæ in general algebraic expressions, and his illustrations are widely different; though the argument of course goes upon the same principles of recondite mathematical science. Mr. Babbage is not a man that would derive advantage from another, and conceal his obligations.

* "—— To those who spread themselves over these opposite lines, each moving in his own direction, a thousand points of meeting, and mutual and joyful recognition, will occur."—Sir John Herschel's *Presidential Address*, at the Fifteenth Meeting of the British Association, at Cambridge, June 1845.

be diminished, so far as to yield a reasonable satisfaction that any remaining obscurity may be fairly imputed to the inherent weakness and the necessary limitations of our imperfect nature. Above all, let us not suffer ourselves to be beguiled into the foolish notion, if it be not an insidious pretence, for the purpose of undermining the foundations of religious truth,—that a position may be false in philosophy, but true in theology; or, inversely, philosophically true and theologically false. It is scarcely conceivable that a sane mind could admit such an assertion: yet it has been made, with some disguise perhaps in the phrase, by persons who apparently expected to be credited.

The sum of objects which we can perceive, or know, or conceive of as existing, falls into two very different classes of description.

The one class is stamped with the proofs of mutability, contingence, and dependence. It presents itself to our senses and our consciousness, in a variety of ways; yet all those ways and their results are limited, but the object itself is to us illimitable. We call it THE UNIVERSE, or more correctly *the Dependent* or *the Finite Universe*. We know not its extent: for, while the microscope, at the one extremity of the scale, and astronomical observations at the other, set before us multitude, magnitude, distance and minuteness, which we feel to become overwhelming to our faculties, we have no reason to suppose that we have reached a term, in either direction of our observations. The vast space into which we look, and the "worlds upon worlds" with which we see it to be filled, may be but the threshold of the finite universe; and in the lowest part of the known scale of being, we gain no evidence of ever touching a boundary.

The other description of what we can know is not presented to our senses; but of its existence we gain an irresistible conviction by reasoning. The former class, however vast its extent and remote its antiquity, impresses us, by many facts and circumstances, with the conviction that *it had a beginning*. This material portion is that alone which is cognizable by our senses. We find it to possess a natural inertness; yet it is in perpetual motion. That motion supposes an impulsive power, as its cause. We can trace the so-called causes of motion, from one to another that is prior, and so continually; and we cannot rationally stop till we have ascended to the idea of a voluntary First Cause. To this originating principle we are compelled, by the manifest evidence of the case, to attribute the properties of being *intelligent, underived,* and *independent;* in other words, of being *self-existent,* spontaneously *active,* and possessed in an infinite degree of *every property that is an excellence;* the One Necessary Being. We combine all other beings into one group, and we call it the dependent universe: but comparing this assemblage with that One Being, it becomes, in the comparison, a shadow of existence, "less than nothing and vanity;" mere emptiness. That Being is GOD; not perceived by our organs of sense, but the Object of pure mental conception. He is Mind, in the highest sense; existing necessarily, and therefore having always existed and always to exist; a free agent, of infinite intellectual and moral perfection; upon whom all other beings depend as their Originator, Preserver, and Benefactor, their Proprietor and Lawgiver, their Judge and Rewarder; the supremely wise, holy, and powerful Basis of the universe. Unbiased reason, no less than the book of revelation, utters the voice of satisfaction and gladness; "Give unto Jehovah the glory of his name; O, worship Jehovah in the beauty of holiness!—For of Him, and through Him, and to Him are all things; to whom be glory for ever!"

Of the existence and perfections, the providence and efficient activity, of this glorious Being, we have every kind and degree of evidence that can warrant the reception of any moral truth whatever. If any honest-hearted inquirer entertain a doubt, it is sufficient to refer him to the volumes of Ray and Derham, Bentley, Clarke, Paley, and the authors of the Bridgewater Treatises.

Neither is this the place for adducing evidence that rational creatures are *accountable,* and that the Supreme Being exercises a moral government over them. The writings of Butler alone are sufficient for this purpose. We are convinced also, upon the most satisfactory grounds, that this Wise and Gracious Being has been pleased to give the elements of positive knowledge to mankind, sufficient to inform us upon subjects which it most highly concerns us to know, but of which, without such information, it would be utterly impossible for us to have any other than conjectures, vague and painfully uncertain. The proofs that God has thus made known these facts and truths, and the realities of an eternal futurity; and that the communication is contained in the series of ancient books called the Holy Scriptures; are also to be found in many easily accessible works.

It plainly follows, that a serious attention to those books is the most important duty, and the most interesting occupation to which we can apply ourselves.

Our great object is, to understand them in their true meaning; that is, to take them in the sense in which they were *intended* by the Spirit of truth from whose inspiration, mediately or immediately, they have proceeded. This true sense and meaning must be brought out by an impartial application of the same means which men use, from a conviction of their necessity and adequacy, in order to obtain a just understanding of any writings composed in long past times and in ancient languages.

The study of revealed religion, thus pursued, cannot but be in perfect harmony with all true science. The works and the word of God are streams from the same source, and, though they flow in different directions, they necessarily partake of the same qualities of truth, wisdom, and goodness. Geology, in an especial manner, possesses its place in this beneficent association. It holds also the most interesting connexions with every other branch of Natural Science. It attracts and renders subsidiary to itself, the entire domain of Natural History; it is indissolubly combined with Chemistry, with which it participates in reciprocal advantages of the most important kind; [it possesses intimate relationships with Meteorology and Terrestrial Magnetism;] it has connexions, which to many have been unexpected, with the sublime science of Astronomy, but which the genius and attainments of Babbage, Herschel, and Hopkins, both anticipated and have demonstrated,—connexions of peculiar interest, and which go far to vindicate for Geology a place among the exact sciences. The facts on which it rests have, since the beginning of the present century, and especially since the establishment of the Geological Societies of London, Dublin, and Paris, and kindred institutions in many parts of Europe, and in America, been collected by the assiduous labour of many men of the finest talents; and those facts have not only been brought together and freely exposed to examination, but they have been subjected to the most jealous scrutiny and the most rigorous tests that can be imagined. Philosophers, whose previous opinions were very discordant, but whose qualifications for the task were of the highest order, of different nations (and there was a time when national rivalry even violated the sacred ground of science and letters,) and who had been trained and raised to the first stations in all the other departments of physical knowledge and the liberal arts; have concurred, and have emulated each other, in sifting and scrutinizing to the utmost every announced discovery, and every theoretical deduction. Can it be then supposed that a scientific edifice thus framed, and in the fundamental doctrines of which all who have a claim upon our confidence, are agreed,* possesses not the elements of stability, and has no claims upon our confidence?

But we are compelled to make the unwelcome admission, that the rules of reason, with regard to evidence, have been not a little disregarded, in relation to the proposed subject of these Lectures, It would not, I am persuaded, be possible to point out any department of scientific investigation, in regard to which persons have rushed to the forming and proclaiming of strong opinions, with so scanty a portion of knowledge, yet at the same time so fearlessly, as in relation to Geology. There have been and perhaps still are persons who, not judging it necessary to use hard-working pains and long perseverance, to obtain a competent acquaintance with facts, have, with much dignity, framed their systems of the world: and have not shown the most charitable dispositions towards those who decline to bow down to the idols thus set up. Let it, however, be recollected that the disposition to make these assumptions, and the facility of admitting them, have risen, in a great measure, from a cause which is entitled to our reverence and esteem, religious feeling; though mistaken in its application. The opinion, or suspicion, is roused to meet us, on almost every occasion, that Geology and a religious regard to the Scriptures are opposed to each other. This notion has been diligently held up to the christian public, and in a style well adapted to excite alarm. Hence, some have been led to propose and others to receive, for the overcoming of the apprehended difficulties, theories which, either, on the one hand, have grievously misrepresented principal facts in the natural history of the earth, or, on the other, have exercised arbitrary power upon the sacred books, in despite of the fair methods of interpretation by which alone we are warranted to treat ancient writings.

* "I need not dwell upon the extreme danger of representing, as necessarily subversive of a faith in revelation, physical conclusions received, I believe, by all those who are generally considered as competent judges, as *firmly established* truths."—Rev. W. D. Conybeare, F. R. S. &c. in the *Christian Observer*, for 1834, p. 307.

When we are compelled, by the force of conviction, to make observations of this kind, it is proper to show that we do not stand alone. I consider it to be an advantage for aiding the mind in the pursuit of truth, and therefore to be eminently my duty, to adduce a small number of citations from Christian Philosophers, whose knowledge on these subjects is the hard-earned fruit of fair labour in toiling over hundreds of miles of rocky mountains, and of close study for the rigid scrutiny of results.

I shall first take a few paragraphs from a most diligent and laborious investigator, and a devout Christian. A regard to brevity will oblige me to select detached passages; but they will represent, without perversion or exaggeration, the meaning and design of the continuous pages. Certain English authors are those referred to, but their names need not be introduced.

The hypotheses of those writers have been "defended with no small ability of a certain kind, and with the most dogmatic assurance.—— They were compelled to pay so much deference to the advanced state of science at the present time, as to knock off some of the Hutchinsonian protuberances; yet they have not gone into the core of the system, to make any reformation there. Their works are distinguished——by great positiveness of opinion. Where the ablest Geologists wait for further light, they cut the knot at once.——The relative importance of facts is often presented by them in such a manner, as to betray at once their want of practical acquaintance with the subject.——These works are distinguished by very great severity and intolerance towards the leading Geologists of the last half century. A powerful attempt has been made to exhibit the 'Mosaical and Mineral Geologies' (to borrow the unfair phraseology which figures in one of their titles,) as at variance in their fundamental principles; so that the one or the other must be abandoned: and, in doing this, they have sadly misapprehended the views of Geologists. Because the latter have imputed the changes in the earth's condition to secondary causes, they are charged with Atheism." One of them "says, 'It is manifest that the Mineral Geology, considered as a science, can do as well without God, though in a question concerning the origin of the earth, as Lucretius did.' Now, such a sweeping charge would never have been made had" the writer "not entirely misunderstood the Geologists; or had he been practically familiar with the structure of the earth's crust: for they have referred to second causes those changes, which no man thoroughly acquainted with them would regard as miraculous, any more than he would the existence of such a city as London or Paris. And they have had no idea of *doing without God*, because they suppose the world to have had an earlier origin than" the censurer "admits: for, at whatever period it began to exist, it would alike require infinite power and wisdom to create and arrange it. Geologists, with scarcely an exception, have decidedly and boldly opposed such views" as these imputations of atheism.—— "The course which" those opponents "have taken, will inevitably produce, among pious men, not familiar with science, a prejudice against it and a jealousy of its cultivation. How disastrous such a result would be, let the painful history of the past testify."—Further "these works are distinguished by the adoption of very extravagant theories, and very great distortion of Geological facts, as well as of the language of Scripture.——None but a Geologist can know what absurdities must be received, and what distortions made of facts, before such opinions can be embraced.——To the Geologist they appear a thousand times more extravagant and opposed to facts, than any opinions that have been entertained by the cultivators of this science. ——But these hypotheses require scarcely less perversion of the Sacred Records."—After giving an instance of this bold dealing with the Bible, the Professor adds, "This, in the matter of interpretation, is 'straining at a gnat and swallowing a camel.'——We have no doubt that" these and similar writers "are sincerely desirous of vindicating Revelation from the attacks of scientific sceptics, and that this desire prompted them to write as they have done. But we cannot doubt that the effect of their works on [those] real Geologists who are sceptical, will be very unhappy. Such persons will see that these authors——do not understand the subject about which they write; and they will see a spirit manifested which will not greatly exalt their ideas of the influence of Christianity."*

I next ask attention to a passage, conspicuous for the beauty of its language, and the justness of its reasoning, from one of the ornaments of the University of Cambridge, the Woodwardian Professor of Mineralogy and Geology.

"A philosopher may smile at the fulminations of the Vatican against those who, with Copernicus, maintained the motion of the earth; but he ought to *sigh* when he finds that the heart of man is

---

* *Historical and Geological Deluges compared;* in the *American Biblical Repository*, vol. ix. passages from p. 108 to 114; 1837. By the *Rev. Edward Hitchcock, L. L. D.*, Prof. of Chemistry, &c. Amherst College, New England.

no better than it was of old, and that his arrogance and folly are still the same.——There are still found some who dare to affirm that the pursuits of natural science are hostile to religion. An assertion more false in itself, or more dishonourable to the cause of true religion, has not been conceived in the mind of man.

"The Bible instructs us, that man and other living things, have been placed but a few years upon the earth; and the physical monuments of the world bear witness to the same truth. If the Astronomer tells us of myriads of worlds not spoken of in the sacred records; the Geologist, in like manner, proves (not by arguments from analogy, but by the incontrovertible evidence of physical phenomena [presented to the plain cognizance of our senses,]) that there were former conditions of our planet, separated from each other by vast intervals of time, during which man, and the other creatures of his own date, had not been called into being. Periods such as these belong not, therefore, to the moral history of our race; and come within neither the letter nor the spirit of revelation. Between the first creation of the earth and that day in which it pleased God to place man upon it, who shall dare to define the interval? On this question, scripture is silent: but that silence destroys not the meaning of those physical monuments of his power which God has put before our eyes, giving us, at the same time, faculties whereby we may interpret them and comprehend their meaning.

"In the present condition of our knowledge, a statement like this is surely enough to satisfy the reasonable scruples of a religious man. But let us, for a moment, suppose that there are some religious difficulties in the conclusions of Geology: how then are we to solve them?—Not by shutting our eyes to facts, or denying the evidence of our senses; but by patient investigation carried on in the sincere love of truth, and by learning to reject every consequence not warranted by direct physical evidence. Pursued in this spirit, Geology can neither lead to any false conclusions nor offend against any religious truth. And this is the spirit in which many men have of late years followed this delightful science; devoting the best labours of their lives to its cultivation; turning over the successive leaves of nature's book, and interpreting her language, which they know to be a physical revelation of God's will; patiently working their way through investigations requiring much toil of both mind and body; accepting hypotheses only as a means of connecting disjointed phenomena, and rejecting them when they become unfitted for that office, so as, in the end, to build only upon facts and true natural causes. All this they have done, and are still doing: so that, however unfinished may be the fabric they have attempted to rear, its foundations are laid upon a rock.——

"But there is another class of men, who pursue Geology by a nearer road and are guided by a different light. Well-intentioned they may be; but they have betrayed no small self-sufficiency, along with a shameful want of knowledge of the fundamental facts they presume to write about. Hence, they have dishonoured the literature of this country, by 'Mosaic Geology,' 'Scripture Geology,' and other works of cosmogony with kindred titles; wherein they have overlooked the aim and end of revelation, tortured the book of life out of its proper meaning, and wantonly contrived to bring about a collision between natural phenomena and the word of God.——They have committed the *folly* and the SIN, of dogmatizing on matters which they have not personally examined, and, at the utmost, know only at second-hand; of pretending to teach mankind on points where they themselves are uninstructed. Authors such as these ought to have first considered, that book-learning (in whatsoever degree they may be gifted with it,) is but a pitiful excuse for writing mischievous nonsense; and that, to a divine or a man of letters, ignorance of the laws of nature and of material phenomena is then only disgraceful, when he quits his own ground and pretends to teach philosophy.——A Brahmin crushed with a stone the microscope that first showed him living things among the vegetables of his daily food.——

"It would indeed be a vain and idle task, to engage in controversy with this school of false philosophy; to waste our breath in the forms of exact reasoning unfitted to the comprehension of our antagonists; to draw our weapons in a combat where victory could give no honour.——Their position is impregnable, while they remain within the fences of their ignorance.——"*

Another eminent author, after largely discussing this class of subjects, Dr. Chalmers, says: "We conclude with adverting to the unanimity of Geologists in one point,—the far superior antiquity of this globe to the commonly received date of it as taken from the writings of Moses. What shall we make of this? We may feel a security as to those points in which they differ; and, confronting them with one another, may remain safe and untouched between them. But when they agree, this security fails. There

* *Prof. Sedgwick's Discourse on the Studies of the Universities of Cambridge;* passages from p. 148 to 152; 1834.

is no neutralization of authority among them as to the age of the world; and Cuvier, with his catastrophes and his epochs, leaves the popular opinion nearly as far behind him, as they who trace our present continents upward through an indefinite series of ancestors, and assign many millions of years to the existence of each generation."* This eloquent writer cannot have intended to signify "ancestors" and "generations" of the human kind, nor of the existing species of animals; for this would involve a groundless imputation. He probably used those words, without adverting to their proper meaning, and designing only to express animated creatures and the succession of different families and genera.†

* *Edinburgh Christian Instructor*, April, 1814.

† *Sec. ed.* The friend of Dr. Chalmers, mentioned in a former note, has honoured me with a remark on this passage. "Dr. C. does not mean animated creatures at all, but *former* continents: which may be looked upon, by a poetical eye, as the *ancestors* of the present ones. You are not accustomed to his imaginative modes of expression: but long attendance in his class-room, and familiarity with his works, enable me to vouch for my correctness here."

LECTURE II.

DEUT. XXXIII. 13, 15, 16. *Blessed of the Lord be his land; for the precious things of heaven, for the dew, and for the deep that coucheth beneath,——and for the chief things of the ancient mountains, and for the precious things of the lasting hills, and for the precious things of the earth and the fulness thereof.*

THIS beautiful passage, from the dying benedictions of Moses, the faithful servant of God, is not recited from any supposition that it has an immediate reference to the subjects of this lecture. Yet, such an application may be made, upon the ground of a fair and unforced analogy. The passage is a sublime thanksgiving to the Most High, acknowledging the eminent advantages which he had prepared for the tribes of Ephraim and Manasseh, in the approaching partition of Palestine. Their allotment had a moderate line of sea-coast, on which was Joppa, at that time and long after a good port; an ample portion of rich land for pasture and cultivation; and numerous high grounds and hills supplying streams of water, and containing excellent stone and lime for building, with iron and copper in the northern mountains. Thus the description may be properly adduced as comprehending, along with other objects, the class of providential blessings which belong to the mineral kingdom, and which are of so great importance to the wealth and prosperity of a nation. That class of blessings, God has conferred upon our country in a far superior degree: and it certainly becomes us to understand our mercies and be grateful for them. Geological knowledge, if pursued in a right state of mind, will much assist us in this duty.

All observation and every experiment prove, that the sensible world around us is in a state of incessant motion and change, upon all points of the scale, from the internal movements of the matter composing the simplest and minutest body that we can observe, to the motions of the astral orbs and nebulæ, so overwhelming to our power of conception, or even in imagination to follow them.

These changes take place not in a fortuitous and confused manner, but in a regular subjection to principles, mechanical and chemical; which, though few and simple, lead to results, very complicated indeed and recondite, yet ever harmonizing with each other and with the whole system of the universe: and thus these changes are supplying employment to the highest powers of mathematical investigation.

Throughout organized nature, the characters of species approach to each other, group themselves into genera, and those again into families and orders, associated by points of resemblance; and thus they constitute a continuous series of structural forms, functions, and operations, which exhibit, in all their variety, a principle of mutual adaptation reigning throughout; and indicate an entire dependence upon an all-comprehending, and all-arranging Intellect. The machine of the universe is thus maintained in being and action, by an intelligent Cause and Preserver. It would involve a contradiction to say that the universe is itself that cause. The marks which it bears of dependence on a supreme reason of existence, are incontrovertible. Whether that dependence be conceived of as strictly proximate, or whether the efficiency of the divine power pass through one or ten, ten thousand or ten thousand millions, of intervening agencies, can make no difference. Let the unceasing activity of operation move subordinate causes whose number could not be put down in figures, and whose complication no created intellect could follow; it is still the same. "The excellency of the power is of God." Indeed the latter supposition exalts the more highly our view of the divine perfections; the knowledge, wisdom, and power, to which complication and simplicity, remoteness and nearness, an atomic point and all space, —are the same. "God is a spirit.—Do not I fill heaven and earth? saith Jehovah—He is all and in all.—In Him we live, and move, and have our being."

Of this dependent universe, our planet is a part so small that no arithmetician can assign a fraction low enough to express its proportion to the whole. God has appointed it for our habitation, till the great change of death: and, on every account, natural and moral, it is to us full of interest. Its constitution, the alterations of structure and arrangement which are incessantly taking place upon it and within it, its living inhabitants, and those races of creatures once possessing vegetable or animal life, but which have ceased to live,—set before us subjects inexhaustible for examination and delight.

The object of this lecture is not to lay down a digest of geological facts. Such a pretension would be absurd, unless we could work upon a larger scale. But I may well feel assured that my friends will not do themselves so much injustice, as would be the neglect of studying diligently some of the best works, and which may easily be obtained.* I have only to present, as concisely as I can make intelligible by merely verbal description, an enumeration of those truths which are necessary to be known for the purpose of our present investigation. I call them *Truths*, because they appear so to myself, after having taken, I shall be pardoned for saying, no inconsiderable pains, and during not a few years, in examining the evidence of these positions. To detail that evidence would be altogether impracticable, except we could devote many days to it; but my friends will give me credit, that I would not utter what I do not believe to rest upon good ground of certainty or high probability.

I. Concerning the Structure of the Earth, we are acquainted, by sensible evidence, with about the four hundredth part of the distance from the surface upon which we dwell, taken at the sea-level, to the centre. This portion may be called ten miles. But every one must be aware that no such distance can be reached by direct descent. To the bottom of the deepest seas, from the water-surface, may be seven miles: The average depth of the sea is pretty well ascertained to be about three miles: the highest of the European mountains, Montblanc, is not quite three miles: the highest peak of the Himalaya mountains falls short of five miles:

* If, for the sake of my younger friends, I mention the works which I can with most satisfaction recommend, omissions must not be understood as intimating any disparagement. Lyell's *Elements*, and his earlier and larger work, the *Principles of Geology*; let the inquirer obtain the last edition of each; also Mr. L.'s two volumes, full of miscellaneous as well as geological interest, *Travels in North America*, 1845; Phillips's *Guide to Geology*, his *Treatises* in the Edinburgh Encyclopædia and the Cabinet Cyclopædia, both works published separately, and that in the Encyclopædia Metropolitana; his *Yorkshire Geology*, two quarto volumes; his *Geological Map of the British Isles*; his *Palæozic Fossils of the West of England*; Conybeare and William Phillips's *Outlines of the Geology of England and Wales*; a work, to our great regret, not yet finished, and of which a revised edition and the completion are earnestly looked for; Buckland's *Bridgewater Treatise*, with the Supplementary Notes published separately; Sir Henry de la Beche's *Researches*, his quarto volume of *Geological Sections and Views;* his *Manual*, and his *Report of the Geology of Cornwall, Devon, and West Somerset;* Mantell's works on *Sussex*, and the *S. E. of England*, his *Wonders of*

each of the two deepest mines in Great Britain, one in Cornwall, the other at Monk Wearmouth in the county of Durham, is stated upon the authority of the Treasurer of the Geological Society,*

Geology;(1) *Medals of Creation; Thoughts on a Pebble*, a beautiful little book, adapted for young inquirers; *First Lessons*, an *Introduction to the Phenomena of Geology; Thoughts on Animalcules*, 1846; Fitton's *Geology of Hastings;* Murchison's small treatise on the *Geology of Cheltenham*, his splendid works on the *Silurian Region*, and the *Geology of Russia*. There are many other books written with sound knowledge and accurate judgment. An inestimable accession to the stores of Geological information, and the aids for labour in the field and study in the closet, is made by the new edition (1840) of Mr. Greenough's *Geological Map of England and Wales*, the fruit of twenty years' application in the improvement of the first, though that was the object of universal admiration. Mr. Charles Maclaren's *Geology of Fifeshire:* Prof. Hitchcock's *Elementary Geology*, second ed. 1841, a work peculiarly adapted to theological students; Mr. Richardson's (of the British Museum,) *Geology for Beginners*, a volume which, without the slightest disparagement of any other, is entitled to be universally read and studied by proficients as well as "beginners." Prof. Ansted's *Geology, Introductory, Descriptive, and Practical;* his *Ancient World, or Picturesque Sketches of Creation;* the *Mosaic Creation, viewed in the light of Geology*, by the Rev. George Wight, of Doun in Perthshire; 1846. *Index Geologicus*, a large Tablet, proper to be mounted on cloth and rollers; by Mr. George Bartlett of Plymouth. It presents a Synoptic View of the Mineralogy of the Formations, their geological characters, and succession, ample lists, parallel with each formation, of the Organic Remains, Vegetable and Animal, properly arranged, with their geographical position, and agricultural notices. As a concomitant aid, and a subsequent review of geological treatises, it will be found of signal use. To those who have not, or who could not use, the Five noble Tablets with Figures (*Geologische General Karte; oder Synoptische Uebersicht des Zustandes der Erde, in ihren verschiedenen Altern;*) published at Weimar in 1838, Mr. Bartlett's elaborated arrangement will be an excellent substitute.

As a valuable companion to these interesting studies, and possessing the closest relation to Geology, I feel no little pleasure in recommending the *Præ-Adamite Earth*, by the Rev. Dr. John Harris.

---

(1) This Work of Dr. Mantell's is peculiarly adapted to serve not merely as an attractive introduction to geological science, but as a comprehensive manual of the principal facts already known, and lines of inquiry which invite pursuit. It has rapidly passed through six editions; besides one (and probably more) in New England, to which Dr Silliman has prefixed a large and instructive Introduction. In it, that distinguished philosopher says, "The title is appropriate: but it would be great injustice to consider this work as a mere collection of *mirabilia*. It embraces in truth a *regular system* of Geology, exhibiting its leading facts, and clearly elucidating its philosophy, which is the great object of the work."

* John Taylor, Esq. in *Report III. of the British Association for the Advancement of Science*, 1833, page 427. [From which I derive the following particulars:

	Eng. ft.
The Kitspühl copper mine, not worked for the last seventy or eighty years	2764
The Sampson, Hartz; silver	2230
Monk Wearmouth; coal. *Auth. of Prof. Johnston*, 1838	1620
Pearce's Cornwall; copper, &c.	1464
Ecton, Staffordshire; copper	1380

But it must be observed that these depths are measured from the mouth of the mine, which, as the countries are mountainous, is always much above the height of plains.

at a little more than three-tenths of a mile: and the deepest mine of which we have any correct measurement, and which may fairly be regarded as the deepest in the world, at the village of Kitspühl in Upper Austria, is a little more than half a mile.

It may then be asked, upon what grounds we regard the distance, or to speak more correctly the thickness, of nearly ten miles of the external part of the earth as known to us by ocular observation. Not a fortieth part of this could have been excavated, or in any way, penetrated, if the surface of the earth were what Dr. Thomas Burnet and some other theorists of the last century imagined to have been its pristine, and, according to their notions, beautiful, and sacred condition, before it became deformed by the sin of man; that is, if the earth's surface were that of a perfect mathematical sphere, without seas and islands, without valley, rock, or mountain, with "not a wrinkle, scar, or fracture," (to use the learned dreamer's own words;)—and which, he seems never to have thought, would be to the eye of a spectator a universal plain, a dead flat. Little knew those speculatists that what they deemed deformity, was the cause of all the life and beauty of our lower world; that without it we should have had no springs of water, no rivers, no stone or lime to build with, no metals to make tools of, no healthy condition of the atmosphere, and but a very scanty and low existence of vegetable and animal life. Happily for the human race, the Creator of the earth did not see fit to form it upon this plan. Its rind, shell, or crust (each of which terms is used, but none of them is free from impropriety, though the last is the best,) consisting of a number of extended masses of various thickness, and spread out one over the other, has been raised up by a power acting from below; and, from the horizontal position which originally but at different times belonged to the larger number, they have been inclined in all degrees, so that the lowest in order have been elevated to form the summits of the

The Woolf's, in Cornwall, is 1350 feet deep, of which 1230 descend below the sea-level: "while the bottom of the shaft of Valenciana in Mexico" (depth 1770) "is near 6000 feet in absolute height above the tops of the shafts in Cornwall. The bottom of the shaft at the Sampson mine, is but a few fathoms under the level of the ocean.—We have only penetrated to the extent of one thirty-two-thousandth part of the earth's diameter."

From the *American Journal of Science*, by the Professors Silliman, (March 1846, p. 264,) we learn that an Artesian well at Mondrop is above 2200 feet deep, and is still in boring, the water rising at the temperature of 95°; and that the Artesian well at Grenelle near Paris, through the chalk, is above 1794 feet; the temperature of the water, 82°.]

loftiest mountains, and their ridges constitute the edges of the basins or troughs in which subsequent deposits have been laid. The masses, beds, or layers, technically called *strata*, so upraised, present of course their broken edges; and, by following these out-croppings, (as they are significantly called,) with careful search and scientific discrimination, through extensive tracts of country, the series is disclosed, from the crystalline rocks upon which the first or lowest stratum rests, up to the last or newest which, in plains for the greater part, lies immediately under the soil on which we live, build our habitations, and cultivate our food.

All strata follow antecedent ones in an order which is certain and invariable for every region of the earth, so far as investigation has been carried; and it has been carried, with great care and skill, far enough to render any exception from this rule extremely improbable. If the entire series exist in superposition in any places, it must be on a line of perpendicular descent, under low plains, which would admit of but a trifling depth of penetration, as water must soon fill the shafts, and the utmost depth to which any well can be sunk is but a small fraction of the perpendicular descent necessary to be explored. But this impracticable proof is utterly unnecessary; because the demonstration of the facts is incomparably more perfect from the out-cropping of strata, and their exposure upon large surfaces, highly inclined or even vertical, in mountainous countries and sea-cliffs. No where, however, is the entire series found. Some member or many are wanting in every assignable locality; but they are never put in a violated order. Also, exact mineralogical identity of composition is not necessary to constitute what I may call the right and title to a given station: analogy of composition, order of succession, and (which is the most interesting and decisive evidence,) similarity of organic remains, produce a sufficient equivalence; and when these three kinds of proof concur, we have a complete demonstration.

It may be objected that our data are insufficient; and that, unless we possessed a knowledge of the terrene matter, whatever it may be, and into whatsoever formations it may be subdivided, through the whole interior, and under every part of the superficial circumference to the centre, we are not in a capacity to draw safe conclusions, concerning the contained materials, their composition, their arrangement, their relations to each other, and any rationally conceived mode in which subordinate causes may have operated, initially, successively, or concurrently, in the production of the matter of our globe.

The objection would be weighty, if there were reason to suppose that the body of the globe, beyond the boundary-line of our inspections, were similar to the part already explored. If, for example, the objector could say to us, "You have arrived at no term. You cannot show us the indications of a cessation of the materials which you say have been deposited, and which form the portion through which you have passed. The series may be repeated, possibly again and again: or there may be another series, of entirely different composition, such as precipitates from suspension in water, or products of chemical action, or results of igneous fusion; and so on indefinitely. Unless you had penetrated through all these, you can draw no conclusion on which dependence can be placed."

But the objector cannot say this. He would be guilty of a false assumption. The true state of the facts is the very contrary to what he supposes. We are acquainted certainly, I might almost say perfectly, with the character and succession of the deposited substances which, laid upon each other with a remarkable degree of uniformity over the whole surface, compose the crust of our globe; and we know the totally different constitution of the materials which lie underneath.* We see demonstrated with satisfactory clearness, the distinct character and the opposite mode of production of these two classes of mineral formations. We have all the evidence that can reasonably be desired of the previous condition of those underlying rocks, their ancient, and at a depth not great their present, liquidity by heat, their boiling up, their extrusion both in the melted state and in different degrees of advancement towards being cooled and hardened, their being driven upwards through the overlying formations of deposited layers, their sometimes insinuating themselves between the previously contiguous surfaces of those deposits, their filling long furrows of outbursts, and their being laid bare in many cases to open daylight. It is therefore no presumption to affirm that we do know, with the

* "Geological investigation may, at the present time, be considered as having fully exhausted Europe, and the greater part of America; and the general uniformity of the geological series, in all the various regions hitherto explored, extending as they do, over a full third of both the Eastern and the Western hemispheres, reduces to a very low degree of probability the anticipation that we shall hereafter discover any new and important term of that series."—*Quart. Rev.*, March, 1846, p. 350.

clearness of sensible evidence, the constituent formations of the crust of the earth, their modes of production, their relations to each other, and the fact of their enveloping a mass of materials, similar in composition to the lowest rocks, and which we have much reason to think are, at certain depths, still in a state of constant fusion. The consolidated crust, with its superincumbent masses, is constantly undergoing elevations and depressions, in different districts; shewing, by those undulations, that it rests, or rather floats, upon a liquid surface.

Those who bring forward this objection are, perhaps, not aware of its bearing. Were it well founded, its effects would be to augment, by immeasurable degrees, the antiquity which must be attributed to the earth.

In replying to this objection, which is brought up at the very threshold of geological inquiry, I have been led into an anticipation of several positions, which must be stated more in regular detail.

II. There are good grounds for supposing that, beyond a certain thickness for the solid crust of the earth, which can hardly be estimated at so much as thirty miles,* the next contiguous matter is in a state of fusion, at a temperature probably higher than any that man can produce by artificial means; or any natural heat that can exist on the surface. Whether, in like manner, the whole interior of our planet be composed of melted matter; or whether there be a solid nucleus; and whether such nucleus be close-grained, or more probably cavernous, the solid partitions being infusible and the disseminated vesicles filled with gaseous substances at a very high temperature; thus presenting an analogy to the appearance of ordinary boiling liquids;—are parts of the problem upon which eminent geologists are not agreed. But in this they are agreed, that they will not put conjecture, however probable, in the rank which is due only to decisive evidence; and that they will wait with patience till such evidence shall be attained. In the mean time the highest efforts of mathematical genius are on the stretch for the resolution of the problem. But that a large part of the interior matter of the earth, and that part in contact with the solid crust on which we dwell, is in the state of fusion by heat, appears to be a doctrine established by most

* Supplementary Note B b; on the thickness of the solid crust of the earth.

satisfactory proofs. It should be considered, that the mean density of the earth is not quite five-sevenths of that of iron,* nor half that of silver, nor one-fourth of that of gold: facts utterly inconsistent with the supposition that the interior is a solid mass, or occupied by vast bodies of water, in its ordinary liquid state, united or detached; or indeed any thing but a fluid or fluids maintained in that state by the action of heat as an antagonist power to gravitation. This mean density is rather more than double that of granite.

III. The rocks which lie the lowest in the descending order, and which of course are under all the stratified deposits, are in the state which has been produced by the prodigious heat that has been mentioned, acting under a pressure from above so great as incomparably to exceed any familiar weight or force that we could mention as a measure of comparison. Those rocks bear clear marks of having crystallized in structure, and contracted in mass, by cooling from a state of fusion. It has been objected, that the component parts of those rocks melt at unequal degrees of heat; as in the constituents of granite, which are quartz, mica, and felspar, the last of these ingredients is fused at about half the temperature which the first requires.

But they who make this objection overlook the fact of the extreme pressure under which the power of heat was exerted; which would prevent the most fusible substance from being volatilized at the highest point that could exist: neither can they argue from the inequality of the points of fusion of the minerals when extricated, that the compound would not melt even in far less favourable circumstances; for most persons are acquainted with the ready fusion of metallic compounds, though at a point considerably different from that which each ingredient would require singly.

IV. The rocks which lie above these, though partial crystallization, generally aqueous but sometimes igneous, is found in them, are demonstrably of a different origin. They are all composed of earthy matter, that is, different mixtures of sand, clay, and lime, with minor proportions of some other interspersed minerals. These have been washed away from the previously elevated rocks by the action, first, of the atmosphere and variations of temperature,

* After the admirable labours of Maskelyne and Cavendish, it has been determined, beyond the chance of any further correction, by the late Mr. Francis Baily, to be five times and sixty-hundredths that of water.

disintegrating and loosening the surfaces; and then of dropping rain and running rills and streams, washing off the materials, in fine particles or coarser grain, through all degrees of attenuation; carrying them down into lower situations; and finally, after perhaps a very long succession of these transporting and sedimentary processes, depositing them on levels of rest, in the quiet bottoms or local depressions of lakes and seas. Each sediment or deposit is called a layer, or bed; for conveniency using the Latin word *stratum*. These stratified formations may be called about forty in number; in thickness, sometimes only a few feet or even inches, but usually many hundreds or several thousands of feet. Stratification must be distinguished from homogeneous lamination, which is a frequent character of single strata, presenting at their edges the appearance of leaves, like those of a book or a bundle of pasteboards. Taking some general resemblances of mineral composition as a principle of classification, the whole of the existing beds may be distributed into a small number of groups, in a measure according to the convenience of the geological observer, describer, or reasoner; though most acquiesce in making about twelve divisions, which, for the most part, have very distinct natural characters. Such a distribution is, at least, useful as an aid to the memory.

V. These beds of deposited earthy substances are not to be conceived of as concentric spheres, spread universally over the earth, the outermost including lower ones, and thus embracing the globe; as the paper and varnish which cover artificial globes, or the coats of liliaceous bulbs, commonly but inaccurately called bulbous roots. Such an idea would be quite erroneous, and would betray into great misapprehensions. But each layer is of some limited extent; considerable, it may be, in reference to the superficial divisions of country, but not exceedingly great in comparison with the whole surface of the earth. Each usually thins off towards its edges, or the edges are abruptly broken by the upheaving and dislocating force: and the highest strata generally lie in hollows of various form and extent, which may be called troughs or basins, the edges of which are made by the elevated ridges of the oldest formations, so beautifully called in scripture, "the great mountains, the everlasting hills, the pillars of heaven."

VI. The lower strata, manifestly the most early, are generally of the greatest extent in length and breadth, and very much the deepest in thickness.* The higher and newer are severally of less magnitude in every dimension. Yet, in no case, must the idea of size or extent be taken upon a trifling scale. Even with the more recent, the area of one formation is often some hundreds of square miles.

VII. Thus are formed the earthy beds called by the general name of *rocks;* but this term must not be understood as it is in common language, to denote a stony mass necessarily very hard. The consolidation of the formations, is in all degrees, from the loose sand and gravel under our feet, or the friable Hastings sand-rock, and the soft coherent texture of the ink-coloured clay which lies beneath our gravel; to the finest close-grained marble and the heaviest hornblende. The degree of hardness, the result of consolidation, is upon the whole the greater, the lower we descend; as must appear probable to the mind of any reflecting person. It is produced by the action and reaction of two opposite forces; the one, derived from the mere weight of the materials, which must press more heavily as the depth is increased; and the other, one whose power is principally exerted upon the lowest class of strata, and which, it scarcely needs to be said, arises from the expanding property of the interior heat. Chemical affinities, also, and electrical action, have had, and continually have, a considerable share in the producing of texture.

VIII. Those lower strata, and in the proportion of their distance from the surface, which is the same as their proximity to the focus of heat, bear the more abundant proofs of having been, not only urged upwards by the expansive power below, but in other ways acted upon by the immensely high temperature. The source of that heat can be no other than the fires which had melted and driven upwards the materials forming the rocks of fusion. We have great reason to believe that these deep-seated fires (—scarcely however to be so called, when we reflect how near they must be to the surface,—) or, as some eminent geologists are disposed to think, certain remainders of them, are perpetually in action.

* On the margin of Mr. Phillips's Geological Map of the British Isles (a model of clearness and beauty) is a proportionate scale of the thicknesses of the whole series of strata; from which it appears that all the formations from the superficial soil to the lowest part of the New Red Sandstone, constitute but about one-sixth of the entire depth (geologically) of the stratified masses. The remaining five parts are the Carboniferous, the Devonian (Old Red Sandstone,) the Silurian, the Cambrian, the Cumbrian, the Chlorite and Mica Schists, and the Gneiss. See *Edinb. Rev.* July, 1839, p. 434; part of a valuable article on Mr. Lyell's Elements.

Consequently, the order of production, in those rocks of fusion, must be the reverse of that which is seen in the rocks of deposition and stratification. The uppermost masses are the oldest; and the newest, so long as they remain in their proper place, must be deep-seated beyond the reach of human inspection, and lying in contact with the amazing mass of melted mineral matter. There are also examples innumerable, and upon a grand scale, of the melted mineral matter having been driven up with a force so great as to have overcome every resistance, breaking through all the hard and thick rocky masses (which must also have been full of cracks from the shrinking while cooling,) that lay over it, bending, bursting, uplifting, and overturning strata, filling the chasms made, running in those lines of crack or fissure, separating strata and entering between their previously close-lying surfaces, so as to form flat tablets, often also coming to the surface and towering above all that it had displaced. These cases are of frequent occurrence, and they form an exception to the observation just made with respect to the relative antiquity of the fused rocks, of which these projected kinds have come up from the lowest depths and the most recently. In fact, those fused rocks may be of all ages; the most recent being of course at the lowest depth, till violent ejection takes place.*

* It would be mean injustice to refrain from acknowledging the obligations under which Geology lies to Dr. James Hutton. His *Theory of the Earth*, published in 1788, propounds the doctrines of the igneous action, its propulsions, and its effect on deposited masses, by felicitous anticipations and reasonings of extraordinary sagacity; the most important of which he lived to see confirmed by visible facts. He died in 1797. Few persons, during his life-time, could appreciate the value of his discoveries and the force of his arguments; and still fewer were willing to do so. The charge of impiety and infidelity was made against him; and he seems to have given himself little disquiet about it. Whether he was really a disbeliever in religion, I know not. His day of life and his connexions were extremely unfavourable to the just treatment of religious questions, and the cultivation of enlightened faith. Inferences which his adversaries drew from his writings, but which were not just inferences, they spared not to lay upon him. His manner of expression was often inconsiderate, obscure, or unguarded; and sometimes exposed to just censure. But the fact ought not to be lost sight of, that his fundamental principles are now admitted, and their great importance felt, by all geologists; few, if any, being excepted. The impartial lover of truth would do well to read the article in the Edinburgh Review, (No. cxl. July, 1839,) upon Mr. Lyell's Elements of Geology; both for its general value and for its discursion on the merits of James Hutton. That any physicists and philosophers are hostile and scornful with regard to Christianity, is deeply to be lamented. Such a fact, in whatever degree it may exist, is due to prejudice, ignorance, irreligious education, or other moral causes: but to treat them with injustice is not the way which Jesus Christ would have adopted, and it can only tend to render their prejudices more inveterate. There is another admirable article in

IX. As we ascend in the order of the strata, we find the appearances of the action of fire become fainter. The pervading influence of a high temperature diminishes, till little or no sensible effect from it remains; and, though the mechanical displacements are still perceptible, they are remote and often secondary results of the power that has acted so far below; and the intensity of the action is weakened, in proportion to the distance from its source.

X. By that mighty action from within, the extruding tendency radiates generally, but with unequal force, to all points on the spheroidal surface of the earth. It follows, that the earlier strata with scarely any exceptions, and in smaller degrees the less ancient, have been raised up, shattered, and left in various positions of fracture and inclination. Of those dislocating movements, the mode has been different; and as to the time of production, the process has been generally very slow; though, in some cases, there are evidences of the disturbing force having acted suddenly and violently. From the portions thus elevated, and left with an irregular outline, the waters in flowing off carried down the loosened materials, and, in different extent and degree, left bare the stony masses.

XI. But it is upon reflection obvious, and the geological evidences of the fact are numerous and decisive, that the ebullient action of the fire-melted liquid below is likely to produce undulations of the surface, and therefore, in some places, to cause diminutions of density, and perhaps vast caverns filled with aëriform fluids. The crust of the earth, over these less solid spots, will be weakened, and a sinking down will take place through, it may most probably be, a large area of the surface. These subsidences may, in some rare cases, be rapid: but generally they, as the elevations, will be extremely slow.

XII. Now I fear that I must put to trial the patience of my friends in an attempt to describe in words a complicated series of operations which, by arguing from effect to cause, we have sufficient reason to believe must often have taken place, in ways equivalent to what I request you to conceive. But this is not the

the same Review, No. cxxxi. April, 1837, on Dr. Buckland's Bridgewater Treatise, pp. 4—14.——It is highly gratifying to meet with such a sentence as the following, from one who deservedly stands so high as a mathematician and a philosopher: "I would venture to express my belief that, among the most eminently distinguished philosophers of the present day in this country, there exists even a profoundly religious spirit."—Prof. Baden Powell's *Tradition Unveiled*; p. 65. 1839.

forming of an imaginative hypothesis: it is no more than expressing in the form of simple narrative, facts of whose separate reality we have the fullest evidence, and the consecutive occurrence of which we consider as in the highest degree probable.

Let the mind represent to itself a large space of the bed of an ancient ocean, into which the sedimentary materials from the land have been transported, through a period of time to us immeasurable. Along this extended surface the deposits, in the varieties which changing circumstances in both the land and the waters have produced, are spread. By the weight of an ocean five or six miles in depth, and by the antagonist pressure, with intensity varying but always great, of heat from the under-lying fires, this formation is consolidated. A series of movements from below raises up a portion of this deposit; till it is above the water-level, with its hills and dales and susceptibilities of further variation of surface. Ages roll on. Other strata are laid upon the portion of the area which had not partaken of the elevating movements; or which may have moved in the contrary direction; that is, may have sunk down: so that a difference of mineralogical (called also lithological) character is produced over it. The former portion long lies as a part of the dry land, is washed over by rains and rivers, and is subjected to other causes of superficial change; then it becomes subject to the process of slow subsidence, consequent upon fluctuation or some other change in the fiery region below, and it becomes once more the bed of oceanic waters. Here, in due but various process of time, it is overspread with a new stratum, differing from its own preceding surface, and from the one or several strata which had in succession been laid upon the portion not elevated during the whole period; the difference being probably in mineral composition and texture, but more certainly in the character of vegetable or animal remains which are imbedded in it. Now the new body of deposits may be identical over the entire extent first supposed. It is manifest, therefore, that in one part the last stratum will rest upon the foregoing one, which had been long elevated and exposed to causes of change; and thus the surfaces at the junction will be irregular: but, upon the portion which had not been raised out of the waters, or which had sunk, one stratum or several have been deposited throughout the intervening period, and they will probably rest conformably, each upon that below it, that is, their bounding surfaces will correspond to each other in lines nearly parallel. The whole area comes afterwards to be elevated; or only some parts of it. One part, therefore, possesses a series of strata which are not found in the other; and that other, if studied alone, might suggest the idea that two formations naturally came together, or that the upper always followed the lower at once, while yet between them in reality some others have intervened.

These operations of deposition, elevation, subsidence, and elevation again, in application to separate districts, and in different periods through an indefinite duration,—have been repeated a number of times; each repetition producing breaks, fissures, and manifold displacings, erections, and inclinations, of the more hard and consequently frangible strata; and bendings, even to a complete overturning, or contortion backwards of the softer and more coherent ones. The evidence of elevation and that of subsidence occur frequently within moderate geographical limits; so that two districts with their intervening ground may be familiarly compared to a long board, balanced on a fulcrum: when one end sinks the other rises.* Often under the superficial area of less than an acre, and with a descent of but a few feet, may be seen, even in beds very similar in earthy composition, such disconformity of the bounding surfaces, with respect to their deviation from the horizontal position, as carries demonstration that each member of the series had been formed, elevated, and afterwards inclined; so that the next deposit came to be laid upon a dipping surface, while its own upper part was on the level: yet this also, with its under-lying neighbours, has received another impulse from below; repose has succeeded, a new layer is deposited, the inclination has taken another change; and this succession of unconformable strata is displayed several times. Such is the case in the Oolitic formations:

* *Sec. ed.* Of this operation examples have recently occurred in the landslips, or rather subsidences, at the cliffs of Dowlands and Whitlands; of which a very instructive elucidation is given in Mr. Lyell's sixth edition of his Principles, vol. ii. p. 78. But the inquirer will find the fullest information upon the facts, and the most satisfactory opinions as to the causes, briefly and luminously stated in a *Descriptive and Geological Memoir of the Subsidences of the Land, and the Elevation of the Sea-bottom, between Axmouth and Lyme, Dec.* 26, 1839, *and Feb.* 3, 1840; with Sections by Mr. Conybeare, a Ground Plan by Mr. Dawson of Exeter, and seven faithful and beautifully picturesque Views of the scenes, two of which are from the pencil of Mrs. Buckland, and five from that of Mr. Dawson: the whole revised by Dr. Buckland. Annexed are accounts of similar phenomena, in the same neighbourhood in 1790, and at various times in Dorsetshire, the Isle of Wight, Kent, Hampshire, Gloucestershire, Shropshire, and other places.

and how much more must this be the case when a number of strata, of differing composition, is taken into the account?——By an abundance of various and complicated evidence, it is proved, that there is probably no spot on the face of the earth, both the dry land and the seas as they at present exist, which has not gone repeatedly through the conditions of being alternately the floor of the waters, and an earthy surface exposed to the atmosphere and occupied by appropriate tribes of vegetable and animal creatures. At the next engulfing, that loose surface has been swept off by the power of the waters. In some cases, the bounding surfaces of differing but nearly allied strata seem to have been produced while under the water; by a rapid change of temperature, or an immission of carbonic acid gas, or some other physical agent.

The miscellaneous result might seem to baffle all attempts at arrangement and safe induction; but the labours of distinguished men, most of them our admirable contemporaries, in the field of actual investigation, with astonishing toil and perseverance, guided by cautious judgment and habits formed in the study of the exact sciences, have triumphed over what might have appeared a hopeless confusion; and have reduced to a certainty scarcely short of sensible and mathematical proof, the modes of deposition, the order of original succession, and in many cases that of subsequent change.

From the description which I have endeavoured to give, it will be easily understood, that the order of succession is never transgressed; though particular formations, one, two, or more, in a system or subdivisional group, and of course many in the whole series, may and must be wanting. Those formations either have never existed, in consequence of modifying causes affecting the operations which I have attempted to describe; or they have been removed by the nearly horizontal action of water, washing away large masses of strata, scattering and spreading their materials upon the floor of the ocean, and thus producing new formations.

XIII. To such removals, occasion has been given by the elevations and depressions so frequently before mentioned. These have exposed the softer or previously loosened materials, to the incursion of mighty bodies of water, which have washed them away, carried them out to shorter or longer distances, dropping the coarser and heavier portions the earliest, holding longer in muddy mixture and transporting to the greater distances the fine and light particles, and spreading them out under the great seas. There these new strata have been disposed variously, according to circumstances arising from the form and constitution of the bottom, the direction of currents, volcanic action below the bed of the sea, molecular aggregation of similar substances, and chemical attractions. This kind of change, in relation to the area from which the surface has been swept off, is called Denudation.

XIV. While these mineral formations were thus in progress, their masses yet soft were replenished with the remains of animals which had lived in the waters; skeletons, coverings, shelly habitations, and even soft parts still exhibiting their vestiges. In all the formations, (or we might say groups or systems of strata,) excepting the earliest two or three, those remains occur of organized creatures, chiefly animal, but in some cases vegetable. The absence or paucity of vegetable remains in the older strata,* except in the beds connected with coal, is reasonably ascribed to the more ready destructibility of vegetable fibre, especially as the earliest species appear to have been of soft structure, though of great size. In the Lias beds, fragments of wood approaching to the harder structure, are abundant: and in the still later formations there are very remarkable instances. But an abundance of vegetable remains does not occur, *except in the coaly strata,* till we arrive at the very recent formations; of which fact geological science affords satisfactory explanations.

Even with respect to those earliest beds, just mentioned, we cannot be absolutely assured that organized nature, vegetable or animal, never existed in them: for their vestiges would [most probably] be destroyed by the heat communicated from below.

XV. As a general assertion, it might be said that the animal remains become more abundant, as we depart from the older strata: but such an assertion would be far from being universally and exactly correct.† In this respect, many interesting circumstances of [extreme] diversity present themselves to the laborious explorer of fossil remains, especially in the department of Conchology.

XVI. With respect to their forms of organization, there is so much general analogy as gives a sufficient ground for the observation that all belong to Classes and Families *similar* to those

[* In the Old Red Sandstone, and even earlier formations, are found some obscure impressions or even scanty remains of sea-weeds;—Fucoides.]

† Supplementary Note, C.

which now exist; but in Genera and Species there are remarkable differences.

XVII. The earliest of known organic remains are the most widely different from animals and plants of the existing creation, in generic, and of course still more in specific characters; and throughout the vast succession there is a gradual approach, in all classes, to the type of recent forms.

XVIII. The duration of existence, in both genera and species, presents many remarkable facts. A few genera, each genus containing perhaps but one species or a very small number, are found to have their respective lengths of time for existence, in some single stratum. In general, they extend through several strata; but then there is a greater multiplication of species, giving proof of periods of remarkable fecundity.

XIX. Each system of strata has species which belong to itself, so that both the mineral formations and those certain species are reciprocally *characteristic.* This fact is among the greatest discoveries of modern times. For it we are indebted to one whose conduct and character should be held up as a model for the imitation of young men, in all the walks of life, that they may aim at the highest excellence and diffusive usefulness;—Dr. William Smith, to whom by general accord, the designation has been given of the *Father of English Geology.*

Fifty years ago, when a very young man, he began his course; he quietly and without ostentation pursued it, in the most laborious examinations of the stratified formations throughout England, chiefly the southern and midland counties. He announced not his discovery till the patience and perseverance of many years had placed it beyond the reach of doubt. He might, by reserve and management not dishonourable, have built up for himself fortune as well as fame; by the benefits which his discovery and his practical knowledge conferred upon the economy of mines, and the surveying of ground in order to building, road-making, and agriculture; besides the firm foundation which he laid for geological science. But with the most open and ready generosity, he communicated all, to men of science and to the world at large.* He

*In and before 1799, "By maps and sections, and arranged collections of Organic Remains, Mr. Smith endeavoured to explain to many scientific persons those views regarding the regular succession and continuity of strata, and the definite distribution of animal and vegetable forms in the earth, which are now the common property of Geo-

constructed the first Geological Map that was worthy of the name, opening the way to Mr. Greenough's disinterested labours; he gave to the world several and most valuable works on the systematic relations of Organized Fossils; and he deposited in the British Museum, for universal instruction, the Collection which verified his doctrines. Long may he enjoy, in his retirement, the happiness most congenial to his liberal mind, and add to that the sublime joys of christian piety and heavenly anticipation!*—But from this tribute of justice, I must return.

Upon this great fact, which Professor Sedgwick happily calls "the Master-Principle of our Science,"† the *Characterism* of Fossils, a number of other truths are dependent, and those of the greatest value both practically and theoretically. A well-prepared Conchological Geologist looks to the succession of strata as the possessor of a cabinet does to the order of his shelves; and with a certainty as precise, knows what species are to be found on every layer.

XX. A small number of genera may be called (if we may imitate one of the pleasantries of Linnæus,) Royal and Noble Families. Comprehending numerous species, they have a truly wonderful range. The genus Leptæna (or Producta) is one of the first that have been ascertained; and, in about fifty species, it is found through the immense series of formations, known as the Cumbrian, the Cambrian, the Silurian, the Old Red Sandstone [or Devonian], and the Carboniferous Limes, Shales and Sands. Spirifer, about equal in origin, passes still higher, through the remarkable varieties of the New Red System; and is found in the Lias. The Am-

logy. Among those who heard his explanations at this early period, may be mentioned Dr. James Anderson of Edinburgh, Mr. Davis of Longleat, the Rev. Joseph Townsend, [of Pewsey,]—and the Rev. B. Richardson of Farley. The *two last-mentioned* gentlemen were *remarkably able* to appreciate the truth and novelty of such views, from both their general attainments in Natural History, and their exact knowledge of the country [Somersetshire and Wiltshire] to which Mr. Smith directed their attention. Both of them possessed large collections of Organic Remains; and both were astonished and incredulous when their new friend, taking up one fossil after another, *stated instantly from what particular rock*, and even *bed of stone or clay*, the specimens were derived. Nor were they less surprised when, in the field, *Stratum Smith* (as he was termed) traced with ease and accuracy the ranges of the rocks, by following the courses of springs, and many other indications of a change of the substrata."—Biogr. Notice, by Prof. Phillips, in Charlesworth's *Magazine of Natural History*. May, 1839; p. 216.

* W. Smith, LL.D., died at Northampton, after a very short illness, Aug. 28, 1839; in his 71st year. As this sentence had been delivered six months before, I do not expunge it.

† *Proceedings of Geol. Soc.* Feb. 18, 1831.

monite, in an amazing number and diversity of species,* appears in the Silurian System, and is found in every formation till it terminates in the Chalk. Terebratula has a far wider range: it begins among the earliest, its numerous species scarcely fail, if at all, till we reach the Chalk, in which they are more abundant than in any other formation; other of its species occur, though in diminished number, throughout the Tertiary System; and it is represented by some twelve or more species in the living creation. Thus each species has a definite period of existence. The succession proceeds. One species dies off, and its place is taken by another of the same genus; till at last, in many cases, the whole genus ceases. Some genera have a confined range, if we may use such a word for periods of probably many thousand years: others have continued through more numerous formations, and some even to the living state of the creation. But, be it observed, I am speaking only of *families* and *genera*. Of *species*, none are found in the Chalk nor in the more early strata, which exist in the present condition of the earth.† Above the Chalk, a small number of the now living species begin to appear: and the proportional number increases through the six or seven Tertiary formations; so that the formation which, as far as has been ascertained, is the last prior to the existing state of nature, contains about ninety-five in the hundred of living species; while the oldest of even these Tertiary beds scarcely yields four living species to ninety-six extinct ones.

* The distinguished conchologist, Mr. Searles Wood, is of opinion that the number of species, including, however, some forms which may be only varieties, approaches to a thousand.

† That none of the now existing *species* of vegetable or animal nature is found so early in geological sequence as the Chalk formation, was the general persuasion of naturalists at the time when these Lectures were first published. But now, an exception must be made of remarkable interest. Of the world of microscopic insects with their shelly coverings (usually called *shields*,) calcareous and often purely siliceous, which have been brought to light by the researches of Prof. Ehrenberg and those who are treading in his steps, it has been discovered that many *species still existing have left their fossil remains in the chalk*, and I believe also in the *green sand*, *the Oolites*, and even earlier rocks: and not only are these found *in* those rocks, but they actually constitute a principal constituent of the mass.

That this should be the fact with respect to these creatures, whose organization is not less complicated, while their diversity of form is far greater, than that of large animals, and their minuteness would for ever have concealed them from man's unassisted eye,—is indeed a surprising disclosure. It cannot but impress us as a new and most unlooked for demonstration of the Mysterious Wisdom, which is "high as the heavens, what canst thou do? deep as the unseen world, what canst thou know?" Job xi. 8. *Fourth ed.*

XXI. The areas, or regions, over which characteristic organic remains are found, though often of great extent, even to the embracing of opposite hemispheres, yet are not universal; thus manifesting that groups of species had their geographical limits: a most important fact, since it establishes a correspondence with that law or condition of the existing animal and vegetable kingdoms, by which species are grouped together, and appropriately confined within geographical districts, man being almost the only exception.

XXII. It is also apparent, that the variations of organization, which form the distinctive characters of species, as those of any given genus succeed each other, have been adapted to the varying condition of the earth's temperature, the atmosphere, and the waters; and undoubtedly made suitable to each other, in their reciprocal relations as partakers of organic life.

XXIII. Besides the fossils which are strictly characteristic of the great systems of strata, there are others which may be considered as subordinate, and which connect the particular formations with those proximate to them, below or above.

XXIV. Strata containing shelly, crustaceous, or coralline remains, generally present appearances which prove to a demonstration that the animals lived and died on the muddy or sandy bottoms of the waters. Those appearances consist in the posture of individual specimens; in the juxtaposition of numbers, as they lie in what may be called tribes or family groups, spread in beautiful order over considerable areas; and in the preservation of their slender, delicate, and fragile parts.

There are other cases, in which the organic remains, be they plants, shells, or bones, exhibit proofs of having been washed away from their native seats, by streams of fresh water, or by tides and currents of the sea; and thus transported into new situations, in which depressions of the bottom, or some obstacle, or the cessation of the force of the water, allowed them to rest; and there the separated parts have become imbedded in the muddy bottom. Those lake or ocean bottoms have been consequently elevated and dried. Again they have sunk and been submerged, so as to form new ocean-beds; over which new alternations of deposition and elevation and depression have taken place. This vast succession of changes presents much and various evidence of having required indescribable periods of time for being effected;

and it should never be forgotten that the same processes are still in operation, and have been so without intermission since the Almighty gave its present form to our habitable earth. There can be no doubt that, from the earliest date of man's brief history, the Nile, the Ganges, and the more mighty rivers of America, have been pouring their waters into the seas at their respective mouths. The quantity of earthy matter (with infinite multitudes of dead animals and portions of them, and the vegetable spoils of the land,) which is without ceasing floated down and added to the formations at the bottom, cannot but be astonishing. By careful experiments it has been ascertained, that the Ganges carries into the Bay of Bengal, annually, the average of 355,361,464 tons' weight; an amount difficult in our imagination to estimate; but to bring it to some auxiliary standard for comparison, Mr. Lyell has calculated that it nearly equals the weight of sixty times the greatest pyramid of Egypt.* The base of that pyramid covers an area equal to that of Lincoln's Inn Fields, and its summit is 150 feet higher than the cross of St. Paul's Cathedral. Yet that sea is not sensibly rendered more shallow; and the river is navigable for large ships to Calcutta. So the Thames and the Severn have been bearing down their sediment for near six thousand years: but how far are their estuaries from being silted up? And, how many thousand years longer will be required to produce that result; should it not be accelerated by a movement from below?

It must, however, be stated, that there is both geological and historical evidence of rapid and even sudden elevations and depressions having taken place in many parts of the globe; but those occurrences have been comparatively rare, and to a limited extent.

XXV. There are two other descriptions of rocks which are neither igneous nor stratified, and which have been from early periods, and still are, in formation. The first of these comprehends two kinds; one consisting of carbonate of lime, deposited by water, generally warm, which had held it in solution, but which drops it on emerging from the earth. This is found abundantly in limestone countries; it is the *travertine* of Italy: the other kind, formed in like manner, by hot water taking up silica (the earth of flints), and depositing it when coming to the air:—the

* *Princip. Geol.* vol. ii. p. 13, sixth ed. in which striking passage are presented other aids to our conception.

great example is in the Geyser springs of Iceland. The second consists of the Coralline Rocks, of many fathoms in depth, and many hundred miles in extent;—the coral rocks of the Red Sea, and the Indian and Pacific Oceans.* These amazing formations are the work of minute insects, which have the property of secreting from sea-water its small quantity of carbonate of lime, and with these apparently petty contributions composing the mighty masses.

XXVI. Every stratum is itself a proof that dry land existed contemporaneously, above the level of the waters: for the mineral materials composing strata are the wearings and washings down, coarse and fine, from the surfaces of the exposed land. Thus were produced areas, formed by each kind of the matter brought down, and having their peculiar characters and boundaries.

XXVII. From the mineral characters of those areas, and from the vertical penetration by various organic species through several strata of different composition, which thus indicate long periods of succession and different conditions of deposition, it is an inference highly probable, if not certain, that there never was a period when the surface of the globe was continuous dry land; nor entirely covered with water, or any mixture of detrital matter in water. In other words: the stratified structure of the earth presents evidence that there have never been universal contemporaneous formations, but that, from the period of the production of the igneous rocks, and the commencement of the stratified, the surface has always consisted partly of limited areas depressed and holding water, and partly of lands rising up from the boundaries of those depressions.†

To this fact in the former periods of the earth, its present condition affords a clear resemblance. The actual Zoology and Botany of its surface exhibit several distinct regions, in each of which the indigenous animals and plants are, at least as to species and to a considerable amount as to genera, different from those of other zoological and botanical regions. Natural agency (such as that of winds and currents) and artificial means have done something

* The classical work on this subject is *The Structure and Distribution of Coral Reefs*, by Mr. Darwin; 1842. A luminous epitome of it, by Mr. Charles Maclaren, is in the *Edinburgh Philos. Journ.* Jan. 1843.

† See the Tabular View; Supplementary Note D.

towards confounding the distinctions of characters; but in the case of countries widely separated, the plants and animals proper to each region so differ from those of every other, as to impress us with the conviction that they have not been derived from a common ancestry for each species, in any one locality upon the face of the earth. They are respectively adapted to certain conditions of existence, such as climate, temperature, mutual relations, and no doubt other circumstances of favourable influence which men have not yet discovered, or which never may be discovered in the present state. These conditions cannot be transferred to other situations. The habitation proper to one description of vegetable or animal families would be intolerable, and speedily fatal, to others. Where the extreme of incongruity does not exist, there are causes of unsuitableness, whose action is less powerful, but slowly and surely effective. Even when, as in many parts of the two hemispheres, and on the contrary sides of the equator, there is apparently a similarity of climate; we find not an identity, but only an analogy, of animal and vegetable species.

It is confessedly difficult to fix with absolute precision the lines of demarcation for these independent domains of living organized nature. The general fact is established beyond the reach of doubt; but naturalists are waiting for a more complete acquaintance with the plants and animals of every part of the globe, before they deem the natural divisions finally determined. According to the degree of knowledge already attained, the following may be accepted as an approximation. A distinguished christian physiologist and philosopher, Dr. Prichard, was the first to bring forward correct views upon this interesting subject; and he proposes *seven* regions for the distribution of animals.* Mr. Swainson pleads for *five*, but upon a ground of analogy which he has assumed without proof, and which is contrary to impregnable truth.† Others make *eleven*.‡ With regard to the vegetable kingdom, some eminent naturalists have given their opinion in favour of ten for the old continents, and six for America:§ but the great philosophical botanists of Geneva, Messieurs de Candolle, father and son, "than whom," says Professor Hitchcock,

* *Researches into the Physical History of Mankind;* vol. i. pp. 68—97, third ed.

† *Geography and Classification of Animals;* pp. 14—18.

‡ Prof. Hitchcock, in the *American Biblical Repository*, vol. xi. p. 17; 1838.

§ Von Schouw's *Fundam. Princip. of a Universal Geography of the Veget. Kingd.* German Transl. from the Danish, by the author, with an Atlas; Berlin, 1824.

"no better judges can be named, reckon the number of distinct "botanical provinces at *twenty-seven.* This estimate was the re- "sult of an examination of seventy or eighty thousand species."* The Rev. J. S. Henslow, the Professor of Botany in the University of Cambridge, a man to whom Geology, as well as the professional science which he adorns, is under great obligations, remarks that "We do not as yet possess any very accurate in- "formation respecting the number and exact extent of the well- "defined botanical regions into which the surface of the earth may "be mapped out:"† but he proposes *forty-five* as an approximating estimate.

Hence it follows that there must have been separate original creations, perhaps at different and respectively distant epochs. Man, whom the Creator formed to "have dominion over the "works of his hands," to a wide extent of the inferior natures, was brought into being in ONE pair; from which all the varieties of our kind have descended. They are only *varieties,* effected by circumstances, and not *species,* which would imply separate primary ancestors. This position, unhappily rejected by some persons, is not only a fact which lies at the foundatian of revealed religion, but it is confirmed by an accumulation of proof from anatomical structure, from history, from the theory of language, and from the philosophy of intellectual and moral qualities. For this assertion I may appeal to the authority of the veteran Blumenbach,‡ who occupies a station among the highest, in the Comparative Anatomy of the different races of men; and to both the authority and the luminous arguments of Dr. Prichard in the work before referred to.§

Man, and a small number of animals peculiarly serviceable to man, are endowed with a capacity of adaptation to all the differences of climate and other circumstances, not indeed unlimited,

* *Amer. Bibl. Repos.* as above. Lyell's *Principles of Geology*, vol. iii. p. 7. Distribution into more numerous groups are ascribed to Von Schouw and De Candolle, in the *Abridgment of Malte Brun's and Balbi's Geogr.* Edin. 1840, part i. pp. 90—93: and into a smaller number, twenty, by De Candolle, as stated by Dr. Prichard in his *Researches*, vol. i. p. 32, third edit.; these differences may be owing to the consultation of different works or editions of the authors, independently of the inherent difficulties of the subject.

† *Descriptive and Physiological Botany;* p. 305.

‡ Born 1752; appointed Professor of Medicine in the University of Göttingen in 1778; and died, Jan. 22, 1840.

§ Supplementary Note E, on the Varieties of the Human Species.

but extending through a wide range.* This capacity requires for its complete developement, a gradual proceeding in subjection to the agents of change; for which the life of no individual is sufficiently long, nor even the duration of several generations. The process must be carried on through many steps of descent; and in its course, considerable alterations of structure are slowly produced.

XXVIII. In every part of the earth, the succession of the strata, and the character and effects of the non-stratified rocks, are the same. Of this fact, the actual observation has been so extensively accomplished, and the operation of mechanical and chemical causes is so certainly understood, that no jealousy or scepticism can avail to prevent the induction from being made universal.

"A few years ago only, when unable to indicate the first created animals, or the exact relative places occupied by some of the earliest formations, we were compelled to trace the sequence downwards, by commencing with deposits previously analysed, proceeding thence to those of anterior date;" [—of which method Sir Roderick's *Silurian System* furnishes a luminous example;—] "but now, having learned to decipher the very first letters in the long records of animal life, we assume a more distinct position as historians, and exhibit in their natural order, the successive organic features which appear in the *stony legend* of the earth, from their earliest dawn to the present condition of the planet.

"In a word,—we can now fearlessly assert, that the geological history of sequence of the earliest races of fossil animals is firmly established. Its truth is sustained by the display of forms, which

* *Sec. ed.* On the borders of the sandy deserts of Africa, and in many other portions of the hot regions of the globe, men live where the ground under their feet is often 140° and even more (Fahr.), and the mean heat of the air around them is from 80° to 90°. On the other hand, in the inhabited country of the Tschutschoi, a little within the Arctic circle, Admiral Von Wrangell, in the winter of 1820, had in his house, — 40°, *i. e.* 72° below the freezing point of water. "The people moved about in the frost of — 41°, as gaily as if it were summer. The Yakuts are still more hardy than the Tschutschoi: lying on the ground in the open air, and often insufficiently protected by clothing, they can endure, without the least injury, a degree of cold which would be inevitably [and almost instantaneously] fatal to a European.—*Athenæum*, June 13, 1840; Review of Von Wrangell's Expedition to the Polar Sea; edited by Colonel Sabine from the Translation of his accomplished lady.

The greatest natural cold known is, from the observation of Sir Edward Parry, — 55°, or even, — 59°; of Sir John Ross, but the accuracy is not quite free from question, — 60°.

mark the period when the first vestiges of life can be discovered, as well as the following SUCCESSIVE CREATIONS; and thus, whilst, with the exception of one sacred record, we can truly say that the origin of the greatest empires of man is buried in fable and superstition, the hard and indelible register, as preserved for our inspection in the great book of ancient nature, is at length interpreted and read off with clearness and precision." *Sir Rod. Murchison's Geol. Russ.* vol. i. p. 9.* 1845.]

The eminent geologist Alcide d'Orbigny, has ascertained, by extensive and accurate study of the requisite authorities, that the geological structure of South America bears a strong resemblance to that of Europe, and that the differences are few and not very striking. *Report to the Paris Acad. of Sc.* stated in the *Athenæum*, Sept. 9, 1843. Combining this information with the labours of the North American geologists, Sir R. M. says, "We can now therefore affirm that, throughout the western hemisphere, from the far north to isles almost within the antarctic circle, the palæozoic deposits succeed each other in the same order as in the British isles." *Geol. of Russia*, vol. i. p. 6. Observation has also shewn that the same characters and succession obtain in Asia both North and South, in Africa, and in Australasia. *Ib.*

LECTURE III.

ROMANS XI. 36. *Of* HIM, *and through* HIM, *and to* HIM, *are all things: to whom be glory for ever.*

SOME of the most important positions affirmed in the preceding lecture could not fail to be perceived by my attentive hearers, to be at variance with certain sentiments or interpretations, which are extensively received under the supposition of their being declared, or at least implied, in the Holy Scriptures. It is now my duty to state, in particular detail, what those sentiments and opinions are; and in what manner they stand in contradiction to the facts in the natural history of the earth, to which we have adverted.

My auditors will do me the favour to observe, that I speak of opinions and *interpretations;* the sentiments which *men have taken up,* and promulgated as the declarations of the Bible. We have not yet arrived at the part of these lectures in which we shall have to examine whether those interpretations are the genuine sense of the divine oracles. It would not be proper to anticipate that inquiry: yet I cannot but be anxious that my friends should keep constantly in mind the avowal made in the first lecture; namely, my conviction that *those interpretations are erroneous.* I solicit this favour as a protection to myself from being understood, in this and the following lecture, to cast any doubt upon the truth and authority of the Scriptures. It is not the word of God, but the expositions and deductions of men, from which I am compelled to dissent.

I. It is a prevailing opinion that the dependent universe, in all its extent, was brought into existence by the almighty power of its Creator, *within the period of the six days* laid down in the first portion of the Book of Genesis; chap. i. throughout, and ii. 1—3, where the editorial division should have been made, as the whole is evidently a connected and complete narrative. The same conclusion is also drawn from the language of the fourth commandment; "In six days the Lord made heaven and earth, the sea, and all that in them is." Exod. xx. 11.

To this mode of understanding the Scripture, the discoveries of geological science are directly opposed. Excepting, [possibly but not certainly,] the higher parts of some mountains, which at widely different epochs have been upheaved, and made to elevate and pierce the stratified masses which once lay over them, there is scarcely a spot on the earth's surface which has not been many times in succession the bottom of a sea, and a portion of dry land. In the majority of cases, it is shown, by physical evidences of the most decisive kind, that each of those successive conditions was of extremely long duration; a duration which it would be presumptuous to put into any estimate of years or centuries; for any alteration of which vestiges occur in the zoological state and the mineral constitution of the earth's present surface, furnishes no analogy, (with regard to the nature and continuance of causes,) that approaches in greatness of character to those changes whose evidences are discernible in almost any two continuous strata.* It is an inevitable inference, unless we are disposed to abandon the principles of fair reasoning, that each one of such changes in organic life did not take place till after the next preceding condition of the earth had continued through a duration, compared with which six thousand years appear an inconsiderable fraction of time. Among other facts, it is to be observed that the instances referred to often involve an increase of temperature to a great amount. For example, it is proved, by the clearest evidence of vegetable remains, that, in what are now temperate or extremely cold climates, there prevailed, during the periods of the earlier secondary rocks, a mean of temperature equal to that of the hottest region upon the present surface of the globe, or probably greater.† It is also shown, by such evidence as every physiologist and every chemist knows to be satisfactory, that, at the periods referred to, the earth's atmosphere (by being loaded with carbonic acid) must have been so different from that which we possess, that the present kinds of animals breathing by lungs, and many kinds

* *Sec. ed.* As the term *stratum* is used with some latitude, so as to be applied to both the greater divisions and those which are less marked, I beg to have it understood here as denoting the principal classes.

† Another evidence of this fact has been adduced by Prof. Edward Forbes, in the characters of the fresh-water shells which are found in the more recent strata preceding the present surface. These prove, by abundant instances, that Britain possessed a

which do not so breathe, could not have existed. Now the evidence, from various points of physical reasoning and from well-known historical facts, is ample, that the same state that now subsists, as to temperature and the constitution of the atmosphere, has belonged to our planet ever since the day that God created man and the animals connected with man. An objection may arise from the recollection that some commentators have supposed, as the mediate cause of the longevity of the antediluvian patriarchs, a peculiarly salubrious quality in the atmosphere, which they also suppose to have been destroyed by the deluge, or in consequence of it. But this is an imaginary hypothesis involving heavier difficulties than what it professes to remove; and, if it were to be accepted, it would add to the weight of reason for the interposition of an immensity of time between the deposition of the carboniferous lime-stone, for instance, and the present epoch; because the condition of the atmosphere which geological evidence evinces to have belonged to the remote period of which we have been speaking, was the reverse of salubrious, or better fitted to support life than our present common air; it would have been instantly, or in a few moments, fatal to man or to any such lung-breathing animals as now exist.

But, while the general evidence for an antiquity of the earth, so great as to set at nought our attempts at estimation, may be compendiously understood by any one who will take moderate pains in studying the appearances of stratification and the characters of organic remains; it ought to be kept in mind that there is a multitude of facts, of a more minute description, and which present themselves on every hand to the practised geologist, each of which has great importance, but the sum of which amounts to an irresistible body of argument. It would be unreasonable to expect that all, of even liberally educated and well informed persons, should be sufficiently versed in Natural History, Chemistry, and the doctrines of mechanical force, to be able readily to apprehend and duly to weigh those facts and the deductions from them: but the claim is reasonable that, in such cases, we should satisfy our-

warmer climate that can be assigned to the human period. *Zoo-Geological Considerations*, &c. in the *Annals and Magazine of Natural History;* vol. vi. 1841, p. 242. Many such evidences occur in the fossil animal remains of older periods.

[It is maintained by Prof. Agassiz and others, as probable, that there has been one at least intercalated period, in which our northern hemisphere has been subjected to a temperature very much lower than its present mean.]

selves by giving credit and honour where credit and honour are due. We feel no difficulty in thus relying upon conclusions drawn, in the way of mathematical reasoning, by Newton, Bradley, Laplace, and the Herschels; and, were we to indulge the monstrous supposition that such men were willing to deceive, we know that there are thousands able and ready to detect the minutest error, and expose any misstatement, if such there were. Upon this ground, therefore, I may take a few sentences from a mathematician and man of science, from whom, in the first lecture, I derived an important citation, and who, till his recent resignation, filled the chair of Newton. In his work, "The Ninth Bridgewater Treatise," Mr. Babbage has the following words:

"In truth, the mass of evidence which combines to prove the great antiquity of the earth itself, is so irresistible, and so unshaken by any opposing facts, that none but those who are alike incapable of observing the facts and appreciating the reasoning, can for a moment conceive the present state of its surface to have been the result of only six thousand years of existence.——Those observers and philosophers who have spent their lives in the study of Geology, have arrived at the conclusion, that there exists irresistible evidence, that the date of the earth's first formation is far anterior to the epoch supposed to be assigned to it by Moses; and it is now admitted by all competent persons, that the formation even of those strata which are *nearest the surface*, must have occupied vast periods, probably millions of years, in arriving at their present state." Pp. 67, 78.

As another example, I may mention that Mr. Charles Maclaren, in a valuable contribution to Geology, very recently published, estimates a single period of volcanic quiescence, during which strata of coal, shale, sandstone, and limestone were deposited over the site of the basaltic hill called Arthur's Seat, at Edinburgh, at five hundred thousand years.* Let it be observed that these are not random guesses, but founded upon knowledge and consideration.†

This is indeed a cumulative argument. It arises from a number and variety of considerations which, without exaggeration, we may call inexhaustible. The active geologist can scarcely enter

* *Geology of Fife and the Lothians;* p. 37. Edinb. 1839.
† See Supplementary Note F, on the Antiquity of the Earth.

upon any new field of observation, or repeat his survey of former ones, but he meets new proofs, or the strengthening of what he before possessed. The evidences, taken separately, are not equal in clearness and cogency. Some of them have a vast amount of independent weight: others are less striking, particularly to an unpractised observer: but they all bear in one direction: and their united force is such as to awaken surprise that any intelligent person can be found, who is capable of resisting it. It is the case, as in all arguments of this description, that the multitude and diversity tend to embarrass us, and the difficulty lies chiefly in selection and arrangement.

II. Another opinion, which has been and perhaps still is received extensively, not only by those who hold the former position, but by many who disallow it, is this: that the state of the earth's surface, immediately before its being brought, by the wisdom and power of God, into the condition destined for the reception of man and his contemporaneous living creatures and plants, was one of universal dissolution from a former condition; and which consisted in a mixture of water and much earthy matter, producing an ocean of muddy substance, half liquid, half solid, completely enveloping the globe: and that also the atmosphere was perfectly dark, or nearly so; either because its constitution, as a regulated compound of nitrogen and oxygen, and endowed with the properties of transmitting and refracting the rays of light, was not yet effected; or because it was so filled with the densest watery vapour as scarcely to allow a passage to the light, so that, if not absolutely yet comparatively and sensibly, had a human being existed to employ his eye upon it, it might be called "darkness." This sentiment has been supposed to be contained in the words of the sacred record; "And the earth was without form and void, and darkness was upon the face of the deep: and the Spirit of God moved upon the face of the waters." Gen. i. 2.

Now this interpretation will not consist with facts briefly stated in the preceding lecture; (Prop. xxvii.) Those statements I am happy in being enabled to confirm and illustrate by the authority of one whom talent and science, unwearied personal toil in the exploring of many of the most important districts of Great Britain and Ireland, and a mind disciplined by severe studies, have formed into one of the most eminently accomplished Geologists.

"The earliest forms of life known to Geology are not, as might perhaps be expected, *plants*, but *animals;* they are not of the lowest grade of organization merely. Zoophyta far advanced in structure, (lamelliferous corals,) and Brachiopodous bivalves, of three genera, were found by myself on Snowdon, but no *distinct* traces of plants. The number of species of this early fauna is extremely small, but there is about them no mark of inferiority, no extraordinary simplicity.

"From this [apparent] origin of organic life, there is no break in the vast chain of organic developement, till we reach the existing order of things: no one geological period, long or short, no one series of stratified rocks, is every where devoid of traces of life. The world, once inhabited, has apparently never, for any ascertainable period, been totally despoiled of its living wonders. But there have been many changes in the individual forms; great alterations in the generic assemblages; entire revolutions in the relative number and developement of the several classes. Thus the *systems* of life have been *varied* from time to time to *suit* the altered condition of the planet, but never *extinguished.* The earth, once freed from its early inadequacy to support life according to the appointed laws of life, has since been prolific of vegetable and animal existence.

"The *proportionate number* of organic forms has gone on, even gradually; augmenting from the dozen species of the Snowdon slates, through the twelve hundred and more species of the Oolite, the four thousand forms of the tertiary eras, to the multitudes of [now] existing things. The *change* of organic structure is also, in some degree, *proportioned* to the time elapsed. Tried by the Cephalopodous Mollusca, we see perish, first the Orthoceratites, then the Belemnites and Ammonites; while Nautilus and Sepia exist to represent this class in [the present families of] existing nature. The developement of the different *classes* of animals is usually thought to exhibit a similar relation; as if nature had been continually improved, from the moment of the origin of life: but this opinion is, if taken generally, one of the least certain of all the general notions now current, because of a radical defect in the reasoning. This defect consists in assuming into one induction, the terrestrial and the marine races of animals. Now, as the higher forms of life are terrestrial, and the remains of terrestrial things are only by accident mixed with the spoils of the sea, it is no wonder that mammalia and birds are rarely even suspected to occur among the buried spoils of the ocean. However, the Didelphys of Stonesfield is enough to cast a doubt on this notion, which should be more critically examined by a logical process.* It should be inquired what is the order of developement, among the marine races on one hand, and the terrestrial groups on the other. The latter are too few, in a fossil state, to justify any decision; the former supply certain evidence. The order of developement is,

"1. Zoophyta and Brachiopodous Conchifera.

"2. The same groups, with the addition of Plagiomyonous Conchifera, Gasteropoda, Cephalopoda, Fishes.

"3. The same, with the addition of Reptiles.

"4. The same, with one solitary Didelphys.

"5. The same, without Didelphys or any other quadruped.

"6. The same, with marine and terrestrial quadrupeds.

"7. Existing creation.

"Is the present creation of life a continuation of the previous ones; a term of the same long series of communicated being? I answer, Yes; but not as the offspring is a continuation of its parent. The present crocodiles are not thus derived from the Teleosaurus of Caen, [nor the alligators, monitors, or any other lizards, from any of the Saurian species of fossil zoology,] by indefinite change through time and circumstances; as St. Hilaire's and Lamarck's (and Goëthe's?) speculations might lead to suppose. But the existing forms of life RESEMBLE those of times gone by, because the general aspect of the physical conditions of the world has always been, since the origin of life on the globe, decidedly *analogous:* and they DIFFER from them because the correlation of life and physical conditions is strict and necessary, so that all the *variations* of these conditions are represented in the phases of organic structure; while all their general *agreements* are also represented by the conformity of the great principles of structure in the beings of every geological age, and the often repeated analogies and parallelisms of series of forms, between different geological periods, which we now hail as a law of nature, when we compare America or Australia, with Africa, Asia, or Europe.

"We are not, then, in a different system of nature, properly so called, from those which have been created, and have been suffered to pass away before the birth of man. But [we are] in a forward part of the same system, whose law of progression is fixed, though from time to time the signification of the terms varies. The full and complete system of organic life now on the globe, includes all the effects

---

* This very curious and perplexing subject has been recently investigated, with exquisite science and labour, by MM. Valenciennes and De Blainville, and by distinguished men in our own country; in particular Mr. Owen, who appears to have brought the completing evidence in favour of Dr. Buckland's opinion, that the animal was a small marsupial, that is, of the opossum family.

of land and sea, warmth and cold, divided regions, and all the other things which are the diversifying causes of nature; and it is no wonder if, before this land was raised from the deep, and the present distinction of natural regions was produced, there was not the same extreme variety of natural productions. Till that variety was occasioned on the globe, it was not the fitting place for intellectual man that it now is: for, surely among the other uses and correlations of the visible creation this is one,—by its inexhaustible diversity and growing newness, to interest with a perpetual charm the growing mind of a rational being, and lead him by a flowery path to the cultivation of the divine thing within him, which raises him above all that his senses make known; and thus to fit him for the highest contemplation of which he is capable, namely, the relation which he bears to the unseen AUTHOR of all this visible material world.

"Thus, to the mind of a geologist, nature is one glorious book: one system of appointed and associated law, independent of time, and exempt from change, but operating under conditions which vary with time and place. The past has prepared the present: the present explains the past and points to the future."*

III. A prevalent, though not universal interpretation of the archaic narrative, is that the sun and all the other heavenly bodies were created on the fourth day after the creation of the earth.

* The Supplementary note, contributed by John Phillips, Esq. to the Rev. Prof. Powell's "Connexion of Natural and Divine Truth:" p. 309. On account of the pressure of other scientific engagements, in which he is rendering important services to Government and the country, Mr. Phillips has been obliged to resign his professorship in King's College, London. [But he is rendering important services to science and to his country, in association with Sir Henry de la Beche, and Prof. Edward Forbes, by conducting the vast work of a Geological Survey of our island, under the authority of Government.]

The high reputation of M. Deshayes as a palæontologist entitles the following statement to great consideration (though it awaits the test of examination by other qualified men), in relation to the doctrine which has been repeatedly advanced in this volume, that few species of organized beings can be traced through more than one formation; and, of those belonging to the present state of the earth, none at all so low as the chalk. Though the statement is derivative, the ability and accuracy of the relater cannot be questioned.

"M. Deshayes has lately [in a paper read to the Philomathic Society, of Paris, Feb. 10, 1838], announced that he had discovered, in surveying the entire series of fossil animal-remains, *five* great groups, so completely independent that no species whatever is found in more than one of them. It is not at present in my power to investigate this subject so completely as the case requires; I shall therefore only recite, that the first of those groups is that to which Trilobites give the character, that the three succeeding belong to the system of the large Saurians, and that the fifth includes the systems in which I have pointed out the Palæotheria, the Mastodons, and the Elephants." D'Omalius d'Halloy, *Elem de Geol.* p. 187; Paris, 1839.

An obvious objection to this opinion is, that *light* is mentioned in the account of the first day; "God said, Be light; and light was." But to this, the common answer is, that light was created in a diffused state; and that, on the fourth day, it was condensed and collected into a centre, for the solar system of planets; that this centre is the sun, or within the sun; and that in some similar way the luminous property of the fixed stars was produced.

Those who adopt this hypothesis, either with or without the modification annexed to it, are perhaps not aware, that the spheroidal figure of the earth, its position in the planetary system, its rotation producing the nights and days which the Mosaic narrative expressly lays down in numerical succession, the existence of water, and that of an atmosphere, both definitely mentioned, and the creation of vegetables on the third day,—necessarily imply the presence and the operations of the sun: unless we resort to some gratuitous supposition of multiplied miracles of the most astounding magnitude. Such as can satisfy themselves with such suppositions, made without evidence and at their own good pleasure, are beyond our reach of reasoning. No difficulty, no improbability, no natural impossibility, appals them. They seem to have the attribute of Omnipotence at their command, to help out any hypothesis, or answer any exigency. But I must confess that such modes of resolving difficulties do not approve themselves to my conviction. The Creator has formed a finite and dependent world, the extent and complication of which overwhelm our faculties: but, in all that extent and complication, we have demonstrations without number that the great Sovereign and Conservator of the universe rules it according to a PLAN; and that plan, in its physical aspect, presents the one grand and simple law of attraction, with its correlates and consectaries. That plan is but the method of the divine agency pervading, upholding, and efficiently directing all beings and all events. God "worketh all things after the counsel of his own will:"—and his "counsel standeth for ever." It would be blasphemous to doubt whether his method of proceeding be the perfection of wisdom. A miracle is not a destroying, nor even a suspending of it; it is not an amending, or repairing, or correcting it; it is not a break in the chain; not an occurrence for which no provision had been made in the construction of the eternal purpose. A miracle is an event which, supposing a given connexion of time, place, and persons, would not have come to pass in the ordinary course of things; but for the instrumental causality of which *the divine plan had fixed* the requisite provision. It is no less a part of "the immutability of his counsel," than is any other fact in the series of God's operations. It is a deviation from the ordinary course of events, but accomplished by the determining will of the Supreme Being, through the agency of the instruments proper in every case, and for purposes of the highest wisdom and goodness requiring such an interposition. The scriptures abundantly shew that the Divine Wisdom has not lavished away miracles; but, so far as we know, has wrought them only for the purpose of accrediting the claim of some one who professed to be the bearer of a revelation from God. To every reflecting person this must appear to be a purpose of pure and exalted benevolence, and most worthy of the Supreme Being, the infinitely Wise and Good. The undeniable evidence of our entire dependence; the consciousness, which each of us carries in his own breast, of wants, capacities, and desires, stretching out of the sphere of our present existence, expanding the more as the more they are gratified, thus proving their illimitable character, and authorizing the expectation of another life with improved faculties of action and sensibilities to enjoyment or suffering;—these and their associated considerations MUST impress us with the desirableness of obtaining something more than that sentiment of the Deity which we derive by inferences from what we see of his works, in their monuments of the past, or their displays of the present; the universal and unceasing manifestations of knowledge and power, of consummate wisdom in the application of knowledge and power, and of beneficence, appearing in so many beautiful forms, yet chequered with so many dark shades of sin and pain and woe. The wondrous evidence thus set before us of the physical government of God, warrants our belief that he exercises a *moral* government; and that, in proportion as mind is a nobler object than insensible matter, or, according to some, mere ideas impressed upon an unknown substratum, so must the LAWS and the action of that moral government be superior to all the grandeur of the sensible world.

But of the MORAL perfections of God, and the laws which belong to this department of his empire, we can have no certain knowledge, unless he be pleased to communicate it. Yet such knowledge is what we *need;* knowledge which shall have the character of *certainty*, so that our anxious minds may rest upon it with confidence; and that we may attain, not a vague and precarious presumption, which may be no better than an illusion of selfishness, but a rational assurance of escaping the just penalties of our offences against the eternal law of morals, and of rising to an immortal perfection of all that is holy, happy, and glorious. Nothing short of a positive communication from the great Being himself, to whom our fears and our desires point, can be satisfactory; and we cannot conceive of any method by which such a communication could be attested as genuine, except a miraculous intervention, a *sensible proof* that the God of the universe is addressing us. Miracles therefore, as well-known and valuable writers upon the evidence of Revelation have shewn, are at the same point on the scale of probability as is the fact of a revelation from God, of grace and mercy and peace. But I must say that this wise and gracious design is beclouded and the evidence is weakened, by those who plead for an exuberance of miracles, and are prompt to resort to them on every occasion which their hypotheses require. If they more deeply considered the sublime objects of revelation, and if they were better informed concerning the order and operations of the physical universe, often called the laws and the powers of nature, but which are no less the results of constant Divine agency than is an act of immediate creation;—if they were thus intellectually and morally prudent, they would cease to fancy such requirements. I humbly think that, for the honour of God and the interests of genuine religion, it is our duty to protest against the practice of bringing in miraculous interpositions, to help out the exigencies of arbitrary and fanciful theories. No: our "God is the Rock," eternal and unchangeable in his attributes; "his work is perfect." He has constructed a system of connexion and dependence, of succession, collateral relations, and harmony; a system which has no shocks, no breaks, no failures, to need the interposition of correcting and repairing. That system does indeed include the constitution of *remedial* adaptations, both physical and moral. But the corrective and restorative character of these provisions arises from the condition of created beings, weak, changeable, and some of them morally depraved. With respect to the Deity, his purposes, and his operations, they are parts of a *continuous system:* and "this also cometh forth from the Lord of hosts, who is wonderful in counsel and excellent in working." Above all, these remarks apply to the constitution and accomplishment of the method of redemption and salvation which Infinite Benevolence has provided for our apostate and ungrateful race. "God so loved the world, that he gave his Only-begotten Son, that whosoever believeth," that is, cordially reposes, "on him, should not perish, but have everlasting life."

IV. It is very generally assumed, as a matter included in the description of creation given in the Mosaic narrative, that all land-animals were created in pairs or other suitable modes of progenitorship, on one spot upon the earth's surface, and that of very moderate extent; which was also the seat of the first human beings, the ancestors of the entire human race. It is also supposed that, from this point, not only did men multiply and diffuse themselves more and more widely, but that the various species of animals did the same. With relation to the vegetable kingdom, the correspondent theory is commonly maintained, as consistency requires. If there be any who do not explicitly declare it, the omission is more likely to have arisen from inadvertence, than from a perception of incongruity.

It is not Geology merely, but other branches of Natural History, that are contradicted by this interpretation of the Scriptures. The fossil remains, whether animal or vegetable, which are found imbedded in the strata of different formations, are in general spread over a large surface; especially so, as we go back to the earlier classes of rocks: but the extent of surface is limited, in both latitude and longitude. This also is the case in the most striking manner, with respect to the present distribution of the earth's vegetable and animal tenantry; the condition to which the subject before us precisely refers. Eden, the region occupied by the first human pair and the animals and plants associated with them, provided for their use, and subjected to their dominion, was in the finest part of the temperate zone. The persons who implicitly receive the opinion just mentioned, have perhaps never asked themselves how animals, which the Creator has formed with the most precise and perfect adaptations to widely different conditions of habitation, could subsist, even for a few days, in or around the original paradise: or, if this difficulty be evaded, by a presumptuous evocation of miracles, or some other arbitrary supposition, the further inquiry presents itself, by what means the respective races, whether progenitors or descendants, could make their way to congenial climes; some to the regions of fierce equatorial heat, others to those of eternal ice and a rigour of cold which no animal can endure for but a few hours, if not protected by the power and skill of man, excepting those which are fitted for it by a wise and wonderful variety in the forms and functions of their bodily structure, internal as well as external. In all the species of animals, the entire anatomy, and the outward provision of covering, defence, and mode of obtaining food, are adapted to their indigenous locality, with a power and precision which richly display the inexhaustible resources of creative wisdom. A few species, indeed, are formed to enjoy a very wide range, they being among the animals readily domesticated and the most serviceable to man. Yet even they, we have much reason to think, were originally indigenous in particular places: and it is worthy of observation that some of these species, by being brought into widely different circumstances as to climate and treatment, acquire, through the lapse of many generations, alterations of form so remarkable, that uninstructed persons might take them for specifically different animals: but that these differences constitute only varieties, and not species, is established by clear anatomical evidence, and by the test of continuous progeny.

Having made these by no means considerable allowances, we find abundant proofs that the habitable surface of the dry land, and even the vast extent of the waters, are divided into districts, the native plants and animals of which have characteristic peculiarities.* This fact was stated in our last lecture. An example of it has been rendered familiar to reading persons, by the enlarged attention of late years to such subjects and the wonderfully increased means of communication; in the instance of the Australasian countries. There has not been sufficient time for any of the species of plants or animals, which have been introduced by Eu-

* The more extensively and accurately researches are made, as they have been by our contemporary Botanists and Zoologists, the more completely has this fact been put out of doubt. *Apparent* exceptions are satisfactorily accounted for. With respect to the one class of the animal kingdom which may be regarded as least under the dominion of man, the inhabitants of the ocean, the constancy with which the boundaries of the different provinces (as I may justly call them) are observed by the teeming population of each, is marked with inviolability. Yet superficial observers may imagine that the free swimmers in the waters which cover nearly three fourths of the surface of the globe, possess and actually use the most unlimited domain of habitation. But this is not the case. The range of some species is very extensive, yet the principle of distribution is remarkably preserved. *Fourth ed.*

ropean settlers, to throw a shade upon the question as to what species are indigenous and what are naturalized foreigners. That region, which includes some of the islands of the South Sea, is marked, by characters of the most manifest and indubitable kind, as a region whose *flora* and *fauna* (terms used as abbreviations, to designate the collection of vegetable and animal productions that belong to any place,) are completely distinct from those of any other portion of land upon the face of the globe.*

If therefore it were maintained, that the first instances or parents of each animal species, which the Creator has formed to dwell upon the earth, were found associated with the first man in paradise, we should be obliged to say that here was a doctrine, alleged to come under the sanction of scripture-authority, but which is at variance with demonstrated facts. [The correlate of this opinion is that all the inhabitants of the dry land, mammals, birds, reptiles, and insects, were, by pairs and septuple pairs, first collected into the ark of Noah, and then issued out of it to spread themselves over the earth.] In a subsequent part of these lectures, we shall have to examine the assumptions upon which these opinions rest, and I venture to affirm that we shall find it to be destitute of any foundation in the fair construction of the Sacred Writings.

V. A difficulty of great moment arises from the supposition that, upon the authority of divine revelation, pain and death had no place in any part of the sensitive creation, at least in this our world, till after the sin of the first human beings.

* "Various opinions have been formed on the original or primitive distribution of PLANTS over the surface of the globe: but since Botanical Geography became a regular science, the phenomena observed have led to the conclusion, that vegetable creation must have taken place in a number of distinctly different centres, each of which was the original seat of a certain number of peculiar species, which at first grew there and no where else. *Heaths* are exclusively confined to the old world; and no indigenous *rose tree* has ever been discovered in the new, the whole southern hemisphere [also] being destitute of that beautiful and fragrant plant. But this is still more confirmed by multitudes of particular plants, having an entirely local and insulated existence, growing spontaneously in some particular spot, and in no other place; as, for example, the *cedar of Lebanon*, which grows indigenously on that mountain and in no other part of the world. The same laws also obtain in the distribution of the ANIMAL creation." Mrs. Somerville's *Connexion of the Physical Sciences;* p. 285. This distinguished lady, of whom a beautiful bust is appropriately placed in the Library of the Royal Society, carries on this observation with respect to the classes of animals; Zoophytes, Mollusks, Fishes, Reptiles, Insects, Birds, and Mammals. *Fourth ed.*

Who has not felt the solemn tenderness of our great poet's invocation?

> "Of man's first disobedience, and the fruit
> Of that forbidden tree, whose mortal taste
> Brought DEATH into the world, with all our woe;
> Sing, heavenly muse;"

——and the sentiment is very natural, and engaging to a mind of sensibility; prior to having any acquaintance with the natural history of the animal tribes, that approaches to comprehensiveness and accuracy. It seems also to be sustained by the infallible authority of the Scriptures. "By one man, sin entered into the world, and death by sin.—The creation has been subjected to vanity:" it is labouring and suffering under "the bondage of corruption: the whole creation groaneth together, and is in pangs together, until now." Rom. v. 12; viii. 20—22.

But, when we come to examine this interpretation or inference, by the light which undeniable facts afford, we are taught a different lesson. We find that all organized matter, that is, every thing that has life, vegetable and animal, is formed upon a plan which renders death *necessary*, or something equivalent to death. The first step to life in the corculum of a vegetable seed, or the atomic rudiment of the animal body, in both cases so minute and recondite as to be inaccessible to human cognizance, commences a course of changes which imply an inevitable termination. [Plants derive their nourishment from inorganic matter, and they thus make the first step in the system of existence to which we attribute material life. But, in animals it is not so. They cannot be supported by any substances except such as have had life, vegetable or animal.] The mysterious principle of their life is universally maintained by the agency of death. From dead organic matter, the living structure derives its necessary supplies. [But those supplies do not bring a perpetuity of existence: their very nature and operation imply the contrary.] The processes of nutrition, assimilation, growth, exhaustion, and reparation, hold on their irresistible course, to decay and dissolution; in another word, to death. Some persons have dreamed of sustaining animal life by exclusively vegetable food; ignorant that, in every leaf or root or fruit which they feed upon, and in every drop of water which they drink, they put to death myriads of living creatures, whose bodies are as "curiously and wonderfully made" as our own, which were full of animation and agility, and enjoyed their mode and period of existence as really and effectively under the bountiful care of Him "who is good to all, and whose tender mercies are over all his works," as the stately elephant, the majestic horse, or man, the earthly lord of all. By far the larger portion of the animal creation is formed, in every part of its anatomy, internal and external, for living upon animal food; and cannot live upon any other. The carnivorous nature, in a thousand instances, is the immediate cause of inestimable benefits to man. Of this fact a familiar example is constantly presented before our eyes, in the speedy removal of the putrescent carcases of animals, by the industry of millions of the minor tribes; creatures which many of us can scarcely look at without disgust; yet they are saving us from being poisoned by a fetid and infectious atmosphere; and after a further change, striking emblem of our future resurrection, they come forth beautiful and admired insects, to enjoy the brilliance of a summer's day, to sip the flowers, to provide a posterity, and then to die.

Geology unfolds to us similar scenes, upon the most magnificent scale, and occupying the recesses of an unfathomable antiquity. Few of the formations above the micaceous slate are destitute of the remains of animals, and in a less degree (which is easily accounted for) of vegetables: but the larger part of those formations is filled with such remains, constituting in some cases nearly the entire substance of rocks which are hundreds and thousands of feet in thickness and many miles in extent. Some of the Egyptian pyramids are built of Nummulitic Limestone, itself entirely composed of chambered shells, of very small size and of exquisite construction. Other rocks there are, whose very substance consists of microscopic shells of extraordinary beauty, once the habitations of living beings. Among these are our English chalk, the Bergmehl of Sweden, and the polishing stone, first obtained from Tripoli, but since found in many other places. Of this last, the exquisite shells, almost entirely siliceous in their composition, which appear to constitute the whole rocky masses, are so minute, that a cube of one-tenth of an inch is calculated to contain five hundred millions of individuals.* In the series of the Oolite and Lias rocks, which come under the Chalk, and, in England and many other countries, overlie the New Red Sandstone, are found,

* Supplementary Note G; on the Fossil Animalcules.

in immense numbers, not only the shells of smaller sea-animals, but the skeletons of formidable creatures, some of gigantic size, formed for swimming in the sea and crawling near the shores.* We can see and examine their powerful teeth; the structure of their bones for the insertion, course and action of muscles, nerves, and the tubes for circulation, indicating the function; and their very stomachs beneath their ribs, replenished with chewed bits of bone, fish-scales, and other remains of animal food.

Thus, not only the characters of the recent animal creation, but those of races which have occupied the earth through past periods of immeasurable duration, demonstrate it to have been the will of the All-wise Creator that life and death should minister to each other throughout the whole extent of the animal tribes; both in the actual condition of nature, and in those states of our world which are past, but have left their monuments inscribed with characters that cannot be mistaken.

Whether these positions militate against any thing that is asserted or implied in the Holy Scriptures; and whether they are at all inconsistent with the impressive declaration, "By man came death;" it will be our duty, in a future lecture, to consider.

* The attentive inquirer, if he have the opportunity, will contemplate with deep interest the skeletons and detached bones of the ancient lizard-like animals, in the British Museum; or the engravings of many, on a large scale, in the *Memoirs of the Ichthyosauri and Plesiosauri*, 1834; and the *Book of the Sea Dragons*, 1840, by Thomas Hawkins, Esq. F. G. S.

LECTURE IV.

GENESIS VI. 17. *And behold, I, even I, do bring a flood of waters upon the earth, to destroy all flesh wherein is the breath of life from under heaven: and every thing that is in the earth shall die.*

ANOTHER point remains, with regard to which the discrepancy between the belief that is held by some, at least, of the most eminent geologists, and the testimony of the word of God, as it is commonly understood, appears most serious and alarming: this is the historical fact of the Deluge.

Fifteen hundred years had nearly elapsed since the creation of man, and his fall into sin and sorrow: and now human depravity had grown to an awful magnitude. So far as we can form a judgment from the concise but emphatic terms of the history, it appears that universal discord prevailed, mutual injustice and exasperation, malignity, oppression, and cruelty. Such a habit of mind from men to their fellow-men, could not but break the bonds of society, destroy confidence and hope, and poison the springs of human happiness. Nor was it less certain, that such a state of mind and character would be associated with an impious contempt of the Creator and Supreme Ruler. The condemnatory testimony therefore is, "The earth was corrupt before God, and the earth was filled with violence." The expression "before God" denotes a contempt and defiance of the Divine Majesty. It is also evident that "the earth" is put, by a frequent scriptural metonymy, for the inhabitants of the earth; whence it is reasonable to infer that the universal terms in our text have their proper reference to mankind, the subjects of guilt, whose flagitious character cried for a condign manifestation of Jehovah's displeasure. His holy perfections were insulted, and perhaps derided with atheistic scoff. It was now become eminently proper that there should be some demonstration of the justice and power of God, which should admit of no doubt; for the supplication of a following age could never have been more appropriate, "Lift up thyself, thou Judge of the earth: render a reward to the proud. JEHOVAH! How long shall the wicked, how long shall the wicked triumph!" (Ps. xciv. 2, 3.)

Yet the Most High shewed himself merciful and gracious. He sent warnings and threatenings, by "Noah, the preacher of righteousness;" and thus his "long-suffering waited" one hundred and twenty years. (I Pet. iii. 20. 2 Ep. ii. 5.) But despised mercy must be vindicated by righteous punishment. God therefore made known his determination to inflict that punishment, in a revelation to his faithful servant. "Behold, I, even I, do bring a flood of waters;"—I will demonstrate my holiness and wisdom, in such a manner as shall admit of no doubt with regard to its judicial intention.

Of that awful event, the sacred narrative is clear and circumstantial.

"In the six hundredth year of Noah's life, in the second month, the seventeenth day of the month," [answering to about the middle of November,] "the same day were all the fountains of the great deep broken up, and the windows of heaven were opened. And the rain was upon the earth, forty days and forty nights.——The flood was forty days upon the earth. And the waters increased and bare up the ark; and it was lifted up above the earth. And the waters prevailed, and were increased greatly upon the earth; and the ark went upon the face of the waters. And the waters prevailed exceedingly upon the earth; and all the high hills, that were under the whole heaven, were covered. Fifteen cubits upward did the waters prevail; and the mountains were covered. And all flesh died that moved upon the earth, both of fowl, and of cattle, and of beast, and of every creeping thing that creepeth upon the earth, and every man: all in whose nostrils was the breath of life, of all that was in the dry land, died. And every living substance was destroyed which was upon the face of the ground; both man and cattle, and the creeping things, and the fowl of the heaven: and they were destroyed from the earth. And Noah only remained [alive,] and they that were with him in the ark. And the waters prevailed upon the earth a hundred and fifty days. And God remembered Noah, and every living thing, and all the cattle that were with him in the ark: and God made a wind to pass over the earth, and the waters assuaged. The fountains also of the deep, and the windows of heaven were stopped, and the rain from heaven was restrained. And the waters returned from off the earth continually; and, after the end of the hundred and fifty days, the waters were abated. And the ark rested, in the seventh month, on the seventeenth day of the month, upon the mountains of Ararat. And the waters decreased continually until the tenth month. In the tenth month, on the first day of the month, were the tops of the mountains seen.——In the six hundred and first year," [that is, of the life of Noah,] "in the first month, the first day of the month, the waters were dried up from off the earth. And Noah removed the covering of the ark, and looked; and, behold, the face of the ground was dry. And in the second month, on the seven and twentieth day of the month, was the earth dried." (Gen. vii. 11 to viii. 14.)

Thus is the tremendous fact related, by the writing which, independently of its divine authority, is the most ancient and the most credible in the world. The histories and traditions of all nations, ancient and of recent discovery, furnish ample proof that this great event is indelibly graven upon the memory of the human race. The ancient systems of mythology and polytheism are filled with idolatrous commemorations of the deluge. Those significant rites, and the traditions and historical fragments which have not entirely perished, make us acquainted with memorials of that event, as having existed among the Egyptians, Chaldeans, Phœnicians, Greeks, Celts, and Scythians, to the farthest antiquity of which we have any documentary knowledge. Also, the discovery of what was long called the New World, three centuries and a half ago, brought to the view of Europeans not only traditionary notices as possessed by the nations, at that time very numerous, and many of them comprising a large population, of North and South America; but, still further, among the Mexicans and Peruvians, historical and emblematical pictures, which preserve, with more exactitude than could have been expected, the general event itself, and various particulars reflecting as it were an image, distorted, indeed, but well capable of being recognised, of the narrative which we possess, in its native simplicity, in the book of Genesis. Even the inhabitants of the South Sea Islands, so recently brought to the knowledge of Europeans, are not destitute of their tradition, bearing its measure of testimony to the universal impression.* That a statement thus attested by the con-

* The evidences of these traditions are detailed in the late Mr. Jacob Bryant's *Analysis of Ancient Mythology*, several works of the Rev. G. Stanley Faber, and the recently published *Doctrine of the Deluge*, by the Rev. L. Vernon Harcourt. It may be regret-

sent of mankind, did not rest upon a foundation of truth, it would be the extravagance of absurd scepticism to doubt.

Yet it is remarkable that learned writers have not perceived the absence of any logical connexion between the universality of historical tradition, and a geographical universality of the deluge itself. Immense pains have been taken, and very laudably, to collect the traditions of tribes and nations deposing to the fact of an overwhelming deluge in the days of their remotest ancestors; and it has been hence concluded, since those traditions existed in every quarter of the globe, that the deluge had belonged to every region. But it seems to have been forgotten, that each of these traditionary and historical notices referred to one and the same locality, the seat of the family of Noah, the cradle of the human race. The progress of population and dispersion, however rapid we may suppose it, could never have been such as would establish any correct idea of geographical distance, from the recollection of space travelled over. Of all notions of longitude and latitude, and determinations of distance by observation of the heavenly bodies, the migrators must have been destitute. Their abandonment of monotheism and pure religion awfully accelerated the reign of barbarism and ignorance. Hence it became a matter of next to inevitable certainty, that later generations would attach their narratives of the flood to their own immediate districts.

The connexion of this distinguished event in the history of mankind, with the phenomena presented to geological study, has long been a favourite object of attention to many persons. But few of them have been aware of the perilous course into which they had entered. To pursue it with any rational hope of success, would require an extensive collection of particular facts, an accurate estimation of each one, a power of comparing, a sagacity in drawing inferences, and a comprehension of knowledge, both physical and biblical, the thought of which cannot but fill me with anxiety. But I shall submit to my friends the statements and deductions which appear to me to be founded on sufficient evidence, in the fear of God, and with the desire of promoting the interests of truth.

That the spoils of the ocean are to be found in all parts of the dry land, is a fact which, one would think, could hardly have

ted that these estimable authors have not been guarded against the too common error of weakening an argument by an excess of amplification.

failed to force itself upon the attention of mankind in all ages and all countries; and that the proper deduction would have been drawn from it. But such a conjecture has not been realized. Just views on this subject have not prevailed, till recent times; though some remarkable glimpses of the truth, and indeed more than glimpses, are to be found in the fragmentary remains of oriental and Egyptian antiquity, and more completcly in the doctrines of Pythagoras and of other illustrious men who followed him at long intervals. Strabo, the Grecian philosopher, historian, and traveller, lived in the reigns of Augustus and Tiberius. Of his writings only a large geographical work has survived the wreck of the middle ages, but it is invaluable, though the existing copies of it are imperfect. In several parts of that work he displays his sagacity and diligence in making observations, and extraordinary justness in his reasonings upon them. He describes geological phenomena, particularly elevations of land, alterations of the lines of coast, and the existence of the remains of sea-animals at considerable distances from the sea: and he shews that he entertained very good ideas upon their instrumental causes.*

These subjects, however, appear to have been forgotten or neglected, during the long night of intellectual darkness till the revival of letters. In the age of the Reformation, and through more than the century which followed, the powerful and active minds of Europe were occupied with other inquiries, of the highest importance; so that few of the great men of those days seem to have sought "sermons in stones," and science in frightful ravines, pits, and precipices. A small number of naturalists, chiefly in Italy, rose above the prejudices which, however ridiculous, were supported not by vulgar minds only, but by persons of high cultivation; yet who could seriously believe that the bones and shells, and the impressions and casts of animal and vegetable fragments, had never belonged to living creatures, or been moulded from them; but had been formed just as we find them, by a *plastic power* in nature, or by some kind of *abortive effort* (*nisus naturæ,*) to produce something which never ascended above a mineral condition, or by *freaks* of nature (*lusus naturæ,*) as if this same nature were a fitful sprite, amusing herself with beguiling and

* *Strabonis Res Geogr.* pp. 71, 73, 79, 89; ed. Falconer. An interesting summary of the testimonies from him and other ancient writers upon this class of facts, is given by Mr. Lyell, in his *Principles of Geology*, Book I. chap. ii.

puzzling the learned industry of poor mortals. We are now surprised that the impiety, as well as the folly, of this jargon did not procure its instant rejection. Yet let us not overvalue ourselves. It is an unhappy fact, and far less excusable, that some men of science in our own days are not ashamed to speak and write of a thing which they perpetually call Nature; of which they speak as if it were a goddess, an intelligent, designing, and active being; and which they without scruple introduce, when the marks of consummate design, benevolent wisdom, and beautiful adaptation in the sensible world, are so striking that we cannot shut our eyes to them. So painfully is it evinced, that "the carnal mind is enmity against God," and that men under its influence "do not like to retain God in their knowledge."*

* *Sec. ed.* I would not that this remark should give pain to any sincere and devout person; and I am aware of the reasoning in defence of the practice, that a too frequent mention of the Deity tends to produce either a heartless formality or a fanatical freedom, each inconsistent with true piety. Dr. Roget has indulgently stated this apology. Upon the passage of his Bridgewater Treatise, "It would almost seem as if Nature had been thus lavish and sportive in her productions, with the intent to demonstrate to Man the fertility of her resources, and the inexhaustible fund from which she has so prodigally drawn," &c. that admirable physiologist has the note; "In order to avoid the too frequent, and consequently irreverent, introduction of the Great Name of the SUPREME BEING into familiar discourse on the operations of his power, I have throughout this Treatise, followed the common usage of employing the term *Nature* as a synonym, expressive of the same power, but veiling from our feeble sight the too dazzling splendour of its glory," vol. i. p. 13. But I would, with all respect, reply to the candid philosopher, that it is not hypocrisy or any sort of affectation that we seek; but the honest and filial affection which is opposed to the state of mind described by the apostle, "they like not to retain GOD in their knowledge." (Rom. i. 28.)

A noble father enriches his mansion with everything that can instruct, improve, and delight his children. They enjoy his munificence with exquisite pleasure; and they spend their lives in displaying and explaining the wisdom and goodness and variety of his provisions for them. But they studiously avoid the mention of his name; any allusion to his titles, his honours, and the homage which he has required of them: and for this purpose they resort to all kinds of circumlocution and evasion.—Would not an observer say, either that his name was not producible because of some dire blot upon it, or that his children were unworthy of him?

The most cutting part of our grief for this practice is, the meanness of surrender which it involves to the irreligious. It is showing them that we are desirous of doing without God as much as we can; plainly, that we are ashamed of HIM! Cowper writes,—

"Why did *all-creating Nature*
Form the plant for which we toil?"

But he was personifying the poor heathen slave. Another poet has shewn us the right order of sentiment, and its due expression :—

"*Nature* with open volume stands,
To spread her Maker's praise abroad;

To all the mental movements and the beneficial progress of the human mind, as well as to times and dwellings, we may apply the principle of the apostle's declaration; "God, who made the world, and all things therein,—the Lord of heaven and earth,—hath made of one blood all nations of men, for to dwell on all the face of the earth, and hath determined the times before appointed, and the bounds of their habitation." (Acts xvii. 24—26.) A time must have been fitted, and an habitation, so to speak, provided, in order that a science or an art might be born, and live, and grow to manly vigour. Geology could not have been studied, without exposure to fatal errors, till the exact sciences had been raised to their present state of cultivation; till NEWTON had led the way; till Astronomy had been perfected by the Bradleys, the Laplaces, and the Herschels; till Chemistry had come into existence, (for it could scarcely be said to have existed before the days of Priestley and Davy;) till Cuvier had made his wonderful use of Comparative Anatomy; and till the exquisite calculation of Dynamics had been established by those living men to whom we look with feelings of, not admiration only, but amazement. In a word, the wisdom of Providence had prepared the combinations, for taking effect in our own time, by which Geological Science should rise and flourish.

There was one distinguished philosopher, Leibnitz, the contemporary and rival of Newton, the man of universal application, and of wondrous attainment in Theology, Jurisprudence, Mathematics, and Philosophy generally; whose penetrating sagacity looked beyond his time. It is instructive and delightful to meet with such instances of the power of mind; recollecting *from* WHOM the talent comes, and the high responsibility which is inseparable from it, before HIM in whose sovereign disposal "is power and might, and in whose hand it is to make great." (1 Chron. xxix. 12.) I cannot resist the wish to cite the words of a judicious author, and one of our first-rate geologists. "Leibnitz honoured this branch of physical speculation by devoting to it a portion of his attention; and anticipated, with the prophetic sagacity of a powerful mind, its future progress, and the very methods of investigation which

And ev'ry labour of his hands
Shews something worthy of a GOD.

But, in the GRACE that rescued man,
His brightest form of glory shines."

would most effectually contribute to its successful developement."—He "exhibits a clear anticipation of the importance and the prospects of the new science of which he foresaw the dawn. Leibnitz proceeds even distinctly to indicate the line of future research into the geographical distribution and extension of the various formations, which might be expected to place this new science on a firm basis."*

Notwithstanding these few exceptions, the common resort of those who took any notice of the bones, shells, and other remains, presenting themselves so profusely in the bowels of the earth, has been to the Deluge of Noah.† In what situations soever the remains of animal and vegetable beings were found, it was at once assumed that they were antediluvian relics, brought thither by the flood. It seems never to have entered into men's minds, to consider the condition of these organic remains, their place in natural history, their relations to each other and to the particular strata in which they occur, and the presence or absence of marks of transport. Scarcely an appearance of entombed organization could be presented, but it was at once set down to the account of the deluge. The contents of all caves containing bones, were supposed to have been floated or driven into them by those mighty waters. The scooping out of valleys, whether with the most abrupt sides and tortuous courses, or in smooth and gentle undulations of outline, found forthwith a ready explanation; without any exercise of mind upon the inquiry whether such a diversity of effects does not imply a proportionate diversity of causes in nature, intensity and duration. All or nearly all, the superficial drift, consisting of sand, gravel, and rolled pebbles of all sizes, up to the bowlders of some thousand cubic feet, were, implicitly and without further examination of cases and circumstances, ascribed to one and the same cause, the diluvial waters. In short, persons have not been wanting, even down to the present

* The Rev. W. D. Conybeare's Report on Geology, in the *Reports of the British Association for the Advancement of Science;* vol. i. p. 368.

† This theory was propounded with ability and a good measure of science such as the time afforded, by John Woodward, D. D. (the founder of the Professorship and the Museum of Mineralogy, Univ. Cambr.) in his *Essay towards a Nat. Hist. of the Earth*, 1695. Animadversions and objections were published by Leibnitz, Martin Lister, Kämmerer prof. at Tübingen, and others. But it required another century to obtain a sufficient knowledge of the facts. Dr. W. maintained that all the rocks and contained minerals were deposited by the diluvian waters, as a common solvent, and in the order of their specific gravity. *Fourth ed.*

day, who have maintained that all the remarkable appearances on the surface and beneath the surface of the earth, the depositions, the fractures, the dislocations, the denudations, the transport of materials, and the entire formation of strata, are the effects of the deluge.

By acting upon the common infirmities of our nature, these pretensions have led to an excess of doubt and objection in the opposite direction. Shunning the violation of reason and evidence on the one side, in attributing too much to the flood, distinguished men, friends of revelation and religion, among whom we must reckon the great Linnæus, seem to have been led into the extreme of too much diminishing their estimate of its power and influence. It has been passed over as an event of but small importance, and which therefore might be altogether neglected in our attempts to trace the natural history of the earth; as having been only a gradual and tranquil rise of water, fatal to life on an awful scale, and extirpating the guilty race of man, excepting one small family; but incapable of working any material effect upon the disposition of even the superficial materials.* To my own apprehen-

* "That great event has left no trace of its existence, on the surface or in the interior of the earth." Prof. Jameson's *Notes on Cuvier's Theory of the Earth*, fifth ed. p. 457. The Professor is a decided friend of revelation. The Rev. Dr. Fleming also, a divine of the Church of Scotland, has largely vindicated the same opinion. I select the following from his paper in Jameson's *Philos. Journ.* No. xxviii. April, 1826. After describing the attempts of some to extract from geological phenomena a corroboration of the scripture narrative, and the crumbling away of their hypotheses under a searching investigation, he says; "The geologist beheld his theories vanish like a dream; and the admirer of revelation felt (though very unnecessarily) as if a pillar of his faith had become a broken reed. Geology, by those premature attempts at generalizing, fell into discredit as a science among philosophers; and by the Christian it was viewed with suspicion. The former had witnessed opinions and assertions substituted for facts; and the latter had reaped the fruits of misplaced confidence." P. 206. "There is reason to believe from the writings of Moses, that the ark had not drifted far from the spot where it was first lifted up, and that it grounded at no great distance from the same spot." P. 213. "I entertain the same opinion as Linnæus on this subject; nor do I feel, though a clergyman, the slightest reason to conceal my sentiments, though they are opposed to the notions which a false philosophy has generated in the public mind. I have formed my notions of the Noachian deluge, not from Ovid, but from the Bible. There the simple narrative of Moses permits me to believe, that the waters rose upon the earth by degrees; that means were employed, by the Author of the calamity, to preserve pairs of the land animals; that the flood exhibited no violent impetuosity, displacing neither the soil nor the vegetable tribes which it supported, nor rendering the ground unfit for the cultivation of the vine. With this conviction in my mind, I am not prepared to witness *in nature* any remaining *marks* of the catastrophe; and I find my respect for the authority of revelation heightened, when I see, on the present surface, *no memorials* of the event." P. 214.

sion, the truth lies between these extremes. During both the increase and the subsidence of the waters, a considerable action, from rushing among obstacles, would seem inevitable; but the admission of this by no means necessitates the further position, that those effects would be distinguishable to men, after the lapse of many ages: and, that they should have produced the stratifications of the earth, is a notion which must appear impossible to any one who has a tolerably correct idea of what those stratifications really are.

A remarkable passage relating to this subject, by one of the finest minds and most eminent philosophers, the late Baron Cuvier, has been often quoted, and it has a strong claim upon our attention.

"I think therefore, with Deluc and Dolomieu, that, if there be any thing settled in geology, it is this, that the surface of our globe has been subjected to a great and sudden revolution, the date of which cannot be carried much farther back than five or six thousand years; that that revolution broke down and made to disappear the countries which had been before inhabited by men and the species of animals with which we are now best acquainted; that, on the other hand, it laid dry the bottom of the immediately preceding sea, and formed the countries which are now inhabited; that it is from the epoch of that revolution that the small number of individuals whom it had spared, have spread themselves and multiplied over the newly dried ground; and consequently that it is from that epoch alone that human societies have resumed their progressive advancement, have formed [social] establishments, have erected memorials of themselves, have collected the facts of nature, and have combined those facts into scientific systems. But the countries now inhabited, which had been laid dry by that last revolution, had been inhabited before, if not by men, yet at least by land animals. It follows, that preceding revolutions, one at least, had buried those regions beneath the waters; and, so far as we can judge of the question from the different orders of animals whose remains are found, it is probable that two or three such irruptions of the sea had taken place."*

It is consistent with our admiration and reverence for this great man, to remark that these observations attach to a state of geo-

* *Discours sur les Révolutions de la Surface du Globe, et sur les Changemens qu'elles ont produit dans le Règne Animal;* p. 138. Third Edition, Paris, 1826.

logical knowledge considerably inferior to that which it has now attained. The chief design of the work from which the passage is taken, was to explain the manner in which the author has applied his knowledge of Comparative Anatomy, to the determination of the masses of bones dug up from the quarries of Paris; and which, by cautious proceeding, but in the end with the clearest demonstration, he proved to be the remains of animals *analogous* to many in the existing creation, but all *differing* in species, and many generically. Now those formations, in various mixtures of chalk, sand, and gypsum, belong to different parts of the Tertiary rocks, and not even its earliest divisions: none of them go lower. The subjects which were thus presented to the illustrious naturalist, in numbers so vast, and in a confusion which would have been overwhelming to minds of less knowledge, industry, and power than his, were more than enough to occupy his thoughts and labours, in the most unremitting manner, during every moment of his life, had it been prolonged to this hour: yet he devoted himself to the efficient performance of many other and those most arduous duties, as a philosopher, an academician, a politician and statesman, and a most active labourer in the walks of beneficence. The number and greatness and comprehension of his exertions were such as to fill us with even astonishment. It can excite no surprise, therefore, that he did not carry his researches farther into general Geology; that in this respect he was behind many of his inferiors; and that he appears not to have had the least idea that many of the points upon which, in this very work, he had put sagacious queries and had suggested decisive methods of research, were at the very time under successful examination in our country, by Dr. William Smith. That indefatigable explorer, *the father of English Geology*, at the time when Cuvier was employed in his own department and was conferring the richest benefits upon natural history, was completing his patient labours of thirty years; the result of which was to fix upon a firm basis, the study of the Secondary rocks, by demonstrating the sure characterism of their imbedded fossils.

The design of these observations is to intimate that the Baron's general conclusion, relative to that which he justly calls the last great and sudden revolution affecting the earth's surface, must not be taken without modification. To this the strict evidence of the case compels us. Though, with his dignified caution and moderation, he speaks of only two or three alternations of land and sea prior to the great deluge; yet the tenor of his work, where he draws rapid sketches of what to him appeared probable theory, with respect to the earlier strata and the under-lying crystalline rocks, and some particular expressions which he uses, afford no slight grounds of belief that, had his investigations been continued over the field on which he could do no more than glance, he would have given his still more decided suffrage in favour of the doctrine of an immensely long succession of changes affecting the earth and its living inhabitants; affecting, not the whole circumambient surface at the same time, but large districts in respect of space, and in separate periods in respect of duration. Speaking strictly, Mineral Geology was not his domain. His empire consisted of the Natural History of the living world, Comparative Anatomy, and the Palæontological department of Geology; and in this wide sphere he had not, while living, a superior, nor scarcely a rival. He was the originator of the science: all others were his followers. No man possessed a more liberal mind than he. To open and widely distribute his accumulations of knowledge, was his heart's delight: and he would have bounded with joy, could he have foreknown the structures which naturalists and geologists, whom I should perhaps displease were I to name them, have built upon the foundations by him so firmly laid.

Here, it is appropriate to our subject, and just to the illustrious foreigner, to repeat a paragraph from Mr. Murchison's eulogium, delivered from the President's chair of the Geological Society.*

"The death of such a man has called forth deep lamentations from every land upon whose children the rays of science have shed their light; and the eulogies poured forth in his honour are heard in almost every language of the civilized globe. How are we to limit our praise of one whose ample mind was matched only by the benevolence of his heart; and whose whole life was passed in unremitting exertions to enlarge the domain of science by blending it with civil polity, and by infusing it into the principles of education? With an almost incredible knowledge of the structure and functions

* On Feb. 15, 1833. George Leopold Christian Frederick Dagobert [but he disused this parade of names beyond the first,] CUVIER died May 6, 1832, of a general and rapid paralysis, probably brought on by his extraordinary mental and bodily labours, in his 63d year.

of every part of organized nature, he possessed a power above that of every other man of emancipating himself from mere details, and of ascending to lofty generalizations, which were ever recommended by him with all the charms of eloquence; so that in his hands, Natural History became adorned, for the first time, with the highest attributes of pure philosophy. To him we owe the most important of the laws which have regulated the distribution of the animal kingdom, and by the application of which we have been made to comprehend many of the mutations of the surface of our planet. He it was, who, removing from GEOLOGY the incumbrance of errors and conceits heaped on it by Cosmogonists, contributed more than any individual of this century, to raise it to the place which it is assuming amongst the exacter sciences. Unlike our precursors, we no longer have to wade through the doubts and perplexities which retarded their acquaintance with the lost types of creation; to his skill we are indebted for a knowledge of their analogies with existing races: and he it was who, from their scattered bones, remodelled the skeletons of those wondrous originals which have successively passed away from the surface of our planet."

Another beautiful and instructive passage of Baron Cuvier's work, more than justifies the supposition which I have ventured to make.

"If, in studying the infancy of our species, we take an interest in following the almost obliterated traces of numerous nations which have gone out of existence, can we fail to feel an equal interest in piercing the darkness of the earth's infancy, and finding there the marks of *revolutions prior* to the existence of all nations! We admire the powers by which the mind of man has measured the motions of worlds which nature seemed to have placed for ever out of our view: but genius and science have burst the limits of space; and a small number of observations, unfolded by reasoning, have disclosed the mechanism of the world. Would it not be also a glorious object for man, to learn how he may clear the boundaries of time; and, by means of [well directed] observations, recover the history of our globe, and display the succession of events which preceded the birth of human kind? The astronomers have indeed advanced faster than the students of nature upon earth; and, at the present moment, the theory of the earth somewhat resembles that of some philosophers [of old], who thought the sky to be built of hewn stones, and the moon to be even as big as the Peloponnesus. But Anaxagoras

began: Copernicus and Kepler came to clear the way for Newton: and why may not Natural History one day have her Newton?"*

These aspirations have been realized; so that I may, with propriety, introduce a paragraph from one who is entitled to write in this strain.

"The gradual advance of Geology, during the last twenty years, to the dignity of a science, has arisen from the laborious and extensive collection of facts, and from the enlightened spirit in which the inductions, founded on those facts, have been deduced and discussed. To those who are unacquainted with this science, or indeed to any person not deeply versed in the history of this and kindred subjects, it is *impossible to convey a just impression* of the nature of that evidence by which a multitude of its conclusions are supported: evidence in many cases so irresistible, that the records of the past ages, to which it refers, are traced in language more imperishable than that of the historian of any human transactions; the relics of those beings, entombed in the strata which myriads of centuries have heaped upon their graves, giving a present evidence of their past existence with which no human testimony can compete."†

One of the ornaments of Geology, in our own country, has indeed gone through a course of sentiment not much unlike that which I have been supposing in relation to Cuvier. Dr. Buckland, in his Reliquiæ Diluvianæ, published in 1823, quoted a part of the passage which I read a few minutes ago; and gave the sanction of his so deservedly high authority to the idea that the

* *Discours*, p. 2. I cannot but here borrow the words of a masterly writer: "The geologist was prohibited from looking beyond the Mosaic chronology,—and the peaceful deluge of the Scriptures was the only catastrophe to which he durst ascribe the convulsions and dislocations which had every where shaken the interior of the earth. While our [*i. e.* English] geologists were thus working in chains, the unfettered genius of CUVIER was ranging over those primeval ages when the primary rocks rose in insulated grandeur from the deep, and when the elements of life had not yet received their DIVINE COMMISSION. From the age of solitude he passed to the busy age of life; when plants first decked the plains, when the majestic pine threw its picturesque shadows over the earth, and the tragic sounds of carnivorous life rung among her forests. But these plains were again to be desolated, and these sounds again to be hushed. The glories of organic life disappeared, and new forms of animal and vegetable being welcomed the dawn of a better cycle. Thus did the great magician of the charnel-house survey from his pyramid of bones, the successive ages of life and death; thus did he conjure up the spoils of preexisting worlds, the noblest offering which reason ever laid upon the altar of its SOVEREIGN." *Edinburgh Review*, vol. lxv. p. 12.

† *Ninth Bridgewater Treatise;* p. 47.

present surface of the earth is the effect of the diluvial waters. While he was enriching his own pages with the pleasing citation, he was furnishing his illustrious friend at Paris with a *seeming* corroboration of the opinion. Speaking of the mud, gravel, and bones of the Kirkdale Caves, Baron Cuvier proceeds;

"Most carefully described by Prof. Buckland, under the name of *diluvium*, and exceedingly different from those other beds of similarly rolled materials, which are constantly deposited by torrents and rivers, and contain only bones of the animals existing in the country, and to which Mr. Buckland gives the name of *alluvium;* they now form, in the eyes of all geologists, the fullest proof to the senses of that immense inundation which came the last in the catastrophes of our globe."*

This testimony was just. Dr. Buckland had indeed put forth his zeal, his characteristic patience, and his never wearied exertions, in exploring the drift, or, as it was usually called, *diluvium*, of the British Isles: and after careful inductions from his own observations, he proceeded with the following passage, in reference to that mighty action of water to which such effects were attributed.

"An agent thus gigantic appears to have operated universally on the surface of our planet at the period of the deluge: the spaces then laid bare by the sweeping away of the solid materials that had before filled them, are called Valleys of Denudation; and the effects we see produced by water in the minor cases I have just mentioned, by presenting us an example, within tangible limits, prepare us to comprehend the mighty and stupendous magnitude of those forces by which whole strata were swept away, and valleys laid open, and gorges excavated in the more solid portions of the substance of the earth, bearing the same proportion to the overwhelming ocean by which they were produced, that modern ravines on the sides of mountains bear to the torrents which, since the retreat of the deluge, have created and continue to enlarge them."†

* *Discours*, p. 141.
† *Reliq. Diluv.* p. 237.

LECTURE V.

2 PETER ii. 5. *God spared not the old world,—bringing the flood upon the world of the ungodly.*

IN this sentence of the holy apostle, it is manifestly declared, that the design of the deluge was to inflict a deserved punishment upon that generation of men, whose awful impiety had defied the power of the Most High, and scorned his mercy. This defining of the object warrants the conclusion, that whatever amount and extent of the diluvial waters would suffice to execute the sentence of excision, would also be adequate to fulfil the moral purpose of the Righteous Judge in ordaining this infliction. If the universality of the flood extended to the human race, "the world of the ungodly," it is all that was requisite to satisfy the purpose of the visitation.

In the last lecture, we had set before us some account of the mistaken views which had been extensively entertained concerning the effects of the deluge, as supposed to have left their permanent impressions upon the surface of our globe: and we listened to the opinions of some of the most illustrious naturalists and geologists in favour of that hypothesis, under different modifications.

But the lapse of not more than ten years has brought a vast collection of observations to bear upon this interesting subject: and I conceive it may, with the strictest truth, be said that the annals of science, or of literature, or of theology, do not present a nobler instance of fairness and mental integrity, than was shewn by the most perfect geologists that our country, or any other, can boast, in yielding up a favourite and long cherished opinion, to which they had committed themselves in the most public manner, and for which they had been hailed with flattering applause; knowing also, by a very sure anticipation, that the concession to the power of evidence, the avowal of honest conviction, would expose them to the censures of some, who "understand neither what they say, nor whereof they affirm," though they speak and write with a confidence in the direct proportion of their incompetency to say or affirm upon good grounds.

The observations which, in their legitimate deductions, have produced this remarkable result, have been made by many persons, and those the best qualified, from their high attainments in all science, and the skill for making observations which long practice alone can give: they have been made in many countries, near and far distant; and they have been made with a circumspection, an exactitude, and an anxious watchfulness against the causes of mistake, which ought to command our admiration and gratitude.

Those laborious researches were chiefly directed to the *drift* of which we have been speaking, and to which was commonly assigned the name of *diluvium*. This is found to spread widely over the surface in many countries, either visibly covering the ground, or barely concealed by the turf and cultivable soil. During the more early period of geological progress, this diversified mass was, implicitly, and rather hastily, though the error was natural, regarded as of one formation; and thence it was an easy step of advance, in drawing the conclusion that a universal flood was the active and immediate cause of the whole, that this flood was among the most recent events affecting the exterior crust of the earth, and that it must have been identical with the great deluge of universal tradition and of sacred history. But the need was felt of closer examination, minutely distinguishing, and carefully classifying. The constitution, mineralogical, or lithological (for we cannot altogether avoid using the technical terms), of the small grains of sand, the pebbles, the bowlders, and the masses of all sizes, which compose the so-called diluvium, was scrutinized, and compared with the character of rocks at every point on the lines of distance, till the parent rocks were demonstrated from which the fragments had been broken or rubbed off. The mineralogical constitution thus traced up to a commencing point, gave a sure indication of the extent of each kind of drift; and a measure of the varying water-power, by which the detached bodies of stony matter had been moved onwards. Hence were perceived the different degrees of force and velocity which characterised the streams as they flowed; the earlier or later dropping of the mud, sand, pebbles, and larger pieces, on their course; the greater or less rolling at the bottom before a resting-place was obtained; the extent of the deposit in breadth, and where it terminated by the moving power's being exhausted, or being checked by some obstacle; and the deductions which could be drawn as to the time requisite, under different degrees of water-power, for wearing the rough and sharp fragments of rocks of various hardness and tenacity, till they could be brought into rounded forms with smooth surfaces.

To any mind not practised in such inquiries, it is not easy to conceive what a wide field this was for investigation; and it could not be occupied by studies only in the closet; it required painful and patient toil in flood and field, over wide plains, in river-beds, on the sea-coasts, in the windings of large and small valleys, and up the mountain-sides; and all this to be effected over many miles of surface, and in different and distant regions of the earth. No one person could be competent to more than a limited share in this field; though we cannot but be astonished at the extensive portions of it which have been individually explored by distinguished geologists: but they are men in whose circumstances have been combined eminent science, disengagement from other occupations, health, bodily strength, ample fortune, and such attachment to these pursuits as made them shrink from no labour. It is not given to every man to be a De la Beche, a Buckland, or a Griffith; a Murchison, a Phillips, or a Sedgwick. The investigations however have been carried on, over the larger part of Europe, and a great breadth and length in North America; and the observations made by individuals have been brought together, rigorously sifted, mutually compared, and their combined results wrought into an harmonious whole. Yet the class of men of whom I am speaking have not sat down satisfied with even the best proved inferences. They have continued their efforts; and their instructions and example have excited others. Many parts of Eastern Europe, Asia, and South America, have been explored by experienced geologists: and their Reports, not seldom brought by themselves and subjected to searching criticism in assemblies of able and acute examiners, have thus been added to the common treasury.

One of the first results established was that the outspread masses of which we are treating, sands, gravel, and bowlders, were not of one formation nor of one age. The separate divisions into which they had been traced, put upon each a sort of historical mark. Some were found to belong to origins almost on their own spot, that is, the rocks of the locality within but a few miles; others were traced to a considerable distance, yet in the same country. Others were shewn to have been derived from mountains in remote lands, from which they were now divided by lofty ridges or by seas, which are thus proved not to have existed when the passage was free. The order of priority or posteriority has been evinced by palpable proofs. The course of a more ancient drift has often been overlaid by a more recent one. In many instances, or I might more correctly say in most, it is evident that the masses of drift have been formed by action long continued under water; that is, by currents, eddies, and tides, working for unknown ages, at the bottom and on the shores of the ocean; thus standing opposed to the idea of any short-lived inundation. Frequently large tracts of country have been stripped bare of their drifts and underlying strata, evidently by the action of an elevating movement from below, and a vast body of water on the surface: and sometimes considerable masses of the materials which had thus been swept away, occur heaped up in a corner, so to speak, or where an obstacle was presented to their further distribution. The idea of sea-beaches covered with shingle is graphically presented, and their successive elevation by slow rising of the land.* The respective ages, in relation or comparison to each other, are determined, by the position of the distinguishable kinds of drift, that of one character lying under or over that of another; by relations to movements of underlying or neighbouring rocks; and by the geological constitution of the parent rocks whence the mass had been derived.

These summary remarks might suffice for the purpose of these lectures, which is not to deliver a system of Geology, but only to state clearly, if I can, those doctrines which to my conviction stand upon solid grounds of proof, but which may have the appearance of being contradicted by something said or implied in the Holy Scriptures. Yet, considering the specially interesting

* See Sir Henry de la Beche's *Geological Manual;* pp. 172—178; third ed. 1833. Since that time, many examples have been brought before the Geological Society, by Prof. Sedgwick and others. Mr. Darwin, describing vast formations of this kind in South America, observes that the doctrine of slow elevations (a demonstrated fact) "will account, without the necessity of any sudden rush of water, for the general covering of mixed shingle, so common in many parts of Europe." *Voyage of the Beagle*, vol. iii. pp. 206; see also of that interesting volume, pp. 381, 411, 423.

character of this subject, I may be excused for briefly describing some of the actual facts which have been brought to light.

In our own island various and extensive bodies of drift are found, to which a more detailed attention is necessary. That which I shall first mention extends over a district to which Mr. Murchison, by a well-judged application of our early history, has given the name of Siluria.* It may be generally described as comprehending a considerable part of Wales, and of Monmouthshire, Herefordshire, Gloucestershire, Worcestershire, Staffordshire, and Shropshire. There is good reason to believe that this body of drift is the most ancient of all that have been formed on the surface of what is now land, but was then the bed of the sea, afterwards elevated, and, in the season ordained by Divine Wisdom, made to constitute the island of Great Britain. The region over which it had been spread when under the waters of an ancient sea, was raised and became dry land, while the ocean still covered the adjoining districts to the east and north. Since that elevation it has not been again submerged. Its dried surface was clothed with vegetation, and became the abode of land animals; scattered bones of which are dug up, containing anatomical proofs that they had belonged to species not existing in the present state of our earth. There are several distinct formations of this drift, but they are all local, derived from rocks existing within the region.

Another more extensive body of drift spreads over a large tract from Lancashire southwards; and it possesses characters of the most decisive kind, shewing its perfect distinctness from the former. Its contents are derived, principally from the crystalline rocks and trappean insertions, which form the great mountains of Westmoreland, Cumberland, and part of Scotland, but with underlying beds and intermixtures of local drifts, indicating previous formation, and being of less extent. It proceeds from its origin, tapering southwards, and turned by the mountains of North Wales, till it comes up to the boundary of the South Welsh and Severn region just mentioned; and there it stops. It skirts that region along its northern and western limit, but does not ascend into it; and it has

* Admirably detailed in the magnificent work, *The Silurian System;* 2 vols. in quarto, with a splendid and most instructive map; 1839. This division of the subject is treated in chap. xxxvi.

also an eastern limit, which proves that a large portion of our island on that side then stood above the water. Between these limits, this drift is contracted, till it terminates in a roughly-pointed form upon the river Severn, where was either the point of a bay, or the straits might be prolonged into a wide sea towards the south. Hence some conclusions of importance force themselves upon our conviction.

The first is, that the country occupied by the local drift had been raised above the level of the sea which flowed up to its northern and eastern frontier.

The second, that the waters bringing this newer drift from the north, did not flow over the region already occupied by the local and more ancient drift. But there is evidence that both these formations were effected in periods much more remote than the date of the flood in the days of Noah, and even before the creation of man and his contemporary animals. We are therefore compelled to the conclusion that the flood of Noah was not absolutely universal: for had it been so, the diluvial waters must have carried forwards the northern drift, mingled with other stones, gravel, and mud; and so have overspread the previous Silurian bed.

Thirdly; this newer drift carries further evidence that it was not deposited by any transient rush of a body of new waters, over a surface which had been previously dry land: for such would have been a deluge rising for 150 days, and then beginning to subside, and in a little more than the same period coming completely to an end. On the contrary, the rounded forms of the pebbles and bowlders, and their diminishing sizes as they advance, evince a very long time of rubbing and grinding by currents, eddies, and tides at the bottom of the sea; and the occurrence of sea-shells, in considerable variety and abundance, affords evidence that the area itself had not been dry land, but the regular bed of the ocean.

It was mentioned above that the newer or northern drift was bounded on its eastern flank by a range of elevated land. It must be added, that the eastern portion of our island affords copious evidence of having received several other deposits of drift, at different and distant periods, brought from nearly all the primary and secondary rocks in the northern parts of Great Britain, from the mountains of Sweden and Norway, and probably from land which once occupied that which is now the bed of the German Ocean.*

In another European region, the effects have been traced of a series of phenomena more magnificent and astonishing still. To bring into view the physical reasons for the conclusions is impossible, in this brief sketch; nor indeed could they be made intelligible to a general audience. A statement of the results must suffice.

Some will perhaps be surprised and incredulous at hearing the position, which many appearances render *probable*, that, for countless ages after the elevation of the great mountain-chains of Great Britain, the region of the Alps, in the heart of Europe, was a champaign country, in many parts marshy, and enjoying a mean temperature not much if at all lower than that of tropical regions in the present condition of the earth. Subsequently, the elevatory movements which have operated so variously and powerfully upon the crust of the earth, greatly altering the forms and proportions of land and sea, pushed up the previously horizontal beds, and raised that large district into ranges of mountains considerably higher than is their present state. This effected an extreme reduction of temperature, and established a polar climate. The valleys were filled with stupendous glaciers; which, as do those of the present day, broke off and slowly bore away as along inclined planes, fragments of rock, of all sizes, from that of mere grains to bowlders weighing hundreds of tons. These, by the known progressive motion of those immense masses of frozen snow, were driven over surfaces of denuded rock, in the way of dry grinding. [Under circumstances of advanced temperature, they became icebergs, bearing on and in their masses and holding fixed to their bottom surfaces, those sharp fragments; and pro-

* Paper of Dr. Mitchell's, read to the Geol. Society, Nov. 7, 1838. Confirmed by Mr. Lyell, in a Paper read Jan. 22, 1840, which contains much important matter upon the Drift-formations, on the coast of Norfolk. It is published at length in the Philosoph. Mag. for May, 1840. Since the depositing of the most recent parts of the drift, the chalk and all the beds over it, (crag, drift, both stratified and not stratified, marine clay, fresh-water deposits, and again marine,) have been subjected to elevation and depression again and again after vast intervals, fracture, inclination at all angles, overturning and convolution; demonstrating the occurrence of repeated and mighty action, but most probably very slow, and all during a period in a geological sense recent.

[See also a brief but graphic and lively illustration of this subject, by the Scottish geologist, Mr. Hugh Miller, in his *First Impressions of England and its People*, 1847, p. 194.]

ducing similar rubbings and tracings upon the rocks over which they were driven by the force of mighty waters.] The mechanical results of such operations, repeated thousands of times, are "written as with the point of a diamond." Grooves, slighter markings, and the interposed small pebbles and fine sand, prove the kind and manner of the operation. In a subsequent period, the great system of mountains is supposed to have sunk down, to the average of seven thousand feet. Consequently, the snows melted below a certain altitude. In time the valleys were cleared, and the whole face of the country became nearly what it is at present. One of the results was, that the blocks of the Alps are now found on the tops and opposite descents of the Jura mountains, separated from the origin of those blocks by several deep valleys, running crosswise, each ten or fifteen miles in width, and the entire distance at least fifty miles. Several local deluges appear then to have taken place, commencing in some part of the higher Alps. The earlier of these were probably produced from the melting of the snow and ice made redundant by the subsidence of the ground, and the dissolution of which would become very rapid in consequence of the rock-fissures inevitably produced, and through which steam and volatilized minerals would rise at a high temperature. The courses of these floods appear to have been principally to the east, towards the plains of Italy, and in a northerly direction, where now is the bed of the Rhine.*

There are evident indications of another deluge, which had washed over Lapland and Norway, but especially Sweden, in a direction from north or north-east, to the south, spreading its stony burden, in accommodation to the receiving surfaces, over vast districts of Denmark, Poland, and the north of Germany, in some parts as far as the 51st degree of latitude;† and presenting

* Venetz and De Charpentier; in Jameson's Philos. Journ. vol. xxi. p. 210. and xxii. p. 27. Agassiz; in the same Journal, xxiv. pp. 176, and 364. Important modifications of this theory, see in Supplementary Note H.

† [Illustration is supplied by Sir Roderick Murchison, in describing the wide extent of this "great Scandinavian drift, by which all the low countries of the north have been covered by far-transported materials." "—To obtain a due consideration of the vast area over which the detritus is spread out, as well as to understand the very irregular dispersion of the blocks,—sometimes placed at wide distances from each other, at other times in heaps,—here quite upon the surface, there entangled in mud,—he [the observer] must traverse not only the northern tracts, but also the great central region of Vologda and its continuous governments. In doing this, he may for a while be led to speculate upon the former existence of basins of sand in one tract, and of clay in another. But, the more he extends his survey, the more will he find that all these accumulations and

the polished surfaces of rocks, marked with fine linear scratches, larger grooves, and even furrows, evidently produced by the passage of immense masses of rock over them.* In other places, the streams of stones have been borne in different and opposite directions, radiating from a point of upheaval. Similar proofs, and those upon a grand scale, of a flood, or rather of several floods, exist in North America. These were variously local, yet extensive and powerful to an amazing degree, and having, in like manner, a direction from northerly points to the southward.†

their associated blocks are parts of one great system of operations, and that they have all been formed in *one long period* of time:—he will conclude with us, that this great northern drift (by whatever power transported) was deposited *on the bottom of a sea.*——The southern limits of these erratics is by no means uniform,—but on the contrary very devious. The detritus does not in fact occupy an equably shelving southern talus; but, though often on plateaux, it has in many instances followed, even to great distances, the course of the existing north and south valleys at its southern extremity.——This ancient detritus has usually been propelled in an opposite direction to the present course of the waters.——We feel confident that there are no other parts of Europe in which foreign materials have been transported so far as from Russian Lapland and Finland to Voroneje and Putievil; points, from 700 to 800 English miles in straight lines from the nearest crystalline rocks whence such fragments can have proceeded."—*Geol. of Russia*, vol. i. pp. 9, and 524.—*Anno* 1845.]

* De la Beche's *Geol. Manual*, third ed. p. 189. Poggendorf, in Jameson's *Journal*, vol. xxiii. p. 69.

["The superficial detritus of Russia, Poland, and Prussia, like that of other regions which we have examined, is referable to the great mountain-chain in its vicinity. The chief, if not the only, distinction between it and all other far-borne drift, consists in the great breadth and length of the dispersed detritus, in reference to the low mountains from whence it has been derived; for, whilst in other parts of Europe various local centres of elevation have shed their detritus in different directions (England, France, and the Alps offer sufficient examples,) the vast regions under consideration have been uniformly covered with crystalline materials" [see Sect. II. prop. iii.] "which have proceeded from Scandinavia and Lapland only." Sir Roderick Murchison's *Geology of Russia and the Ural Mountains;* vol. i. p. 509; 1845. This magnificent work, in two imperial volumes, pours a flood of light upon geological science generally and in most of its great particulars. "This monster-publication may be considered, in more senses than one, as the *opus magnum* of Geology.—The importance of the work more than rivals its gigantic bulk. It embraces the physical geography, the mineral structure, and the history of the ancient organized beings of nearly two-thirds of Europe; and the information thus communicated, for the first time, to the scientific public will enable them to form more complete and just views on all the geological relations of this vast portion of our continent, than we could possibly have obtained concerning our own little island alone, when the Quarterly Review had reached its twentieth volume:" i. e. in 1818. *Quart. Rev.* vol. lxxvii. p 348; March, 1846.]

† "That a transient deluge, like that described in the Scriptures, could have produced, and brought into its present situation, all the diluvium which is now spread over the surface of this continent, will not (it seems to me) be admitted for a moment by any impartial observer. It has obviously been the result of different agencies and of different epochs; the result of causes sometimes operating feebly and slowly, and at other times violently and powerfully. But the conclusion to which I have been irresistibly forced, by an examination of this stratum in Massachusetts, is, that *all the diluvium, which had*

Those torrents have borne upon their bosoms numerous icebergs, broken off from vast glaciers; and which, both from their former action in separating portions of rock of all sizes, and from the accompaniments of their disruption, must have involved large masses of rocky materials. These materials are of all sizes, from small pebbles and moderate bowlders to blocks of thousands of cubic feet in dimension and hundreds of tons in weight. As the icebergs melted away, after the retiring floods had left them, these stones were deposited. Some of the masses received additional periods of long-continued water-wearing, and are now exhibited to us in the graduating forms of blocks separate or in continuous heaps, smaller bowlders and pebbles, gravel and sand. It must be borne in mind, that the reducing of angular fragments into rounded and smooth forms, especially of the extremely hard rocks which have furnished this drift (quartz, granite, syenite, hornblende, porphyry, basalt, and the like,) could not be effected in a short time, nor probably by any one land-torrent, or sea-current: so that we are led to the admission of long action, previous to the great transport, or subsequently, or both; and that not merely in progressive motion in straight lines, but by gyrations in basin-like

been previously accumulated by various agencies, has been modified by a powerful deluge, sweeping from the north and north-west over every part of the State, not excepting its highest mountains; and since that deluge, none but alluvial agencies have been operating to change the surface." Hitchcock's *Geology of Massachusetts;* p. 148. Amherst, 1835.

"If it be true that continents and vast chains of mountains were elevated at different periods, and by paroxysmal efforts, it is impossible but that deluges of tremendous violence and universal (1) extent, should have been the consequence. Accordingly, we find traces of such deluges in the vast beds of conglomerates that exist in the sedimentary deposits; and also in the frequent extinctions and renewals of animal and vegetable life, which appear to have taken place on the globe. For such deluges must have been fatal to organized existence: at least to a great extent.——Our rocks [those of Massachusetts] shew the occurrence of several very powerful deluges in early times.——The new red sandstone affords evidences of numerous deluges during its deposition; in the many alternations of coarse and fine materials of which it is composed. Two periods, during its production, appear to have been particularly distinguished for powerful diluvial action. In the first, those conglomerated beds, made up chiefly of the ruins of granite, and associated with the lower beds of sandstone, were accumulated. In the second, that very coarse conglomerate, chiefly composed of various schists, and connected with the higher shales and sandstones, was brought into its present situation. The osseous conglomerate connected with the plastic clay, indicates diluvial action, perhaps, though not of the most violent kind, during the deposition of this formation." Hitchcock's *Geology of Massachusetts;* p. 250. Amherst, 1835.

(1) He probably means *very wide;* for a strict universality is not required by the reasoning, nor quite consistent with what follows.

spots which abundantly shew themselves in the regions of which we have been speaking. The heavier fragments, having, by the force of gravity, originally taken their places at the bottom of the icy masses, would, upon the melting away of the under-surface, present sharp angular points; for when they were first enveloped in the ice they had been just broken off from their parent rocks. These under surfaces, acting under the pressure of many thousand tons weight, rubbed and ground smooth the rocks upon which they slid; and their points made grooves, or deep scratches, which present themselves to the laborious observer, and are truly inscriptions "graven in the rock for ever," and furnishing unerring indications of the direction in which those vast masses were carried. The torrents must soon have ceased, the waters subsiding into the seas and lakes in the respective regions. The icebergs grounded; and, being now in climates which kept them continually melting, at last disappeared, and the blocks, often exhibiting their original sharpness of outline, remain to this day, attesting, by the identity of the stone, which is often remarkably characteristic, the mountain-ridges whence they had been torn. Those mountain-ridges are frequently within a few miles, but often at the distance of some hundreds, from the areas over which the derived pebbles and bowlders are spread.

Here, then, we have evidence of the origin and the direction, the breadth (though the edges which would shew the boundary are often lost in the ocean), and the gradual termination, of the astonishing bodies of water which had thus been put into a violent and long-acting motion.

To my auditors, notwithstanding their candour and patience, I fear that these details have appeared dry and tedious; and to those who are not accustomed to such verbal descriptions, it may perhaps be difficult to estimate their argumentative value. But this object will be attained in a manner highly advantageous and illustrative, if I here cite the declarations of those eminent Geologists, who have frankly and honourably relinquished their former opinion.

I begin with Dr. Buckland, because I have already quoted from his elegant and deeply interesting Reliquiæ Diluvianæ, the passage expressing what were his sentiments seventeen years ago. In his Bridgewater Treatise, he mentions, with a brevity which we cannot but lament, the "deposits of diluvial detritus, dispersed over the surface of formations of all ages." These he classes with the newest or latest geological formations, called in Mr. Lyell's nomenclature those of the Pliocene period, that is, *the newer* of the Tertiary series; though in fact it is older than the state of the surface which we can, with any reasonable appearance of evidence, regard as contemporary with the human race and the present vegetable and animal creation. Dr. Buckland also shews that the bones of large quadrupeds, which are abundantly found in these strata, have belonged to species which no longer exist in a living state, though we have other species of the same genera: thus warranting the belief that we live under a different order of creation than that of even the latest of the past periods: he then subjoins the following passage:

"The evidence which I have collected in my Reliquiæ Diluvianæ, 1823, shews that one of the last great physical events that have affected the surface of our globe, was a violent inundation, which overwhelmed great part of the northern hemisphere, and that this event was followed by the sudden disappearance of a large number of the species of terrestrial quadrupeds, which had inhabited these regions in the period immediately preceding it. I also ventured to apply the name *Diluvium* to the superficial beds of gravel, clay, and sand, which appear to have been produced by this great irruption of water.

"The description of the facts which form the evidence presented in this volume, is kept distinct from the question of the identity of the event attested by them, with any deluge recorded in history. Discoveries which have been made, since the publication of this work, shew that many of the animals therein described, existed during more than one geological period preceding the catastrophe by which they were extirpated. Hence it seems more probable, that the event in question, was the last of the many geological revolutions that have been produced by violent irruptions of water, rather than the comparatively tranquil inundation described in the inspired narrative.

"It has been justly argued, against this attempt to identify these two great historical and natural phenomena, that as the rise and fall of the waters of the Mosaic deluge are described to have been gradual, and of short duration, they would have produced comparatively little change on the surface of the country they overflowed. The large preponderance of extinct species among the animals we find in caves, and in superficial deposits of diluvium, and the non-discovery of human bones along with them, afford other strong reasons for referring these species to a period anterior to the creation of man. This important point, however, cannot be considered as completely settled till more detailed investigations of the newest members of the Pliocene, and of the diluvial and alluvial formations shall have taken place."*

My next citation is from an equally distinguished philosopher, the correspondent ornament of the University of Cambridge. Though the passage be long, its importance for our present object and its comprehensiveness in relation to others, not to mention the felicity of its expression, render any apology unnecessary.

"At our former Anniversary I ventured to affirm, that our diluvial gravel was probably not the result of one, but of many successive periods. But what I then stated as a probable opinion, may, after the Essays of M. de Beaumont, be now advanced with all the authority of established truth: and among the many obligations we owe to this accomplished observer, I may mention the new and instructive views he has given us of the origin of the great masses of old detritus lying scattered over the lower regions of the earth. We now connect the gravel of the plains with the elevation of the nearest system of mountains; we believe that the Scandinavian bowlders in the north of Germany are of an older date than the diluvium of the Danube; and we can prove, that the great erratic blocks, derived from the granite of Mont Blanc, are of a more recent origin than the old gravel in the tributary valleys of the Rhone. That these statements militate against opinions, but a few years since held almost universally among us, cannot be denied. But theories of *diluvial gravel*, like all other ardent generalizations of an advancing science, must ever be regarded but as shifting hypotheses to be modified by every new fact, till at length they become accordant with all the phenomena of nature.

"In retreating where we have advanced too far, there is neither compromise of dignity nor loss of strength; for in doing this, we partake but of the common fortune of every one who enters on a field of investigation like our own. All the noble generalizations of Cuvier, and all the beautiful discoveries of Buckland, as far as they are the results of fair induction, will ever remain unshaken by the progress of discovery. It is only to theoretical opinions that my remarks have any application.

* *Bridgewater Treatise*, vol. i. p. 94.

"Different formations of solid rock, however elevated and contorted, can never become entirely mixed together; and the very progress of degradation commonly lays bare all the elements of their structure. But diluvial gravel may be shot off from the flanks of a mountain chain, during one period of elevation, and become so confounded with the detritus of another period, that no power on earth can separate them: and every subsequent movement, whether produced by land-floods or any other similar cause, must continually tend still further to mingle and confound them. The study of diluvial gravel is, then, not only one of great interest, but of peculiar difficulty and nice discrimination: and in the very same deposit, we may find the remains of animals which have lived during different epochs in the history of the earth.

"Bearing upon this difficult question there is, I think, one great negative conclusion now incontestably established—that the vast masses of diluvial gravel, scattered almost over the surface of the earth, *do not belong to one violent and transitory period.* It was indeed a most unwarranted conclusion, when we assumed the contemporaneity of all the superficial gravel on the earth. We saw the clearest traces of diluvial action, and we had, in our sacred histories, the record of a general deluge. On this double testimony it was, that we gave a unity to a vast succession of phenomena, not one of which we perfectly comprehended, and under the name diluvium, classed them all together.

"To seek the light of physical truth by reasoning of this kind, is, in the language of Bacon, to seek the living among the dead, and will ever end in erroneous induction. Our errors were, however, natural, and of the same kind which led many excellent observers of a former century to refer all the secondary formations of geology to the Noachian deluge. Having been myself a believer, and, to the best of my power, a propagator of what I now regard as a philosophic heresy, and having more than once been quoted for opinions which I do not now maintain, I think it right, as one of my last acts before I quit this chair, thus publicly to read my recantation.

"We ought, indeed, to have paused before we first adopted the diluvian theory, and referred all our old superficial gravel to the action of the Mosaic flood. For of man, and the works of his hands, we have not yet found a single trace among the remnants of a former world entombed in these ancient deposits. In classing together distant unknown formations under one name; in giving them a simultaneous origin, and in determining their date, not by the organic remains we had discovered, but by those we expected hypothetically hereafter to discover, in them; we have given one more example of the passion with which the mind fastens upon general conclusions, and of the readiness with which it leaves the consideration of unconnected truths.

"Are then the facts of our science opposed to the sacred records? and do we deny the reality of an historic deluge? I utterly reject such an inference. Moral and physical truth may partake of a common essence; but as far as we are concerned, their foundations are independent, and have not one common element. And in the narrations of a great fatal catastrophe, handed down to us, not in our sacred books only, but in the traditions of all nations, there is not a word to justify us in looking to any mere physical monuments as the intelligible records of that event: such monuments, at least, have not yet been found, and it is not perhaps intended that they ever should be found. If, however, we should hereafter discover the skeletons of ancient tribes, and the works of ancient art buried in the surperficial detritus of any large region of the earth: then, and not till then, we may speculate about their stature and their manners and their numbers, as we now speculate among the disinterred ruins of an ancient city.

"We might, I think, rest content with such a general answer as this. But we may advance one step further.——History is a continued record of passions and events unconnected with the enduring laws of mere material agents.—The progress of physical induction, on the contrary, leads us on to discoveries, of which the mere light of history would not indicate a single trace. But the facts recorded in history may sometimes, without confounding the nature of moral and physical truth, be brought into a general accordance with the known phenomena of nature: and such general accordance I affirm there is between our historical traditions and the phenomena of geology. Both tell us, in a language easily understood, though written in far different characters, that man is a recent sojourner on the surface of the earth. Again, though we have not yet found the certain traces of any great diluvian catastrophe which we can affirm to be within the human period; we have, at least, shewn that paroxysms of internal energy, accompanied by the elevation of mountain chains, and followed by mighty waves desolating whole regions of the earth, were a part of the mechanism of nature. And what has happened, again and again, from the most ancient up to the most modern periods in the natural history of the earth, may have happened once during the few thousand years that man has been living on its surface. We have therefore taken away all anterior incredibility from the fact of a recent deluge; and we have prepared the mind, doubting about the truth of things of which it knows not either the origin or the end, for the adoption of this fact on the weight of historic testimony."*

I shall add one more to the mention of eminent Geologists who, upon the point before us, have shewn their loyalty to the laws of evidence and the dominion of truth, by surrendering favourite, long cherished, and diligently elaborated sentiments. It is scarcely twenty years since Mr. Greenough, at that time President of the Geological Society, of which he was one of the founders, published his Critical Examination of the First Principles of Geology, in which he investigates at great length the phenomena which have detained us so long, the state and connexions of gravel and transported bowlders. It is right to say of this gentleman that he has been always distinguished by his comprehensiveness of knowledge, and his caution, I might say extreme reluctance, and even jealousy, in acceding to new opinions, till they were substantiated by very satisfactory evidence. In that large and careful disquisition, he repeatedly declares himself in favour of one great and universal deluge. But in the year 1834, we find him thus addressing that Society.

"Allow me —— to say a few words upon a subject in connexion with which my name has of late been brought forward much more prominently than I could have desired;—I mean *Diluvial action.*

"Some fourteen years ago I advanced an opinion, founded altogether upon physical and geological considerations, that the entire earth had, at an unknown period, (as far as that word implies any determinate portion of time,) been covered by one general but temporary deluge. The opinion was not hastily formed. My reasoning rested on the facts which had then come before me. My acquaintance with physical and geological nature is now extended: and that more extended acquaintance would be entirely wasted upon me, if the opinions which it will no longer allow me to retain, it did not also induce me to rectify. New data have flowed in, and with the frankness of one of my predecessors, I also now read my recantation.

"The varied and accurate researches which have been instituted of late years throughout and far beyond the limits of Europe, all tend to this conclusion, that the geological schools of Paris, Freyberg, and

* *Geol. Soc Proceed.* vol. i. pp. 312—314. 1831.

London, have been accustomed to rate too low the various forces which are still modifying, and always have modified, the external form of the earth. What the value of those forces may be in each case, or what their relative value, will continue for many years a subject of discussion; but that their aggregate effect greatly surpasses all our early estimates, is I believe incontestably established. To Mr. Lyell is eminently due the merit of having awakened us to a sense of our error in this respect. The vast mass of evidence which he has brought together, in illustration of what may be called *Diurnal Geology*, convinces me that if, five thousand years ago, a deluge did sweep over the entire globe, its traces can no longer be distinguished from more modern and local disturbances. The first sight of those comparatively recent assemblages of strata, which he designates the *Eocene*, *Meiocene* and *Pleiocene* Formations, (unknown but a few years ago, though diffused as extensively as many which were then honoured with the title of universal,) shews the extreme difficulty of distinguishing their detritus from what we have been accustomed to esteem Diluvium. The Fossil Contents of these formations strongly confirm this argument. M. Deshayes has shewn that they belong to a series unbroken by any great intervals, and that if they be divided from the secondary strata, the chasm can have no relation to any such event as is called *The Flood*.

"Further, the elephants and other animals once supposed to be exclusively *Diluvial*, are now admitted to be referrible to two or three distinct epochs; and it is highly probable that the blocks of the Jura mountains, of the North of Germany, of the North of Italy, of Cumberland, Westmoreland, &c. are not the waifs and strays of one, but of several successive inundations."

In addition to these vestiges of deluges, wide in their extent, and mighty in their effects, but yet limited and marked with characters of independent action and diversity of time, geological research has brought to light other facts and evidences, which we cannot enlarge upon. The phenomena are chiefly in the northern hemisphere.* As far as my reading has enabled me to get infor-

* *Fourth ed.* In North America, vast tracts of country are described by scientific observers as overspread by drift, containing massive bowlders and of all inferior sizes down to pebbles and sand, and masses of clay. They have been borne from the mountains of the northerly regions (Upper Canada, &c.) to distances of 50 or 60, 100 to 200, and in some directions, above 400 miles. The thickness of these *streams* of stones varies from about 10 feet to 100, and in some places 200 or 300, and more. On this subject, see Dr. Hitchcock's *Elementary Geology*, sec. ed. pp. 192—219; the same author's *Geology of Massachusetts*, in two large quarto vols. 1841, vol. ii. p. 350—406; Mr. Lyell's *Travels*

mation, and if the recollection do not fail, they are much less frequent and extensive in the equatorial regions. In Jamaica, Mr. De la Beche found considerable masses of drift-pebbles, conglomerates, and breccias, derived from the rocks of the island, and evidently of various ages.* But in the farther latitudes of South America, the plains of Patagonia, an area of two or three thousand square miles is covered with drift derived from the chain of the Andes by the washing of the ocean upon ancient coasts, which, in successive geological periods, have been raised above the waters, leaving a series of beaches which form terraces hundreds of miles asunder, and marked with the intervention of vol-

in North America, 1845, passages referred to in the Index under *Drift*, especially vol. ii. p. 99. From the Geology of Massachusetts, I cite an appropriate passage.

"Another theory, which has long been a favourite one, imputes diluvial action to the Deluge of Noah. The freshness and apparent recency of the effects of this action, and its apparent universality, give at first view a strong probability to this supposition, if we understand the language of Scripture in its most literal sense. But many distinguished Biblical writers regard the description of the Noachian Deluge as an example of the use of universal terms with a limited meaning," [as is often the case, especially in ancient writings and the sacred books, but *this is only when the limitation is suggested by the context, or by the nature and conditions of the subject:*] "and hence regard that deluge as not universal over the globe, but only over the region inhabited by man. Again; if the diluvial action of Geology resulted from the Deluge of Noah, why are the organic remains found in diluvium, mostly of extinct animals? And why is not man among the number? Finally, the diluvial action of Geology must have occupied a much longer period than the hundred and fifty days, or at longest the year, of the Noachian Deluge. It is difficult, if not impossible, to make any one feel the force of this objection, who is not familiar with diluvial phenomena. But he who has seen where the hardest rocks have been worn away many feet at least, and probably sometimes many hundred feet, by diluvial action, cannot but see that many years must have been required for the work, even though the waters were driven over the surface with the greatest violence." Vol. ii. p. 403.

"The structure of the Appalachian mountains (and, by analogy, those of other countries), implies the operation of far greater and more sudden forces than the gentle secular changes observed in modern times; and they (H. D. and W. B. Rogers,) consider it impossible to avoid the conclusion that *all the more extensive evolutions of the earth's crust have involved*, to a greater or less extent, *the agency of vast earthquake waves*. [They mean an 'actual *billowy pulsation* in the molten matter,' upon which they suppose the crust of the earth floats; 'engendered by a linear or focal disruption and immediate collapse of the crust, accompanied by the explosive escape of highly elastic vapour:'—p. 775.—] To the action of these waves, in different geological epochs, they attribute the formation of the vast masses of conglomerate and detrital deposits distributed in the various groups of strata; also the transport of the great northern drift, and the polished and furrowed surfaces of rocks both in Europe and in N. England. *Athenæum*, Aug. 26, 1843, p. 776.

Mr. Griffith,—on vast erratic block and bowlder deposits in Ireland,—thinks that they have been carried by currents from at least two foci, in Ireland. *Ib.* 776.

* *Geol. Soc. Transact.* Second Series; vol. ii. Article xiii. 1827. See also his *Geol. Manual*, p. 142.

canic eruptions. The mind is overwhelmed by an attempt to reduce these periods to any comparison with our puny measures of time: and yet they belong to the most recent class of geological operations.*

It must not be forgotten that, in some situations, the characters of the rolled stones are thought to warrant the supposition of their having been driven and agitated upon the bottom of the deep ocean, by under-currents, acting during vast periods of time, when it is probable that the region, which now constitutes Europe, was occupied by the sea, and studded with a multitude of small islands.

The inference to which all these observations and reasonings lead, is that geological evidence is adverse to the admission of a deluge simultaneous and universal for every part of the earth's surface. Indeed I must add that, in proportion to the care and accuracy with which the investigation of physical facts has been carried on, so the proofs have accumulated that there never was a period, since any vestiges occur of the existence of organized creatures, when the earth did not possess a varied face; partly dry land with its vegetable and animal occupiers, and partly the wide domain of the waters possessing their numerous inhabitants.

Another fact, which has an interesting reference to our present inquiry, must not be passed over, though I can only treat it with the utmost brevity. There is a district in the southern part of the centre of France, more than forty miles in length, and twenty in breadth, comprised in the ancient provincial divisions of Auvergne and Languedoc.† In this district are the unquestionable cones, craters, and other characteristic remains of more than two hundred volcanic hills and mountains. These, in former periods of our planet's history, have projected their tremendous fiery masses, ashes, and water, into the air; and vast streams of the melted rocks along the ground. Some of the smaller hills may have been secondary vents, burst open at the same time with a great mountain-eruption, with whose interior a series of minor cones might be connected, in a way well known to those who

*For this information I am indebted to Mr. Darwin's instructive and delightful volume, the third of the *Narrative of the Voyages* of Captains King and Fitzroy; p. 201, &c.

† Supplementary Note I; which will be a welcome refreshment to the Christian's heart, giving an authentic account of the Revival of True Religion in that district.

have studied the structure and action of volcanoes. But, when every allowance is made for this supposition, there remains the astonishing spectacle of many contiguous burning mountains, some of them fairly comparable to Vesuvius.* All the accompaniments of volcanic action, are here presented in the most perfect manner. The craters, the ejected ashes and cinders, the characteristic fragments of stones, and the consolidated but once liquid masses of various lavas, which have flowed in all directions, dispossessing rivers of their channels, filling up those channels and other valleys to heights of fifty, one hundred, and many more feet, and spreading in their various flow, over many miles of area. The different and distant periods which separated these eruptions from each other, are shewn by the interposition of stratified formations, and by numerous other circumstances, appropriate marks of volcanic districts. Subjacent and alternating beds of different material demonstrate the succession of distinct mineral formations, and a rich abundance of what was once vegetable and animal life in species of creatures which belong not to the present condition of our globe. Vast forests, and those of the largest chestnut trees, now clothe many parts of the slope. "Rivers have, since the flowing of these lavas, worn themselves new channels; and have sometimes not only exposed on each bank a precipitous wall of columnar basalt one hundred and fifty feet in height, but even to a considerable depth eaten into the granite rocks beneath; the whole excavation being of course entirely subsequent to the volcanic eruption, the lava of which flowed at the bottom of the then existing valley."†

Yet when did these fires burn? When took place this amazing combination of volcanic eruptions and their terrible accompaniments? How long ago was the last of them? And by what intervals of time could we ascend, from that last, to the earlier eruptions; and to the earliest of the—astounding number?—These questions cannot be answered by any assigning of our measures of time; years and centuries. Such analogies as may be inferred by comparative examinations of the condition of Ætna, Vesuvius, and other active volcanoes, carry us to the contempla-

* The summit of Vesuvius is 3900 feet above the level of the sea. Of these extinct volcanoes, one is 3956, another more than 4000, another nearly 5000, and many are from 500 to 1000.

† *Quarterly Review*, vol. xxxvi. p. 464; 1827.

tion of a period which runs back not to the age of Noah merely, but immeasurably beyond the date of the creation of man and his contemporary plants and animals. In mountainous countries many facts are presented to the eye which approach to a standard of measurement of the average action of the atmosphere and of running water, in decomposing and washing off the surface of granitic and basaltic rocks. That action is sure and constant: but it is slow, to such a degree, that not years but centuries are requisite for its chronicle. Even the abrading of that description of rocks when they form the boldest sea-coast, by the violence of storms added to the ordinary action of water and weather (an addition of great power), has not materially altered the outline of such shores in Cornwall, the west and north of Scotland, Norway, and many other countries, since the beginning of our historical knowledge. But the action of a fresh-water river, impinging upon hard rocks, is much more feeble. Yet, in the district of which we are speaking, such streams have made themselves a way, in several places, between the granite and the lower part, indeed the most porous and friable, of the lava, which had formed rocks of more than one hundred feet in thickness, overlying the granite. Such an operation must have been slow, almost beyond conception. In whatever way we may contrive to imagine a reduction of the time necessary for this purpose, the mind cannot rest upon a period less than many thousands of years.* Also, in this re-

* "These ancient currents [of basalt] have since been corroded by rivers, which have worn through a mass of 150 feet in height, and formed a channel even in the granite rocks beneath, since the lava first flowed into the valley. In another spot, a bed of basalt, 160 feet high, has been cut through by a mountain stream.——The vast excavations effected by the erosive power of currents along the valleys which feed the Ardèche, since their invasion by lava-currents, prove that even the most recent of these volcanic eruptions belong to an era incalculably remote." Mr. Poulett Scrope's *Memoir of the Geology of Central France.*

"The time that must be allowed for the production of effects of this magnitude, by causes evidently so slow in their operation, is indeed immense: but surely it would be absurd to urge this as an argument against the adoption of an explanation so unavoidably forced upon us. The periods which, to our narrow apprehension and compared with our ephemeral existence, appear of incalculable duration, are in all probability but trifles in the calendar of nature. It is Geology that, above all other sciences, makes us acquainted with the important, though humiliating fact. Every step we take in it forces us to make unlimited drafts on antiquity.

"There are many minds that would not for an instant doubt the God of nature to have existed *from all eternity*, and would yet reject as preposterous the idea of going back a million of years in the history of his works. Yet, what is a million, or a million million, of solar revolutions to an ETERNITY?" *Ib.* p. 165.

markable region, in places where time has laid bare large perpendicular surfaces, are presented series of strata of different rock; and laminations of the same kind of rock, which amount to the thickness of one hundred feet, and two hundred, and still more. One of the laminated formations just mentioned may be said to furnish a chronometer for itself. It consists of sixty feet of siliceous and calcareous deposits, each as thin as pasteboard, and bearing upon their separating surfaces the stems and seed-vessels of small water-plants in infinite numbers; and countless multitudes of minute shells, resembling some species of our common snail-shells. These layers have been formed with evident regularity, and to each of them we may reasonably assign the term of one season, that is a year. Now thirty of such layers frequently do not exceed one inch in thickness. Let us average them at twenty-five. The thickness of the stratum is at least sixty feet; and thus we gain, for the whole of this formation alone, eighteen thousand years.

Further: many of these hills in the form of sugar-loaves consist of, or are coated with, pumice-stone and other loose and light substances, which every person knows to be volcanic products. It is self-evident that these could not have withstood the action of a flood: they must have been broken down and washed away with the first rush of water. Either, then, the eruptions which produced them, took place since the deluge; or that deluge did not reach to this part of the earth. Against the former side of this alternative, the argument from analogy is very strong. All that we know of the history of volcanoes impresses us with the vast *improbability*, that such an intensity and extent of volcanic action as belonged to the later series only, of these eruptions, could begin, run their course, and come to an end by settling in perfect quiescence, within the period from the deluge to our first historical notices of this district, which is about 2300 years.* Supposing

* *Sec. ed.* A paper of great interest was presented to the Geological Society, on Nov. 2, 1836, by Mr. H. E. Strickland and Mr. W. J. Hamilton, upon the Geology of the Western part of Asia Minor. This includes the country anciently called *the Burnt* (ἡ κατακεκαυμένη. Strabo. ed. Falc. p. 900, &c.); on account of the marks of volcanic combustion with which it abounds. It is the region of the ancient Sardis and Philadelphia. It presents a strong resemblance to "the volcanic district of Central France. In each country are extensive lacustrine formations, cones of scoriæ of different ages, *coulées*," [rocks preserving their pristine form of lava-flowings,] "sometimes forming plateaux on the summits of isolated hills" [consequently that which originally filled the intervening valleys must have been worn off and washed away; a series of operations

the eruptions in question to have commenced immediately upon the subsiding of the diluvial waters, it would be contrary to all known instances of volcanic action, to suppose that they would finally cease within a less period than many centuries. Now Julius Cæsar, in his Gallic wars, was encamped in this very district, at the closing part of the period just mentioned. His writings furnish abundant evidence of his observant, inquisitive, and acute character. Notwithstanding his vicious habits, he had a mind deeply imbued with literature, and the love of philosophical pursuits; and he made considerable attainments in science so far as in his day was practicable. Had he found in this place any tradition of volcanic action as having formerly existed, it is morally certain that his curiosity would have been powerfully awakened, and that we should have had in his Commentaries the result of his inquiries. But nothing of the kind exists, though he indicates his acquaintance with the features of the country, as having surveyed it with the eye of a general.*

The geological difficulties are not the only ones which present themselves, in relation to the admission of a strictly universal deluge, and some of the circumstances which are *commonly supposed* to be affirmed or implied in the sacred narrative. It would be a failure in the service which I have undertaken, were I to pass these by without notice: but I must renew my entreaty that my auditors would not permit any conclusion unfavourable to the perfect verity of the Mosaic narrative, *correctly interpreted,* to lodge in their minds; for I trust that, in a future lecture, satisfactory proof will be brought that such conclusion would be erroneous.

The mass of water necessary to cover the whole globe to the depth supposed, would be in thickness about five miles above the previous sea-level. This quantity of water might be fairly calculated as amounting to eight times that of the seas and oceans of the globe, in addition to the quantity already existing. The

requiring time to us immeasurable!] "at others continuous streams, and thick beds of lava worn through by the action of running water." There are thirty distinct volcanoes, whose craters are filled up and covered with vegetation; and which are therefore evidently the oldest. "The newer volcanoes, of which there are only three, must have been extinct for at least 3000 years" [otherwise history would almost certainly have preserved some memorial of them]; "yet their craters are perfectly defined, and their streams of lava are black, rugged, and barren."

* *Comment.* vii. 4, 9, 36. Supplementary Note, K.

questions then arise, Whence was this water derived; and how was it disposed of, after its purpose was answered? These questions may indeed be met, by saying that the water was created for the purpose, and then annihilated.——That Omnipotence could effect such a work, none can doubt: but we are not at liberty thus to invent miracles, and the narrative in the Book of Genesis plainly assigns two natural causes for the production of the diluvial water; the incessant rain of nearly six weeks, called in the Hebrew phrase the "windows of heaven," that is, of the sky; and the "breaking up of all the fountains of the great deep." By the latter phrase some have understood that there are immense reservoirs of water in the interior of the earth, or that even the whole of that interior, down to the centre, is a cavity filled with water; a notion which was excusable in the defective state of knowledge a century ago, but which, from the amplest evidence, we now know to be an impossibility. The use of this expression, in other parts of Scripture, sufficiently proves that it denotes the general collection of oceanic waters. It is scarcely needful to say, that all the rain which ever descends, has been previously raised, by evaporation from the land and water that form the surface of the earth. The capacity of the atmosphere to absorb and sustain water is limited. Long before it reaches the point of saturation, change of temperature and electrical agency must produce copious descents of rain: from all the surface below, evaporation is still going on: and, were we to imagine the air to be first saturated to the utmost extent of its capacity, and then to discharge the whole quantity at once upon the earth, that whole quantity would bear a very inconsiderable proportion to the entire surface of the globe. A few inches of depth would be its utmost amount.* It is indeed the fact, that upon a small area of the earth's surface, yet the most extensive that comes within experience or natural possibility, heavy and continued rain for a few days often produces effects fearfully destructive, by swelling the streams and rivers of that district: but the laws of nature, as to evaporation and the capacity of atmospheric air to hold water in solution, render such a state of

* Seven inches, according to Mr. Rhind, in his *Age of the Earth*, p. 100. Edinb. 1839. [Atmospheric air holds in solution 3-5 of its own quantity. Therefore,—"supposing the vast canopy of air, by some sudden change of internal constitution, at once to discharge its whole watery store, this precipitate would form a sheet of scarcely *five* inches thick over the surface of the globe."—Sir John Leslie's Dissertation on the Progress of Mathematical and Physical Science. Encyclop. Brit. vol. i. p. 650; edit. 1843.]

things over the whole globe, not merely improbable, but absolutely impossible.

If we then turn to the waters of "the great deep," we obtain the idea of an irruption of the sea, spreading desolation and death over the land. Such irruptions have often occurred over low countries bordered by flat coasts. But all the water that could be derived from this cause would produce only an increased diffusion over the land, which would be accompanied by a substraction of water from the sea, to the same amount. The absolute quantity of water, for the entire globe, would remain precisely the same.

But we are especially called to take notice of the terms used in the sacred narrative, which appear to exclude the idea of a sudden and violent irruption; and to present that of an elevation and afterwards a subsidence, comparatively gentle, so that the ark was lifted, floated, and borne over the awful flood in a manner which we might call calm and quiet, if compared with an in-burst of the sea by the immediate breaking of the barrier. The words are, "The waters increased, and bare up the ark, and it was lifted up above the earth: and the waters prevailed, and were increased greatly upon the earth; and the ark went upon the face of the waters." In relating the subsidence, the words used are such as remarkably suit the conception of a large body of water undergoing a process of evaporation from the surface, and of a gradual draining off by outlets beneath: "God made a wind to pass over the earth" (—an expression which definitely conveys the idea of a local field of operation; extensive it might be, but totally inapplicable to the surface of the whole globe;—) "and the waters assuaged; the fountains also of the deep and the windows of heaven were stopped, and the rain from heaven* was restrained; and the waters returned from off the earth continually—(literally, *going and returning*) and, after the end of the hundred and fifty days, the waters were abated."

If we suppose the mass of waters to have been such as would cover all the land of the globe, we present to ourselves an increase of the equatorial diameter by some eleven or twelve miles. Two new elements would hence accrue to the action of gravity upon

* This "rain" is not to be considered as a third cause; but, according to the frequent style of Scripture, exegetically intended, or upon the principle of the *hendiadys*, which is abundant in the Hebrew Scriptures.

our planet. The absolute weight would be greatly increased, and the causes of the nutation of the axis would be varied. I am not competent to the calculation of the changes in the motions of the earth which would thus be produced, and which would propagate their effects through the whole solar system; and indeed to the entire extent of the material creation: but they would certainly be very great. To save the physical system from derangements, probably ruinous to the well-being of innumerable sentient natures, would require a series of stupendous and immensely multiplied miracles.

Again, pursuing the supposition, the ark would not remain stationary: "it went upon the face of the waters." Its form was adapted to secure slowness of motion; so that it should float as little a distance as possible from the place of human habitation. But, by the action of the sun upon the atmosphere, currents would be produced, by which the ark would be borne away, in a southerly and then a western direction. To bring it back into such a situation as would correspond to its grounding in Armenia, or any part of Asia, it must first circumnavigate the globe. But, this was impossible in the time, even if it had possessed the rate of going of a good sailing vessel. It might, perhaps, advance as far as the middle of North Africa, or the more westerly part; and *there* it would ground, at the end of the three hundred days.

Upon the supposition that the words of the narrative require to be understood in the sense of a strict and proper universality, another difficulty arises with respect to the preservation of animals. Ingenious calculations have been made of the capacity of the ark, as compared with the room requisite for the pairs of some animals, and the septuples of others: and it is remarkable that the well-intentioned calculators have formed their estimate upon a number of animals below the truth, to a degree which might appear incredible. They have usually satisfied themselves with a provision for three or four hundred species at most; as in general they shew the most astonishing ignorance of every branch of Natural History. Of the existing mammalia (animals which nourish their young by breasts,) considerably more than one thousand species are known; of Birds, fully five thousand: of Reptiles, very few kinds of which can live in water, two thousand; and the researches of travellers and naturalists are making frequent and most interesting additions to the number of these and all other classes.* Of Insects (using the word in its popular sense) the number of species is immense; to say one hundred thousand would be moderate: each has its appropriate habitation and food, and these are necessary to its life; and the larger number could not live in water. Also the innumerable millions upon millions of animalcules must be provided for; for they have all their appropriate and diversified places and circumstances of existence.† But all land animals have their geographical regions,‡ to which their constitutional natures are congenial, and many could not live in any other situation. We cannot represent to ourselves the idea of their being brought into one small spot, from the polar regions, the torrid zone, and all the other climates of Asia, Africa, Europe, America, Australia, and the thousands of islands; their preservation and provision; and the final disposal of them;—without bringing up the idea of miracles more stupendous than any that are recorded in Scripture,§ even what appear appalling in

* Among the numerous and satisfactorily authentic works of this description, it is a pleasure to mention two as an honour to our country, which are now publishing under the authority of Her Majesty's Treasury: the *Zoology of the Voyage of H. M. S. Beagle*, Capt. Fitzroy, by Mr. Darwin, Naturalist to the Expedition: and the *Illustrations of African Zoology*, by Dr. Andrew Smith, who conducted an exploring expedition into the Interior of South Africa. Both these enterprises were effected in the years 1832 to 1836.—Since, completed.

† *Fourth ed.* To the best of my remembrance, these numbers were given, in the delivery of the Lecture, from general recollection, or when I had not the time for accurate research. I therefore adduce the following as more perfect statements. The sentence upon animalcules was intended to refer to individuals, not to species.

From the *Encyclopædia Britannica* (1842,) upon the authority of Mr. Swainson:—

	SPECIES.		SPECIES.
Mammalia	1,000	Conchylia and naked Mollusca	5,100
Birds	6,000	Insects	550,000
Reptiles and amphibious animals	1,500	Vermes, &c.	2,500
Fishes	6,000	Zoophytes, &c.	2,500

"Besides these, there exist innumerable hosts of Infusoria." Vol. xvii. p. 549.

To Dr. Beard's *Bible Dictionary*, vol. i. p. 422, I am indebted for another passage:—

"Greatly has our acquaintance with the animal world been extended by the labours of Cuvier. Linnæus, in the last edition of his *System of Nature*, described altogether six thousand species of animals. [Linnæus died in 1778.] Whereas the following numbers have been known for a long time, and every year is making some addition.

	SPECIES.		SPECIES.
"Mammalia	800	Conchylia	15 to 20,000
Birds	6,000	Insects	80,000
Amphibious animals and Reptiles	1,000	Intestinal worms	1,500 to 2,000
Fishes	5 to 6,000	Zoophytes, including 600 Infusoria	6,000

‡ See Lect. II. prop. xxvii.

§ Some one may adduce Josh. xi. 13, the sun and the moon standing still: but the obvious reply is, that the whole effect wanted in that case, and fully answering to the de-

comparison. The great decisive miracle of Christianity, the RESURRECTION of the LORD JESUS,—sinks down before it.

The persons of whom we are speaking have probably never apprehended any difficulty with respect to the inhabitants of the waters; supposing that no provision was needed for their preservation. It may therefore be proper to notice some particulars. Such an additional quantity of water as their interpretation requires, would so dilute and alter the mass as to render it an unsuitable element for the existence of all the classes,* and would kill or disperse their food; and all have their own appropriate food. Many of the marine fishes and shell animals could not live in fresh-water: and the fresh-water ones would be destroyed by being kept even a short time in salt water. Some species can indeed live in brackish water: having been formed by their Creator to have their dwelling in estuaries and the portions of rivers approaching the sea; [or they may be brought to endure it:] but even these would be affected, fatally in all probability, by the increased volume of water and the scattering and floating away of their nutriment.†

Thus, in a variety of ways, it is manifest that, upon the inter-

scription of the apparent phenomenon as recorded, would be produced by an alteration in the refracting and transmitting properties of the atmosphere, immediately over the part of Judea where the victory was obtained. Such an alteration would be an indubitable miracle. But if any exclaim, 'All miracles are alike; the smallest and the greatest are equal to Omnipotence;' I request their kind attention to some remarks in a former lecture, (pp. 60—63.) Upon this particular case, to suppose that the diurnal rotation of the earth was interrupted, is to bring in a shock which would have disturbed the functions of not only every part of our earth, and the planetary system, but would extend through the astral spaces, rendering necessary three continuous and universal miracles, one for the disturbance, a second for preserving all creatures from being ruined by the shock, and a third for the restoration of order.

* *Third ed.* A very moderate proportion of salt water will dilute a much larger quantity of fresh, if it be introduced suddenly, in such a degree as to destroy life. In the dreadful hurricane of Barbadoes, Aug. 10, 1831, the spray of the sea was carried by the wind for many miles inward, so that its falling was called a *salt-water rain;* and "all the fresh-water fish in the ponds of Major Leacock were killed." Gen. Reid on the *Law of Storms;* 1838, p. 34.

† *Third ed.* The larger number of land-plants, and those the most important for size and utility (as timber and fruit trees, and the different kinds of corn and grasses,) lose their vitality by a short submersion in water; so that, in a period equal to the duration of the Deluge, they would have become putrescent and in a great measure decomposed. Thus, upon the supposition of a strict universality, a new creation of the chief part of the vegetable tribes would have been necessary, after the waters had subsided. In this view, the existence of an *olive-leaf* (Gen. viii. 11) is an observable circumstance. It was probably a fresh germination, but the stem must have grown very near the highest point to which the waters ascended, and could not have been long under water.

pretation which I conceive to be erroneous, the preservation of animal life in the ark, was immensely short of being adequate to what was necessary.

Further; if we admit that interpretation, and also accede to the usual opinion that the Ararat upon which the ark rested was the celebrated mountain of that name in Armenia, and which tradition points out as being such,—we are involved in another perplexity. That mountain is nearly the height of our European Mont Blanc,* and perpetual snow covers about five thousand feet from its summit. If the water rose, at its liquid temperature, so as to overflow that summit, the snows and icy masses would be melted; and, on the retiring of the flood, the exposed mountain would present its pinnacles and ridges, dreadful precipices of naked rock, adown which the four men and four women, and with hardly any exception, the quadrupeds, would have found it utterly impossible to descend. To provide against this difficulty, to prevent them from being dashed to pieces,—must we again suppose a miracle? Must we conceive of the human beings and the animals, as transported through the air to the more level regions below: or that, by a miracle equally grand, they were enabled to glide unhurt down the wet and slippery faces of rock?

One fact more I have to mention, in this range of argument. There are trees of the most astonishing magnificence as to form and size, which grow, the one species in Africa, the other in the southern part of North America. There are also methods of ascertaining the age of trees of the class to which they belong, with satisfaction generally, but with full evidence after they have passed the early stages of their growth. Individuals of these species now existing are proved, by those methods, to have begun to grow at an epoch long before the date of the deluge; if we even adopt the largest chronology that learned men have proposed. Had those trees been covered with water for three-quarters of a year, they must have been destroyed: the most certain conditions of vegetable nature, for the class (the most perfect land-plants) to which they belong, put such a result out of doubt. Here then we are met by another independent proof that the deluge did not extend to those regions of the earth.†

* The most recent statements make it much higher: Mont Blanc, 15,668 English feet: Ararat, 17,000. *Black's Atlas*, 1840.

† See Supplementary Note L; on the Longevity of Trees.

Such are the objections which present themselves against the interpretation which, with grief I acknowledge, is generally admitted, in relation to the scriptural narrative of the deluge. It is a painful position in which I stand. I seem to be taking the part of an enemy, adducing materials for scepticism, and doing nothing to remove them. But this situation for me is inseparable from the plan of these lectures; the only plan that appeared practicable. The apparent discrepancies, between the facts of science, and the words of Scripture, must be *understood,* before we can make any attempt at their removal. I confide in the candour of my friends, that they will suspend their judgment till I am enabled to lay before them the way, in which I conceive that *independent* and *unforced* philological evidence will enable us satisfactorily to dispose of those difficulties.

LECTURE VI.

PART I.

1 THESSALONIANS V. 21. *Prove all things: hold fast that which is good.*

WE are born for great and noble purposes. The object of existence, to every rational creature, is to enjoy a conscious union, in approbation, delight, and conformity, with the Being who is supreme in all excellence. To love and obey him is to secure our own happiness, and to acquire the best means of promoting that of every other being within our influence. If our minds be not dead to just feeling, we must be sensible that this is a necessary truth: and its undeniable concomitants are accountableness and retribution, stretching out into immortality. To that immortality of moral purity and happiness, the Revelation from God, contained in the Scriptures, is our only guide. Clearly then, it is the duty of every man to apprehend, with the most complete intelligence and satisfaction that he can attain, the contents and evidences of that Revelation; and to remove out of the way every obstacle to a complete "assurance of faith." Among the Christians of the apostolic age, there was a variety of talents for the understanding of sacred subjects, their explication, and their communication to others. Some of these were of an extraordinary kind, depending for their existence and exercise upon peculiar communications from the Sovereign of all minds, who, in order to give the fullest proofs of divine authority, in the introduction of Christianity, confirmed it by wisely adapted miracles. Among these was the gift of Prophecy. The meaning of this word was not restricted to the foretelling of future events, in such a manner as evinced an emanation from the Omniscient; but it comprehended a faculty of communicating divine knowledge, by public speaking, with remarkable attractions of fervid eloquence: in fact, it was *preaching*. But the matter thus declared was not necessarily and in all cases the result of inspiration or any divine influence. Even in the hands of the wise and holy, it was not infallible; but was exposed to the intrusions of error in judgment and imperfection in representation. Therefore the apostle Paul gave precepts for the regulation, controul, and correction of this "gift for the edifying of the church."* In the words preceding our text, he enjoins a respectful and reverential treatment of all those means of instruction; while yet, in the text itself, he directs to a faithful examination of them, by bringing them to the standard of truth, and then firmly to retain whatever sentiments had endured this searching scrutiny. The standard of truth, in religious matters, lies in the unchangeable perfections of God, and the revelation which he has made of himself: and, in matters of science respecting the sensible world, it is to be elicited by observation, experiment, and induction. The obligations, then, to which we are here remitted, are comprehensiveness and diligence in our inquiries, openness to conviction, right estimation of evidence, and a steadfast adherence to its results.†

* 1 Cor. xiv. A similar precept is in 1 John iv. 1

† "—See; here St. Paul determines that no position should be admitted, till, before the community which hears it, it has been examined and found to be sound. This duty of examination does not belong to teachers only; but" [implies that] "they must openly propound their sentiments, in order that they may be subjected to every man's examining. Thus, by the authority of this passage, the exercise of judgment upon doctrines is not reserved to Christian teachers, but is given to the learners: so that it is altogether a different thing among Christians, to what obtains in the world. In the world, sovereigns command what they please, and their subjects yield compliance. 'But,' says Christ, 'it shall not be so among you.' Among Christians, every one has the right of forming a judgment concerning others; and is also himself subjected to the same right in them: though spiritual tyrants have made a worldly dominion out of Christianity." Luther's *Larger Catechism;* a work of 2756 columns on the quarto page, written in 1528: in Walch's ed. of *Luther's Works*, in 24 quarto volumes; Halle, 1744, vol. x. col. 1799.

"Because rash men and impostors often cover over their absurdities with the title of *prophecy*, there was some danger of true prophecy being brought into suspicion, or cast into odium. As, in the present day, many persons almost nauseate the very name of a sermon, because there are so many silly and ignorant men (*insulsi ac imperiti*) who babble out from the pulpit their own inventions; and also ungodly men and contemners of religion, who preach execrable blasphemies. Wherefore, because, by the faults of such teachers, prophecy" [or preaching] "might be brought into dislike, or even be almost entirely rejected, Paul commands the Thessalonians to *prove all things;* intimating that, although all teachers are not unexceptionable in their adherence to the perfect rule, and the propriety of their expressions, still we are not to condemn or reject any doctrine till we have fairly put it to the trial. In this respect, two opposite errors are common. Some persons, finding that themselves, or the bulk of men, have been imposed upon, reject in the mass all" [religious] "doctrines. Others, with weak credulity, indiscriminately embrace whatsoever is proposed to them in the name of God. Each extreme is wrong. The former class, filled with proud prejudice, bar themselves out from the way of im-

We have seen that formidable difficulties present themselves to a man who looks seriously at the relations between the records of Revelation and the monuments of Natural History. Yet such a man cannot but feel assured, that the difficulties lie only in our want of sufficient knowledge. Nature and Revelation are both beams of light from the same Sun of eternal truth; and there cannot be a discordance between them. If that which is announced as a revelation be indeed what it professes, and if the facts in nature be satisfactorily ascertained, it must be impossible that any real discordance should exist. The appearance of it, however, we have seen. We know that this appearance of things has attracted, and continues to attract, the most earnest attention, to a very wide extent among reading and inquiring persons. Serious Christians are alarmed: unbelievers and irreligious persons exult. But to both classes we say, Ye are too hasty: the Christian may dismiss his apprehensions: the hopes of the infidel are a spider's web. The voices of nature, and reason, and revelation are in harmony. We want only that facts be correctly stated, and that the words of Scripture be interpreted upon the principles of just philology; and we fear not the result. We will search out the objects of science, "the works of the Lord," by the most careful investigation and rigorous induction, as if we had never heard of his word: and we will apply ourselves to the study of his word, with the strictest observance of the rules of interpretation, just as if we knew nothing of the physical world. We do not therefore speak of bringing about a *conciliation* between these two lines of fact and doctrine; for we anticipate the conviction that it already exists.

It will not, I trust, be presumptuous in me to express some regret in finding an expression used by one of the most accomplished geologists of our own or any other country, Dr. Buckland; believing, at the same time, that it was introduced by him more from oversight than with deliberate intention. He says, "If, in this respect, geology should seem to require some little

provement; the others, rashly expose themselves to every wind of error. From these two extremes, Paul recalls the Thessalonians to the middle path; forbidding the condemnation of any sentiment, till it be first duly examined; and admonishing that we should exercise a just judgment before we receive as certain that which is proposed to us.—— Nothing is more hurtful" [to intellectual and religious improvement] "than the petulant and conceited disposition, by which we take up a dislike to any sentiment, without taking the trouble of a fair examination." Calvin, in his *Comment. in Epistolas;* ad locos.

concession from the literal interpreter of Scripture, it may fairly be held to afford ample compensation for this demand, by the large additions it has made to the evidences of natural religion, in a department where revelation was not designed to give information."* The testimony of the word of heaven does not lie at our disposal. We have not the power of conceding any thing from it; and I am confident that the distinguished Professor did not intend to intimate that mortals have such a power or right. He was referring indeed to the *interpretation* of Scripture; but, in this view, the expression is unhappy. Interpretation, as well of the Bible as of other ancient writings, is to be conducted by a rigorous process of examination into words and phrases; a process solely grammatical, and which must not be checked or turned out of its straightforward course by any foreign considerations.†

The design of this lecture and the following, is to enumerate methods that have been proposed for removing the difficulty, or apprehended inconsistency, which arises from a survey of God's visible works and comparing them with the declarations of his word; and to submit those remarks which they respectively seem to require.

It cannot be without some anxiety that I enter upon this part of my duty, being perfectly aware of the strong sentiments which exist in the minds of many upon this class of objects; and of the suspicion and disapprobation, I might even say horror, with which some excellent persons view any deviation from those interpretations which they have been accustomed to hear and read. Scarcely less sensitive are the authors of different hypotheses with regard to their respective views. Many estimable men, who have published their opinions upon the question before us, lay the

* *Bridgewater Treatise;* vol. i. p. 14. I cannot too much recommend the diligent study (not an indolent running over) of this admirable work, to all who desire to gain true and accurate information. Such students, however, will consult their own advantage by *previously* acquiring a satisfactory acquaintance with the Mineralogical part of Geological science. Dr. Buckland's work is chiefly occupied with the description of the animal and vegetable remains found in the successive strata of the earth; conveniently called the Palæontological department of Geology.

† The excellent Bishop of Chester has perhaps approached to the same inadvertence in saying, "The concessions, if they may be so called, of the believers in revelation on this point, have been amply remunerated by the sublime discoveries as to the prospective wisdom of the Creator, which have been gradually unfolded by the progressive improvements in astronomical knowledge. We may trust with the same confidence as to any future results from Geology." This was written in 1813 or earlier. Dr. Bird Sumner on the *Records of Creation;* vol. i. p. 271.

greatest stress upon their own views, and find it difficult to tolerate, or even to excuse, any dissent from them. For many of them I entertain a sincere esteem; and I equally respect the motive by which they are excited, a jealousy for the honour of revelation and the interests of religion. But it becomes us all to take the utmost care that our godly zeal may be according to knowledge. If it be not so, we shall inflict no slight disservice upon the cause of truth and righteousness, while we may imagine that we are promoting it.

I. There are some who feel no difficulty at all in the case, or at least, none from which they cannot disembarrass themselves with the utmost ease. Of geological subjects, truly they possess but little knowledge; yet they persuade themselves that they know much, or certainly as much as qualifies them to give a peremptory judgment upon the whole matter. They afford reason enough to believe that, of the most important facts, those upon which the decision of the question principally depends, they are far from being well informed: and with regard to other geological facts and doctrines, a partial acquaintance with which they have derived from a light and easy perusal of a few books, or perhaps of only one, they make it evident that they have acquired no more than some confused and incoherent notions. But their confidence rests upon the assumption, that the interpretation of the Sacred Records which they have adopted, and in which they can certainly strengthen themselves by the suffrages of eminent commentators, none of whom had the least acquaintance with these subjects, is the only true one. Some of them reckon it among the highest points of the christian faith, that the first sentence in the book of Genesis is not an independent proposition, a simple, majestic, and complete enunciation of one grand truth; but that it is connected with the recital of the six days' work, in such a manner as to allow of no interval of time between the facts related. To have a doubt upon this matter is represented as characteristic of a criminal state of mind, not deserving to be refuted by kind and calm argument, but which ought to be put down by awful rebukes and threatenings. I shall transcribe a few words of a fervid writer of this school.

"This 'first day' is THE BEGINNING: and, if we fix that beginning by the eternal testimony of the same truth (which the same God of truth will do, and has done, for us,) all the vain 'nebulosities' of a graceless philosophy are dispelled for ever.—[This is] the self-evident definition of the *beginning* which God himself has given.—And we here defy all the combined ability of infidelity, philosophy, and geology, to *prove* the 'beginning' to have been anterior to the 'first day' God here intends.—No geologist who may read these pages will henceforth remain ignorant of his war against Omnipotence and everlasting Truth. And we again sacredly defy all the combined ability of sophistical geologians, to the end of time, to prove either our Scriptural positions false, or their geological positions true.——We have insubvertibly established it from the lips of Eternal Veracity, that neither the earth, nor the material of which it was formed, nor any creature that is found therein, had existence before 'the first day' of the revealed creation: that truth we have undeniably and everlastingly established, insubvertible and immoveable by human ability. ——Certainly, of all the lately discovered or extended sciences, which the enemy of God and man has thus pushed to his destroying ends, no one has been found so appropriate to his purposes, nor has been so insidiously and industriously driven forward to the accomplishment of his aims, as the popular 'new science' of Geology.——To enumerate all the infernal artillery, which the subtle enemy of God and man has put into the hands of his vassals, to aim at this everlasting monument of revealed truth, would require his own unspent breath and unwearied tongue. Suffice it to say, that sophisticating geologians have been allured, by his implacable subtleties, to enlist themselves in the service of his infernal policy.——This awful evasion of the testimony of Revelation, by denying its concernment with the Creation, and indeed by denying in fact its inspiration altogether, runs through the whole race of geologists, and is the principle set up in both our National Universities.——As to the fear of not satisfying, or of making, infidels; if the word of God does not satisfy them, no scientific hypothesis will. If a man acknowledge not the divine and eternal authority of that word, he is not worthy with whom to argue on any subject which involves its sanction. Let such be turned out of the field of sacred argument, as they have often nobly been from a court of justice, as not worthy of being heard."—*

I have thought it right to quote these passages, that I may not do injustice to their author; who is, I indulge no doubt, a zealous maintainer of the gospel according to his own conceptions of it,

* *Popular Geology subversive of Divine Revelation*; and *Two Letters to the Editor of the Christian Observer*; by the Rev. Henry Cole. Pp. 21, 35, 37, 54, 91; 6, 34, 42.

and desirous of promoting the best interests of mankind, which undoubtedly can be promoted by no other means than the truth and power of religion. These declarations of his are adapted to make a deep impression on the minds of uninformed persons, who are upright and pious: and it is always a duty to protect such persons from being grieved or offended.

1. I present then my solemn protest against the *assumption* which runs through and characterizes the whole structure of the book and the supplementary pamphlet just cited. The impassioned author of them *ought not* to put his own interpretations, supported though they be by the expositions of eminent scholars and divines, upon a level with the express declarations of Scripture itself. That he believes his interpretations to be just, cannot be doubted: but he ought not to affirm, in so high and peremptory a tone, that they are infallible and incapable of being subverted; at least till the other side has been heard. Also, on my own behalf as an humble geologist, (and I confidently join with myself men of the greatest eminence in geological attainments,—) I disown and reject with the strongest abhorrence the imputation of evading, or denying, or in any way perverting the Holy Scriptures, or taking away their inspiration: and I maintain also that those persons do no honour to the word of God, but are unwittingly serving the designs of its enemies, who judge of it in the superficial, hasty, and flippant manner here exemplified; who choose not to search out its true sense by those means of criticism and explication which God has put into our hands; and who bury the christian dispositions of humility and meekness under their imperious dogmatism and assumed infallibility. It will be the business of a future lecture to explain and apply those principles of honest philology by which we are bound to study and interpret the Scriptures, and which, it is my full conviction, will shew that the true sense of the beginning of Genesis does not contradict the geological doctrines which are made the objects of these unmeasured reproaches.

The reverend gentleman to whose observations I have been compelled to advert, makes large extracts from Luther's Commentary on the Book of Genesis; and displays, with exultation and triumph, that great man's opinion of the creative act, described in the second sentence, as having immediately followed upon the primary one declared in the first. I yield not to that gentleman in veneration and love for the illustrious Reformer; for his devoted piety, his noble independence of mind, his simplicity and perspicuity, the ingenuity and liveliness of his remarks, his judgment and even his taste: but I do not see the propriety of attributing to him, or to any man of his day, such a knowledge of Natural Philosophy as was necessary for the application of the Hebrew phraseology to the objects under description. It is no disparagement to Luther that, for instance, in his Comments on the work of the fifth day, he shews his want of correct ideas concerning the atmosphere and the heavenly bodies; that he implicitly rests on the common notions of his time; that he speaks copiously upon the four elements and the ten spheres, (according to the doctrine of one atmospheric, seven planetary, the ninth crystalline, and the tenth empyreal;) that the stars, taken universally, derive their light from the sun, for he intimates no distinction between the fixed stars and the planets; and that the sun and all the other heavenly bodies move round the earth in twenty-four hours. All this was quite natural, and we may say unavoidable, under the circumstances of the time. Unless a miraculous communication had been made to the mind of Luther, it could not have been otherwise. Yet the author who has compelled me to make these observations brings forward his citations from the blessed and immortal man, (as he justly calls the Reformer,) as if they possessed a kind of divine inspiration. He writes, "What a faithful, simple, unphilosophizing, convincing, and self-evident exposition is the holy man thus *instructed by the Holy Spirit* to leave to the world!—I cannot describe the gratitude of spirit and union with the holy Luther which I found, when in turning to his exposition of the Book of Genesis, I found that his faith and understanding respecting some particulars of the creation-work (in addition to his fixed faith regarding the main point at issue,) exactly and sweetly accorded with my own."

This writer so cites, with just apprehension, a part of Luther's introductory paragraph. It would have been well if he had given the passage entire; and had reflected whether, in his fiery positiveness of assertion and his ruthless condemnation of philosophers and geologists, he was not violating the admonition before his eyes.

"There has not hitherto been any one in the Church, that has, with the sufficient propriety and exactness, expounded the whole of these subjects. For expositors have so mixed them up with various, diversified, and never-ending inquiries, as to make it apparent that God has reserved to himself alone this majesty of wisdom, and the sound understanding of this chapter; leaving to us the general knowledge, that the world had a beginning, and was created out of nothing by God. This general knowledge is clearly derived from the text. But with respect to the particular things, there is very much that is involved in difficulty and doubt, and about which questions without end are agitated."*

Thus temperately and wisely wrote "the blessed man." Most plainly has he laid down the very position which will be *the foundation* of my reasoning, when I arrive at the part of these lectures in which it is proposed to search out the declarations of divine truth upon our subject. Other passages might be adduced from the writings of Luther,† in which he vindicates scientific researches,

* Luther's Works, ed. Walch, vol. i. p. 1.

† *Sec. ed.* For instance. "Reason is a very great and inestimable gift of God, and its sagacious directions and discoveries in human things are not to be despised."——"It is absolutely certain that reason is among all things the most excellent, the best of all other things in this life, yea, something godlike: as it is the inventress and directress of all sciences, the medical art, jurisprudence; and even of all wisdom, energy, virtue, and honour that men possess in this life.——God has not deprived reason of this glory since the fall of Adam, but rather has confirmed it. Yet, what is the [most] majestic and excellent reason knows nothing of itself, but only from the Scripture.——Of human nature we know scarcely any thing, more than that into its material causes [no doubt meaning what would now be called *physiological*,] we can scarcely carry a glance. Of efficient causes little is known to philosophy; and of final causes, nothing." Upon such considerations, this great man proceeds, from the limitation and imperfection of the human understanding, to urge the duty of valuing and improving the light of the glorious gospel.——"Reason indeed comprehendeth not what God is; but it does comprehend, with great certainty of evidence, [inferior things] that which is not God." He then adduces examples of the Lord Christ and the Apostle Paul, appealing to the dictates of reason.——"What then is contrary to reason, is certainly much more contrary to God. How can that which is opposed to the reason and truth of man, be other than opposed to the truth of God?"——"That man fails in some things; but thou, in more. I enter into a subject which others have not penetrated; but I also well know that, at some future time, others will see what I have not attained to perceive. What remains then but that we should extend a helping hand to each other?——Our present life is a beginning and a progress, but not a completion and perfection. The more closely any one attains the mind of the Holy Spirit, the greater advantage hath he for interpreting the holy Scripture. If I have reached the moon, I must not fancy that I have also grasped the sun in my hand: no, nor should I despise the smaller stars. There are steps and degrees in life and action; why not also in the faculty of understanding?"——After correcting the error of interpretation which applies Isaiah xiv. 12, to the fall of the chief apostate angel, he says, "This so weighty error should stimulate us to enjoin the studies of the learned sciences and the philosophy of language, as [*höchst nöthig*] in the highest degree necessary to a theologian in his discussions upon holy Scripture." Walch's ed. vols. vi. 181; xix. 1778, 1940; iv. 2679; vi. 391.

and supports the kind of principles for ascertaining the sense of Scripture, on which we are proceeding; those of a strict and impartial grammatical investigation.

2. I likewise raise my protest against the constant strain and tone of this gentleman, respectable and worthy as he may be, in his holding up the friends and professors of Natural Philosophy in general, and of Geology in particular, as either open infidels, or, what would be worse, secret traitors to the cause of Christianity. There is a deplorable want of both wisdom and justice in this style of representation. It is not *wise;* for it tends to foster the suspicions and objections which unhappily exist in many minds, imbued with scientific knowledge, but ignorant of the evidences and the divine grandeur of religion, and unhappily averse to a free examination of them. How must such persons be confirmed in their prejudices, and in the sinful condition of mind which is the substratum of those prejudices, when they hear christian ministers declaiming against the knowledge of what they are convinced is certain and valuable truth; and reviling the only possible means of attaining that knowledge! It is not *just:* for the sciences and all their investigations for which we are pleading, are not the "philosophy and vain deceit" against which the apostle gives a solemn warning. That was no other than a compound of Oriental and Grecian doctrines; referring to the mind of man and to invisible beings; founded, not upon observation and experiment, but on the play of imagination and the dictates of assumed authority: it was an impostress under the name of philosophy, entangling men in a web of idle and visionary speculations, destitute of evidence, having no practical applications, and opposing itself to that purest reason which is displayed in the authority and grace of the gospel. The Natural Philosophy of our times is of the opposite character, as to both its constitution and its tendency. It consists in the honest "*searching out* of the works of Jehovah," (Ps. cxi. 2,) in obtaining the facts of sensible nature, in admitting nothing as data without adequate evidence, and in receiving no conclusions till they have been substantiated by the most cautious reasoning: and if its proper effects be not counteracted by our own perverse depravity, it leads to a devout veneration of God, and to practical benefits without number to ourselves and our fellow-creatures. This philosophy may be abused: and so may any of the gifts of God; health, strength,

property, family, education, talents, the esteem of our friends, the advantages of our social position, and even our heavenly religion itself. All our enjoyments of the divine beneficence may be abused, by some kind or other of an association with unworthy principles, or a subserviency to wrong pursuits. But does any man abandon these blessings on that account; or declaim against them as sinful, or in their own nature pernicious? The oppugners of philosophy do not act so with their own favourite enjoyments. They ought to reflect that the pursuits which they misunderstand and misrepresent, and then decry, are no other than obedience to the divine command, "Consider the works of God:—remember that thou magnify his work which men behold." If, to any attainments which we may make in the study of physical objects, we do not add sincere love and devotion and obedience to the Lord of nature and grace, the blame is our own; and no slight blame and guilt it is. But let not the good principles be condemned for the bad practice. Does it not so much the more become sincere Christians, to labour to "add to their faith—knowledge;" to acquire, so far as they have opportunity, that true science which diffuses innumerable benefits among men, unfolds many of the divine glories, and is the proper handmaid of vital piety?

3. Though our interpretations of the word of God must rest upon their own intrinsic evidence, in grammatical construction, suitableness to the connexion, and agreement with other parts of Scripture; still it is a useful assistance, in cases of difficulty, to know what sentiments have been entertained, and expositions given, by persons whose opportunities of knowledge, and whose character for learning and judgment, constitute a reasonable presumption that they have not taken up opinions from supine ignorance, unexamined custom, or any other prejudice. Upon this ground, therefore, and not because we attribute to the sentiments of uninspired men any commanding authority, I bring some instances to shew to our opponents that it is not a novelty in the Church of Christ, to consider the first sentence in the Book of Genesis as an independent proposition: and the succeeding portions as taking up our habitable earth at a crisis of its existence, and describing a series of operations by which God was pleased to make it fit for the exercises of his wisdom and goodness in relation to a new order of creation: and consequently that those

persons have no right to charge us with impiety, even if our interpretation were erroneous: since we stand upon the same ground with so many eminent Christians, who were led to their conclusions by reasons purely critical, and without the least tincture of geological knowledge.

Some of the ancient christian writers, usually called the Fathers of the Church, intimate this idea, under the opinion that the first verse states generally the creation of matter, out of which the formations and distributions of the six days were afterwards educed. It is evident that the former idea is distinct and separable from the latter; though it is not probable that Clemens of Alexandria, Origen, and others who adopted the sentiment, conceived of the commencement of the former order of action as having preceded that of the latter, by any long interval. Augustine, in two passages, though he does not always maintain consistency, writes copiously upon this interpretation; representing the former state of the earth as being to the latter what the seed of a tree is to the root, the trunk, the branches, leaves, and fruit.* Basil says; "It is probable that something existed before this world; which we may conceive of in our understandings, but of which no narrative has been left."† Chrysostom lays down, as a principle for the interpretation of the beginning of Genesis, that Moses designed to write only of the sensible appearances of things, adapting both the matter and the expression to the capacities of the Israelites, a people recently delivered from the oppression of Egyptian slavery, and whose minds had not been elevated above low and common conceptions.‡

* *De Genesi, contra Manichæos*, lib. i. cap. 6. *Confessiones*, lib. xii. cap. 17, 29.

† *Homil. I. in Hexahemeron; Op.* tom. i. p. 7, Par. 1619.

‡ *Homil. II. et Sermo I. in Gen. Op.* tom. ii. pp. 12, 728; Francof. 1698. "It is indeed singular that all ancient cosmogonists should conspire to suggest the same idea, and preserve the tradition of *an early series of successive revolutions*."——The Hindoos:—Burmese:—Egyptians.——"But I think it much more important and interesting to observe, how the early Fathers of the Christian Church should seem to have entertained precisely similar views; for St. Gregory Nazianzen, after St. Justin Martyr, supposes *an indefinite period* between the creation and the first ordering of all things. St. Basil, St. Cæsarius, and Origen, are much more explicit; for they account for the creation of light prior to that of the sun, by supposing this luminary to have indeed before existed, yet so as that its rays were prevented, by the dense chaotic atmosphere, from penetrating to the earth; [and that] this was, on the first day, so far rarified as to allow the transmission of the sun's rays, though not the discernment of its disk, which was fully displayed on the third day." Principal Wiseman's *Lectures on the Connexion between Science and Revealed Religion*, delivered in Rome, in 1835; vol. i. p. 297.

Calvin considers the design and purport of the first verse, as being to establish this primary truth, that "the world was not from eternity, but was created by God." Thus that acute Bible-interpreter sanctions the general idea for which I am pleading, that the passage is a grand and independent axiom.

Bishop Patrick, in his Commentary, supports the sentiment, which many others have done, that the passage declares a chaotic condition of the earth, between its creation and its being made the receptacle of vegetable and animal life: and he regards this state as having been of an indefinitely long continuance. He thus admits the principle of our interpretation, though we think him to have been mistaken in his method of applying it. There appears to be no reason for attributing any other than a short duration to the state of our planet, or any part of its surface, which is expressed in the words of our translation, "And the earth was without form and void."

Dr. David Jennings, the author of the well-known work upon Jewish Antiquities, and who, in the days of our fathers, was one of the most esteemed Dissenting Ministers of this city, has these observations. "The Mosaic account does not seem to be designed for an account of the whole creation of God;"—but "plainly to be a designed account of the creation of this planet only." He speaks with approbation of the hypothesis, that "our earth,—as that most penetrating philosopher, Dr. Halley, seems to suspect, might be a former world, reduced to a chaos by the shock of a comet."—It may be not improper here to interpose the remark, that this supposition of Halley and others, is exploded by the fact, ascertained but within the few latter years, that comets are not solid bodies, but are composed of brilliant matter, resembling some kind of vapour; but so attenuated that small stars are visible through it, and that it might pass over and envelope the earth without giving a shock, or producing any material effect.—Dr. Jennings goes on to say: "One cannot suppose that this account of the creation was designed to teach the Israelites——such deep points of philosophy as the true motions of the earth and moon: but rather it was designed to teach them to reverence the great Creator of all things, and also to preserve them from the idolatry of the heathen nations around them, who worshipped the sun and the moon, and other creatures which God had made. But yet, as this account was written by inspiration,—it is all agreeable to truth and to the nature of things. And the skill of the Divine Author is in this truly admirable, that the account of the creation is here given, for the use of the people, in such words and phrases as were suited to vulgar conceptions; and yet it is, at the same time, perfectly consistent with true philosophy."*

I may, with propriety, remind my auditors, that in this Lecture for 1833, Dr. Wardlaw had the passage; "*When* creation began, we know not. There were angels, and there was a place of angelic habitation, before the creation of man and of the world destined for his residence. How long these spirits had existed, and how many other orders of being besides, it is vain for us to conjecture.—But of one thing we are certain, that, how far back soever we suppose the commencement of creation carried,—let it be not only beyond the actual range (if a definite range it can be said to have) of the human imagination, but even beyond the greatest amount of ages that figures in any way combined could be made to express;—still there was an ETERNITY preceding."†

Also, in the Lecture for the year 1837, Dr. Redford went into our present discussion at considerable length, and concluded that "we ought to understand Moses as saying, *Indefinitely far back, and concealed from us in the mystery of eternal ages, prior to the first moment of mundane time, God created the heavens and the earth.*"‡

The last year a pamphlet was published by a clergyman whose

* *Introduction to the Globes;* pp. 148, 151, 167. Lond. 1747.

Sec. ed. Rabbi Solomon Jarchi, who lived in the eleventh century, is among the most highly valued of all the Jewish interpreters, both by his own nation and by Christians: and is honoured as "The chief of expositors, the father of the Talmud, and the teacher of the exile," denoting the present state of dispersion. He labours much in the explanation of this chapter, and makes the general remark, "In no case can it be accepted, that the Scripture here [in this sentence] intends to lay down the succession of the objects of creation." His meaning appears to be, that this verse stands as an independent and complete proposition.

"The writer does not amuse or tire his reader with long metaphysical disquisitions, about the nature of the universe, the generation of matter, cause and effect, time and eternity, and other such subtle and insolvable questions; but, with the greatest simplicity and the most imposing air of conviction, tells us that an ALMIGHTY Being made those heavens which we behold, and the earth which we inhabit. 'In the beginning God created the heavens and the earth.' This is *the general proposition.*" Geddes's *Pref. to his Bible;* p. 2.

"——Moses—forbears to speak——even of the *time when* such first creation as he thus briefly mentions, was effected; for he only says that God Almighty was the original Great Creator of all." Edward King's *Morsels of Criticism;* vol. i. p. 90.

† *Cong. Lect.* first series, p. 206.

‡ *Cong. Lect.* fifth series, p. 34.

manner of writing makes a strong demand upon our respect and affection.* His talents are evidently of a superior order; and, which is a far higher recommendation, his book breathes the spirit of reverential piety, and a holy affection for the word of God. From such a man it is painful to be compelled to differ. But I should be wanting in that faithfulness of which he sets the example, if I were not to express concern that he has not escaped the errors of many other good men, with respect to the design of the Scriptures, and the proper method of interpreting them. It will be my duty, in future lectures, to shew cause in reply to his views, upon the subject of the Deluge, and that of Biblical interpretation. At present I have only the pain of saying, that he follows in a style of assumption, less headstrong and vehement, but for that reason more touching to my mind and feelings, than that of another author, before referred to. He hesitates not to charge upon modern geologists, making no exceptions,—even designating them "our Bucklands, our Sedgwicks, and our Conybeares,"—that they are associating their efforts with those of infidels to invalidate the statements of Scripture,—impugning the sacred record,—and assailing the volume of the Great God. On the other hand, with equal boldness, he represents his own interpretations of Scripture as *unquestionable;* and so confident is he in the infallibility of his own deductions as to identify them with the Divine Veracity, and to think himself entitled to take for an analogy to his own reasonings, "Two and two may be five, more easily than the God of Truth can be untrue." He zealously affirms, but makes no attempt at proof, that it is exceedingly "offensive to the plain reader of the Scriptures,"——"not only contrary to the Scriptures but unphilosophical, to resort to such an idea as a series of creations on the same spot:" and he maintains that "our highest conception of creation" (evidently intending to imply that it is the proper conception,) "is that of a world starting into being, perfect and complete, at the command of God; so perfect and complete, that, from the lowest zoophyte to the highest species of living creature, not a single gap could be found into which another animal might be thrust." He looks with evident complacency to the hypothesis "that Almighty God may, by the mere *fiat* of his power, have intentionally brought every rock and

† The Rev. J. Mellor Brown, mentioned in the Note on p. 7.

stratum, every fossil leaf and shell and bone, into its present form and condition."

This kind of argument has been repeatedly brought forwards, even in modern times: but surely those who use it have not considered what havoc they are making; for, if it had any strength at all, it would fearfully weaken the proof for the first truth of religion, from the doctrine of sufficient causes. We find the dead parts of animals, with the marks of muscular attachment, the shelly, or crustaceous, or bony structure, the condyles, the receiving hollows, the grooves and port-holes for the passage of nerves and blood-vessels, the teeth with their sockets in all the variety of the most exquisitely appropriate formation, even the organs and provisions and products of nutrition:—and it is seriously said, that we may sit down with the conclusion that these objects were never the parts of any living creature, but have existed from the beginning of time, just as we now find them!—shall we throw such an advantage as this into the hands of the atheist?—

This respected clergyman has also other suppositions, and certain theories of his own, by which he believes that all the geological appearances may be accounted for, within the limits of time which he holds it an impiety to exceed.

One of these is, to bring forwards, with some spirit and ingenuity, instances of accelerated speed, in motion and mechanical operations, by the steam-engine; and some cases in Natural and Civil History, not well understood: and from the whole, the author asks, "Whether there is any difficulty in believing that the known laws of nature could be so far increased, in power and velocity, as to produce the same effects in six thousand years, for which" geologists "now estimate sixty thousand, or six hundred thousand, to be necessary?"* The querist was evidently not

* "I once shewed to a reader of this cast a solid, lofty, inland rock, composed of one vast mass of shells, often very delicate and brittle, agglutinated with interstitial matter; and asked him whether he thought that these enormous depositions were attributable to the deluge, or were formed during its short duration: and also, whether the various successions of strata, ten miles thick, teeming with the remains of animals and vegetables, from the most complicated in the upper strata down to the most simple in the lower —all arranged in order; now a layer of salt water formation, then one above it of fresh, and then another of sea, and so on in succession,—had really been deposited thus in fifteen hundred years before the deluge. His reply was to the following effect.—'How do I know but that in those early days the powers of nature were so prolific, or rather that there was so constant a miracle, that this rock, which would require an enormous period to grow by ordinary accretion, might be generated in a day; each plant and animal going through all its stages of life and death in the fraction of a moment, if necessary

aware of the want of analogy in his cases. We know that great mineralogical changes may be wrought in a very short time, by the chemical and electric forces which are in constant action: metallic compounds may be produced and veins formed, crystals made to shoot, and lamination or even stratification effected upon a small scale. Let us grant the extension of these effects as largely as can be desired, notwithstanding the insuperable objections which lie in our way: the concession will not benefit the argument. The question is not with regard to mineralogical deposits and formations, as such; but to the remains of once living beings imbedded in them. It is manifest that the worthy author possesses only crude and defective notions upon this subject. He is evidently not acquainted with the *characterism* which connects particular formations with definite fossils; nor with the manner, as to position, in which the principal classes of specimens are found, (the conchiferous and molluscous shells,) proving the quietness and slowness of the processes to which they had been subjected; nor of the numerical amount of the remains, as to species and individuals, (the number of known fossil species of these two classes only, being little if at all less than five thousand;) nor of the nature of the argument as it arises from the gradation of changes, specific and generic, in the subjects of organic life; nor of laws which the CREATOR has disclosed to industrious research with regard to the duration of species. All these topics needed to have been known and well-scrutinized, before any surmise had been hazarded. Our objectors universally appear not to be aware that it is from a long-continued search into the almost immensely numerous particulars, and a contemplation of their parallel relations, that the conclusion appears irresistible, as to the myriads of ages during which the all-glorious God has held on the wondrous course of his works.

Another of his objections is directed against the theory of the internal heat of the earth, and its gradual cooling through a vast period of time. He appeals to the evidence which we possess, that the general temperature, and that of particular climates, has

to produce the effect?' But why should it be necessary? Or, what 'effect' did my friend mean, except the support of a popular interpretation? I almost believe, that if my friend had been pressed with an argument from Euclid, he would have replied, 'But how do we know that antediluvian circles or angles were like ours?'" A Scriptural Geologist; in the *Christian Observer*, April, 1839, p. 212.

undergone no change from the earliest times of history. Had he taken the precaution of understanding what he was writing about, he would have refrained from combating his own shadow. He would have learned that the heat, however intense at no very great depth, has long ago arrived at the point at which the weak conducting power of the earth's rocky crust prevents any further sensible progress, in affecting the temperature at any point of the surface. The process of cooling therefore, though at first and for a long period rapid, must have acquired a stationary condition thousands of years ago: so that our climates now are dependent solely upon the action of the sun, and the superficial causes of radiation. We have reason to regard it as highly probable, and we may hope that the exact researches upon which eminent mathematicians are now engaged will bring an approximating certainty to the conclusion, that this point was reached some time before the creation of man, and that it was a part of the processes by which the earth was adapted to its present destination among the works of God.

With a solemnity and fidelity for which he has my cordial gratitude, this christian monitor sounds the alarm against forgetting "the most valuable axiom of human science, that man is ignorant and weak;" and that he ought therefore "to be thankful for what he is permitted to know," but "submissive where God has been pleased to set a barrier to further knowledge." He comprehends geological investigations among what he considers as not "subjects of lawful inquiry,—shrouded from us by a higher power," to be reckoned "a *dark art*,——dangerous and disreputable." To these cautions he adds the assertion, "Surely an humble mind will be ready to confess that events which took place before the birth of man, or the date of revelation, belong to a forbidden province."

I cannot for a moment doubt the good motive from which this strain of admonition has proceeded. The author's fundamental principle, upon the duty of modesty and humility, is unquestionably of the first importance. The best friends of science will unite with him in deprecating the pride and vanity which pretend to carry researches beyond the limits which the Author of our nature has prescribed. But he has not brought an atom of evidence to prove that the efforts of Geology, or of any other branch of Natural Philosophy, involve any excursion whatsoever out of those limits. His caution is, in itself, only an enforcement of the first principle of the Baconian philosophy. But for this application of it, he gives us nothing but his own assertion. The undistinguishing application of good general principles is one of the most frequent causes of human error, and that to the most dangerous extent. I question whether there is any error or heresy, which may not be traced to this as one of its principal causes. Speculations may indeed be indulged and theories constructed, upon subjects in which we have no data for the support of our conclusions; and in which therefore all the materials are the offspring of imagination. But *that is not the case here.* In Geology and every other part of physical science, the objects of investigation are substantial realities, things presented to our eyes and all our other bodily organs; and the phenomena of change are in many cases perfectly similar, and in others analogous, to what is continually passing before our eyes. True philosophy is not an "intruding into things which we have not seen," the vain inflation of a carnal mind. (Col. ii. 19.) It is the patient ascertaining of actual things and actual events, of which our own senses and those of other men are the witnesses; and it then seeks to find out the connexion of those facts with each other. Such is Geology. It deals in realities, diligently ascertained and faithfully reported: and the reasonings against which this author, pious and amiable as he is, directs his assault, are in all christian uprightness intended to protect the cause of religion against the injuries to which it is exposed from the misunderstanding of natural facts, and from what we believe to be the misinterpretation of the sacred Scriptures. What right has he to say, that "events which took place before the birth of man or the date of revelation, belong to a forbidden province?" He brings no reason in support of his assertion: he adduces no evidence in its favour from the divine oracles: he does not pretend to give us any ground whatever for the reception of it. Can he have expected that any man will receive this dictate, upon his pronouncing of it? Geology unrolls to the eyes of men a glorious book of the works and ways of divine power and providence. Are we to behold these objects; and then turn aside refusing to inquire, or to hear other persons inquire concerning their nature and relations, their causes and consequences? Can we persuade our fellow-men to yield obedience to such a prohibition? Will the unbelieving and irreligious submit to it? Will they retire from the threshold of the temple, after they have been permitted to look in and gain a glance of its grandeur; and will or can they repress every desire of entering to explore its treasures? There are, unhappily, men well acquainted with the natural sciences, but who are disgracefully, because wilfully, ignorant of the real nature of religion, and the grounds of claim which it has on their understandings and their hearts: how will such as they treat this ban of an unproved authority? Will they not regard the futile prohibition as involving an unequivocal confession, that the book of revelation will not endure to be confronted with the book of nature? Or will religious persons, the sincere believers in the authority of the Bible, give in their adherence to it? Will they, can they, shut their eyes and silence their understandings; and suppress the risings of reason and admiration and piety? Can they strike dead the desire for knowledge which the wise and good Creator has implanted in man? Widely different is a simple desire of knowledge, regulated by rational and religious considerations, from that principle of the first transgression with which some unreflecting persons profess to identify it. That was the hankering after a gratification of animal appetite, in despite of a prohibition which the transgressors knew to have proceeded from infinite goodness; it was the giving credit to an unknown pretender, in contempt of the divine veracity: but the studies of Natural Philosophy, (though, like every other of God's benificent gifts, they may be and awfully are abused by ungrateful men,) are, in themselves, only a proceeding in the spirit of the divine declarations; "The works of the Lord are great, sought out of all them that have pleasure therein.—Remember that thou magnify his work which men behold.—Through desire, a man, having separated himself, seeketh and intermeddleth with all wisdom."* The Bible, in numerous places, directs us to the contemplation of God, under the especial aspect of displaying his perfections by his doings; and it affixes no limitations of time or place to the objects of such contemplation. The works which the Infinite Being has wrought, and the ways in which he governs his own creation,

* Ps. cxi. 2. Job xxxvi. 24. Prov. xviii. 1. This last passage is one of those in the Old Testament which, on account of the extremely elliptical character of the Hebrew style, is attended with difficulty. The following paraphrastic translation is submitted as strictly conveying the *sense* of the original. "For gratifying a laudable desire, a recluse student diligently explores and zealously contends for all elevation of knowledge."

may, in a sound and obvious sense sanctioned by the inspired apostle, be called *a revelation of* HIM; "because that which may be known of God (τὸ γνωστὸν τοῦ Θεοῦ) is manifest in them." (Rom. i. 19.) It cannot be held excusable, in any to whom he has given the means of studying this manifestation of himself, to neglect that duty, or to oppose and decry those who endeavour to perform it. This study is, not the rival, but the valuable assistant, of the manifestation which God has granted us in positive revelation; and which is to us practically of infinitely the greatest importance.

> "All nature joins to show thy praise.
> Thus God in every creature shines.
> Fair is the book of nature's lines:
> But fairer is the book of grace."
>
> *Watts.*

PART II.

II. THERE is another and very different class of men, who are not only aware of the difficulties which we have undertaken to discuss, as producing some appearance of contradiction, but who affirm, without hesitation, that there is a real and insuperable discrepancy between the demonstrated facts of science and the unambiguous declarations of the Mosaic writings; and their method of resolving the difficulty is not like that of others who deny the geological facts, (for this, their knowledge makes impossible for them,) but they take the opposite course. The two leaders in this course are Mr. Babbage and Professor Baden Powell. The former of these philosophers, thinks himself compelled to resort to a desperate kind of hypothesis, which is really cutting the knot. He is of opinion that we cannot so depend upon our ability to construe the ancient Hebrew language, as to be sure that we have correctly interpreted the archaic documents before us. Thus, to speak the plain truth, an opening is made for treating the written records of the creation as if they had no existence; or, in the same manner as would be our conduct with regard to some antique marble, inscribed with characters which we might believe to express the words of a lost language, but that language one which we could never hope to recover. We might admire the elegance of its form and the beauty of its sculptured figures; we might lay it up as the most interesting treasure of a museum; but we should not spend our time in attempting to decipher its characters, persuaded beforehand that the attempt would be vain.

The second of those distinguished mathematicians and philosophers goes farther. He has no difficulty in admitting the perfectly intelligible character of the commencement of Genesis and the Fourth Commandment; but he considers it incumbent upon him to maintain that, in both cases, the statement *"was not intended for* an HISTORICAL *narrative;* and if the representation cannot have been designed for *literal history,* it only remains to regard it as having been intended for the better enforcement of its objects in the language of *figure* and *poetry;* and to allow that the manner in which the Deity was pleased to reveal himself to the Jews as accomplishing the work of creation was (like so many other points of their dispensation,) veiled in the guise of apologue and parable; and that only a more striking representation of the greatness and majesty of the Divine power and creative wisdom was intended, by embodying the expression of them in the language of *dramatic action.**

I offer a few remarks upon each of these hypotheses.

Mr. Babbage is careful to state that he has not "any acquaintance with the language in which the sacred volume" of the old Testament is written. This deficiency is much to be regretted. Had it not existed, the acute investigator would never have taken

* *Connexion of Nat. and Div. Truth;* by the Rev. Baden Powell, F. R. S. &c. Savil. Prof. Geom. Oxford: p. 260. A work which I regard as of great value; and cannot but earnestly recommend to those who wish to search deeply and accurately into philosophical subjects and their moral relations: notwitstanding the author's deplorable mistake in his notion of Calvinism, and the appearance of some serious theological errors. But I cannot surrender him to the self-styled Rationalists; men whose just claim would be to a very different appellation. The learned Professor has, more recently, done excellent service to the cause of religion by his masterly exposure of a system, which comes forwards indeed with lofty pretensions, uniting in itself the lamb and the dragon (Rev. xii. 11,) but which he rightly characterizes "as involving in entire ambiguity the land-marks of christian truth:—by neutralizing it *destroys* the whole evidence of the gospel." *Tradition Unveiled;* p. 68. Deeply also are the friends of Scriptural religion and just liberty indebted to him for another contribution to their cause. *State Education, considered with reference to Prevalent Misconceptions on Religious Grounds:* 1840: and more recently still the *Supplement to Tradition Unveiled.*

up his hypothesis, or any approach to it. He would have felt himself assured that, as a consequence of the uninterrupted use of the Hebrew language by the Jews, and the constant public reading of these very writings, from the days of Moses down to our own, we have in fact as firm a hold upon the meaning as we have in regard to the Greek and Latin; that, from its being one of a family of languages, all of which possess literary monuments and those of great antiquity, we are furnished with aids and guarantees, in the comparison of the cognate tongues, by which the correct understanding of Hebrew is made sure to those who will rationally study it; and that, by the aid of the Greek Version, all or most of which was made in the third century before Christ, we have a still further ground of satisfaction for the intelligence of the Hebrew Scriptures. There are oriental scholars, especially in Germany, and of whom some are awfully hostile to the truth and the authority of revelation, who would inform Mr. Babbage that the fact of a clear and certain understanding of the Hebrew Scriptures is above all reasonable doubt. The construction of the language is the most simple and luminous that can well be imagined; its peculiar idioms are well ascertained and illustrated; few very difficult passages occur; the principal obscurities lie in the determination of a small number of words referring to natural objects and operations of art; and the text is settled to a degree of purity more satisfactory than we dare affirm of many of the Greek and Latin classics. All competent scholars, of whatever opinions and parties they may be in other respects, will agree to reject any imputation of uncertainty with respect to the means of ascertaining the sense of the language.

Professor Powell's scheme appears, at first sight, to be a reproduction of the *mythic* hypothesis which the German Antisupernaturalists generally hold; and which we could not *consistently* adopt unless we went with them to the infidel length of denying any positive revelation. This I am persuaded that the Professor would not do. But as a divine, he has involved himself in serious difficulty. His notion, that we have here "the language of figure and poetry," is palpably erroneous. The whole is in the style of plain narrative, evidently intended to be understood as a simple, straightforward, unadorned *history*. The dramatic form, introducing the Creator as speaking, to command an effect; and then stating that the effect followed, and that he was pleased with the contemplation of it;—is a part of *the great characteristic* which runs through all the Hebrew Scriptures and especially the earlier parts of them, the *Anthropopathia;* a mode of expression adapted, by the graciousness of Divine condescension, to the capacity and habits of thought which belong to men in an unpolished state of society, who were totally ignorant of abstract phraseology, and would have been unable to receive spiritual sentiments, unless clothed in language borrowed from sensible objects and from the emotions and actions of men. This is indeed the very principle which will appear, as I trust, in a following lecture, to be both "a *true* cause" in the formation of the ancient scriptural phraseology, and to be *adequate* to carry us out of the difficulty, without sacrificing the reality of the things related, or invading the truth and majesty of Divine Inspiration.

I do cherish much hope that, had Professor Powell more carefully and completely examined the case, he would have found this principle, which indeed he definitely lays down, quite sufficient for obviating all the difficulty; without having recourse to admissions which cannot but be revolting to the calm judgment of any man; as well as to the enlightened piety of a reflecting Christian. We, equally with him, admit the folly of "constructing systems of philosophy out of the Bible,——of attempting to force its language into accordance with philosophical results,"—or of supposing that the senses or applications which, by some engineering of verbal criticism, we might maintain that the words could be made to bear, were actually in the understanding and intention of Moses, or of any other inspired writer;——or of "imagining that the delivery of the Judaical law was really *intended* to embrace the doctrines of Geology, and this too under the guise of expressions which, in their obvious sense, are directly contradictory to those doctrines;" or, in a word, of "saying something plausible to satisfy prejudice, and avoid giving offence to popular belief."* Some persons indeed have been, and still are; who have held notions like these, and have pursued some such fallacious course as is here reprobated. We cannot shield them from the Reverend Professor's censure. We repudiate all such devices. But it is not necessary for us to go into the opposite extreme, and affirm that the language of revelation, when stripped of the conventional

* Expressions of Prof. Powell.

forms of description which were necessary in that state of mind and habits which characterized the people and the age, is *irreconcilably* and *insuperably* contradictory to the truth of facts in nature. I fear that Mr. Powell's expressions are in danger of involving some inconsistency with his own sacred professions and obligations; and, that, if followed out, they would lead to consequences deeply injurious to the cause of Christianity. *He admits the inspiration of Moses,* and the divine origin and authority of the previous patriarchal and the subsequent prophetic revelations; and yet he maintains that the christian system of religion is *independent* of those former disclosures of the will and truth of God, and *distinct* from them, in such a manner that (if I do not misapprehend his meaning,* which I sincerely wish may be the case with me,) we might lawfully and safely give them up, as obsolete ideas, mingled with much that is erroneous. This is a notion which stands in direct hostility to the sentiment that pervades the whole frame of revelation, a *progression* of knowledge and its practical applications; exhibiting a twilight, a dawn, a sunrise, and the perfect day. Moses and the prophets bore testimony to the Messiah, the promised Redeemer of mankind; and that Messiah with his immediate disciples pointed to the completion of the ancient dispensations in the "grace and truth" of the gospel. Nothing can be plainer than that our Lord and his apostles gave honour to Moses as the most faithful servant of God, as an inspired person, and as the initiating prophet of a national dispensation which was constituted by divine authority to be the symbol and preparative of a religion that should be universal and permanent for mankind, the "glad tidings concerning Jesus Christ."†

* *Sec. ed.* It is with great pleasure that I here copy the words of the Professor in a more recent publication. "Dr. Pye Smith—fears [—no,—wishes,] he may have mistaken my meaning. He has certainly done so, if he supposes me to deny any of the positions which he states respecting the *progressive* nature of the divine dispensations. All this is the very view that I take. All that I contend for is the plain fact that these different relations *were addressed*, as they were *adapted*, to *different parties;* one to the Jews, another *to us*. In connexion with the view of such *adaptation*, when I suggested the idea, that the whole description of the creation, *taken as a whole*, might be understood as couched in the language of *mythic poetry*, this was not laid down dogmatically, but *simply suggested* as a less harsh alternative than a naked statement which might seem directly impugning the truth of the narrative.——If the true statement be not boldly made by the friends of Christianity, it will inevitably be perverted and turned against them by its adversaries."——*Suppl. to Trad. Unveiled;* p. 36.——But upon this subject, a few remarks will be offered in a Supplementary Note.

† Besides the whole bearing of the Old Testament prophecies and the writings of the

I trust it will appear in the sequel of these lectures, that we neither torture the Bible to make it speak the language of philosophy, nor suppress or mutilate the facts of nature in order to bring about an agreement with the Bible.

III. An hypothesis was resorted to about thirty years ago by several men of eminence in geological knowledge, such as the late Mr. James Parkinson, Baron Cuvier, and Professor Jameson of Edinburgh; and it has found approvers and advocates more recently; among whom we may reckon Professor Silliman (at least a few years ago,) and the anonymous clergyman who wrote the able Preliminary Essay to Dr. Mantell's Illustrations of the Geology of Sussex, published in 1822: but it is now so generally relinquished that more than a brief mention of it will not be necessary. This is, that the Six Days of Creation may be understood of periods of time, of indefinite though of a very great length. Finding in frequent instances of scripture-use, what is indeed the case in all languages, that the term *day* is put metaphorically to denote any portion of time which has been marked by the accomplishment of some great event or series of events, it was concluded that the same figurative application might be resorted to here. The mind was thus left at liberty to attach to each of these periods any length that the exigency of the case might require, in order to obtain the protracted time which the supporters of this hypothesis knew to be an indispensable provision for the mineral and palæontological formations. They went further, and supposed that the succession of geological beds, with respect to organic remains, exhibited a correspondence with the contents of the sacred narrative in describing the several operations of divine power. Upon this theory a few remarks are submitted.

1. More accurate investigations have proved that the correspondence just mentioned does not exist. Though, to a superficial view, some plausable appearances of this kind present themselves, the scheme fails when it is attempted to be carried into detail.

2. Admitting, what indeed every person must be aware of, that the word is often used in the wide acceptation, as when we speak of "the day of the Son of man,"—"the day of salvation,"—the day of human life;—it is evident that this figurative use is em-

New Testament, particular evidences are Matt. xvii. 3; Luke xvi. 31; xx. 37; xxiv. 27; John i. 17, 46; iii. 14; v. 46, 47; Acts iii. 22; vii. 35; xxvi. 22, 23; xxviii. 32; Rom. iii. 2, 21, 31; iv. throughout; ix. 4, 5; 2 Cor. iii.; Heb. throughout; Rev. xv. 3.

ployed, more generally indeed in poetical or oratorical diction, but always when the connexion in any given instance makes it unquestionably manifest that a figurative sense is intended. No examples need be brought in proof of this fact: it must be familiar to every person.

Yet there is one instance which is peculiarly important, because it occurs in another of the archaic records with which Moses the inspired and faithful servant of God,* was directed by the Divine Being to commence his narrative. For, it is not irrelevant here to remark, that the earlier part of the Book of Genesis consists of several distinct compositions, marked by their differences of style and by express formularies of commencement.† It is entirely consonant with the idea of inspiration, and established by the whole tenor of the scriptural compositions, that the heavenly influence operated in a concurrence with the rational faculties of the inspired men; so that prophets and apostles wrote from their own knowledge and memory, the testimony of other persons, and written documents, to which indeed express appeal is often made.‡ From the evidence of language and of matter, we have no slight reasons for supposing that Moses compiled the chief parts of the Book of Genesis, by arranging and connecting ancient memorials, under the divine direction, and probably during the middle part of his life, which he spent in the retirements of Arabia. Thus, though it is impossible to affirm with confidence such a position, yet it appears far from improbable that we have, in this most ancient writing in the world, the family archives of Amram and his ancestors, comprising the history of Joseph, probably written in great part by himself; documents from the hands of Jacob, Abraham, Shem, Noah, and, possibly, ascending higher still, authentic memorials from Enoch, Seth, and Adam.

* "My servant Moses is not so [on an equality with other prophets,] who is faithful in all my house. With him will I speak mouth to mouth, even apparently [*Heb.* in visible form,] and not in dark speeches [obscure representations:] and the similitude of Jehovah he shall behold." Numb. xii. 7, 8; and compare Heb. iii. 2, 5.

† The following appear to be the distinct compositions, yet it must be observed that the evidence is not equally clear in every case. I. Gen. i. 1, to ii. 3. II. ii. 4, to iii. 24. III. chap. iv. IV. v. 1, to vi. 8. V. vi. 9, to ix. 29. VI. chap. x. VII. xi. 1—9. VIII. xi. 10—26. IX. xi. 27, and all that follows may be regarded as the records of the house of Abraham. Chap. xxxvi. a separate document, inserted in the most suitable place.

‡ We have these instances in the Old Testament, Numb. xxi. 14, 17, 18, 27—30. Josh. x. 13. 2 Sam. i. 18. 1 Kings xi. 41. 1 Chron. ix. 1; xxix. 29. 2 Chron. ix. 29; xii. 15; xx. 34. In the New Testament many of the anecdotal portions in the first three Gospels; and see Luke i. 1, 2.

At the fourth verse of the second chapter, commences a new narrative in these words, "These are the generations" (—the Hebrew word is that commonly used to introduce an historical relation, and learned translators render it, in numerous places, by *origin, history, account,* or some similar word,—) "of the heavens and the earth, in their being created, in the day of Jehovah God's making earth and heavens." I read this in the most closely literal version. Undoubtedly the word requires to be understood here, in the less restricted sense of a period of time. But one obvious remark puts an end to all difficulty in the matter. The word used in this place and in chapter v. 1, 2, is not the simple noun; but it is a compound of that noun with a preposition, formed according to the genius of the Hebrew language, and producing an adverb, requiring to be rendered by such words as *when, at the time, after.**

3. Upon the very face of the document, it is manifest that in the first chapter the word is used in its ordinary sense. For this primeval record (terminating, as was remarked in a former lecture, with the third verse of the second chapter,) is not a poem, nor a piece of oratorical diction; but is a narrative, in the simple style which marks the highest majesty. It would be an indication of a deplorable want of taste for the beauty of language, to put a patch of poetical diction upon this face of natural simplicity. But, one might think that no doubt would remain to any man who had before his eyes the concluding formula of each of the six partitions, "And evening was, and morning was, day one;" and so throughout the series, repeating exactly the same form; only introducing the ordinal numbers, till we arrive at the last, "And evening was, and morning was, day the sixth."

4. If there were no other reason against this, which I may call device of interpretation, it would appear quite sufficient to require its rejection, that it involves so large an extension in the liberty, or license, of figurative speech. Poetry speaks very allowably of the day of prosperity or of sorrow, the day of a dynasty or of an empire: but the case before us requires a stretch of hyperbole which would be monstrous. A few hundreds, or even thousands, of days turned into years, would not supply a period sufficiently ample to meet the exigency of geological reasoning; while this

* Examples are numerous; as Exod. xiv. 57; Numb. xxx. 5, &c.; Deut. xxi. 16; 2 Sam. xxii. 1; Neh. xiii. 15. Many other instances are adduced in Noldii *Concord. Partic. Hebr.*

way of proceeding, to obtain the object desired, is sacrificing the propriety and certainty of language, and producing a feeling of revolt in the mind of a plain reader of the Bible.

IV. We advance to the consideration of a theory, which has been held with strong attachment by persons of talent and piety, upon many of whom we cannot think without the feelings of christian affection. At the same time, it is incumbent on me to make an observation which is entitled to be well considered. It is, that the persons to whom I advert, and especially those who have most distinguished themselves as the advocates of this theory, are not practical men, not geologists who have devoted the continuous labour of weeks and months, I might justly say years, in exploring those regions of Europe and other parts of the earth, which are the most important in a geological sense, because they present the greatest extent of natural sections, elevations, fractures, and outcrops, and the largest abundance and variety of organic remains. But the writers who have most signalized themselves in the advocacy of this view, appear to have chiefly derived their knowledge of geological subjects from the study of books and their own reflections in calm retirement. I am not so presumptuous as to imagine myself qualified to bear this testimony concerning those estimable persons, so as to exclude all liability to mistake. I utter only the impression made upon my mind, by a small degree of actual knowledge, by credible information from other persons, and above all from the indications of their own writings.

The hypothesis referred to is that which, first, considers the Mosaic record as indubitably affirming the creation of the universe, within the period of six natural days, at an epoch about six thousand years back; then, it regards the interval from the creation to the Deluge, as affording a sufficient lapse of time for the deposition of the chief part of the stratified formations; and finally it considers the remainder of the phenomena as adequately accounted for by the action of the diluvial waters.

That interval, according to the chronology calculated from the Hebrew copy of the Bible, was 1656 years; according to the Greek translation usually called the Septuagint, it was 2262; but according to the estimate in the "Analysis of Chronology" of the late Dr. William Hales of Dublin, the period was 2256 years. Professor Wallace brings out, from laborious investigation, 2262.*

* On the *True Age of the World*, and its *Chronology*; p. 298. 1844.

1. The first thought that strikes our minds, on a survey of the inquiry, is this; that the materials, of which the advocates of this theory have framed it, are what they have derived from the labours of the very men who hold the opposite doctrine. The men whose persevering toils have brought to light the great facts of Geology, who have traced them through their vast extent, and who have described them with careful precision by their pens and pencils, are represented by this hypothesis as the worst interpreters of those facts; either incapable of drawing logical inferences from their own observations or unwilling to declare what the honest inferences are. Upon the former supposition, it must appear a strange thing that the persons, who have given such distinguished proofs of their general ability, and of their acuteness of penetration in this particular department of scientific study; who possess the resources of those auxiliary sciences which are the best guides in physical inquiry, and the most stern checks upon sanguine minds, to guard them against precipitance or inaccuracy in drawing conclusions;—it must appear a strange thing, that such persons should labour under an obliquity of judgment, so peculiar and so obstinate that they cannot see the just conclusion from premises which they have obtained by so much expense of time and fortune, of mental and of bodily toil. It should also not be omitted that, of these persons, some, probably the larger number, had the prepossessions of education originally fixed in their minds in favour of the very opinion which they are now rebuked for rejecting. Could we imagine that one such human mind was in existence?—It would appear a prodigy: but that many, that all who fall under the former part of my description (for I know not of one exception,) should be thus mighty to do the greater thing, which every logician knows to be the gaining of true premises, yet so wretchedly feeble to perform the easiest part of all, the perceiving what conclusion is contained in those premises!—This does indeed surpass belief!—

But the other part of the alternative is that, the men so qualified, with the evidence on the case spread before their eyes, are unwilling to announce that conclusion which dispassionate bystanders see to be the right one, and which they themselves were quite aware of, yea, probably had before maintained; that they have been seduced into a confederacy,—though many of them never saw each other,—to violate conscience, honour, and truth, to support an opinion which they know *is not* the fair deduction from the facts by themselves elicited; an opinion which they themselves had once disapproved,* which shocks many of their friends, which is denounced as of an irreligious and sceptical character, and which therefore forces them to lie under suspicion and reproach; and, finally, that some of these men, and those the most ready to make the avowal, are consecrated ministers and zealous advocates of the Christian Religion:—this side of the supposition does indeed involve such an amount of deliberate baseness,—that it exceeds my capacity of belief!

2. The worthy persons who oppose what I may, not assumingly, call the whole body of geologists, have had no very difficult task to perform. There may be two or three exceptions: but we may safely affirm that they in general have not spent those years of patient application which the case demands in order to have the prerequisites for forming a correct judgment: but they take up an alluring book, Professor Buckland's Bridgewater Treatise, perhaps, or Mr. Lyell's Principles; or, more probably, they may have been content with some of the older and very defective authors. From this they select a few statements, which, by their want of previous knowledge, they are exposed to no small risk of failing to understand. Of the great number of facts necessary to be known, many are overlooked, and many are forgotten; and among them are some which make no very prominent appearance in a verbal description, but the omission to grasp and apply which

* "When I first heard of the conclusions of Geology, I thought them very unsafe, for they opposed my conscientious interpretation of the scripture-narrative; and I concluded (as was right and just, for I knew scripture to be infallible, and I had never considered any other interpretation,) that geological science was an 'aberration.' But, upon farther scrutiny, I found its main conclusions impregnable. I then considered whether my interpretation was of necessity the right one; and I found, as many scriptural geologists have shewn, that the sacred text might, without any violence, be differently interpreted, and that thus the supposed difficulties vanished. I was not reckless of consequences,—very far from it; but I saw that there might be bad consequences in two opposite ways; and I fear that some well-meaning and truly pious writers *are exposing* scripture to one of them." Letter of a Scriptural Geologist, in the *Christian Observer*, August 1839, p. 473.

On the question, Whether these phenomena can "be comprised within the short period usually assigned to them," the Rev. Samuel Charles Wilks long ago observed: "Buckland, Sedgwick, Faber, Chalmers, Conybeare, and many other christian geologists, strove long with themselves to believe that they could; and they did not give up the hope, or seek for a new interpretation of the sacred text, till they considered themselves driven from their position by such facts as we have stated.——If, even now, a reasonable, or we might say *possible* solution were offered, they would, we feel persuaded, gladly revert to their original opinion." *Christ. Observ.* Aug. 1834; p. 486.

will vitiate the entire body of conceptions which the hasty compiler is forming. He finds incoherences, and has no suspicion that they are produced only by the fragmentary character of his own attainments: he puts them down and surveys them: to him they appear to involve positions or to warrant inferences fatal to the geologists: and then our well-pleased considerator marshals his doubts and objections, forms a theory of his own which delightfully harmonizes with his views of the scriptural cosmogony: he favours the world with it: and, in the end, he is surprised and grieved, and perhaps irritated, that the geologists do not adopt his views.

With reluctance and pain I acknowledge myself under the obligation of mentioning some principal writers of this description.

Some twelve or thirteen years ago, a gentleman entitled to our high esteem, Mr. Granville Penn, published a large work which he entitled "A Comparative Estimate of the Mineral and the Mosaic Geologies." He endeavours to prove that the phenomena of stratification may be accounted for by referring them to the accumulated deposits of the antediluvian ocean, which he supposes to have become the habitable earth after the Deluge; and then introducing tremendous disruptions, and forcible transportations of those accumulations, by the action of the diluvial waters. While professing, and I have no doubt with the utmost sincerity, to hold the authority of Scripture in the supremacy of honour which is its due, Mr. Penn makes no scruple to deal with it in a very arbitrary manner. He even cashiers and rejects as spurious, in the face of all critical evidence, the entire passage which gives the topography of the country of Eden; because it is incompatible with his theory. Pleasing and in some respects useful as his volumes are, I am compelled to regard them as calculated to mislead the confiding reader.

Considerably later, another of our countrymen, Mr. Fairholme, published a work on the "Geology of Scripture," which he has lately amplified and republished. He is evidently versed in some parts of recent Natural History; and, in this respect, he may be put into the same class with a respectable clergyman, the Rev. William Kirby, who, in his Bridgewater Treatise, having wandered out of his proper province, has introduced some of the wildest speculations upon geological subjects that ever germinated in the brain of man, while, in the same work, he generously relieves our astounded minds by acknowledging that he has not studied Geology. Surely this is a lesson and a monitory example for us all, to refrain from hazarding opinions upon subjects with which we are conscious of being but insufficiently acquainted.

Mr. Fairholme exercises great ability, I might call it adroitness, in the whole strain of his work; with a strong tincture of severity and sarcasm upon the objects of his censure; and with a boldness of assertion and the frequent assumption of a triumphant tone which is likely to lead captive an uninformed reader. He rests most confidently upon an argument derived from the forms of valleys, which Dr. Buckland had before laid before the world, but which he has since, with equal publicity, retracted, or so modified as to render it incapable of warranting the conclusion in favour of which Mr. Fairholme avails himself of it: yet he does not, so far as I have observed, take notice of such modification, though the fact itself, under all its circumstances, had surely no little claim to respectful notice. Dr. Fleming also, a zealous advocate of the authority of Scripture, had long before maintained the futility of this argument.

In preference to resting upon my own opinion of the productions of Mr. Penn, Mr. Kirby, and Mr. Fairholme, I will quote that of Professor Hitchcock; a man whose religious character, his candour and fairness in discussion, and his extensive acquaintance with geological subjects,—an acquaintance gained not merely by studious reading and reflection, but by the hard labour of years in river-beds, ocean-coasts, gorges, and mountains,—entitle him to the confidence which is due to a man who understands what he is writing about.

"Will it be believed, that a really able and scientific man, writing by appointment of the President of the Royal Society—in the year 1835, should have revived and adopted, with slight modifications, the essential features of this hypothesis" [Thomas Burnet's] "of dissolution and reconsolidation of the earth by the deluge?"——"It is not necessary to go into a formal exhibition of the absurdity of such views as these: for, unless a new school of Physico-Theologists should arise, and Geological Science as well as Biblical Criticism revert to their condition one hundred years ago, they will not be adopted.—We do no injustice to that gentleman by saying this; while *justice* to the cause of science as connected with religion requires us to do it. ——Such exhibitions can have no other than a bad effect upon the cause evidently so near Mr. Kirby's heart, the defence of Natural and

Revealed Religion. For the inevitable effect upon the Sceptical Geologist will be to make him throw aside the work, and we fear the whole series" [of the Bridgewater Treatises,] "in disgust. We have before us a letter from one of the ablest living Geologists of this description, which well exhibits the effects of such productions. 'It gives me pain (says he) to find a man so estimable in every respect as * * * [not Mr. Kirby,] compelled to cling to theories impossible to defend, from reasons unconnected with science. It has injured his well-earned reputation; and I think *has injured* the great cause he has at heart, the interests of the Christian Religion: for this must be the effect of connecting it with opinions which are manifestly no more than the best conclusions that wise and good men of former days were induced to adopt, when they had but few facts, inaccurately observed, to reason from.'——There is another bad effect resulting from the adoption of such untenable and exploded opinions by a standard writer. The greater part of even educated men have not the leisure requisite for pursuing the subjects of natural science, so accurately as to be able to form independent opinions upon difficult questions connected with it. Hence, when a man like Mr. Kirby, of acknowledged distinction in science, and evidently jealous for the honour of Natural and Revealed Religion, advances opinions on the connexions of science with revelation, they will have a wide influence and be extensively adopted: and, if they happen to be wrong, they will powerfully arrest the progress of truth. Now, Mr. Kirby's reputation as an Entomologist, and perhaps we may add also as a Helminthologist, is deservedly high. But this does not prove that he is at all qualified to decide difficult Geological questions; especially when he himself testifies that he is not. Yet his opinions on Geology will have nearly as much influence, except among Geologists, as if he were well acquainted with the science. Nay; with not a few, there exists no small jealousy respecting the views of Geologists, as if hostile to revelation; and such will be very glad to range themselves under the banner of a leader in Natural History, especially of one whose great object appears to be, to bring philosophers back to the word of God."*

With regard to Mr. Penn and Mr. Fairholme, I must now say that a passage of Professor Hitchcock which was quoted in the first lecture, but suppressing the names, referred to those authors. It needs not to be repeated. The tenor of it is to complain of them

* *Americ. Biblic. Repos.* Jan. 1837; pp. 100—104.

for their unreasonable positiveness of opinion upon subjects in which they betray their want of practical acquaintance, their intolerant spirit and injurious language, their wrong representation of facts, and their calling upon us to receive theories of their own which, says Mr. Hitchcock, "appear" to a person acquainted with Geology, "a thousand times more extravagant and opposed to facts, than any opinions that have been entertained by the cultivators of this science, and which Penn and Fairholme so violently oppose." This comparison shews the strong sense which Hitchcock entertains of the folly and presumption which provoked his censure; but I ought to caution my hearers against understanding it too largely. The Professor did not design to cast a veil over the irreligious opinions of some foreign geologists, which, in the Dissertations from which I have quoted, he has strenuously exposed and refuted. But his observation is strictly correct in relation to the subject upon which he is treating, the theories of really well-informed geologists.

Two years ago, a venerable clergyman, of whom it would not be easy to speak in terms of too high respect, the Rev. Thomas Gisborne, one of the Prebendaries of Durham, published his "Considerations on the Modern Theories of Geology." If christian piety, good temper, fine talent, and elegant expression, could alone secure correctness of sentiment upon a subject of natural knowledge, we should have had nothing to regret in relation to this work. But the sources of error, which have been already described, have unhappily poured their influence into Mr. Gisborne's mind. The prevalent and deeply working prejudice against the modern Geology, that it seeks to undermine the authority of the Scriptures, and consequently to destroy our faith in Christianity, has led Mr. Gisborne into the adoption of most imperfect views of geological facts, and into the pleasing fallacy of what Professor Sedgwick calls "making a world after a pattern of our own." He employs his great ability in finding or in imagining faults and inconsistencies in the doctrines advanced by geologists, while it is manifest that his acquaintance with the subjects of their attention is extremely limited; and that his perusal of their writings has been but cursory, and far from being comprehensive, or such as could be made the basis of safe argument. The inconsequence of reasoning, into which this excellent man has allowed himself, I am sure unconsciously, to be drawn, we can scarcely hope that, in his very advanced age, he will be brought to discover: but it has subjected him to the cutting suggestion of a clergyman of his own communion, who concludes a page of criticism upon the Prebendary's pamphlet, with the words, "This is surely not an age, in which dignitaries of the Church should be found arraying themselves in hostility to science."*

Yet another dignitary has not withheld himself from the peril of joining this array. The last year, the Dean of York published "A Letter to Professor Buckland;" in which, by the expenditure of a very few pages of loose paragraphs, he actually represents himself as having overthrown some of the principal doctrines which the most cautious geologists regard as indubitably established; and then he brings forward a theory of his own, of which I will only say that it manifests a degree of ignorance next to incredible upon the phenomena under his consideration, the very nature and most obvious facts of stratification: and, to crown all, the Dean of York does not observe even common courtesy towards Dr. Buckland. Probably that eminent man may think this attack beneath his notice; and, scientifically considered, it is so. But, as not only the Dean's pamphlet, but the productions of Prebendary Gisborne, Mr. Mellor Brown, and some other writers, are directed against Dr. Buckland by name; and as multitudes read those pamphlets who are totally unqualified to detect their errors and escape the impression of their vehemence; it is greatly to be wished that he would confer upon the public a service so valuable as would be a calm exposure and refutation of the whole genus.

PART III.

A GENTLEMAN who has illustrated the history of our country in a manner which proves diligent research, fidelity to moral principles, and a pleasing talent for narration, Mr. Sharon Turner, has also written a work for the use of young persons, and containing stores of valuable matter, "The Sacred History of the World." This work, in a manner well adapted to inform and

* Prof. Powell's *Connexion*; p. 281.

religiously to benefit the readers, introduces many facts of Natural History and principles of Natural Philosophy: yet one may wish that the author had accumulated his materials with more discrimination. He has also taken notice of geological subjects, in several of the Letters of which the work consists. He has consulted many books and philosophical journals; and has brought together, in rapid, but not always correct, sketches, a numerous body of interesting facts. In many of his details and descriptions, I humbly think that his work is mistaken and defective; the apparent result of having been compiled too hastily, by multifarious reading, without personal observation and practical knowledge. This is particularly the case in his opinions upon stratification; and in his account of vegetable and animal remains. He supposes all the stratified formations, from the lowest to the highest secondary, to have been produced in the 1656 years from the creation of man to the deluge; and the tertiary, to have been the effects of the deluge itself: notions which, one might well think, would be impossible to be received by any person who had examined with his eyes any large extent of stratified masses, and observed the vast thickness of many, and the regularity and order which belong both to the earthy deposits and to the organic remains imbedded in them. But, with all the deficiencies and errors which appear in this part of the work, Mr. Turner has sufficiently conceded the position, that, in any fair interpretation of the commencing portion of Genesis, "the Sacred Historian gives the largest latitude for the investigations and deductions of geological science."——"What interval occurred between the first creation of the material substance of our globe, and the mandate for light to descend upon it, whether months, years, or ages, is not in the slightest degree noticed. Geology may shorten or extend its duration, as it may find proper. There is no restriction on this part of the subject. In this portion of time or eternity, we may place the formation of our elementary matter; the composition and arrangement of the vast central and interior contents, whatever they may be; and the construction, circumambiency, and consolidation of all the primordial rocks; and indeed the production of all things to which light was not essentially necessary."* If this be admitted, the chief point is secured; and we may indulge

* *Sacred History of the World;* vol. i. pp. 491, 490.

the hope that more ample examination, and its results in more accurate knowledge, will shew to this respectable writer the perfect untenableness of the theories which he has advanced on the formation of strata and the character of imbedded remains. I may be allowed also to add, that the beautiful sentence of the archaic record,—"Be light, and light was,"—upon which Mr. Turner expatiates with just feeling, will be perceived by no means to signify a first creation of light, or a first production of the conditions of which it may be an effect; but is perfectly reconcilable with the belief that the phenomena of light had existed long before, and that the instance under consideration declares only a new developement and application of it.

A book has been lately published by some one who honours himself with the appellation of "Biblicus Delvinus;" entitled, "Facts, Suggestions, and Brief Inductions in Geology." The apparent rapidity of composition, the unscrupulous facility of assertion, and the tone of self-complacency, which distinguish the book, would appear ludicrous; were it not that our minds are wounded and mortified by the reflection, that errors so egregious and reasonings so inconsequent as are found here, united with professions of pious reverence for the Bible, are not unlikely to work great mischief. That mischief may be immediate, by misleading the honest but uninformed; and remote, by producing a revulsion, to the injury of faith in the Scriptures, when those persons may come hereafter to be better informed. Indeed, I may express the belief that this is a common character of certain books and papers, which seem to be mutual copyists, in the qualities of blind and obstinate blundering, and vehement censuring of others who take some pains to understand before they write and publish; while these easy writers allow themselves no narrow indulgence in the formation of purely ideal and often very ignorant theories, by which they fancy that they can account for every thing.*

* There have been in the Christian Observer for 1832, 1834, 1839, and at other times, many valuable remarks of the Editor and communications from his correspondents, upon the studies of Geology. Many of those papers might be particularized as pre-eminently valuable: but to attempt such a discrimination would be digressing too far, in this incidental notice. I may, however, recommend *con amore*, the poetical *jeu d'esprit*, "The Fossil Shell," by the Rev. Samuel Charles Wilks, in the vol. for 1834, page 219; and republished in a volume of the author's Poems, "Rescued Rose Buds." From an article published since these lectures were delivered, I feel happy in taking a citation. "The anti-geologists taunt the geologists with their diversities of opinion, but keep back that no two of themselves agree: whereas the geologists, amidst all their contro-

A gentleman entitled to our high regard as a christian minister and a cultivator of natural science, Dr. George Young of Whitby, has recently published a small work with the title, "Scriptural Geology." He possesses the advantage of having resided many years in a most interesting district for this branch of study; and he has acquired, what long observation and practice only can give, an extensive acquaintance with mineralogical structure and organic remains in some of the northern counties, both on the eastern coast and in the upland. In former works of greater magnitude, he has furnished valuable materials to the antiquary and to the geologist.* The design of this recent treatise is to maintain the production of the earth, at least as a place of habitation for living creatures, to have been coeval with the creation of man, that the materials of all the strata were collected during the period from that epoch to the deluge, that the deposition of those materials and the formation of all the strata took place about the same era, that this was effected by the waters of the deluge, and that all the organic remains are those of vegetable and animal beings, which lived in the antediluvian period.

It is with reluctance and pain that I say any thing in disparagement of a writing by so good a man: but I am sure that he is far from wishing that any person should sacrifice conviction to respect and friendship. To me, I must confess, it appears, that he often errs in stating the opinions of other persons; that his arguments upon the disputed points are quite insufficient to bear their conclusions; that he commits the great fault of drawing universal inferences from particular facts and occasional circumstances, without any sufficiently comprehensive induction; and that, if we were to rest upon the statements by him made and the doctrines which he draws from them, our knowledge of premises would be essentially defective, and our conclusions from them very far from the truth.†

versies, are unanimous, as to the main points which their opponents represent as heretical; namely, [1.] the impossibility of condensing the actual phenomena of the fossil strata into the space of six thousand, or many times six thousand years; or [2.] of admitting, with due regard to the voice of truth, that the death of animals is not to be traced to a much more remote period.——A man only betrays his own ignorance or incapacity, who affects to sneer at modern physical science." A letter signed Fides; *Christ. Obs.* for July, 1839, p. 404. In the same work for the month of August, p. 473, is a just and gentlemanly castigation of Biblicus Delvinus.

* In his *History of Whitby and the Vicinity;* 2 vols. 8vo, 1817; and his *Geological Survey of the Yorkshire Coast;* 4to, 1828.

† See Supplementary Note, M; on Dr. Young's Scriptural Geology.

Mr. Rhind of Edinburgh is a writer respectably known by a brief treatise entitled "The Elements of Geology," and by other works on natural science. The last year, he published "The Age of the Earth, considered Geologically and Historically." He understands his subject far more than some of whom we have been obliged to speak, and discusses it with calmness and candour. He lays down facts, too briefly and generally indeed, and not always, I fear, accurately, but with the nature and relations of which he is acquainted; and he is far from being dogmatical in his manner. Yet I must own that, to my apprehension, he seems to be labouring under the disadvantages of an inquirer whose mind is filled beforehand with the idea that he absolutely must establish a previously dictated doctrine. I cannot with full satisfaction accord to him the praise of impartiality. He brings forward facts and phenomena that may be made to look favourably upon the views which he is anxious to confirm; and touches very lightly or entirely passes over others which are necessary to a more complete view of the evidence.* His mind is imbued with the idea, that the voice of the Eternal and Omniscient Being, speaking by the instrumentality of his inspired servants, has clearly fixed a limit to physical research, and has positively revealed the commencement of universal creation to have been nearly coincident with that of the human race. He affirms, that "the most obvious and general impression of these revelations on the human mind cannot be mistaken or controverted;" [as being to this effect,] "that the world was created, and furnished with plants and animals, for the express habitation of man, within a definite period; that, after a time, it suffered a partial destruction and change by some great catastrophe; and that, ultimately, *it will be totally destroyed*, after it has ceased to be needed as the theatre of moral probation for the human race." (Page 115.) Of these three positions, the first is the question under our actual consideration: and the middle one is expressed in terms not discrepant from the views concerning the Deluge which are supported in these lectures. With respect to

*As many of Mr. Rhind's arguments are drawn from the geological structure of the country round Edinburgh, considerable advantage would be derived by a careful student from the far more comprehensive and exact descriptions of the same region, by Mr. Charles Maclaren, in his *Sketch of the Geology of Fife and the Lothians;* 1839. The results of his investigations, as applied to the time elapsed since the deposition of even the carboniferous strata, are in striking contrast to Mr. Rhind's opinions.—See also the Addition to Suppl. Note, F.

the third, I cannot but feel astonishment that any serious and intelligent man should have his mind fettered with the common, I might call it the vulgar, notion of a proper destruction of the earth; and some seem to extend the notion to the whole solar system, and even the entire material universe; applying the idea of an extinction of being, a reducing to nothingness. This notion has indeed been often used to aid impassioned description in sermons and poetry; and thus it has gained so strong a hold upon the feelings of many pious persons that they have made it an article of their faith. But, I confess myself unable to find any evidence for it, in nature, reason, or Scripture. We can discover nothing like destruction in the matter of the universe as subjected to our senses. Masses are disintegrated, forms are changed, compounds are decomposed; but not an atom is annihilated. Neither have we the shadow of reason to assert that mind, the seat of intelligence, ever was or ever will be, in a single instance, destroyed. Should any man ask me, What I presume to think concerning the principle of intelligence in the inferior animals? What becomes of it, when they die? Does that principle in an elephant or a sparrow, in a bee, an ant, or an animalcule, retain its consciousness after death? Or, into what state does it pass? Or, does it absolutely cease to exist?—I reply, that I pretend not to know, nor do I presume to conjecture; that an impenetrable veil prevents our obtaining this knowledge; but yet that, if there be mind, I can find no ground for believing in its annihilation. The great naturalist of Geneva, Charles Bonnet,* distinguished also by his piety as a Christain, maintained the reality of a future life for all sentient natures. No man who thinks seriously upon the infinite perfections of God, can imagine that difficulty can lie in his path, whether of purpose or of action; or that there is not space in the universe to contain such assemblages of beings, and to furnish

* *Fourth ed.* Other distinguished men have been, at least, inclined to this hypothesis. See a most able and cautious *Dissertation on the Mind of the Lower Animals*, by John Sheppard, Esq., appended to his poem, *An Autumn Dream*, a deeply interesting volume for its poetical merits, and eminently so for its copious Notes, in which theology and practical religion, criticism and metaphysics, receive rich contributions. Gladly also do I recommend the other writings of this excellent author. They possess the same classes of good qualities, invaluable aids to knowledge, taste, and piety. As allied to some of the subjects of this volume, I would particularly mention his *Lecture on the Arguments for Christian Theism from Organized Life and Fossil Osteology;* 1845. It contains penetrating remarks, yet always candid and kind, upon the book, entitled *Vestiges of the Nat. Hist. of Creation*

them with the fullest scope for useful and happy existence. If an expression in one of the Psalms be held to imply the annihilation of inferior animals, such interpretation will carry with it also that the souls of wicked men are annihilated: "Man that is in honour and abideth not, is like the brutes that perish."—Where our Maker has not given us the means of knowledge, our duty is to be humbly and thankfully ignorant.* The declaration in Scripture, that "the heavens and the earth shall flee away, and no more place be found for them," is undoubtedly figurative, and denotes the most momentous changes in the scenes of the divine moral government. If it be the purpose of God that the earth shall be subjected to a total conflagration, we perfectly well know that the instruments of such an event lie close at hand, and wait only the divine volition to burst out in a moment.† But that would not be a destruction; it would be a mere change of form, and, no doubt, would be subservient to the most glorious results. "We, according to his promise, look for new heavens and a new earth; wherein dwelleth righteousness."‡ Upon the whole, Mr. Rhind's chief intention

* Quærunt arguti sed parum sobrii homines, an immortale futurum sit omne animalium genus. His speculationibus si frænum laxetur, quorsum tandem nos abripient? Hac ergo simplici doctrina contenti simus, tale fore temperamentum et tam concinnum ordinem, ut nihil vel sit deforme vel fluxum appareat. "Some persons, more curious than wise, ask whether the inferior animal creation will be endowed with immortality in the future state. If we give unlimited indulgence to such speculations, to what lengths will they hurry us? Let us be satisfied with the plain doctrine, that the adjustment and disposition of the universe will be so beautifully adapted as to leave no room for disorder or decay." Calvin, on Rom. viii. 21.

† *Sec. ed.* "When we consider the combustible nature of the elements of the earth, so far as they are known to us, the facility with which their compounds may be decomposed and made to enter into new combinations, the quantity of heat which they evolve during these processes; when we recollect the expansive power of steam, and that water itself is composed of two gases which by their union produce intense heat; when we call to mind the number of explosive and detonating compounds which have been already discovered; we may be allowed to share the astonishment of Pliny that a single day should pass without a general conflagration. 'Excedit profecto omnia miracula, ullum diem fuisse quo non cuncta conflagrarent.' *Hist. Mundi,* lib ii. cap. 107." Lyell's *Princip.* B. II. ch xx. vol. ii. p. 451, sixth ed.

‡ 2 Pet. iii. 7, 10. Many critics and expositors, probably the majority, understand this passage of a literal conflagration of our planet, to take place immediately after the universal resurrection and the final judgment. But it would be wrong to withhold the observation, that some of the most eminent Bible-scholars have entertained a different opinion: in particular, John Prideaux, Bishop of Worcester in the time of Charles I, a man never to be thought of without affection for his learning, magnanimous humility, piety, and sufferings as a conscientious royalist; (*Fascicul. Controv. Theol.* cap. vii.) Dr. Lightfoot; (*Works*, ed. 1684. vol. ii. pp. 626, 1073—6.) and Dr. John Owen; (Θεολογούμενα, ed. Bremen, 1684, p. 147.)

I will attempt a summary of Owen's disquisition. "The apostle treats upon three

appears to be the moderate and pious one of promoting the due reverence to divine authority, a modest sense of our ignorance, and a cautious abstinence from lofty positiveness. His candid admission does him honour. "*It is true*, even the Mosaical record *does not definitely settle* this question.——May we not be permitted to think—that the period for forming a true theory of the earth, has not arrived, and may never come; that we must content ourselves in this, as in most other cases of human inquiry, with an investigation of facts and phenomena, without diving into causes which are to us inscrutable?" (Pp. 114, 111.) Thus he concedes what nullifies the purpose and the title of the whole book.

Three years ago, Dr. Nicholas Wiseman, Principal of the English (of course Roman Catholic) College in Rome, published a work eminently valuable, "Twelve Lectures on the Connexion between Science and Revealed Religion." The course advantageously comprehends Philology, Civil History, Antiquities, and some branches of Natural Science. The view which he gives of Geology, he professes to be historical rather than scientific,* but it

worlds, or states of the world; the ancient one, which had perished by water; the one *then present*, which was to be consumed by fire; and a third, the *new heavens and earth*, the abode of righteousness. He is not referring to the visible heaven or earth, considered with respect to its substance. For the destruction of the ancient world by water did not take away the material frame of the heavens and the terrene globe. The term *world* is used to signify *the human inhabitants* of the world. They were extirpated by the flood; and another world of men was to be established, for maintaining true religion and the right worship of God. Of this *world* he laid the foundations in the family of Noah; and its fabric was completed by the erection of the Church of Israel. That was the world whose immediately impending dissolution by fire St. Peter here predicts: but we must observe that he uses the *prophetic style*" [of emblematical imagery;] "corresponding with Isa. li. 15, 16;" [lxv. 15, 17, 18; lxvi. 14—16.] "When God *divided the sea* and brought his people out of Egypt, he intrusted them with his law and the solemn institutions of his worship, and formed them into a church for himself: that was establishing and completing *this new world, the heaven and the earth*. But, when Peter wrote, this *world*, the Jewish church, had become apostate, and was hastening to the destruction of *fire*; just as the ancient world plunged itself into the destruction of *the deluge*. By the burning of the temple and city of Jerusalem, the frame of that world was dissolved. The apostle directs believers to another world, as a matter of expectation, *to be looked for*; because ἡ συντέλεια τοῦ αἰῶνος [the completion of the period, Matt. xxviii. 20.] was not yet accomplished; and which would be *new heavens and a new earth, according to the promise of God*. That promise is in Isa. lxv. 17; lxvi. 22; in which passages the prophet draws as it were a picture of the coming of the Messiah.——The state of the Church, after the conflagration of the second world, was called *the age or world to come*: Heb. ii. 5; vi. 5. Thus the first or ancient world, was that which perished by the deluge; the second, was the actually present, which the apostle declares was about to perish by fire; and the third, the *world to come*, is declared to be that which shall endure to the end of time."

* "I am not guided by a personal predilection for any system. I have no claim to be called a geologist. I have studied the science more in its history than in its practical principles." Vol. i. p. 299.

is very able, candid, and judicious; and, in a mild but effective manner, he vindicates Geology and many modern geologists from the opprobrium which some have endeavoured to throw upon them; he convicts those accusers (some of whom we have had occasion to refer to,) of inconsistency and vicious reasoning; he shews that the time implied between the first action declared in the Book of Genesis and the ensuing facts is left undecided and indefinite; he expresses himself very favourably to the doctrine of the central heat; he has just views of the difference and disposition of strata and the characters of the imbedded vegetable and animal remains; and though he maintains the universality of the deluge of Noah, he considers its effects and vestiges as merely superficial, and that it is utterly absurb to ascribe to it the formation of strata. Throughout this part of his interesting volumes, he proves how vain are the fears of those who apprehend injury to religion from geological discoveries, he exposes the false reasonings of infidel pretenders, and he manifests the consistency of those very positions which have been vehemently condemned, upon the antiquity and mutations of the earth, with the testimony of the sacred writings. The impartiality, good temper, and equity of this Romish priest ought to put to shame some Protestant animadverters.

A pleasing exception therefore is made by these volumes of Principal Wiseman, to the larger part of books like those upon which I have thought myself called to animadvert. Of them it may be said that, however dissimilar in some respects, they agree in certain characters: such are, the laying down of facts or statements in a partial manner, thus producing defective and often widely erroneous impressions; the keeping out of sight other facts which would be adverse to their hypotheses, probably from not being themselves acquainted with those facts; a frequent forgetfulness of equity in stating and describing the objects under consideration; their being either insensible to the difficulties which belong to their own schemes, or not feeling any obligation to remove those difficulties; in short, their carrying on their arguments in the way which too much resembles the chicanery of counsel in a bad cause.

Striking is the contrast which this method of reasoning and writing bears to the character of a work which I do not say is unexceptionable, but which, for completeness and accuracy, for fairness of statement and perspicuity of exposition, for force of reasoning and felicity of suggestion, stands forth among the books of our day, very signally distinguished; but which has been made an object of censure and suspicion, by some who have never carefully studied it, and of serious regret by intelligent and candid geologists;—Mr. LYELL's *Principles of Geology*. We cannot but lament that he takes so slight a notice of the bearings of his subject upon the ancient records* of revelation; using general expressions when precise distinctions were called for, and thus laying himself open to painful imputations. The hope had been cherished that, in the editions after the first, he would have obviated serious objections which had been advanced in a spirit so candid and kind as to have possessed a just claim upon his respect.† This, however he has not done. It therefore remains for the readers of his indispensable volumes, to make such explanations and corrections for themselves. It is not, I trust, in me an unbecoming hope, that these lectures may furnish, in some degree, the means of so doing. Yet a work which the Council of the Royal Society, two years ago, honoured by the adjudication of the Royal Medal, a work of which Sir John Herschel says, "I now read it for the third time, and every time with increased interest," a work whose luminous and lively diction makes even so interesting a subject more attractive,—cannot have its merits exploded by a few though serious faults, and from which it is a pleasing and reasonable hope that it will be expurgated. If I may venture on the expression of my own opinion, it is, that the day is not distant when the chief points of difficulty will be satisfactorily cleared up; and that, in particular, the great question between catastrophes and uniformity of action, brought to comparison upon a scale of appropriate amplitude, will be found to shade off into a fair coalescence. All will fall under the universal principle that, through a series of dependent agencies, extensive and complicated beyond our mental grasp, GOD "worketh all things, according to the counsel of his own will." Professor Sedgwick, while he did not spare the language of frank and strong criticism, uttered the impressions of his honourable mind, with impartiality as noble as it was splendid in eloquence. Speaking of Mr. Lyell's first volume in the first edition, he says, "Nineteen twentieths of his work remain untouched

* Supp. Note, N; on the Comparison of the Egyptian and the Mosaic Cosmogonies.
† Supplementary Note O; on some Passages in Mr. Lyell's Principles of Geology.

by these remarks. His excellent and original historic narrative, his dignified philosophic views and clear descriptions, his admirable account of the effects brought about by the great causes, whether aqueous or igneous, now acting on the crust of the globe, contribute to make his volume in the highest degree both popular and instructive: and I cannot but express a wish that, in the future editions of his work, the system of *Geological Dynamics* may be stripped of even the semblance of hypothetical assumption."*

It would be desirable here to give a sketch of the reasons which we have for believing in the high antiquity of the earth: but the length of this lecture and the demands of the subsequent ones, render such an attempt impracticable.† Instead of it, my kind and patient auditors will allow me to conclude by reading a passage, from a paper by an unknown writer, in the Christian Observer for the present month.

"In regard to difficulties, the popular interpretation labours under heavier ones than that of the scriptural geologist; but I fear that such *argumenta ad hominem* are of very little service; for there is a class of minds upon which inductive science makes no impression. Argue with a person of this order of intellect, (he may be a good linguist, a critic, an historian, a man versed in polite literature,) upon the known and incontrovertible facts of Geology; he cannot deny them; but when you press the conclusion, you perceive that his mind has not really grappled with them. He replies, 'How do we know that it was not a miracle?' or, 'How do we know that things were then as they are now?' or, 'I will believe God rather than man;' or, 'We know nothing at all about the matter;' or something equally vague, and to which of course no reply can be given. But the most common resource is, '*The Deluge did it all.*' This reply exhibits either complete ignorance of the facts, or a rejection of the inevitable conclusions which they suggest. No epitome of those facts would do justice to them; for they would require at least a hundred pages of minute detail; and yet, without having even glanced over the outlines, some persons are not ashamed to say, 'It was the Deluge;' or, 'It was a miracle;' and they persuade themselves they do God service by this sort of obtund argument. Geologists have

* Address to the Geol. Soc. Feb. 1831; on retiring from the President's chair.
† To meet this object, the Supplementary Note F. was added to this volume.

carefully examined some ten miles' thickness of solid fossiliferous strata to the number of hundreds, which they are able to do by means of their slanting position, where the edges crop up. These strata are not homogeneous; but consist of successive layers differing widely in their character and contents. They are divided into groups; they are not jumbled confusedly—fresh water productions with salt, land animals with fishes, present with extinct genera or species; but they lie as methodically as the shelves of specimens in a cabinet, being to all appearance successive sedimentary depositions gradually accumulated through a period of very long duration; the footsteps of animals on the once soft moist sand (now hard rock), and the ripple marks of water, being in many cases still visible, and the most delicate and brittle species of shells being unfractured. At the bottom are numerous strata of slate, shell, limestone, and sandstone, containing vegetable and animal sea-water remains now wholly unknown. Over these come sand and clay, interlaid with vast forests of coal, and other land and fresh-water productions. Then come limestone, and sandstone, and clay; all containing organic remains quite distinct from those of the former groups. Then come the upper fossiliferous rocks; in which, for the first time, appear land animals; but even these quite distinct from those that now inhabit the world. These ten miles of strata upon strata bear marks of successive changes in the crust of the earth, both by dislocation and gradual accretion, every particle of clay or sand, for example, being so much pulverized rock; and the vast masses of fossiliferous stone, often composed almost entirely of shells, having every appearance of being the sediment at the bottom of oceans for very lengthened periods; how long no man can calculate; but this we know, not through eternal ages, for the very first announcement of Holy Writ is, that God created all things; they were therefore not self-derived or eternal. But to pretend that there is any proof in Holy Writ, that God created them about six thousand years ago, and that to doubt this is infidelity, is to foist the received interpretation in the place of the inspired word, as well as to deal very harshly by our christian neighbour who thinks otherwise. The geologist only asks a hearing; but he is not heard; he is taunted, declaimed against, and silenced; whilst the infidel stands by and admires the proceedings of the Protestant Inquisition, as often as a new Galileo demonstrates a truth which accords not with some received interpretation. 'Let God be true, and every man a liar;' but we are not to lie for God, or, what comes nearly to the same, to refuse to open our eyes to truth, because we are apprehensive, as the Roman Catholics are in regard to transubstantiation, that our senses and our faith will contradict each other. We may feel quite easy on that score; for the more we know of God's works, the more clearly shall we see their accordance with his word; though not, it may be, with some popular comments on it."*

---

* Baconianus Christianus; in the *Christian Obs.* March, 1839; p. 147.

LECTURE VII.

Psalm xii. 6. *The words of the Lord are pure words; as silver tried in a furnace of earth, purified seven times.*

The connexion of this passage shews that, by "the words of the Lord" here mentioned, we are to understand his promises of mercy and protection to his faithful servants, when they are exposed to sufferings from the treachery of false-hearted men, and when their hopes of aid from their friends are diminished by the death or oppression of the "godly" and "faithful." In opposition to the flatteries and deceitful actions of an unprincipled party, the author of this psalm exults in the fidelity of God, and the assurance that the fullest reliance might be placed on every authenticated declaration of the divine will. This is illustrated by the metaphor of metallic purity. Silver and gold occur native, in the proper metallic state; yet, even in that case, they cannot be got free from the stony substances which inclose or penetrate them, without the art of the refiner: but, when the processes of the hammer, the crucible, and the furnace have been duly performed, the precious metal is obtained in a state of high purity, and fit for completely answering every purpose in the arts of life, for which it is adapted.

That which is thus declared concerning the "exceeding great and precious promises" of divine grace, is equally true of every other part of what God has been pleased to reveal, for the purposes of his wisdom and benevolence to mankind; "for doctrine, for reproof, for correction, and for instruction in righteousness." The most scrupulous student of the Bible will not accuse me of making an arbitrary application of Scripture, because from this particular instance, upon the principle of evident analogy, I deduce a universal truth. That truth is, that every declaration contained in the writings of the prophets and apostles, which has a respect to the faith, the obedience, the consolation, and the usefulness of believers; and when understood in the sense intended by the Author of inspiration; possesses the purity of the best refined silver, the INFALLIBILITY of unmixed TRUTH. The sentiment, in an enlarged form, is given by the son of the writer of this psalm; "Every word of God is pure. He is a shield unto them that put their trust in him. Add thou not unto his words, lest he reprove thee, and thou be found a liar."* Every serious mind will perceive how solemnly this caution bears upon our proceeding, in the endeavour to elicit the sense of the Scriptures. It not less clearly follows, that one of our first duties is to ascertain, by those means which God has put into our possession, *the genuine meaning* of the divine oracles, without prepossession in favour of some interpretations, or prejudice against others. Our honest question must be, "*What* saith the Lord?"

It is not, I trust, in disregard of this caution, that I avail myself of the analogy suggested by our text, as an instructive direction, not of fancy, but arising justly and naturally out of the imagery employed. The use of silver, though it is often found native in metalliferous veins, would be confined within narrow limits, if mankind could employ only the native metal. The quantity obtained, and the capacity of even the best specimens for being applied to the many valuable purposes for which the providence of God has given us that metal, would be very small, were it not for the skill and laborious diligence of the metallurgic workman. So the treasures of the heavenly word, "more to be desired than gold, yea, than much fine gold," require that we should exert our best faculties, in digging out of the mine, (if I may carry on the metaphor,) and in separating the actual SUBSTANCE of divine communication from that which is necessarily human, the *forms* of language, and the condescending *methods of comparison* with the affections and actions of men, by which God is pleased to bring spiritual and divine realities within the sphere of our narrow comprehension. The *matter* is divine, but the *vehicle* is human. "We have this treasure in earthen vessels." Pursuing this train of thought, we arrive at some important *principles* for Theology and the study of the Scriptures.

I. Of the nature and attributes of the Infinite Spirit, of his purposes and his acts, which cannot but have the characters of his

* Prov. xxx. 5, 6.

own perfection, we have *no intuitive* knowledge: and we have *no possible* means of receiving knowledge, though communicated from its own Divine Fountain, except through the medium of RESEMBLANCES to objects of our own thought, or of sensible perception by our own organs. "Behold, God is great; and we know him not!" Of the Divine Nature as Infinite Intellect, PURE MIND, we can form no conception but by reflecting upon, and drawing conclusions from our own consciousness, and the operations of our own minds. In like manner, we gain our knowledge of the *Eternity* of God, by adding the notion of infinity to our perception of the flow of time. By our touch and our sight, we get the ideas of motion, resistance, and impulse; and, by reflecting on the lesson thus taught, we rise to the notion of effects and causes. We look and feel around, we lay hold of bodies extraneous to ourselves, and we discover certain states and alterations of states following upon certain conditions of tangible and visible things; we then rise to a wider survey of the sensible world around us, and we see a vast number of changes taking place, upon a scale of great magnitude; and at last our feeble minds having acquired the idea of *power*, we transfer it, with the highest increase of form, to our conception of the Infinite and Eternal Deity; and we call our new idea *Omnipotence*. In a similar way, we form conceptions of justice and kindness, from the action of parental and infantile feelings, and from the mental phenomena which we experience inwardly and the actions of our fellow-beings observed outwardly; to these conceptions we also annex the qualities of infinity and eternity, and thus we gain some notion of the MORAL attributes of the Supreme Majesty, his *Holiness* and his *Benignity*. But, how faint, how low, are our best conceptions! "Lo, these are parts of his ways: and what whisper-word is heard of him!—The Almighty! We find him not!"*

I humbly think that these positions are self-evident to every reflecting person. Equally manifest it is, that the highest orders of created intelligences, though they may be immeasurably superior to man in their faculties of understanding, can *know* GOD in only the same way: by elevating their minds through aids of

* Job xxvi. 14. The word rendered *parts* signifies the extremities of lines, mere points: but I know not of any good English word which I could venture to substitute. The *whisper-word* is the barest literal rendering; and it is too beautiful to be lost, as in the common version. Chap. xxxvii. 23, also closely rendered.

analogy: unless the TRANSCENDENT ONE, in his boundless goodness, have reserved for them some mode of immediate communication; but to conceive which must necessarily be beyond our powers.

From this general statement some important consequences follow.

1. All the methods of representation, that may be employed to convey notions of the Deity to the mind of man, must, of absolute necessity, be designed to produce only analogical or comparative ideas; and must be adapted to that end. If we may so speak, they are *pictures*, which stand *in the place* of spiritual realities; but the realities themselves belong to the INACCESSIBLE LIGHT.

2. The materials of such comparison must be different, according to the varying states of mental improvement in which different minds are found. Let it, for a moment, be supposed that it had pleased the Divine Majesty to grant an immediate revelation of his authority and his grace to the Athenians, in the age of Socrates, Plato, and Aristotle, and for their use; we may reverentially believe that, in such a case, the communication would have been expressed in the terms and phrases to which they had habituated themselves, and moulded upon a system of references to the natural scenery around them, to their modes of action in social life, and to their current notions upon all other subjects. Not only would the diction have been pure Greek, but the figures, the allusions, and the illustrations of whatever kind, would also have been Attic. The Hebraized style which was adapted to the people of Israel, would have failed to convey just sentiments to the men of Greece; or, though it would not have been absolutely unintelligible, the collateral ideas would have been misapprehended, false bye-notions would have insinuated themselves, and the principal sentiments, to inculcate which was the object of the whole process, would have been grievously distorted. Or, had the favour of a positive revelation been given to the ancient Britons, or to the aborigines of America, it would have been clothed in another dress of representative imagery, and described in other and very different forms of speech.

Yet, in any such case, and under every variety that could occur, the enucleating of the representations, if it were fairly accomplished, would bring out *the same* truths: and the practical benefit to piety and virtue, resulting from each mode, for the classes of mankind to which each was adapted, would be *the same,* if improved with equal fidelity.

3. The earliest revelation which God was pleased to grant to man, whether in the state of pristine integrity, or in that into which by transgression he fell, must have been conveyed by representations of the character which we have described; they must have been composed of materials derived from the *knowledge* possessed by the subjects of those revelations, and the *relations* under which they stood to beings and circumstances around them.

This position is only the correlate of saying that the revelation must have been given and transmitted in the language spoken or written by those to whom the message of God came: or, to say all in one word, it must have been *intelligible.* If any objection be raised against the supposition, that, by this shewing, the revelation would be clothed in the imagery of gross and sensible objects, with the imperfections and misconceptions, under which those objects appeared to men possessing only the rude ideas of a primeval state of society; a corresponding objection would lie against the revelation's being conveyed in a rude and imperfect language. Then, to be consistent, it would be requisite further to maintain, that the terms and style of the revelation must have been in the most pure and abstract kind of phrase that human diction could afford, the most nearly approaching to the spirituality of the Divine Nature, and the majesty of eternal things; and this would be equivalent to saying, that it ought to have anticipated by many centuries the progress of man as an intellectual and social being; that it ought to have been written, not in the language of shepherds and herdsmen, but in that of moral philosophers and rhetoricians; not in Hebrew, but in Greek or English.

It would plainly also follow that, if the prescription, as to the forms of thought and diction, which such presumptions demand as befitting a revelation from heaven, were admitted, a revelation so expressed would have been *unintelligible* to the "ages and generations" of primitive time, and to the generality of mankind in all times.

II. We are thus led to another observation, which will bring us to *the principle* proposed as the solution of the Biblical question, with relation not to Geology only, but to human science universally. It is this.

The revelations, successively given to the fathers of mankind, to the ancestors of the Israelitish nation, and to particular persons of that nation, "at sundry times and in divers manners," were conveyed in *representations to the senses*, chiefly that of *sight*, and in *words descriptive* of those representations.

To the slightest rational consideration, it must be evident that the first human pair were created in the perfection of their bodily organs and mental powers; and that they were immediately endowed by their Creator with a full use of their organs and faculties, and with a competent measure of the habits thence resulting: that use and those habits, which all subsequent human beings have had to acquire, by the slow process of parental training and imitative acquisition. Had these qualifications not been thus infused into them, or made instinctive, at the very commencement of their being, they could not have preserved their own lives, nor have rendered to their heavenly Sovereign any religious homage. The German philosopher Fichte gave the decision of reason, when he asked the question and returned the answer, "Who educated the first human pair? A Spirit took them under his care; as is laid down in an ancient, venerable, original document; which contains the deepest and the sublimest wisdom, and presents results to which all philosophy must at last return."* The certainty of such an order of things nature and reason declare; the actual reality of it we learn from the word of revelation.

"God created man in his own image;" and the christian Scriptures shew us in what that image consisted; "in knowledge, righteousness, and true holiness." That knowledge must have been sufficient for all the purposes of a pure and happy existence, and as the principle of a progressive developement which would undoubtedly have been most glorious, had man abode in his pristine honour. The Deity was pleased to manifest himself to the newly formed and favoured creatures, in ways of the most condescending goodness and wisdom; assuming probably a splendid

* "Wer erzog denn das erste Menschenpaar? Ein Geist nahm sich ihrer an, wie es eine alte, ehrwürdige Urkunde vorstellt, welche überhaupt die tiefsinnigste, erhabenste Weisheit enthält, und Resultate aufstellt, zu denen alle Philosophie am Ende doch wieder zurück muss." Quoted by Dr. Dereser of Breslaw, in the translation of the Bible with annotations, by himself, Brentano, and Scholtz; in 17 vols. Francf. 1820—1833; vol. i. p. 16. John Gottlieb Fichte, whose writings have exercised a very powerful influence in Germany, taught that the arrangement of moral sentiments and relations, that is, the moral order of the universe, *is God;* thus denying a personal and intelligent Deity. He died in 1814, æt. 52; and there is reason to believe that, several years before his death, he renounced his atheism.

human form, and communing with them, in ways and to an extent of the most wise and benevolent purposes, beyond what we can know. But it is not an unreasonable conjecture, that the archives of the human race which open the writings of Moses, are fragments of those communings. The narration of that which took place before man existed to have witnessed it, could have been only from a supernal communication. Yet, to suppose that scientific knowledge was thus imparted, or any knowledge beyond what was necessary for the present welfare of the newly created rational beings, their intellectual progress, and the preservation of their unalloyed but not expanded holiness; has no ground of probability as a subject of conjecture, nor the shadow of evidence as a matter of fact. After the mournful apostasy of man, the condescending Deity was pleased still to grant manifestations of himself; for the increase of moral knowledge, the counteraction of growing wickedness, and the providing of facts and evidences to be recorded as a basis for ulterior revelations. In many of those manifestations, the appearance of a human figure is expressly declared: thus suggesting reason to believe that those appearances were in the person of "the Word, who, in the fulness of the time, became flesh," that is, assumed the human nature, "and dwelt among us;" "who is over all, God blessed for ever."* In this manner, a foundation was laid for the succession of divine communications, to guide wandering man into the ways of peace.

In comparison with the glory of the gospel, the "grace and truth by Jesus Christ," this was a very imperfect proceeding: but it was a rudiment of the moral system which was to be the excelling glory of a future age; and, with all its imperfection, it was as high and spiritual as *the condition of human nature was able to bear*. It was adapted to a state of intellectual and spiritual infancy; and from it was derived *that character* of the Old Testament revelations, which it is our present object to consider more closely.

That character consisted in representing God by the figurative attribution of the human form with its organs and functions, and the human mind with its affections and passions.

In the majestic language of the Church of England, "There is but one living and true God; everlasting, without body, parts, or

* John i. 1, 14. Gal. iv. 4. Rom. ix. 5.

passions."* And does any man need to be told that this article is the echo of the clearest scripture-testimony; in the Old Testament as well as in the New? "Do not I fill heaven and earth? saith the Lord.—Whither shall I flee from thy presence?—God is a spirit:—the King eternal, immortal, invisible;——who only hath immortality, dwelling in the light which no man can approach unto; whom no man hath seen, nor can see."†

Yet it pleased this Being to bring down himself, not to the comprehension, for that is impossible, but to the apprehensive capacity of untutored men, by representations drawn from the circumstances of man, and from other natural objects.

Is it intended to represent the beauty and grandeur of the Divine Nature?—"He covereth himself with light as with a garment.—His glory covered the heavens:—his brightness was as the light:—God is light."‡

His universal knowledge? "The eyes of the Lord run to and fro, through the whole earth."§

The application of his omniscience to the exercises of distributive justice? "God looked down from heaven upon the children of men; to see if there were any that did understand, that did seek God.—The Lord said, Because the cry of Sodom and Gomorrah is very great, and because their sin is very grievous, I will go down now, and see whether they have done altogether according to the cry of it, which is come unto me: and if not, I will know."||

His unfailing notice and gracious attention to the sufferings of his obedient servants? "The eyes of the Lord are upon the righteous, and his ears are open to their cry.—Thou wilt hear me, O God; incline thine ear unto me, unto my speech."¶

His justice upon the wicked and impenitent? "When ye spread forth your hands, I will hide mine eyes from you. Yea, when ye make many prayers, I will not hear.—God is jealous, and the Lord revengeth; the Lord revengeth and is furious."**

His compassion and forgiving grace? "Is Ephraim my dear son? Is he a pleasant child? For, since I spake against him, I

* More impressively in the Latin copy of the articles; "——incorporeus, impartibilis, impassibilis;——"

† Jer. xxiii. 24. Psa. cxxxix. 1—12. John iv. 24. 1 Tim. i. 17; vi. 16.

‡ Psa. civ. 2. Habak. iii. 3, 4. 1 John i. 5.

§ 2 Chron. xvi. 9.

|| Psa. liii. 2. Gen. xviii. 21.

¶ Psa. xxxiv. 15; xvii. 6.

** Isa. i. 15; Nah. i. 2.

do earnestly remember him still: therefore my bowels are troubled for him; I will surely have mercy upon him, saith the Lord."*

His almighty power, and its various exercises? "When I consider thy heavens, the work of thy fingers.—I have made the earth and created man upon it. I, even my hands, have stretched out the heavens.—This is the finger of God.—Thou didst drive out the heathen with thy hand:—thy right hand, and thine arm, and the light of thy countenance."†

In like manner, "the heart of Jehovah" is put to signify his love and approbation; his nostrils, mouth, and breath, his lips and tongue, express his declarations of mercy to the penitent and retributive justice upon the ungodly; his feet and footsteps, designate the proceedings of his government.‡

By a further application of this method of bringing down divine things to the grasp of man, the Scriptures, and most abundantly the earliest books, represent the attributes of Deity and their exercise in the moral government of rational creatures, by ascribing to him the sudden emotions, and the more tranquil yet mutable affections, which, in their literal meaning, can be predicated of only limited and imperfect beings.

To express the wisdom of God in the adaptation of creatures, forms, and structural organs, to the purposes destined; he is represented in the attitudes of a man who has invented and constructed a new machine, or who has made an untried experiment. He watches the working; he looks at the result; he sees the whole to have succeeded to the fulness of his intention; and he sits down contented and happy, to repose after his labour. "God saw" (the word has an intensive meaning, and denotes to *look at* an object with strong feeling,) "every thing that he had made; and behold, it was very good."—"Thus the heavens and the earth were finished, and all the host of them: and, on the seventh day God ended his work, which he had made; and he rested, on the seventh day, from all his work which he had made."§

It deserves observation, that a similar train of ideas occurs in the passage which, with the same kind of graphic simplicity, presents Moses, upon his having completed the construction and utensils of

* Jer. xxxi. 20.

† Psa. viii. 2. Isa. xiv. 12. Exod. viii. 19. Psa. xliv. 3.

‡ In numerous places which must be familiar to the dutiful readers of the Bible.

§ Gen. i. 31—ii. 3.

the tabernacle, as revising the whole work, finding it correctly done, sitting down satisfied, and invoking the blessing which only God could confer.*

The disobedience and ingratitude of mankind to their heavenly Maker and Benefactor, and his abhorrence of every thing wicked, in principle and in act; are expressed by the image of a man who sees a valuable work spoiled, a favourite measure frustrated, his intentions thwarted, and his hopes turned to the reverse of just expectation: he therefore bitterly regrets that he had ever formed such a purpose, and undergone the labour of executing it. "God saw that the wickedness of man was great in the earth; and that every imagination of the thoughts of his heart was only evil continually: and it repented the Lord that he had made man on the earth, and it grieved him at his heart."† In another remarkable passage, this imagery is carried still further, and the Blessed and Glorious Being, "with whom is no variableness nor shadow of a turning," is depicted as changing his mind a second time. "The Lord said unto Moses, I have seen this people; and, behold, it is a stiff-necked people. Now therefore let me alone, that my wrath may wax hot against them, and that I may consume them: and I will make of thee a great nation. And Moses besought the Lord his God, and said, Lord, why doth thy wrath wax hot against thy people?——" He then uses pleas and arguments to urge his petition,—"Turn from thy fierce wrath, and repent of this evil against thy people.——And the Lord repented of the evil which he thought to do unto his people."‡

One instance more only shall be mentioned. After the awful visitation of the deluge, when Noah with his small household came from their ark of safety and saw themselves the sole survivors of the human race, he presented the adoration of gratitude and prayer to his Almighty Preserver: and this, according to what we think there is evidence to regard as a divine institution, was accompanied by a full§ offering of sacrifices, in which sin was acknowledged, repentance professed, and the great propitiation anticipated. The God of mercy deigned to give some sign of assurance, that the act of devotion was accepted; and that the stream of his goodness should now flow uninterruptedly to man,

* Exod. xxxix. 42, 43.

† Gen. vi. 5, 6.

‡ Exod. xxxii. 9—14.

§ That is, of all the kinds requisite to the completeness of the ritual design.

notwithstanding the aboundings of sin which would anew take place. The entire transaction must have been of the most impressive character to the favoured family; and to us and all men, it is full of instruction. Yet observe the child-like simplicity and the boldly figurative language in which it is related. "Noah builded an altar unto the Lord; and took of every clean beast and of every clean fowl, and offered burnt-offerings upon the altar. And the Lord smelled a sweet odour; and the Lord said in his heart, I will not again curse the ground any more for man's sake; although the imagination of man's heart is evil from his youth; neither will I smite any more every living thing as I have done."*

Such was the manner in which the earliest scriptures depicted to men the perfections and the operations of the Infinite Being, his dominion and authority, his justice and his mercy. Was it not most touching and impressive? Was it not well adapted to the mental capacities and the susceptibility of strong affections, which characterised men in a state of rude simplicity? Would a style more chastised, more coldly correct, more philosophical, more theological (if we please so to call it,) have been better fitted, to answer the ends of religious instruction?—*better* adapted! —would it have been adapted *at all?*—Let us elevate its beneficial effect the most that we reasonably can; still it would have been cold, unattractive, and with difficulty comprehended. Try the experiment upon our peasantry, or even the best educated children of our own families. The style of a Moral Philosophy school would arouse no attention, would leave scarcely any impression; the simple imagery of Scripture is instinct with life, and touches every chord of feeling.

But it not the less plainly follows, that it is our duty to *understand* all such passages in modes which shall be worthy of the dignity of God; and so to *interpret* them as to deprive the contemners of revelation of a pretext for censuring and rejecting it. Possibly some Christian may say, 'I will not follow this course: I will take the words of Scripture in their immediate and obvious sense, and let difficulties alone, persuaded that all is true and right, however contrary to my understanding.' If this language proceed from piety, I honour its motive; but I cannot regard the

* Gen. viii. 20, 21.

course which it takes as wise and good. If you do indeed resolve to take up the figurative language of Scripture as if it were literally true, look well to yourself. Think what consequences you are plunging into; what conceptions of the Infinite Majesty you are cherishing in your mind and propagating around you; what effects they are likely to have upon other persons,—yes, your own children, especially in the well educated and inquiring classes of society; and what vantage-ground you are surrendering to the impugners of the Bible, thus giving your aid for undermining the faith of probably the dearest to you in this world.—Know ye not the universal rule of language, that the figurative is always to be explained by the simple; the obscure by the perspicuous? Are ye inattentive to the plain declarations of the sacred word, upon the spirituality, the omniscience, the unchangeableness of the One Living and True God? Or, if ye will not accept of this method of reconciling the apparent discrepance between the two classes of passages, a method fair and reasonable, and consonant to all the use of language; are you provided with any other? Are you able, upon any better grounds, to protect the faith of the Gospel, and to disarm its opponents?*

Nor ought we to forget, in the pride of our philosophy, that our own best conceptions of God, and our most chastised manners of expression, are likewise formed upon resemblances and analogies. In this way only can we have any conceptions of the Infinite One. The difference between us and the ruder children of nature lies only in the degree.

* The Anthropomorphites of the fourth and fifth centuries furnish an example of the danger of adhering to the literal understanding of the passages of the Old Testament which describe the Deity under the analogies of human forms and passions. Upon them, the modern master of Ecclesiastical History, Dr. Neander (Prof. Theol. Berlin,) has this observation: "The coarse and carnal ideas, which attribute human passions to the Divine Nature, were derived by carnally minded Jews and ignorant Christians, cleaving to the letter, from certain misunderstood passages of the Old Testament. Thus occasion was afforded to Marcion to represent the God of the Old Testament as in reality such a being as those persons had pictured him." (*Allgemeine Gesch. d. Chr. Relig.* vol. i. p. 968.) There are some unhappy people, in our own times, who maintain that God is really a being having the shape, limbs, and functions of a man; persons who call themselves Christyans; also some disciples of an Irishman, Alexander Campbell, an emigrant to Virginia. A large account of them is in the *American Biblical Repository* for Jan. and April 1839. *Third Ed.* This assertion has been recently denied, in a publication at Nottingham; but it is fully averred in passages cited in the Am. B. Repos. p. 310, from a Christyan book professing to give their system authoritatively, *Kincade's Bible* Doctrine; and other quotations shew that "the Christyans and Campbellists are here declared by both parties [themselves], to stand upon the same foundation, and to be one people."

III. We have now to consider the manner in which this characteristic style of the Scriptures speaks of *natural phenomena.* The field of this kind which it opens for investigation is very extensive; but we must content ourselves with a small number of instances.

1. With regard to the figure of the Earth, its relation to the heavenly bodies, and its motion or immobility.

So far as I have been able to ascertain, direct information does not occur in the Scriptures, upon these subjects. But there are many passages which, in the way of incidental mention, seem capable of affording us abundant satisfaction. As this is a topic of much interest in itself, and has a close connexion with our ultimate subject, I shall recite passages at some length.

The primary record, in the beginning of the Book of Genesis, will presently be the specific subject of attention. It is only needful now to say, that nothing is there affirmed, nor in any way implied, concerning the figure and situation of the earth. The mention which is made of the heavenly bodies evidently relates to their use to men, as luminaries and as measures of time; and it gives no hint of any other relations and uses.

"He stretcheth out the north over the empty place, and hangeth the earth upon nothing."* The former part of this verse seems to contemplate the expanse of the starry heavens as seen by night, especially distinguishing the northern constellations, and presenting the appearance of a concave surface extended on all sides; or, as it is more fully expressed in the Book of Isaiah; "He stretcheth out the heavens as a curtain, and spreadeth them out as a tent to dwell in."† By "the empty place" (*tohu*, a word applied to any thing supposed to be *waste* and *deserted*,‡) appears to be meant the whole space above the habitable ground, and which, by those, who had no knowledge of the atmosphere or of any aëriform substance, was regarded as emptiness, a mere nothing. The "suspending of the earth upon nothing," comes as the antithesis of the former member, and declares that the solid earth on which men and other creatures dwell, has no visible or known support, but remains in its place fixed by the decree and power of God. I cannot discover that the passage involves any sentiment, or war-

* Job xxvi. 7. † Is. xl. 22.

‡ Used in Gen. i. 1, and there translated *without form.*

rants any conclusion whatever, as to the figure of the earth, or its connexion with other bodies: but it is perfectly conformable to the idea of the earth's being an extended plane; which we shall find to be the sentiment more clearly declared in other places.

Consonant with this, is a verse in the same connexion. "He hath drawn a limiting circle upon the surface of the waters, to the boundary of light with darkness."* The idea is that of a disc drawn with a compass-instrument, consisting of the whole earth, surrounded by water, and beyond which, on every side and beneath, all was perpetual darkness and a dead waste. The same representation is in the Book of Proverbs; "In his cutting out a circle upon the surface of the deep."†

Other passages speak of extremities, as bounding lines of the earth; and of pillars or supports of some kind upon which it rests. In some places these boundaries are represented as points, the summits of angles: but it is not necessarily to be thence deduced that the idea entertained concerning the figure of the earth was that of a four-sided plane; for the expression would naturally arise from contemplating the two opposite points marked by the sun's rising and setting, and the two which lie transversely to them. The Hebrew words for denoting each of these four quarters (called *wings*) of the heavens or of the earth, are several in each instance; and thus they afford us an insight into the ideas of the Israelites upon the characteristics of the cardinal points. The words for the East signify *radiating*, *a luminous space*, and *before*, that is, referring to the position of a person who has his face towards the rising sun: those for the West, express *going away*, *going down*, *behind the sea*, namely the Mediterranean: those for the North, *darkness*, *gloominess*, *the left hand;* and those for the South, *light*, *the shining region*, *dry*, referring to the countries parched with heat, *the right hand.*

"Under the whole heavens he directeth it, [the thunder;] and its light [the lightning] unto the wings of the earth.——Where wast thou at my laying the foundations of the earth? Narrate [it;] since thou possessest full understanding. Who applied measuring rods unto it; since thou knowest? Upon what were its

* Verse 10. The closest translation. That in the Common Version is not sufficiently exact.

† Chap. viii. 27; closely translated.

bases let in? Or who laid a stone for its corner?——He shaketh the earth out of its place, and the pillars thereof tremble.*—— He will collect [the dispersed people] from the four wings of the earth."†

The belief with regard to the figure of the earth, that it is an extended plane, was current among the Christian fathers:‡ but they in general disapproved and avoided attention to physical subjects. By slow degrees the general doctrine of a globular form made its way among men; but, to a much later date, that of the immobility of the earth was strenuously maintained. Considerably within the last two centuries, that opinion was the common belief of all denominations of Christians. Most persons know that threats, persuasions, and a short imprisonment subdued Galileo, and brought him to make a solemn recantation of the Copernican doctrine; and he had to endure the penal sentence of imprisonment for life.§ It is hardly imaginable that his persecu-

* Job xxxvii. 3; xxxviii. 4—6; ix. 6; closely translated.

† Is. xi. 12; and compare Ezek. vii. 2.

‡ *Sec. ed.* Plato, Aristotle, Strabo, Cicero, and others of the heathen, maintained the globular figure of the earth. Hicetas of Syracuse is mentioned by Cicero as holding its motion; and an approach to just views concerning the system of the world appears to have been made by Pythagoras. Socrates regarded this kind of topics as beyond the reach of human knowledge. But the fathers of the church (not very worthily so called) were generally alien from such inquiries. Lactantius diffusely reproves and ridicules those who believed the earth to be round, and to be habitable on opposite sides. "Is any one so foolish," he asks, "as to believe that there are men whose feet are higher than their heads;—trees growing downwards; rain, snow, and hail, falling upwards?" (*De Falsa Sapientia*, iii. 24.)

In the middle ages, the Jews and Mahommedans were the men to whom we might look for philosophical knowledge, rather than to the general mass of those called Christians, but who were the degraded victims of spiritual tyranny, superstition, and ignorance. In the Hebrew Concordance, attributed to Rabbi (Isaac or Mordecai?) Nathan in the fifteenth century, we find this explication, under יָסַד; "—to place, found, build, lay the foundation of an edifice; *applied* to the creation of the earth, which God has placed *in the middle of the universe, a solid, immovable body*."

§ Yet let not a wrong use be made of the example of Galileo. It has been very properly observed, that many a system-maker, "when a check is offered to his crude and inconclusive conceptions,—fancies himself another Galileo, and glories in his imagined martyrdom. Yet no case was ever more exaggerated than that of Galileo; and even assuming it at its worst phase, it was rather the fault of the age than of the individuals engaged in it. How many really wicked attacks have been levelled at sacred things, from the days of Galileo to the present, and successfully refuted by divines laudably on the watch to preserve the purity of that faith which has been entrusted to them; and yet how small praise has been awarded them, compared to the opprobrium of this one case of exaggerated oppression!" Rhind, *on the Age of the Earth;* p. 117.

So much error prevails with regard to this great man and his persecutions, some overstating and others diminishing them, that a few lines of information may not be useless.

tors could believe in his sincerity; even had he not declared, the moment after, his retention of his own belief; which he did. But persecution is the parent of hypocrisy. A consistent Christian would have died, rather than have infringed his integrity. Yet, not hurling condemnation, but pitying the illustrious Florentine, let us turn his history into a lesson for ourselves. In things of every kind, earthly as well as spiritual, "godly simplicity and integrity" is the only right course: and, whatever it may cost, it will bring happiness in the end.——But it is not so much known that, long after that event, pious and learned Protestants viewed

I derive it from the *Allgemeine Deutsche Real-Encyclopädie*, 16 volumes, Leipzig, 1830—1834; and its authorities are the works of Galileo himself, and Lives by Jagemann and Nelli. We usually call him by his baptismal name, though the family name would be more exactly proper. He was the son of Vicenzo Galilei, a Florentine nobleman, and born at Pisa. His talents and industry corresponded to the signal advantages of his education, in mathematics, the sciences, and elegant literature. About 1620, he became involved in a dispute with the Jesuits, which materially affected his subsequent circumstances. Having obtained the legal permission at both Rome and Florence, he published, 1632, his great work, "A Dialogue by Galileo Galilei, in which, through conversations of Four Days, are discussed the two principal Systems, the Ptolemaic and the Copernican." Notwithstanding the extreme moderation of the work, scarcely amounting to an avowal of the Copernican doctrine, it was made the ground of severe proceedings. Pope Urban VIII. had, in private life, been his friend; but he was now drawn over by the monks to become a zealous enemy. A congregation of Cardinals and others, all his sworn enemies, condemned his book, and cited him to the tribunal of the Inquisition. He was obliged to come to Rome, was imprisoned some months, and on the 23d of June, 1633, kneeling and placing his hand upon the gospels, to denote a declaration by oath in the presence of the God of truth, he uttered the dictated words, "With a sincere heart and undissembled fidelity, I abjure, curse, and detest, the aforesaid errors and heresies." Immediately as he rose from this impious mockery, he betrayed the strongest emotion, stamped on the ground, and said, *E pur si muove!* (It moves, however!) He was condemned to perpetual imprisonment in the dungeons of the Inquisition, and to repeat weekly for three years the seven Penitential Psalms. With regard to the place of imprisonment great favour was shown him. Instead of a dungeon, he was confined in the Bishop's palace at Sienna, and afterwards in a similar retreat near Florence. In this condition he prosecuted his investigations on the laws of motion, the planetary phenomena, and other parts of mechanical philosophy; till deafness, blindness, sleeplessness, and excruciating pain, wore out the venerable philosopher. He died, aged 78, Jan. 8, 1642, the year of the birth of NEWTON.—Alas! how low does this great man sink, by the side of many a poor, tender, and delicate woman, who has refused to purchase a release from the most cruel torture of the rack or the flames, by yielding to utter any falsehood or deny any truth. [With this agrees the incidental record of our immortal poet. His description seems to have purposely avoided implying that the scene was *in* the prison of the Inquisition, and it is not probable that the young English Protestant would have been admitted there. "I could recount what I have seen and heard in other countries, where this kind of inquisition tyrannizes; when I have sat among their learned men, for that honour I had.——There it was that I found and visited the famous Galileo, grown old, a prisoner to the Inquisition, for thinking in Astronomy otherwise than the Franciscan and Dominican licensers thought." *Areopagitica*, Hollis's ed. 1780, p. 310. Milton was at that time twenty-nine years old.]

Galileo's doctrine with the same alarm and abhorrence as the Romish Church professed to feel; and they founded their determination upon the following passages of Scripture.

"He hath established the earth upon its foundations: it shall not be moved, for ever and ever.—For upon the seas he hath founded it, and upon the streams he hath fixed it.—O, give thanks unto Him—who hath spread out the earth upon the waters!—the mount Zion" [and therefore, they inferred, the whole earth, of which any hill or mountain is only a part,]—"shall not be moved, for ever and ever.—Generation goeth, and generation cometh; but the earth for ever standeth.——The sun——rejoiceth as a strong man to run a race. From the end of the heavens is his going forth, and his circuit to their uttermost parts.——Praise him, ye heavens of heavens, and ye waters that be above the heavens.——Who stretcheth out the heavens as a curtain, who layeth rafters in the waters, his upper chambers."*

Upon the interpretation which men of the highest ability attached to these declarations of Scripture, they rested the most positive confidence that the sun flies round the earth every twenty-four hours, and that the earth rests immoveably in the centre of the universe. "This," said one of the most eminent men of the Reformed Church, "we affirm, with all divines, natural philosophers and astronomers, Jews and Mohammedans, Greeks and Latins; excepting one or two of the ancients, and the modern followers of Copernicus."† It is in no small degree curious, but it conveys also a serious lesson to us, to observe what was a very great stretch of candour and charity, one hundred and fifty years ago. "That the sun moves and that the earth is at rest," wrote another of that class of learned men, "is testified in Scripture:——that the earth also cannot be moved, being as it were founded and fixed upon bases, pedestals, and pillars. Some philosophers, indeed, both ancient and modern, and Copernicus, the most distinguished among them, have maintained the contrary. Gemma Frisius has taken pains to explain this opinion of Copernicus in the most favourable manner that he could; and some celebrated philosophers have endeavoured to reconcile it to the Bible, by considerations drawn from the ambiguity and various use of lan-

* Psa. civ. 5; xxiv. 2; cxxxvi. 6. Eccles. i. 4. Psa. xix. 6; cxlviii. 4; civ. 3.
† Gisb. Voetii *Disput. Theol.* vol. i. p. 637. Utrecht, 1648.

guage. Others have recourse to the condescension of the style of Scripture, which, upon matters that do not affect faith and religion, is wont to lisp and prattle (συμψελλίζειν,) like a father with his babes. But our pious reverence for the Scripture, the word of truth, will not allow us to depart from the strict propriety of the words; as, by so doing, we should be setting to infidels an example of wresting the Scriptures; unless we were convinced by sure and irrefragable arguments; as perhaps there may be a few so convinced, but they are ambitious persons, though professing themselves to be devoted to sacred studies."*

The length to which these observations have gone appeared necessary, in order to establish the broad and strong foundation of that principle of Bible-interpretation which to my full conviction, will liberate us from difficulty, in relation to the supposed discrepance between the facts of science, especially geological science, and the testimony of the Holy Scriptures.

A few more instances will be useful: but they shall be briefly mentioned.

"Look now toward heaven, and tell the stars; if thou be able to number them.——So shall thy seed be.——In multiplying I will multiply thy seed, as the stars of heaven, and as the sand which is upon the sea-shore."† Here we have two similitudes, to represent the great increase of a national population; a population which, in the most flourishing times of Israel and Judah, cannot be estimated as having reached to more than eight or nine millions. Yet it is represented by two comparisons, which lie in opposite extremes. The one falls immensely short. With a little skill and perseverance, Abraham might have counted all the stars visible, even in his fine climate. They could scarcely have amounted to fifteen hundred. But the second object of comparison presents a number which the most advanced arithmetic could with difficulty write in figures, and which would many times exeeed the number of human beings that have ever lived upon the face of the globe.‡ Will any one say, that these are not figurative ex-

* Joh. Henr. Heideggeri *Medulla Theol. Christ.* p. 136; Zurich, 1696.

† Gen. xv. 5; xxii. 17.

‡ *Third ed.* The same method of expressing a number, large in reference to some object of comparison, but far from being absolutely of immense extent, we find applied to an armament of the Canaanitish confederacy, Josh. xi. 4; to an army of the Philistines, 1 Sam. xiii. 5; to a levy in mass, 2 Sam. xvii. 11; to the population under Solomon, 1 Kings iv. 20; and even to the days of a reasonably protracted human life, Job xxix. 18.

pressions, peculiarities of idiom; which must be interpreted by the rule of common sense, the one by extending, the other by contracting?

A mode of expression to be interpreted upon the same principle is that of representing a long period of time, in relation to the history of mankind, by "a thousand generations:"* whereas all the generations of the human race, from Adam to the present hour, cannot exceed two hundred.

2. Concerning atmospheric phenomena, a few things are to be noticed.

The Hebrew word (*rakía*) is commonly translated *firmament*, after the example of the Septuagint (στερέωμα·) but many modern critics have sought to mollify the unphilosophical idea of a solid concave shell over our heads, by using the word *expanse*. No doubt they felt their minds acquiescing in this term, as expressing very well the diffused fluid which surrounds the earth; and so leaving us at liberty to conceive of its increasing tenuity, till it is lost in the planetary spaces. But this is the transferring of a modern idea, to times and persons which had it not. The Hebrew language has no word for *air*, properly speaking: because they knew not the thing. Their nearest approaches were with words that denoted watery vapour, condensed and thus rendered visible, whether floating around them or seen in the breathing of animals; and words for smoke arising from substances burning; and for air in motion, wind, a zephyr-whisper, or a storm. But of elastic fluids they had no idea. The word under consideration strictly signifies a solid substance, *extended* by beating out, or rolling, or any other mode of working upon a ductile mass.† The old word, *firmament*, was therefore the most proper.‡ Examining

* Deut. vii. 9. 1 Chron. xvi. 15. Psa. cv. 8.

†*Sec. ed.* In Jer. x. 9, the passive participle (Pual) is used;—"silver spread into plates." In Is. xlii. 5, we have the active form as applied to the earth, while another verb which signifies *expanding* and *extending*, as of cloth cords, or the limbs of animals, is applied to the heavens:—"Creating the heavens, and stretching them out, spreading forth the earth and its productions."

‡ *Fourth ed.* "Solid expanse;——I say *solid*, for nothing can be more certain than that the apparent welkin above us, in which the heavenly bodies seem to move, is spoken of in Genesis i. and in other parts of Scripture, as a solid and expanded arch or ceiling over our heads. Yet what reality is there in such a supposition? The scriptural writers were not commissioned to teach philosophy, nor astronomy; and they have always spoken of objects like those just mentioned, merely in an optical manner; in the way in which they present themselves to the eye, either of the body or of the mind." Prof. Moses Stuart, in the *Amer. Biblioth. Sacra.;* 1843, p. 142.

the whole subject, by connecting it with some passages which have been quoted, and some yet to be mentioned, we acquire an idea of the meteorology of the Hebrews. They supposed that, at a moderate distance above the flights of birds was a solid concave hemisphere, a kind of dome, transparent, in which the stars were fixed, as lamps; and containing openings to be used or closed as was necessary. It was understood as supporting a kind of celestial ocean, called "the waters above the firmament," and "the waters above the heavens." This was the grand reservoir containing water to be discharged at proper times in rain, with which were connected "water courses, for the overflowing," or *pouring out.** The idea also was entertained of masses of water being secured in strong bags, which the clouds were supposed to be. Thus we read, as one of the works of Deity, that he "tieth up water in his dark cloud, and the cloud beneath them is not torn."† Here also were the "treasures of snow and treasures of hail."‡ Lightning also was conceived of as produced, and then laid by for use, in the same region; and as consisting of some kind of ignited matter, called in Scripture "coals of fire;" deriving the idea from burning wood, for mineral coal they knew not. Of the nature and cause of thunder, the Israelites had no conception; and therefore they referred it immediately to the Supreme Cause, and called it "the voice of God." This idea coincided with the accustomed mode of representing the Deity, by the analogies of the human form. In one place it seems as if the lightning was regarded to be the effect of thunder: "Who hath divided——a way for the dartings of the voices?"§ As the thunder was conceived to be the awfully majestic voice of God, it was a natural accompaniment of the imagery that "He maketh the clouds his chariots, and walketh upon the wings of the wind."|| In one passage, we find all the parts of this imagery combined, so as to produce the

* Job xxxviii. 25.

† Ib. xxvi. 8. *Sec. ed.* A striking instance of this mode of representation occurs in Prov. viii. 28. "In his fastening the clouds from above, in making strong the fountains of the depth." The second clause, according to the structure of the Hebrew poetry, is the correlate for illustrating the first; so that the sentiment is, that, as the springs of water, before their gushing out on the sides of hills, are contained in hollows of the rock, so water is also contained in the clouds as vessels of capacity, ready to discharge it when wanted, but, in the mean time, hung up by some kind of strong attachment in the vault of the sky. The prototype for the resemblance was most probably the suspending of skins containing water or wine, from the ceiling of a room or the upper part of a tent.

‡ Job xxxviii. 22. § Ib. xxxviii. 25. || Psa. civ. 3.

most magnificent effect. "Then the earth shook and trembled: the foundations also of the hills moved and were shaken; because he was wroth. There went up a smoke out of his nostrils, and fire out of his mouth devoured: coals were kindled by it. He bowed the heavens also, and came down; and darkness was under his feet: and he rode upon a cherub and did fly; yea, he did fly upon the wings of the wind. He made darkness his secret place: his pavilion round about him was dark waters, thick clouds of the skies. At the brightness before him his dark clouds passed, hail-stones and coals of fire. The Lord also thundered in the heavens, and the Highest gave forth his voice, hail-stones and coals of fire. Yea, he sent out his arrows and scattered them; and he shot out lightnings and discomfited them. Then the channels of water were seen, and the foundations of the world were discovered, at thy rebuke, O Lord, at the blast of the breath of thy nostrils."*

3. With respect to the animal system, the knowledge of the ancient Hebrews did not go beyond what might be expected from men in their circumstances. They appear to have ascribed distinct intellectual functions to the region of the *kidneys* (usually rendered the *reins*,) and the *liver*. They referred pain to the *bones;* and they seem to have not had the least knowledge of the *nervous system*. There is no word in Hebrew for the *brain* and *nerves* except that which denotes the marrow of the bones, with which it is probable they confounded the cerebral and nervous substance; and even that word was a derivative from another signifying *fat*. Yet upon this defective physiology the language of Scripture is formed for the expression of sensations and many intellectual operations.†

It was incumbent upon me to go thus largely into the induction of particulars, not merely on account of the connexion of the entire view of Scripture-Idioms with our particular object; but because I venture to hope that the principle thus established will be of use to those who favour me with their attention, as some assistance to the forming of an intelligent and therefore most profitable method of studying the divine word.

* Psa. xviii. 7—15.

† Examples. Psa. xxvi. 2; lxxiii. 21. Lam. ii. 11. (Psa. xvi. 9; lvii. 8; cviii. 1; where the word is usually rendered *glory*, but learned orientalists incline to the opinion that the use of the term is based upon the sensitive properties which were supposed to reside in the liver.) Job xxxiii. 19. Psa. vi. 2.

We have thus seen it placed beyond the possibility of a doubt, that it is *the manner* of the Scriptures, and most copiously in their earliest written parts, *to speak of the* DEITY, *his nature, his perfections, his purposes, and his operations, in language borrowed from the bodily and mental constitution of man, and from those opinions concerning the works of God in the natural world, which were generally received by the people to whom the blessing of revelation was granted.*

That so the fact is, cannot be denied: and will any dare to find fault with it? Is it not sufficient to satisfy any rational man, that it has pleased Him who cannot err to make use of this method? We have no right to demand any more satisfaction. But let it not be forgotten, what has already been stated, that, not only is this style that which alone would have been intelligible in the early ages of the world; but it is still the best adapted for universal use.

An observation now arises to our view, which must, I cannot but think, force itself with irresistible conviction upon any impartial mind. If it was not unworthy of the Adorable Majesty of GOD to permit HIMSELF to be described in terms *infinitely beneath* him, and which require our watchfulness and pious care, lest we take up with conceptions far remote from the spirituality of the Divine Nature, and the purity of christian worship; MUCH MORE may it be regarded as consonant with the honour of his word, that its references to *natural objects* should be, in the character of thought and expression, *such as comported with the knowledge of the age in which they were delivered.**

* No doubt this principle has been often thought of, and happily employed in theological discussions; as by Archbishop King, the German divine Seiler, Mr. John Sheppard, and probably others. Whether it has been distinctly applied to the interpretation of the Bible, in relation to the objects of natural science, by any writers in particular, I am not able to say. I am aware of but two distinguished authors who have expressly pointed it out: and, as they only indicate it in general terms, the effort in this lecture to pursue it into its details, and to shew its application as a shield to scientific investigations, against the misconceptions and alarms of some well-intentioned men, will not, I trust, be held superfluous. The two authors alluded to, are John George Rosenmüller, in a book published more than sixty years ago, and from which the relevant extracts are given in the Appendix, Supplementary Note P; and my honoured friend, Professor Sedgwick, in his Discourse on the studies of Cambridge:—A "source of error, on physical questions, has been a mistake respecting the import of certain scripture-phrases. These writings deal not in logical distinctions or rigid definitions. They were addressed to the heart and understanding in popular forms of speech, such as men could readily comprehend. When they describe the Almighty as a being capable of jealousy, love, anger, repentance, and other like passions, they use a language accommodated to our

Again: the completed manifestations of the Divine Will in the New Testament raise us to a justness and purity of conception concerning "the things of God," far superior to that which the ministrations of Moses and the prophets could supply. The one was obscure, tinctured with the spirit of bondage, only a preparatory and temporary system: but the other is the "ministration of righteousness," in comparison with which the former "had no glory."* We stand therefore upon safe ground, and are fully warranted by divine authority to *translate* the language of the Old Testament upon physical subjects, into such modern expressions, as shall be *agreeable to the reality* of the things spoken of.

PART II.

Upon the principle which has been explained, I now propose to the impartial judgment of Bible-scholars, that method of understanding the Mosaic account of the Creation and the Flood, which appears to me just and safe. The way is sufficiently cleared, and

wants and capacities, and God is put before us in the semblance of humanity." Page 147. Galileo must be added: see the next Note.

* 2 Cor. iii. 10, 11. *Second ed.* A passage of the man who was in scientific respects so wondrously in advance of his age, Galileo, is highly interesting, as shewing that he clearly understood and justly applied this principle of Bible-interpretation.

"I admit and maintain that the Holy Scripture can never depart from what is true, provided we take it in its true and germane sense: but no one will deny, that this often lies deep, and is a good deal removed from the bald signification of the words. If any one think that it is always to be understood according to the letter, he will not only run into error, but he will impute to Holy Scripture numerous contradictions, propositions palpably untrue, even heresies and blasphemies. He would be obliged to ascribe to God feet, hands and eyes, and human properties and accidents both bodily and mental, such as anger, repentance, hatred, forgetfulness of the past, and ignorance of the future. Propositions of this kind have been in this manner expressed by the sacred writers, by the inspiration of the Holy Spirit, in order to accommodate divine truths to the capacity of the uncultivated and ignorant mass of mankind. It is therefore the duty of competent and diligent expositors to bring forth, in every instance, the true meaning; and to explain the ground and reason of their having been expressed in the words which are presented to us." *Novantiqua; alla Serenissima Madama la Gran Duchessa di Toscania, Madre;* p. 10, 11; printed in 1636, at Augusta Trebocca, perhaps Trevi in the duchy of Spoleto.

the principles explained and confirmed; so that little will be necessary in shewing the application to the cases before us.

I. With respect to the account of the CREATION.*

Gen. i. 1. "In the beginning, God created the heavens and the earth."

The phrase "the heavens and the earth," though not always used by the sacred writers in the full sense, is the most comprehensive that the Hebrew language affords, to designate the universe of dependent being; and, on account of the connexion, it requires to be so taken in this place. It thus corresponds to the expressions in the New Testament; "All things that are in the heavens and that are on the earth, the visible and the invisible; ——the all things."† This sublime sentence therefore stands, as an independent axiom,‡ at the head of the sacred volume, announcing that there was an epoch, a point in the flow of infinite duration, when the whole of the dependent world, or whatever portion of it first had existence, was *brought* into being; and that this commencement of being was not from preexistent materials, nor by fortune, chance or accident, nor through the skill of any finite agent, but absolutely and solely by the will, wisdom, and power of the ONE and ONLY GOD. It was a *creation*, in the proper sense; not a modelling or new-forming. The phrase, "In the beginning" is used several times in Scripture, to denote the commencement of whatever flow of time, or series of things, the subject spoken of requires. One of the primary doctrines of the New Testament is, "In the beginning was the WORD;" shewing that the Word was already in existence, at the point of time spoken of, did not then begin to be, and consequently must have existed in all prior time. But here the expression specifies an *action* as *taking place at this point* of time; an act of the Infinite Being. But WHEN that *beginning* was, when that act was put forth, it was not the design of revelation to inform us. Carry it back as far as we may, there is ETERNITY beyond it: and compared with that eternity, all finite duration sinks into a moment.

In the same manner we understand the recapitulation in chap. ii. 1—3; the commencement of the briefer narrative, in chap. ii. 4;

* Supplementary Note, Q.

† *Τὰ πάντα, τὰ ἐν τοῖς οὐρανοῖς καὶ τὰ ἐπὶ τῆς γῆς——τὰ πάντα.* *Sec. ed.* The equivalent phrases in common authors are *τὰ ὅλα*, and *τὸ πᾶν*.

‡ See pp. 120—126.

and the reason of the sabbath given in the fourth commandment, Exodus xx. 11. All that the Israelites could understand by "the heavens and the earth," all that they knew and all that it concerned them to know,* was "made," (adjusted, arranged, appropriated to new purposes, for so the word often signifies,) "in six days." There is just as much reason to interpret that commandment, as representing the Deity to "faint and be weary," in direct contradiction to other parts of the Bible,† as to maintain that it teaches the proper creation of the universe to have taken place immediately before the institution of the sabbath.

Here, I trust that, without assumption or captiousness, I may express regret that Dr. Buckland, in his Bridgewater Treatise, instead of relying on his own sound and clear judgment, obtained a note from one of his learned fellow Professors, which appears very obscure and quite nugatory. If it had any application to the matter at all, it would rather go to darken the evidence of a proper creation being here asserted, or declared in any other part of the Bible. Such aid was not needed.

Whether the original writer of this sacred archive was Moses, or whether he was placing at the head of his work, a composition of an earlier patriarch, the calm majesty and simplicity of the declaration, give, as a matter of internal evidence, the strong presumption that he spoke with authority; that he only repeated what the Omniscient Spirit had commanded him to say and write. The declaration is, in the New Testament, adduced as an object of *faith;* which implies a divine testimony.‡

What was the condition or constitution of the first created matter?—Certainly it falls within the province of General Physics to

* *Fourth ed.* "Whatever worthy and exalted apprehensions of the Author of nature, the infinite perfection of his attributes, or the extent and magnificence of his works, reason and philosophy may dictate and discover to us; to whatever important uses, God, in his infinite wisdom and power, may have destined the planets and the fixed stars (in the discovery of which we have no other light to direct us but bare conjectures, and arguments drawn from congruities,) Moses, by divine direction, has withdrawn our thoughts and speculations from all such far distant objects; not only because we have no visible relation to, nor perceptible connexion with, them, but rather (as we may with certainty and confidence affirm) because they do not measure *our* time, by either their real or apparent revolutions. God has created and ordained two great luminaries, the sun and moon, to be *unto us* 'for signs and for seasons, for days and years;' and to this motion only Moses, with great judgment and accuracy, confines his astronomy." *Scripture Chronology, by John Kennedy, Rector of Bradley, Derb.* 1751: p. 7.

† "Hast thou not known, hast thou not heard, that the everlasting God Jehovah, the Creator of the ends of the earth, fainteth not, neither is weary?" Is. xl. 28.

‡ Heb. xi. 3.

examine this question: and if the investigation be conducted in the true spirit of philosophy, which is modest, reverential, and cautious,—in a word, the spirit of genuine religion,—though it may not be demonstratively answered in the present life, yet valuable approximations may be made to it. The nebular hypothesis, ridiculed as it has been by persons whose ignorance cannot excuse their presumption, is regarded as in a very high degree probable by some of the finest and most christian minds.* If I may venture to utter my own impressions, I must profess it as the most reasonable supposition, and the correlate of the nebular theory, that God originally gave being to the primordial elements of things, the very small number of simple bodies, endowing each with its own wondrous properties. Then, that the action of those properties, in the ways which his wisdom ordained, and which we call

* If the reader be not already acquainted with the nature and the reasons of this doctrine, he owes himself a great duty. Let him consult Whewell's *Bridgewater Treatise*, book ii. chap. vii.: Mantell's *Wonders of Geology*, Lect. i. § 17, 18; and Nichol's *Architecture of the Heavens*, Letters vii. and viii. "The Nebular Hypothesis, in its relations to the Planetary System, may be termed *complete;* it comprehends its *beginnings*, establishes those elements on which its duration depends, and exhibits the causes and mode of its ultimate *transition* into a novel form.——Surely the vision of these unfathomable changes, of the solemn march of these majestic heavens from phase to phase, obediently fulfilling their awful destiny, will be lost on the heart of the adorer, unless—it swells with that humility which is the best homage to the SUPREME!—Between us and the HIGHEST there is still vastness and mystery.—To take wing beyond terrestrial precincts, perhaps, is not wholly forbidden, provided we go with unsandaled feet, as if on holy ground.—— An order hanging tremblingly over nothingness, and of which every constituent—fails not to beseech incessantly for a substance and substratum, in the idea of ONE WHO LIVETH FOR EVER!" Nichol.

Fourth ed. These objects wear the appearance of luminous masses, in various degrees of brilliance and obscurity, of different and what might be called capricious shapes, but which, however irregular in our view, undergo no perceptible change of figure. They are very numerous. Of most of them, the magnitude far exceeds that of our whole solar system. See Sir John Herschel's Astronomy; p. 401-7. Many of them he had scarcely ever a doubt, would be resolved into constellations, clusters, or groups of stars, if a sufficient telescopic power could be obtained. This anticipation has been realized by the Earl of Rosse, in the use of his matchless telescope. He has resolved several of these objects, upon which he has given a short paper, with exact figures, in the *Philosophical Transactions* for 1844. A sufficiently favourable state of the atmosphere is so rare in our climate, as to forbid our hoping for a rapid progress of those observations. Some persons have hastened to the conclusion that all the so-called nebulosities are of the same character, groups of stars: and that, of course, the nebular theory is exploded. But this is a premature judgment: we cannot say that the induction has been carried out far enough. Lord Rosse observes that, though, "as has always been the case, an increase of instrumental power has added to the number of the clusters, at the expense of the nebulæ properly so called; still it would be very unsafe to conclude that such will always be the case, and thence to draw the obvious inference that all nebulosity is but the glare of stars too remote to be separated by the utmost power of our instruments."

laws, produced, and is still producing, all the forms and changes of organic and inorganic natures; and that the series is by HIM destined to proceed, in combinations and multiplications ever new, without limit of space or end of duration, to the unutterable admiration and joy of all holy creatures, and to the eternal display of His glory "who fixed the wondrous frame."

Ver. 2. "And the earth was without form and void, and darkness was upon the face of the deep."

The first inquiry here is, What relation does this paragraph bear to the preceding? Is it the relation of close connexion, and immediate sequence; or does it only express posteriority, without defining the separating interval? My conviction is, not the former, but the latter.

The question will be answered by attending to the connecting particle. As it is rendered in our Version, it naturally excites the idea of immediate sequence. But a few words will shew that this would be an unwarranted inference from the expression in the original. This prefixed conjunction is the general connecting particle of the language; but the *mode* of connexion may be extremely various, and is always to be ascertained by a consideration of the circumstances in every case. It may be copulative, or disjunctive, or adversative; or it may express a mere annexation to a former topic of discourse, the connexion being only that of the subject matter, or the continuation of the composition. This continuative use forms one of the most marked peculiarities of the Hebrew idiom; and it comprehends every variety of mode in which one train of sentiment may be appended to another.* As this prefix is most usually rendered *and*, in our Version, (though frequently by other conjunctions,) the English reader has it in his power to observe the variety in the shades of meaning, and the differing grounds upon which it connects sentiments and expressions. The two sentences are thus rendered by a cautious and judicious critic, the late Dr. Dathe of Leipzig: "In the beginning God created the heaven and the earth. But afterwards the earth became waste and desolate."†

* It introduces the series of history, commencing at Numb. xx. 1; which immediately follows the preceding narrative, from which it is chronologically separated by an interval of thirty-eight years: yet that interval is not indicated by any words; it is left to be made out by the research of the reader. [It often commences an entirely new subject, and even a new composition.]

† See Supplementary Notes, R. and S.

A most important subject of our inquiry is the genuine meaning of the word which we render *earth;* and which, in passing, it may be remarked has an etymological affinity with the words of the same signification in all the Teutonic languages, to which class ours belongs, the ancient Persian, those allied to the Hebrew, and the Sanscrit. I assure my friends that I have not spared time and pains in pursuing this inquiry; and the result I will briefly give. The most general sense of the word is, the portion of the universe which the Supreme Lord has assigned for the habitation of mankind. When it is conjoined with "the heavens," it denotes the entire created world: but it is evident of itself, that the practical understanding of the phrase would be in conformity with the ideas of the people who used it. Frequently it stands for the land of Palæstine; and indeed for any country or district that is mentioned or referred to in the connexion. Sometimes it denotes a mere plot of ground; and sometimes the soil, clay and sand, or any earthy matter. Often it is put, figuratively, for mankind, as the inhabitants of the world. Considering all the evidence of the case, I can find no reason against our regarding the word, subsequently to the first verse, and throughout the whole description of the six days, as designed to express *the part of our world which God was adapting for the dwelling of man and the animals connected with him.* Of the spheroidal figure of the earth, it is evident that the Hebrews had not the most distant conception. The passages which have been quoted, and many others, abundantly convince me that it never entered into the purpose of Revelation to teach men geographical facts, or any other kind of physical knowledge.

I must profess then my conviction that we are not obliged by the terms made use of, to extend the narrative of the six days to a wider application than this; *a description, in expressions adapted to the ideas and capacities of mankind in the earliest ages, of a series of operations, by which the Being of omnipotent wisdom and goodness adjusted and furnished the earth generally,** but, as the particular subject under consideration here, a PORTION *of its surface, for most glorious purposes; in which a newly formed crea-*

* "Geology, therefore, in expounding the former condition of the globe, convinces us that every variation of its surface has been but a step towards the accomplishment of one great end; whilst all such revolutions are commemorated by monuments which, revealing the [proximate] cause and object of each change, compel us to conclude that the Earth can alone have been fashioned into a fit abode for Man by the ordinances of INFINITE WISDOM.' Murchison's *Silurian System;* vol. i. p. 576.

*ture should be the object of those manifestations of the authority and grace of the Most High, which shall to eternity shew forth his perfections above all other methods of their display.**

This portion of the earth I conceive to have been a part of Asia, lying between the Caucasian ridge, the Caspian Sea, and Tartary, on the north, the Persian and Indian Seas on the south, and the high mountain ridges which run at considerable distances, on the eastern and the western flank. I venture to think that man, as first created, and for many ages afterwards, did not extend his race beyond these limits; and therefore had no connexion with the extreme east, the Indian and Pacific clusters of islands, Africa, Europe, and America; in which regions we have ocular demonstration that animal and vegetable creatures had existed, to a vast amount, uninterruptedly, through periods past, of indescribable duration.

This region was first, by atmospheric and geological causes of previous operation under the will of the Almighty, brought into a condition of superficial ruin, or some kind of general disorder. With reverence I propose the supposition, that this state was produced by the subsidence of the region, of which the immediate cause might be the same that we know has often wrought a similar effect in various districts upon the earth's surface; namely, that which is probably the cause of earthquakes, a movement, (which may be in all the degrees of intensity,) of the igneous fluid mass below. Extreme darkness has been often known to accompany such phenomena. This is the unforced meaning of the two words rendered "without form and void." Those words (*tohu vabohu*) are elsewhere in the Hebrew Bible used to describe ruined cities, wild wastes of desert-land, and figuratively any thing that is *empty*, *unsubstantial*, or *useless*.

The sacred record presents to us the district described as overflowed with water, and its atmosphere so turbid that extreme gloominess prevailed. "Darkness was upon the face of the deep," the "waters" mentioned just before. Both this deluge, from the flowing in of a sea or rivers, and the darkness, would be the effect of an extensive subsidence. The Hebrew word does not necessarily mean the absolute privation of light: it is used in relation to various circumstances of partial darkness: and we know that con-

* One of those separate districts, or centres of creation, the certainty of which we have shewn in Lect. II. and III.

ditions of the atmosphere have locally happened, in ancient and in recent times, in which the noon-day has become dark as an ordinary night. The Divine power acted through the laws of gravity and molecular attraction; and, where requisite, in an immediate, extraordinary, or miraculous manner. The atmosphere over the region became so far cleared as to be pervious to light, though not yet perfectly transparent. In this process, the watery vapour collected into floating masses, the clouds; which, as we have seen, the ancient Hebrews expressed by the phrase "waters above the firmament." Elevations of land took place, by upheaving igneous force; and consequently the waters flowed into the lower parts, producing lakes, and probably the Caspian Sea, which manifestly belonged to the very region. The elevated land was now clothed with vegetation instantly created.* By the fourth day, the atmosphere over this district had become pellucid; and, had there been a human eye to have beheld, the brightness of the sun would have been seen, and the other heavenly bodies after the sun was set. Animals were produced by immediate creation, in this succession;† the inhabitants of the waters, birds, and land-

* Gen. i. 11, 12. The enumeration of vegetable kinds here given is both an illustrative example of the earliest botanical distribution, and a confirmation of our *principle* of interpretation, that the language has throughout a simple reference to the wants and conveniences of men. The vegetation intended to be included in this primeval arrangement is put under three descriptions; (1.) grasses, food for cattle; (2.) herbs, for human use, probably referring chiefly to grain and leguminous plants; (3.) trees producing edible fruit: all considered merely in the light of utility to mankind. Of timber-trees and thousands of other important genera, there is no hint. From just analogy we infer, that the first individuals of every other species were produced by an act of immediate creation; but a body of evidence convinces us that these productions took place, respectively at the points of divergence, or centres, of the different botanical districts. The language of the text expresses a creation of these vegetables in a state of maturity, that they might be ready for the immediate use of the human pair and the small number of land-animals formed for the enjoyment of this region. Those who contend for an immediate creation of all the mineral strata with all their contents, precisely as they are (—see Mr. Mellor Brown's positions, page 128 of this volume,—) have sometimes brought forward this question, as including for them a triumphant argument. If the exogenous trees were created in a state of maturity, must they not have had the concentric layers around their pith, indicating, what in all future cases would be years of growth, and which, in order to effect the perfect maturity supposed, would in many instances be numerous?—The answer is at hand; that all the exigencies of the case are satisfied by the condition of trees in an early stage, before the first layers can be distinguished. Serviceable leaves, fruits, and seeds, are produced within that period. Besides, we do not suppose that all vegetable species were thus produced, but only such as were adapted to the climate and requisite for the immediate purpose.

† *Fourth ed.* Combining all the intimations that we can collect, I venture to think that the Mosaic description in this part extends not to all animal and vegetable species,

animals; all in the full vigour of their natures. No mention is made of the thousands of tribes of insects, molluscous creatures, and animalcules; whose number, we know, transcends calculation. It is generally assumed by commentators that they are included in "the things that creep." But this very phrase supplies an illustration of the scripture-style, as condescending to the limited knowledge and the simple associations of comparatively uncultivated men.* Last of all, God formed his noblest earthly creature: "In the image of God created HE him," in the command of physical faculties, the possession of intellect, a dominion over the lower creation, and the noblest enjoyment of all, the image of the divine holiness.†

No rational objection can lie against the statement, that the Creator was pleased to distribute these works through the space of six natural days; instead of effecting the whole by an instantaneous volition. It is sufficient for us to know that Infinite Wisdom chose this method of proceeding: we are sure then that it was *the best*. But we may very reasonably suppose that the gradual character of the process furnished valuable instruction to

but to those only which would be *suitable* to the region under its various conditions, would have a beneficial *connexion* with man, and would, by their forms, habits, and instincts, be *subject* to his dominion. Chap. i. 26, 28.

* *Sec. ed.* In this single verse, the 20th, are several striking illustrations of the principle of interpretation for which I am pleading. It is literally—"And God said, Let the waters breed [*propullascere*, *cause to swarm*, *wimmeln*,] a brood, animated being, and flying [animal which] shall fly over the earth upon the face of the firmament of the heavens." The literal meaning would be that all the smaller kinds of land-animals and birds, had their origin under the waters. In verse 24 it is said of the larger quadrupeds that "the earth brought them forth:" as if they had been created underground, and were then protruded, as many molluscous animals and worms come up to the surface of the mud in which they live. But the plain sense is given in v. 25, where it is said that "God *made*" the land-animals; the words merely expressing that Divine power gave them existence; and we cannot indulge a doubt, but that they were brought into being in the conditions for which their conformation fitted them, land-animals on the dry ground, fishes and other inhabitants of rivers, lakes, and seas, in such waters as they were adapted to. But those expressions were the phrase of the time; and the kernel of truth which they inclose is, that animal and vegetable bodies are organized out of the very materials which constitute water and the commonest minerals. Jarchi's annotation upon verse 20, is curious: "Every living thing which does not raise itself much above the ground is called *sheretz* (creeping thing.) Under the winged creatures, flies; under the impure [creepers] ants, beetles, and worms; under the other creatures, weasels, mice, snails and the like; as also all fishes."

† It will, I trust, conduce to the illustration and establishment of the sentiments here so briefly sketched, and other parts of the general subject, to insert in the Appendix a Letter published some time ago in a periodical work, and occasioned by a Review of Dr. Buckland's Bridgewater Treatise. Supplementary Note, S.

superior creatures, and filled them with devout rapture; "when the morning-stars sang together, and all the sons of God shouted for joy." Nor can we be insensible to the lessons to which the Scriptures apply this part of the counsels of Jehovah, for the religious, and not overlooking the physical, benefit of mankind in all following time.

A consideration, which not merely justifies but renders necessary the interpretation here proposed, arises from the incongruity, and in fact reciprocal ruin, which would have taken place if all plants and animals had been created at the same epoch. Many plants could not have lived, unless time had been given for them to establish themselves, before the introduction of other species into the contiguous soil. Provision also needed to be made for each kind of animal, before it was brought forth to occupy its destined place. Single pairs of each would all have perished in a very short time, some being immediately consumed, and others then dying for want. Take the example of the inhabitants of the waters, fresh or salt. They are almost all carnivorous; and each individual requires, for but a day's sustenance, vast multitudes of the smaller kinds, we must say countless myriads, if we consider the visible insects and the invisible animalcules which constitute the food of many species. In like manner, with regard to reptiles, birds, and land-animals, it was necessary that those species in both the vegetable and the animal kingdoms, on which other animals must have depended for their support, should have been in existence a time sufficient to ensure a multiplication adequate to two purposes; a provision for the unfailing supply of the feeding creatures, and a redundancy sufficient to preserve and adequately increase the stock. It follows that the creation of all species, both vegetable and animal, must have been gradual, and with intervals adjusted by unerring benevolence and wisdom. Therefore the scene of the six days' operations, which I have endeavoured to shew was only one of those districts which in different periods were centres of creation, could not but be very limited.*

The condescending principle of the narrative is manifested, in a striking manner by the description of the fourth day. The sun is mentioned as the *greatest* luminary, the moon as the *next* in

* See a striking passage of Mr. Lyell, illustrating this connexion of things dependent on each other; *Princip.* B. iii. ch. viii. vol. iii. p. 166.

magnitude and importance, and the other shining orbs are grouped together as if they formed, even when all combined, the *least* object of consideration. The heavenly bodies are represented, not as being at that time *created*, (for that word, which occurs in verses 1 and 27, is not the word used here,) but "made," *constituted* or *appointed*, to be "luminaries," for such is the meaning of the word used: and their design is specified with an exactitude very observable: to afford light, and to furnish standards for the divisions of time, the operations of agriculture, and religious or other social observances. Had it been the purpose of revelation, to give a view of creation according to the physical reality, can we imagine that no reference would have been made to superior creatures, of whom the subsequent Scriptures say so much, under an appellative which designates only their work and office,—angels? Or that no mention would occur of the planets, and their satellites, as distinct from the fixed stars? And that all the notice taken of the astral system would lie in two words,—"and the stars?"—If not our earth merely, but the entire solar system, were to be this instant blotted out of existence, it would be no more missed in the aspect of the universe,—EXCEPT TO THE GLORIOUS CREATOR'S EYE,—than a grain of sand blown away from the sea-shore! Yet it is most evident that any person not acquainted with the true system of the world, would, after his most careful study of this portion of the Bible, rest in the conclusions, that our earth is, not in moral importance only, but in physical magnitude, by far the greatest of the Creator's works; and that the entire furniture of the heavens is solely a provision for our convenience and comfort.*

* It is also evident that the completion of Revelation, by the Christian Scriptures, did not include any purpose of teaching the topics of natural knowledge, or correcting the current opinions of the ancients upon this class of subjects. Our Lord himself did not disdain to speak in the common style and according to the opinions of those among whom he lived, when the philosophy of germination and vegetable growth were unknown, and a spontaneous (αὐτομάτη) power of production was attributed to the soil: Mark iv. 27, 28. And the enumeration of the heavenly bodies in Cor. xv. 41, proceeds upon the position, the same as in Gen. i. 16. that the sun is the greatest of all, the moon the next, and the stars taken together compose but the third degree. Would men impartially consider *what* they are demanding, when they claim that the language of Scripture should be an anticipation of modern philosophical discovery, they would see that to insist upon those demands is throwing the evidence of revelation under the feet of infidels. The grand design, above all others in excellence and glory, is thus declared; "These things are written, that ye may believe that Jesus is the Christ, the Son of God; and that, believing, ye may have life through his name."

It is a further evidence that the style of this primitive document was framed in conformity to the phraseology of simple men in unpolished times, that the successive processes are described in a child-like conversation form. "God said, Let there be light;——let there be a firmament;——let the earth bring forth;——let us make man:" the author using in each instance the same formula, first, an introduction of the matter, and then narrating the effect. Now is there a man who seriously believes that the Infinite Spirit exercised vocal organs, the supposition of which would imply a corporeal structure; or that he willed the effect of voice without those organs, creating the impulses upon an elastic medium which, had there been an animal ear to have received the impression, would have duly impinged upon it and produced the effect of articulate words; as "God spake all the words of the law" from the top of Sinai, so as to be heard and understood by a million and a half of people? To my judgment, this circumstance carries with it the force of demonstration.

The same style is shewn in the second and the subsequent narratives.

"The Lord God formed man of the dust of the ground, and breathed into his nostrils the breath of life." To the men of primitive time this statement would be sufficient; and they would probably form a conception of some kind of moulding as in pottery, one of the earliest arts; which indeed we actually find in the Grecian fable of Prometheus: and that, into this mechanical formation the powers of life were infused, as they are indicated by respiration. The style of the Scriptures abundantly shews that the Hebrews derived their conception of the intellectual principle in man, from the phenomena of respiration. So far only could the men of the first ages proceed: but we are enabled to develope, out of this little statement, one of the most interesting facts in physiology, and which could not have been known till the chemistry of our own days was, by God's benignant providence, bestowed upon men. By the Hebrew term (*aphar*) rendered *dust*, is signified the general soil with which men were always familiar; the mingled sand, clay, and lime. Now the fact is, that the human body, as that of all other animals, is composed of the same substances as those which constitute large and essential parts of the mineral kingdom; nitrogen, oxygen, carbon, and hydrogen; potash, soda, phosphorus, sulphur, lime, and iron. Thus does the most accurate science confirm the declarations of Scripture, if we only take care to *understand them rightly.*

Again; "The Lord God said, It is not good that the man should be alone; I will make him a help, meet for him." In the fact itself there is no difficulty; but it is the mode of introduction upon which we are remarking. The statement of the fact has been cavilled at by inconsiderate men. But I would ask any person of reflection and feeling, whether the method described of bringing the female man (*isha, vira, hommesse, männin,*) into being, is not as wise and benign as it is simple? The first female must have been the subject of an immediate creation, in some way: and can imagination frame a mode of origin so well adapted to endear her to her conjugate, as that the creative power should form her out of his actual bodily substance? Under the dress of a child-like narrative, we discover a proceeding of exquisite wisdom and effective tenderness.*

II. We proceed now to inquire what solution the Holy Scriptures afford of that which to many appears a difficulty not only formidable but insuperable; the dominion of PAIN AND DEATH over the animal creation, in all periods of its existence.†

* Upon the genius and character of the initial Mosaic records, I *earnestly solicit* my reader to give his attention to the beautiful and eloquent Address of the Rev. William Vernon Harcourt, to the British Association, at its meeting in Birmingham, Aug. 26, 1839. It is excellently reported in the Athenæum for Aug. 31; and has since been published authentically in the eighth Volume of the Reports of the Association. With all respect for opponents, I cannot but say that this Address and the many other labours in science, especially Geology and its alliances, by which that amiable and accomplished man has distinguished himself, form a mighty shield of defence against the efforts to disparage Geology, which some estimable clergymen and others mentioned in former parts of this volume have unhappily put forth. *Sec. ed.* Yet with the freedom which I am sure that he will not only permit, but encourage, I shall offer a remark on a part of his Address, at the close of the Supplementary Note R, upon Professor Powell's Solution of these difficulties. The following passage, from one of Dr. Chalmers's earliest works, may calm the apprehensions of some pious persons. They sufficiently shew that, in the judgment of that accomplished man, a negative answer to his questions would by no means involve any irreverence to the authority of the Scriptures. "Does Moses ever say that, when God created the heavens and the earth, he did more at the time alluded to than transform them out of previously existing materials? Or does he ever say, that there was not an interval of many ages betwixt the first act of creation, described in the first verse of the Book of Genesis, and said to have been performed at the *beginning*, and those more detailed operations, the account of which commences at the second verse, and which are described to us as having been performed in so many days? Or finally, does he ever make us to understand that the genealogies of man went any further than to fix the antiquity of the species, and of consequence that they left the antiquity of the globe a free subject for the speculations of philosophers?" *Evid. and Auth. of the Christian Revel.* p. 204.

† See an excellent work of christian philosophy, which happily unites free and power-

The nature of this difficulty was stated in Lecture III. and facts were detailed, both in the disclosures of geological investigation and in the present condition of animated nature, which compel us to admit that production and growth in all organized beings have their correlates in decay and dissolution.

But the general opinion has been that, before our first parents fell from innocence and happiness, death and its harbingers had no place in the inferior animal creation. To maintain consistency, it ought further to have been affirmed that the vegetable kingdom was also preserved from decay, withering, and dying. But men have been probably withheld from setting up such a theory, by consideration of the manifest absurdities into which it would have led its supporters; and by the belief that plants, though possessing an irritability to which it is difficult to refuse the idea of some kind of sensitiveness, yet appear not to have any consciousness or intellectual faculties.

Our first inquiry most naturally should be, whether we find any information, direct or indirect, in the original document of inspiration. I think that we do; not indeed directly, but indirectly, and by such an implication as is equal to a formal assertion. The constitution of animated beings, founded upon the divine will, is expressed in the words, "Be fruitful, and multiply." This involves the preservation of species, but a succession of individuals; which would necessarily imply a departure of precedent individuals. The law of organization, from the embryo formation to the animal maturity, is carried on in the way of a continual separation of particles and their replacement by new ones which the

ful reasoning, with the spirit of reverential piety, *Moral Agency and Man as a Moral Agent;* by William Mac Combie: London, 1842. In Part ii. Section iii. this subject is carefully investigated.—"These astonishing disclosures [—those of Geology,—] open to us an entirely new view of the constitution of the universe: and in casting about for a solution of the (as it seems to our notions) awful and anomalous fact of the universal prevalence of suffering and death, the idea presents itself, that trial and pain may be indispensable to the developement of mind, as we have every reason to believe they are in every system of moral agency. It has been generally assumed, but unphilosophically, we think, and *certainly without any authority from Scripture,* that the original state of man must have been one of unmingled enjoyment; and preachers and poets have strained their imaginations and exhausted nature, for images to picture its felicity.——— We are not entitled to pronounce that the most anomalous of all the modes of suffering which come under our view, that of the lower animals, is to them an evil; seeing we know not how far it may contribute to enhance their enjoyment; and are ignorant whether they may not have a future destination, in regard to which it may be subserving the most important purposes."

nutritive process incessantly furnishes. To this process, impassable limits are set, by the most certain laws of the Creator's ordination; those of gravity and chemical action. To suppose that those laws should be abrogated, or what would amount to the same thing, be perpetually suspended, would involve a contradiction; it would be abolishing the very essential condition of organized existence. When a certain point was reached, separation, changed combination, and dissolution of the molecules, must take place; the rudiment and sure introducer of death.

Were it not so, were animated beings to increase and multiply without the departure of the preceding generations, they would, at no immense distance of time, go beyond the provision of nutritive support, and the limits of appropriate habitation: the land, the air, and the waters, would be filled; food would fail, and death with aggravated suffering would be the infallible consequence. This terrible consummation would the more speedily ensue, as, by the supposition made, the only means of nutrition would lie in vegetable matter.

The threatening of death, upon a violation of the easy test of obedience, seems very clearly to imply, that the subjects of this law had a knowledge of *what* death was; otherwise they could not have known what the threatening meant. The idea of their having had set before them, as the penalty of violating the law, an unknown and undefined suffering, does not seem congruous to the wisdom and dignity of legislation.

It would next be proper to ascertain whether there are any passages of Scripture which affirm, or imply, that the animals inferior to man were created in a state not liable to death. This, if supposed, would involve the necessity of all being herbivorous; and further, that there were no minute and even invisible animals, inhabiting the leaves and fruits of plants, and which the feeders on vegetables must kill by myriads. I must own that I know of no such passage.

If, however, any should contend that an insuperable difficulty lies in the occurrence of pain and death to animals, irrespectively of moral evil, I humbly think that they ought to satisfy themselves with the spirit and principle of our Lord's reply to a not dissimilar question; "His disciples asked him, Master, who did sin, this man or his parents, that he was born blind? Jesus answered, Neither hath this man sinned, nor his parents; but [this was appointed] that the works of God should be manifested in him."*

It is indeed an essential part of revealed truth that, "by one man, sin entered into the world, and death by sin;" and that thus "by man came death."† But it appears to me a fair interpretation of these passages, and a full admission of the doctrine concerning death as the penalty of sin, to consider them as declaring that in this manner death acquired dominion over the first man and his posterity; that is, the human race universally. The entire view of the case leads us to believe that, in the state of pristine purity, the bodily constitution of man was exempted from the law of progress towards dissolution which belonged to the inferior animals. It must have been maintained in that distinguished peculiarity, by means to us unknown: and it would seem probable that, had not man fallen by transgression, he and each of his posterity would, after faithfully sustaining an individual probation, have passed through a change without dying, and have been exalted to a more perfect state of existence.

In addition to these considerations, it ought to be especially recollected, that the anatomical structure of the larger part of animal species presents demonstration that they were created to live upon animal food.‡ There are those who have affirmed the contrary, and have supposed that, by persevering practice, lions, and wolves, and all carnivorous creatures might be brought to live on a vegetable diet. Every physiologist must smile at this monstrous absurdity. A few species indeed are omnivorous; and this circumstance has misled some persons. Cases also sometimes occur, in which the violation of natural habits has been imposed upon domesticated animals, by artificial means; but the healthy condition is sacrificed, and the effect is not permanent. It follows, that those predictions of the peace and happiness of the Messiah's

* John ix. 2, 3. † Rom. v. 12. 1 Cor. xv. 21.

‡ *Fourth ed.* "Of any organized being," each part taken separately, indicates and gives the key to a knowledge of all the rest. Thus, if the *stomach* of an animal is so organized as only to digest fresh animal food, its *jaws* must also be so contrived as to devour such prey; its *claws*, to seize and tear it; its *teeth*, to cut and divide it; the whole structure of its *locomotive organs*, to pursue and obtain it; its *organs of sense*, to perceive it from afar; and nature must even have placed in its *brain* the necessary instinct to enable it to conceal itself and to bring its victim within its toils. *Geology, Introductory, Descriptive, and Practical;* by Prof. Ansted: 1844, p. 74. The law of nature stated in the first sentence of this citation comprehends every order of corporeal animated creatures, and is demonstrated in the structure and the habits of every species.

reign, which picture the ferocious and venomous animals as becoming herbivorous and harmless, must be understood, as they are by christian expositors generally, as beautiful poetry, expressing the moral influence of the gospel.*

III. In the fourth and fifth of these lectures, several facts were brought forwards, tending to place the natural history of the earth in a position of variance with the generally received belief concerning the Deluge, which is so important a part of the scriptural history of the human race. As I cannot expect that those facts can be distinctly recollected, it will be proper to recapitulate them in the briefest manner consistent with making them intelligible.

That enumeration brought before us the following statements: that, through the whole process of stratification, from the most ancient to the latest, the mineral character of each stratum proves the existence of contemporaneous dry land, as well as of depressed areas filled with water; that the indubitable relics of once animated creatures, in a great variety of species, from the earlier formations to the latest, penetrate through one or more of the next superincumbent strata, so that there never occur contiguous beds of mineral deposit which fail to be connected, (if I may use the phrase, dovetailed,) with each other: giving the result that, from the unspeakably remote point of time in which vestiges of living nature first occur, there never was a period when life was extinct upon the surface of the globe; or, we might more properly say, when living creatures did not abundantly exist: that the vast masses of rolled pebbles and stones of all sizes which have been spread over large districts, especially of this northern hemisphere, belong, not to any one transient flood, but to different eras of time, at great respective distances; some of the earliest never having been overflowed by a succeeding flood, and each for itself indicating the action of water, in one direction, through very long periods of time, in contradistinction to the idea of a deluge so brief as that of Noah, enduring but little more than three hundred days: that the cones of cinder and other volcanic products, over a considerable district in the south of France, are accompanied by evidences of an antiquity reaching much further back than the date of Noah's deluge; and that these cones of loose and light materials have never been

* Upon this subject, I beg to refer to Dr. Buckland's recently published Sermon on *The Sentence of Death;* and to the Supplementary Note A of this volume.

exposed to the action of a rush or any even moderate force of water, or they would have been inevitably washed away. These geological facts stand thus powerfully in the way of admitting that there ever was a *universal* deluge. Some other circumstances also were briefly alluded to, belonging to other departments of natural science. One of these was the impossibility of either the vegetable or the animal creations having all proceeded from one spot as a centre of ancestry; but that the surface of the earth is distributed into several distinct regions, each of which has its appropriate and exclusive tenantry, both vegetable and animal. It was also remarked how utterly impossible it would be for the inhabitants of many of those regions to have migrated from various others, or even to exist in them, if by an instantaneous miracle they were transported thither. We adverted to the difficulty, arising from the quantity of water requisite to cover the entire globe and to overflow the highest mountains, which would be an addition to the present ocean of eight times its actual quantity. For both the production and the subsequent removal of this body of water, we can imagine no cause but the miraculous intervention of omnipotence; whereas the narrative in the Book of Genesis assigns two natural causes, raised to an extraordinary degree of action. Notice was also taken of the animals preserved with Noah in the ark; the number of existing species, so far exceeding what the commentators on the Bible have taken into their calculations; the very different kinds of receptacle which would be necessary, the amount of food, the necessity of ventilation and the cleaning out of the stables or dens; the provisions for reptiles and insects; the fact that some fish and shell animals cannot live in salt water, and others not in fresh. The difficulty also was mentioned, if we suppose that the resting-place of the ark was the Mount Ararat pointed out by tradition, of conceiving how the eight human persons and their accompanying animals could descend adown the precipitous cliffs; a difficulty which amounts to an impossibility, unless we call in the aid of divine power, operating in the way of miracle.

Another circumstance was adduced as proving that the Deluge of Noah was not absolutely universal: the existence of trees in the equatorial regions of Africa and of South America, which, by the known method of ascertaining the age of exogenous trees, are shewn to be of an antiquity which goes farther back than to the date of the Deluge. What was said in that lecture, and will be advanced in the Note on this subject,* renders it needless to add any more.

I may also remind my auditors that the opinion which ascribes to the Deluge, the vast amount and variety of animal and vegetable remains found in a fossil state, in all parts of the earth, is flagrantly inconsistent with a correct attention to the circumstances in which such remains occur.

From any of these considerations, the probability of a universal contemporaneous flood is, to say the least, rendered very small; but, their united force appears to me decisive of the negative to this question.

I cannot doubt but that some alarm and anxiety may be produced in the minds of many, by the hearing of these statements. They will be thought to be in direct contradiction to the sacred narrative: and we cannot justify to ourselves any twisting and wresting of that narrative in order to bring it into an apparent accordance with the doctrines of human philosophy. But let my friends dismiss their fears. The Author of nature and the Author of revelation is the same. He cannot be at variance with himself. The book of his works and the book of his word cannot be contradictory. On the one hand, we find certain appearances in the kingdoms of nature, which stand upon various and independent grounds of sensible proof; and, on the other hand, are declarations of Scripture seeming to be irreconcileable with those appearances, which are indeed ascertained facts. But we are sure that Truth is immutable; and that one truth can never contradict another. Different parts of its vast empire may and do lie far asunder, and the intermediate portions may be covered with more or less of obscurity; but they are under the same sceptre, and it is of itself and antecedently certain that the facts of nature and the laws that govern them are in perfect unison with every other part of the will of Him that made them. There are declarations of Scripture which seem thus to oppose facts, of which we have the same kind of sensible evidence that we have of the letters and words of the sacred volume; and which we understand by the same intellectual faculties by which we apprehend the sense of that volume. Now those appearances,—facts I must call them,—have been scruti-

* See Supplementary Note, L. But the reader will especially observe the addition to that Note in this [the third] edition.

nized with the utmost jealousy and rigour: and they stand impregnable; their evidence is made brighter by every assault. We must then turn to the other side of our research; we must admit the probability that we have not rightly interpreted those portions of Scripture. We must retrace our steps. Let us resort to this renewed examination in the great instance before us.

I. The expressions of universality, with regard to the extent of the deluge, are these. "The waters prevailed exceedingly upon the earth, and all the high hills that were under the whole heaven were covered."

To those who have studied the phraseology of Scripture, there is no rule of interpretation more certain than this, that *universal terms* are often used to signify only a *very large* amount in number or quantity. The following passages, taken chiefly from the writings of Moses, will serve as instances.—"And the famine was upon all the face of the earth:"* yet it is self-evident that only those countries are meant which lay within a practicable distance from Egypt, for the transport of so bulky an article as corn, carried, it is highly probable, on the backs of asses and camels.—"All the cattle of Egypt died;" yet the connexion shews that this referred to some only, though no doubt very many, for, in subsequent parts of the same chapter, the cattle of the king and people of Egypt are mentioned in a way which shews that there were still remaining sufficient to constitute a considerable part of the nation's property.†—"The hail smote every herb of the field, and brake every tree of the field;" but, a few days after, we find the devastation of the locusts thus described; "They did eat every herb of the land and all the fruit of the trees, which the hail had left."‡—"All the people brake off the golden ear-rings which were in their ears, and brought them unto Aaron:"§ meaning undoubtedly a large number of persons, but very far from being the whole, or even a majority, of the people; as we may reasonably infer from the circumstance that the stroke of punitive justice, for this act of idolatry, fell upon only three thousand persons, but the entire number of the Israelites at that time was a million and a half, and of them six hundred thousand were grown men trained to arms.—"This day will I begin to put the fear of thee and the dread of

* Gen. xli. 56, 57.
† Exod. ix. 6, 10, 19—22, 25; xiv. 26, 28.
‡ Ib. x. 5, 15.
§ Ib. xxxii. 3.

thee upon the face of the nations under all the heavens:"* yet this declaration respects only the nations of Canaan and those lying upon its frontier, all being within a very small geographical district. We likewise find the phrase, "under heaven," employed by the inspired writers to signify an extent of country, large indeed, but falling exceedingly short of a geographical universality: as, "I gave my heart to seek and search out by wisdom concerning all things that are done under heaven.——There were dwelling at Jerusalem, Jews, devout men, out of every nation under heaven." With this passage is combined a geographical enumeration, which points out the extent of country intended, as being from Italy to Persia, and from Egypt to the Black Sea: and thus a probable elucidation is given to the declaration of the apostle, that "the gospel was preached to every creature which is under heaven."†—"Ye shall be plucked from off the land whither thou goest to possess it, and the Lord shall scatter thee among all peoples, from one end of the earth even unto the other end of the earth:"‡ a prophetic description of the dispersion of the Jewish people, as the punishment of their apostasy from God and rejection of the Messiah, but no one can regard the expression as denoting a proper geographical universality.—"The fame of David went forth into all the lands [the plural of the word generally rendered *the earth*], and Jehovah put the fear of him upon all the nations."§ This expression cannot be taken as reaching beyond the range of Syria, Armenia, Mesopotamia, Arabia, and Egypt.—"And all the earth sought the presence of Solomon, to hear his wisdom."|| This cannot be reasonably understood of any kind of resort but that of embassies and complimentary visits, from sovereigns and states within such a distance, as might have appeared immense in those times, but which was small compared with even the then inhabited parts of the earth. The queen of Sheba was, we may think undoubtedly, the principal of these visitants. Our Lord himself condescended to use the style of the Jews, in saying of her, that "the queen of the south—came from the uttermost parts of the earth, to hear the wisdom of Solomon."¶ Yet her country was on either the Eastern or the Western side of the Arabian Gulf, about twelve or fourteen hundred miles south of

* Deut. ii. 25.
† Eccl. i. 13. Acts ii. 5. Col. i. 23.
‡ Deut. xxviii. 63, 64.
§ 1 Chron, xiv. 17.
|| 1 Kings x, 24.
¶ Matt. xii. 42.

Jerusalem; a mere trifle compared with distances familiar to us in our days.

Passages are numerous, in which the phrase "all the earth" signifies only the country of Palestine.* In a few places it denotes the Chaldean empire:† in one, that of Alexander.‡

From these instances of the scriptural idiom in the application of phraseology similar to that in the narrative concerning the flood, I humbly think that those terms do not oblige us to understand a literal universality; so that we are exonerated from some otherwise insuperable difficulties in Natural History and Geology.§ If so much of the earth was overflowed as was occupied by the human race, both the physical and the moral ends of that awful visitation were answered.

Some writers have taken great pains in calculating the numbers of mankind at the epoch of the deluge, and they have brought out an amount for the human population immensely larger than that which has subsisted in any succeeding period, down to the present time. But apart from other errors in the statistical principles upon which they have proceeded, they appear to have overlooked two elements of calculation. The first is the apparent paucity of births which not obscurely shews itself in the genealogical table (Gen. v. 3—28), almost all the history left to us of the period from Adam to Noah. We may not irreverently conjecture that, in addition to other reasons, especially the preservation of a correct tradition concerning the most important religious truths, one motive in the plan of Providence for the longevity of the antediluvian patriarchs was, to compensate by the length of individual lives, for the slowness of multiplication. The second consideration which those calculators have neglected, is the effect of moral depravity in diminishing the fecundity of the human species. There are facts in modern history which exemplify this principle. The rapid decrease of the population of the South Sea Islands, within little more than half a century, is a striking instance. Of such depopulation, there are two causes: the one, extreme licen-

* Deut. xxxiv. 1. Is. vii. 24; x. 14. Jer. i. 18; iv. 20; viii. 16; xii. 12; xl. 4. Zeph. i. 18; iii. 19. Zech. xiv. 10.

† Jer. li. 7, 25, 49. ‡ Dan. ii. 39.

§ Dr. George Young, though his ideas concerning the flood appear to my humble judgment to be very extravagant, feels the necessity of maintaining that "*all*, *every one*, *the whole*, and such like expressions, are very often used to denote *a great many*, or *a large proportion*." *Script. Geol.* p. 27.

tiousness; the other, tyrannous, anarchical, and murderous cruelty. That the latter state of mankind existed in the antediluvian period, is expressly recorded (chap. vi. 11): and the former is not without intimation (verses 2 and 4), as indeed from the too well known tendencies of corruption in society, it may be very certainly inferred. The consequences would be, that few children would be born; many would die of diseases, or of sheer neglect, or by actual murder; and the mutual destruction of grown persons would be very great. It is an instance in confirmation of this reasoning, that no children of Noah are mentioned till he was five hundred years old; and that, a century later, his three sons, each having a wife, had no children. Now we cannot but suppose that the family of Noah was, at least, among the most virtuous of those which then existed; and therefore was, upon the whole, more likely to have become numerous than the generality of others. From the whole, I humbly think it reasonable to infer, that the human population had not spread itself far from its original seat, the country of Eden; that its number was really small; and that it was in a course of rapid progress towards an extreme reduction, which would have issued in a not very distant extinction.

The difficulties also seem to be insuperable, with respect to the animals saved in the ark, on the supposition that every species had its representatives. But why may we not derive our explanation of this part of the statement, from the general rule of the Hebrew and Hebraistic diction, with respect to universal terms? A confirmation of the principle we may find in the description of Peter's emblematical vision, presenting to him, "all the four-footed animals of the earth, and the wild beasts, and the creeping things, and the birds of the heaven."* The design of this revelation was to convince him that the Mosaic distinction into clean and unclean was by the gospel abolished: therefore, a representation of some principal animals, under each of the two divisions, and those such as were well known to the apostle, would be all that was needed. To assume a literal universality would involve the idea of a crowding and compressing such as would destroy all distinctness. In the case of Noah, we may understand the animals preserved with him in the ark as having been those connected more or less with man, by domestication, and by other modes of

* Acts x. 12,—*πάντα τὰ τετράποδα* ——.

subserviency to his present and future welfare. This idea answers to the enumeration given, which only comprises the four descriptions;—"wild animals," such as we now call game, serviceable to man but not tamed;—"cattle," the larger domesticated mammifers, such as the ox, the camel, the horse, the ass, the sheep, and several species of the deer and goat genera;—"the creeping things," the smaller quadrupeds;—and "birds," the peaceable, useful, and pleasing kinds.*

But an important observation presses upon us. If, by the Ararat mentioned in Scripture, be understood the mountain of that name in Armenia, it would inevitably follow that a deluge capable of surmounting that, must have been, by the laws of the motion of fluids, universal with regard to the earth. Against that supposition, the impossibility of descent presents itself, as has been already mentioned. But St. Jerome says that the name Ararat was given generally to the mountains of Armenia: and Shuckford, a judicious writer, who lived long before geological studies were awakened, adduces reasons against the common opinion, and supports the idea of the ark's having grounded much farther to the East.† This therefore might be on a mountain, or a mountainous range, but not so high and precipitous as to preclude an easy descent into the lower and more cultivable grounds.

Let us now take the seat of the antediluvian population to have been in Western Asia, in which a large district, even in the present day, lies considerably below the level of the sea.‡ It must

* Gen. viii. 14.

† *Sacred and Proph. Hist. Connected;* vol. i. pp. 98—104; ed. 1731. A learned writer (but who, I have no knowledge or conjecture) in the Congregational Magazine for May, 1840, has urged other cogent reasons, geographical and historical, against the supposition that the Ararat, usually so called, was the resting-place of the ark.

"Paravay, in his work on the Origin of Arithmetical Figures and of Letters, Introd. p. 5, maintains the position that the ark rested in the western part of the country now called Thibet; and this opinion obtains strong confirmation from Gen. xi. 2. 'They journeyed from the east, and found a plain in the land of Shinar.' Fr. de Paula de Schrank, *Comment. in Genesin;* Sulzbach, 1835. The region thus pointed out is that of the vast Himmalayah chain, a very conceivable boundary on the east for the diluvial waters, and far beyond the probable extent of the then inhabited earth.

‡ The site of Mesopotamia and Persia, and part of Afghanistan and Turkestan, taken generally; the countries laid down in Lechner's Map of Central Asia [*Mittel-Asien*, so called in reference to the knowledge of the ancients;] Leipzig, 1823.

A more precise statement is desirable; and this I derive from the Preliminary Discourses to *Black's Atlas*, Edinburgh, 1840, p. 23; but corrected from Dr. von Schubert's own work (*Reise in das Morgenland, in d. J.* 1836, 1837; vol. iii. p. 87, Erlangen, 1839; a beautiful example of philosophical, tasteful, and christian travel.) "In the S.

not be forgotten that six weeks of continued rain would not give an amount of water forty times that which fell on the first or a subsequent day; for evaporation would be continually carrying up the water, to be condensed and to fall again: so that the same mass of water would return many times. If, then, in addition to the tremendous rain, we suppose an elevation of the bed of the Persian and Indian Seas, or a subsidence of the inhabited land toward the south, we shall have sufficient causes, in the hand of almighty justice, for submerging the district, covering its hills, and destroying all living beings within its limits, except those whom divine mercy preserved in the ark. The draining off of the waters would be effected, by a return of the bed of the sea to a lower level, or by the elevation of some tracts of land, which would leave channels and slopes for the larger part of the water to flow back into the Indian Ocean, while the lower part remained a great lake, or an inland sea, the Caspian.*

W. of Asia there are two remarkable regions, depressed *below the level of the sea.* The one of these comprises the basin of the Caspian Sea and a considerable tract of country to the N. and N. E., the depression of which amounts to 101-2 Russian feet. The other includes the Dead Sea and the valley of the river Jordan; but the exact amount of its depression has not been ascertained. Prof. von Schubert estimated (for his barometer had not sufficient height of tube) the Dead Sea to be 600 French feet (about 640 English,) and the sea of Tabaria (Tiberias, the Lake of Galilee,) by barometrical measurement, for here the instrument would serve, 535 Fr. (=570 Engl.) below the level of the Mediterranean; but M. Russeger estimates the Dead Sea, at its northern end, to be no less than 1319 French, or nearly 1400 English, feet below that level." However, it must be observed, that the result of numerous observations, estimates, and adjustments, by the fore-mentioned and other scientific travellers is to cast doubt upon the accuracy of the preceding statements of number; while the general fact is well established, a low position of the Lake of Galilee and the bed of the Jordan, and much lower still of the Dead Sea. See an elaborate paper on this subject from Poggendorf and Berghaus, in Jameson's *Edinburgh Journal;* July 1840.

It is now (1843) ascertained, by the trigonometrical survey of Lieutenant Symonds, that the Dead Sea is 1311 feet below the level of the Mediterranean. M. Berthou, from barometrical calculation, had stated it to be 1332.

* *Fourth ed.* This is not the only mode in which an elevation of a vast body of waters may be conceived as probable, and as adequate to the production of the effect. It is established by abundant evidence that, through a period geologically recent, a district lying immediately north of the primeval seat of mankind, was occupied by an inland sea, more than equal in extent to the existing Mediterranean. The shores and basin of this ancient sea are incontrovertibly determined by littoral and marine remains. It is also certain that repeated elevations and subsidences of the region still further to the north, have taken place. One such elevation, proceeding gradually for forty days, would throw southward such a body of water as would produce the effect described; and the cessation might leave the separate basins of the Aral, the Caspian, and the Euxine Seas, in a state to be brought to their present form by the progress of evaporation and drying.

I may now adduce citations from divines and sacred scholars whose eminence none will dispute, and who wrote without the least knowledge of geological arguments.

Few men possessed a more powerful understanding or a finer judgment than Bishop Stillingfleet. He makes the following remarks.

"I cannot see any urgent necessity from the Scripture, to assert that the Flood did spread itself over all the surface of the earth. That all mankind, those in the ark excepted, were destroyed by it, is most certain, according to the Scriptures.—The flood was universal *as to mankind:* but from thence follows no necessity at all of asserting the universality of it as to the globe of the earth, unless it be sufficiently proved that the whole earth was peopled before the Flood: which I despair of ever seeing proved. And what reason can there be to extend the Flood beyond the occasion of it, which was the corruption of mankind?——I grant, as far as the Flood extended, all these [the animals] were destroyed; but I see no reason to extend the destruction of these beyond that compass and space of the earth where men inhabited; because the punishment upon the beasts was occasioned by, and could not but be concomitant with, the destruction of mankind. But (the occasion of the Deluge being the sin of man, who was punished in the beasts that were destroyed for his sake, as well as in himself,) where the occasion was not, as where there were animals and no men, there seems no necessity of extending the flood thither."

The bishop further argues that the reason for "preserving living creatures in the ark," was that there might be a stock of the tame and domesticated animals that should be immediately "serviceable for the use of men after the flood: which was certainly the main thing looked at in the preservation of them in the ark, that men might have all of them ready for their use after the flood; which could not have been, had not the several kinds been preserved in the ark, although we suppose them not destroyed in all parts of the world."*

The eminent nonconformist divine, Matthew Poole, wrote as follows, in his Latin Synopsis of Critical Writers upon the Bible.

"It is not to be supposed that the entire globe of the earth was covered with water. Where was the need of overwhelming those

* *Origines Sacræ*, Book iii. chap. iv. ed. 1709, p. 337.

regions in which there were no human beings? It would be highly unreasonable to suppose that mankind had so increased, before the Deluge, as to have penetrated to all the corners of the earth. It is indeed not probable that they had extended themselves beyond the limits of Syria and Mesopotamia. Absurd it would be to affirm that the effects of the punishment inflicted upon men alone, applied to places in which there were no men. If then we should entertain the belief that not so much as the hundredth part of the globe was overspread with water, still the Deluge would be universal, because the extirpation took effect upon all the part of the world which was inhabited. If we take this ground, the difficulties which some have raised about the Deluge, fall away as inapplicable and mere cavils; and irreligious persons have no reason left them, for doubting of the truth of the Holy Scriptures."*

The same pious and learned author repeats the sentiment, in his English Annotations, published after his death. "Peradventure this flood might not be simply universal over the whole earth, but only over the habitable world, where either men or beasts lived; which was as much as either the meritorious cause of the flood, the sins of men; or the end of it, the destruction of all men and beasts; required."†

To the same effect, Le Clerc and the younger Rosenmüller might be quoted; but it cannot be necessary. Yet I may add that my hearers and readers will derive additional satisfaction from perusing the observations on this subject of Dr. Prichard, a man whose amiable and christian character adds a bright ornament to his scientific and philological eminence. He states the difficulties, and methods for removing them. But though he declines giving a decided opinion, the inclination of his judgment appears to be in favour of the limited locality of the deluge.‡

But, I almost hear the exclamation from a thousand tongues, What are you doing? Whither are you driving? Are you not

* Non putandum est totum terræ globum aquis tectum fuisse. Quid opus erat illas mergere terras ubi homines non erant? Stultum est putare ante diluvium homines ita multiplicatos fuisse ut omnes terræ angulos pervaserint, cum ne Syriæ quidem et Mesopotamiæ fines forsan excesserant. Absurdum autem est dicere, ubi nullæ hominum sedes, illic etiam viguisse effectus pœnæ solis hominibus inflictæ. Licet ergo credamus ne centesimam quidem orbis partem aquis fuisse obrutam, erit nihilominus diluvium universale, quia clades totum orbem habitatum oppressit. Sic si statuerimus, jam cessabunt ineptæ istæ et futiles quæstiones quas nonnulli de Diluvio moverunt, et simul im probis de Sacrarum Literarum veritate dubitandi omnis præripietur occasio." *Synops. in Gen.* vii. 19.

† On the same passage. Mr. Poole died in 1679.

‡ See his *Researches into the Physical History of Mankind;* vol. i. pp. 98—102.

trampling upon, not the inspiration only, but the veracity of the Holy Scriptures? Are you not representing the God of truth, speaking through the medium of his inspired servants, as uttering that which is not true? Let it be freely admitted that it is no part of the design of God, in giving a revelation of his moral will, to communicate lessons of physical philosophy; yet this does not involve the admission that, when the instruments of revelation advert to physical causes and operations, they should not speak according to *the reality* of things. A well informed and correct speaker, when he is talking freely about common affairs, and when nothing is farther from his mind than to be teaching history or geography, yet will not so express himself as to imply ignorance of historical or geographical facts. Surely we cannot think less of the inspired writers. "If Moses professes by divine inspiration to give an account of the manner in which the world was framed, he must describe the facts as they occurred."* This may seem an unanswerable objection; but will it stand before a fair examination? I think not; for two reasons.

1. It is impossible to deny that the Scripture does use language, even concerning the highest and most awful of objects, GOD and his perfections and operations, which we dare not say is *literally true*, or that it is according to the reality of the things spoken of. I entreat renewed attention to the evidence which I have adduced. Will any man deny, that the Scripture, in places innumerable, particularly in the earlier books, speaks of God as having the bodily form and members of a man, and the mental passions and imperfect affections of men? Or will any say that such descriptions and allusions are properly true; that they are according to the reality of things? Shall we, *can we*, believe that the Infinite, Eternal, and Unchangeable Being, comes and goes, walks and flies, smells, hears, and sees, and has heart and bowels, hands, arms, and feet? Or that he deliberates, inquires, suspects, fears, ascertains, grieves, repents, and is prevailed upon by importunity to repent again and resume a rejected purpose? Do not the same Scriptures furnish us amply with the proper exponents of those figurative, and, strictly speaking, degrading terms? Do they not, for example, tell us; "God is not a man, that he should lie; neither the son of man, that he should repent. Hath he said, and

* The excellent and amiable man, the Rev. Richard Watson, in his *Theological Institutes;* vol. i. p. 273.

shall he not do? Or hath he spoken, and shall he not make it good?——I am Jehovah: I change not."* What then will ye do, ye worthy men that make this objection? Must ye not admit that the language of inspiration is couched on the plan of the boldest figures? Such figures as, if we were not protected by this authority, we should not dare to employ? And do ye not always explain that language by stripping off the figurative coverings, and drawing forth the simple truth, which ye then express in some kind of abstract phrase, metaphysically more accurate, but far less mighty to impress the human mind?—You are convinced that this is *necessary;* and you do not for a moment admit that, in doing this, you derogate from the truth and inspiration of the Bible. Apply then your just methods of interpretation to this case: I ask no more. Mr. Romaine lays down the principle, in saying, "The Holy Spirit does not reveal God to us as he is in himself, but as he stands related to us:" and this knowledge is best conveyed to mankind in the style of condescension to our own low estate of acts and habits, feelings and language.

If the view of the range of inspiration, that *its proper and sole reference is to religious subjects,* be rejected, it will inevitably follow that we must impute error to the Spirit of God.——Abhorred be the thought!——We must suppose to be physically correct those declarations concerning the astral worlds, the phenomena of the atmosphere, and the human frame, which have been mentioned: we must regard the inferior creatures as "made to be taken and destroyed,"† in defiance of all our knowledge that the whole animal creation is formed for an immense variety of beneficent purposes, partly no doubt unknown to us, but in a very great measure manifest by the clearest and most beautiful proofs.

2. The Mosaic narrative is, manifestly and undeniably as we have seen, so expressed in that style of condescension, and particularly in the manner suited to the men of primeval times. Yet, when read and understood, as all language is required to be, by the conversion of what is figurative and idiomatical into plain diction, *it is a faithful description* of the facts that did occur, and the method and order of their occurrence.

I have now reached the point at which, from the beginning of

* Numb. xxiii. 19. Mal. iii. 6.

† 2 Pet. ii. 12. Not well rendered "natural brute beasts:" for the clause ἄλογα ζῶα, φυσικὰ, strictly signifies, *irrational animals, governed by natural instinct.*

these lectures, I have been aiming. I speak my own conviction, and I trust I have brought forwards sufficient evidence to support that conviction, that the alleged discrepance between the Holy Scriptures and the discoveries of scientific investigation, is not in reality, but in semblance only: in particular, that the Scriptures, fairly interpreted, are not adverse to a belief in an immeasurably high antiquity of the earth; in the reference of the six days' work to a part only of the earth's surface; in the position of several centres of creation, distinct from each other, on the surface of the globe; in the reign of death over the inferior animals, from the earliest existence of organized earthly beings; and in a limited extent of the deluge which swept away the remnant of a self-destroying race, saving one family, which "found grace in the eyes of the Lord."

I have not attempted to do this by affirming that the Scriptures teach the sciences; or that their language can be forced, by any grammatical or critical ingenuity, into a literal accordance with scientific truths: but by adducing abundant evidence to shew that the AUTHOR of revelation spoke to mankind in such language as they were accustomed to use, such as they could most readily understand, and such as must ever remain the most affecting and impressive to the human heart.

Let it also be observed, that the principle of interpretation here brought forwards is entirely independent of facts in Natural History, or doctrines of Geology or any other branch of Natural Science. If those facts be denied and those doctrines disapproved, still this mode of understanding the figurative language of Scripture will not be affected; it stands upon its own evidence, and cannot, I conceive, be overthrown.

It follows then, as a universal truth, that the Bible, faithfully interpreted, erects no bar against the most free and extensive investigation, the most comprehensive and searching induction. Let but the investigation be sufficient, and the induction honest. Let observation take its farthest flight; let experiment penetrate into all the recesses of nature; let the veil of ages be lifted up from all that has been hitherto unknown, if such a course were possible; ——religion need not fear, Christianity is secure, and true science will always pay homage to the Divine Creator and Sovereign, "of whom and through whom and to whom are all things; and unto whom be glory for ever."

LECTURE VIII.

ECCLESIASTES XII. 13. *Let us hear the conclusion of the whole matter: Fear God, and keep his commandments: for this is the whole* [*duty*] *of man.**

"THE whole of man:" instruction for his duty, direction in his difficulties, consolation in his sorrows, triumph in death, and the boundless bliss of knowledge and holiness to eternity. But the fear of God and the observance of his commandments are no servile and narrow habits of mind. The Scriptures abundantly shew that they comprehend, or by just deduction lead to, all that is true in knowledge and noble in feeling. "The High and Lofty One, who inhabiteth eternity," builds also his temple in "the contrite heart." He has made it our duty, and a part of the filial "fear" which we owe to him, that we should acquire all that we can of sound information concerning his perfections and his works. "He giveth to a man that is good in his sight, wisdom and knowledge and joy;" and it is laid down as one of the characters of the impious, that, "they regard not the works of the Lord, nor the operation of his hands."†

When the Committee of the Congregational Lecture did me the honour of the invitation to deliver the course of this year, I could not but feel grateful for the opportunity thus afforded, of making an attempt to rescue from misapprehension a branch of research into the works of God, which at the present time attracts the attention of men, beyond all former example; and of offering an humble contribution for advancing the influence of religion, as the rightful asssociate of all other knowledge.

It is incumbent upon me to state that, beyond a general appro-

* It will not be unwelcome to the serious reader to have this passage laid before him in a close translation. "The finishing lesson, the total, let us hear; Revere God, and keep his commandments: for this [concerns] every one of mankind."

† Eccl. ii. 26. Psa. xxviii. 5.

bation of the subject, the Committee is not answerable for any thing that has been advanced. The sentiments and arguments which have been submitted to you, rest upon the responsibility of the lecturer alone.

There are some remaining subjects respecting which I am desirous of obtaining the approbation of my indulgent auditors; especially of the young persons, who are the delight of our families and the hope of our churches;—"for ye are our glory and joy."

I. I congratulate you upon the increasing ATTENTION which is evidently paid to the objects of sensible SCIENCE. By the studies of Natural History, my young friends, you become acquainted with "the wondrous works of HIM that is excellent in knowledge;" and, by those of Natural Philosophy, you investigate the causes and results of the changes which you or others have observed in the objects noticed by your senses. This is a part, at least, of what the wise man describes as "applying the heart to know, and to search, and to seek out wisdom and the reason of things."* It is a subject for much thankfulness to the Author of all good, that so many of you have been furnished, by the affectionate liberality of your parents, with the means of laying a foundation for these acquisitions, and of commencing to build worthily upon that foundation. Yet those who have been thus favoured in a less degree ought, by no means, to be discouraged. It is an humiliating fact, that the class of persons which has enjoyed such opportunities in their most perfect form, is not universally found to make a correspondent improvement of them. On the other hand, the honours of science have been sustained, and its bounds enlarged, in the greater number of directions, and in superior degrees, by those who, nearly or altogether unaided, have risen to eminence by their own diligence and perseverance in the cultivation of talent.

The advice has been often and very properly given, that you should beware of satisfying yourselves with superficial acquirements. But this recommendation needs to be better understood than it sometimes is. A vicious superficialism is when self-fondness persuades a man, and urges him to endeavour to persuade others, that his knowledge is something great; that he has studied to an extent which he has not done, and has made attainments

* Eccl. viii. 25

which he has not made. Such affectation involves the guilt of falsehood; and it is sure to defeat its own end, and bring its merited punishment.

But there is a sense in which it must be said that most, even of cultivated minds, possess but superficial knowledge. It is one of our blessings, by God's kind providence, to live in a time when literature, science, and the arts are cultivated so assiduously; and their results are proclaimed so widely; that the necessity of acquiring general knowledge is strongly impressed, and the means of the acquisition are afforded with unexampled facility. To many, however, the measure of such acquisition must be imperfect. The indispensable cares and labours of our earthly condition present insurmountable obstacles: and there are duties of personal religion and of social life which possess an infinitely higher obligation, and the neglect of which would bring guilt upon our own consciences, and injury upon our dearest connexions. Far from happy would be the possession of even great attainments, purchased at such a cost.

Let us then never be reluctant to acknowledge the ignorance, which we have not been able to remove. Let us not put on the flimsy shew of a knowledge, which we do not possess. Let us be ever open to the confession, that such or such a subject is one with which we have not been favoured to obtain an accurate acquaintance. The ingenuous state of mind which thus expresses itself, will bring no shame; and it will very often be the means of opening a valuable door of information and improvement; partly by its exciting influence on ourselves, and partly by its conciliating the attention of our more accomplished friends.

These considerations not only impress upon us some admonitions, but they justify the exhortations which I am presuming to give, that (in subordination to the richest jewel and sweetest charm of life, the RELIGION OF CHRIST, and in a well regulated connexion with all domestic and social obligations,) my young friends would invigorate their minds by literary, mathematical, and scientific pursuits. This must, generally and chiefly, be accomplished by what Milton so strenuously eulogizes, as the education which a man gives himself.

Let us suppose that a foundation has been laid in a good general education, in which the rudiments of the Mathematics have been solidly taught; for without that preparation the exact sciences cannot be efficiently pursued.* Young persons then enter upon some course of life which claims their chief earthly attention. Some are privileged to enjoy a good measure of evening hours: let them not neglect the gift which the benignity of Providence thus confers upon them. Their leisure is a talent too precious, and its responsibility is a weight too awful, to be treated lightly. The cultivation of Natural History and the Sciences will be a dignified means of excluding those modes of abusing time which are the sin and disgrace of many young persons; vapid indolence, frivolous conversation, amusements which bring no good fruit to the mind or the heart, or such reading as only feasts the imagination while it enervates the judgment, and diminishes or annihilates the faculty of command over the thoughts and affections, a faculty whose healthy exercise is essential to real dignity of character.

But, there are many of the most estimable men who cannot enjoy this advantage. The connexions and claims, whether of business or of professional life, leave them scarcely any leisure; and, at the close of each day, both the mind and the body are wearied to exhaustion. Yet let them not be discouraged. Let them take unceasing pains to cultivate the habit of close observation and exact attention. Let them make up by repetition what they lack in continuity. Small portions of time, linked together by constancy of return and closeness of succession, will form, in months and years, a noble amount of improvement.

May I then be permitted to advise my young friends to select that department of solid knowledge, for which each may possess the best means and opportunities? Let this *one* thing be the body of the building. "This one thing, do."† You will see the ne-

* The observation of Sir John Herschel concerning Astronomy is also applicable to all other departments of Natural Philosophy, and it ought to be engraven on the mind of every aspirant after scientific knowledge. "Admission to its sanctuary, and to the privileges and feelings of a votary, is only to be gained by one means, *a sound and sufficient knowledge of Mathematics, the great instrument of all exact inquiry, without which no man can ever make such advances in this or any other of the higher departments of science, as can entitle him to form an independent opinion on any subject of discussion within their range.*" *Treatise on Astronomy;* p. 5.

† Not till after the composition of these lectures was I made acquainted with a circumstance, full of hope and promise; and which presents a motive for determining, among objects that may seem equally inviting, that which shall be the first choice. The University of London has made a *Regulation* that every student, before being admitted to Examination for his first Degree, (and, after 1840, at his matriculation,) shall be examined, among other subjects, in "The characters and differences of the Natural Classes and Principal Orders belonging to the Flora of Europe, according to the botanical classification of De Candolle." This then *fixes the first step* in a scientific education; and a

cessity of obtaining completely and securing firmly, those first truths in any science which make its foundation: and you will be

more judicious determination could not well be conceived. It will now be the duty of parents and instructors everywhere to lay this foundation in early life. From their tenth or twelfth year, boys and girls should be led to acquaint themselves with every species in the fields, hedges, and woods within their reach. It will be the most salutary recreation from the toils of school; it will be a strong barrier against indolence and dissipation: and it will draw on to Zoology and all other departments of natural knowledge, by obvious and even necessary bands of affinity. Though but a small number of our young men through the land may come to be examined for degrees, the spirit of the Regulation ought to operate to the widest extent; and I trust it will. It has led Dr. Lindley (Prof. Bot. Univ. Coll. Lond.) to compose his new work, "School Botany;" for the express purpose of promoting this object. He gives the monition: "It is *necessary* that boys should prepare themselves for it, before they leave school; and therefore it will be a part of the duty of schoolmasters to cause their highest classes to be taught the kind [i. e. the system] of Botany required by the University." Undoubtedly it has been from mature consideration that the Council has fixed upon M. De Candolle's System, instead of the more operose and difficult one of Dr. Lindley himself: but it has the unwelcome result of counteracting in some measure the use of his own valuable works. It was hoped that the System which he has elaborated through so many years of study and exertion would have come into universal and permanent use. However, for inconveniences like this, there is no remedy but acquiescence: and let it be our consolation that De Candolle's System has already made sure of acceptance among all nations. Perhaps Dr. Lindley will give the necessary modifications to his principal works, to the great benefit of students. It will be needful and easy for them to add a competent acquaintance with the Linnæan System, for many indispensable purposes.(1) To this study there is a delightful Introduction expressly for young persons, by Mr. Francis, just published, *The Little English Flora;* (2) but they must not dispense with the works of Dr. Withering,(3) or Sir James E. Smith, or

(1) *Sec. ed.* At the same time the young student must come to his enterprise with a resolute heart, and should never forget the monition of Prof. Lindley:——"After all that has been effected [for giving facility to the acquirement of an incipient knowledge of Botany,]——or is likely to be accomplished hereafter, there will always be more difficulty in acquiring a knowledge of the Natural System of Botany, than of the Linnæan. The latter skims only the surface of things, and leaves the student in the fancied possession of a sort of information which it is easy enough to obtain, but which is of little value when acquired: the former requires a minute investigation of every part and every property known to exist in plants, but, when understood, it has conveyed to the mind a store of information of the utmost use to man in every station of life. Whatever the difficulties may be of becoming acquainted with plants according to this method, they are *inseparable* from Botany." *Synops. of Brit. Flora;* pref. p. xi

(2) That gentleman had before conferred on young Botanists a benefit of no little value, to assist their study of a peculiarly interesting and beautiful Order, and to which a minute attention has, in the present day, become an elegant fashion, *The British Ferns and their Allies*, in 1837: and, but a few weeks ago, he has published a still more important pocket volume, *The Grammar of Botany*, 1840, a necessary introduction to the Flora, or to any other Synopsis of the Linnæan Botany. Mr. Francis's works have the merit of aiding the student with regard to his literary taste and the attractions of anecdotal facts, thus adding greatly to the pleasure of scientific acquirements: and he has benevolently considered the logic of the pocket. He has also rendered a service of great value, to both young and advanced Botanists, by his *Catalogue of British Plants*, exhibiting on a large sheet all the Linnæan Genera and Species; and the price is *sixpence!*

(3) The condensed and otherwise improved edition, by Dr. Macgillivray, in a single volume, will be found the most useful.

convinced also of the need of minute accuracy in all details. This one science,—or you may have chosen a department of solid and elegant literature, then I would say, this one object,—make your dwelling place; and let others be viewed as accessories of convenience and stability. Avenues will open into other departments of valuable knowledge. Affinities will present themselves of the most pleasing kind. Mutual illustrations will multiply. Delight will supersede difficulty. Every position taken up will give a new extent of command; and by degrees a noble allotment will be enclosed from the field which divine goodness has made the common property of mankind. Thus, a most desirable amount of literary or scientific acquirement will be laid up in the stores of memory. The very labour of getting these intellectual possessions will be a pleasure, and its own reward; and results will probahly be obtained, of immediate value in the arts of life. Your attainments will not be superficial; they will be solid and safe, so far as they have proceeded; you will have always in your hand good instruments, and you will know how to use them, for making progress in any direction that may invite. But forget not the heavenly axiom, "The fear of the Lord is the beginning of wisdom."

II. As a branch of knowledge to which I request these remarks to be especially applied, I invite you to the studies of GEOLOGY.

Here I avail myself of a paragraph, expressed with his usual felicity and force, by one of the most favoured sons of science, and to whom already I have been largely indebted.

"By the discoveries of a *new* SCIENCE (the very name of which has been but a few years engrafted on our language,) we learn that the manifestations of God's power on the earth have not been limited to the few thousand years of man's existence. The geologist tells us, by the clearest interpretation of the phenomena which his labours have brought to light, that our globe has been subject to vast physical revolutions. He counts his time, not by celestial cycles, but by an index he has found in the solid framework of the globe itself. He sees a long succession of monuments, each of which may have re-

Sir W. J. Hooker.—Besides the sentiment which has occasioned this too long note, we ought not to be insensible to the *direct* benefit of botanical knowledge, economically and in agriculture, as well as in relation to Medicine and general science.

[But, now (1847) I must earnestly call attention to Prof. Lindley's vast work, to which his former labours, great and numerous have been culminating; *The Vegetable Kingdom;* sec. ed. with above 500 wood engraved illustrations of admirable beauty; 8vo. 979 pages closely printed.]

quired a thousand ages for its elaboration. He arranges them in chronological order, observes in them the marks of skill and wisdom, and finds within them the tombs of the ancient inhabitants of the earth. He finds strange and unlooked for changes in the forms and fashions of organic life, during each of the long periods he thus contemplates. He traces these changes backwards, through each successive era, till he reaches a time when the monuments lose all symmetry, and the types of organic life are no longer seen. He has then entered on the dark age of nature's history; and he closes the old chapter of her records.——This account has so much of what is exactly true, that it hardly deserves the name of figurative description."*

We have seen, however, that this science brings us into a situation which we cannot but feel most unwelcome and even distressing. In these lectures it has been sufficiently shewn, that some of the most evident geological facts carry the appearance of being at variance with the declarations of Holy Scripture; and that many of our friends, men of ardent piety and christian excellence, not perceiving any mode of conciliation, deny and reject, with great vehemence, our statement of those facts.

In the last lecture, a principle was explained and established which to me appears capable of removing the difficulty, in a way that ought to satisfy impartial minds. But it would be too presumptuous in me, to indulge the hope that this mode of solution

* Sedgwick's *Studies of Cambridge;* p. 25. My reader will thank me for introducing here a passage from another ornament of the same University. "The spirit of geological observation is so widely diffused and so thoroughly roused, that I trust we need not anticipate any pause or retardation in the career of Descriptive Geology. I confess indeed, for my own part, I do not look to see the exertions of the present race of geologists surpassed by any who may succeed them. The great geological theorizers of the past belong to the *Fabulous Period* of the science; but I consider the eminent men by whom I am surrounded as the *Heroic Age* of Geology. They have slain its monsters and cleared its wildernesses; and founded here and there a great metropolis, the queen of future empires. They have exerted combinations of talents, which we cannot hope to see often again exhibited; especially when the condition of the science which produced them is changed. I consider that it is now the destiny of Geology to pass from the heroic to the *Historical Period*. She can no longer look for supernatural successes: but she is entering upon a career, I trust a long and prosperous one, in which she must carry her vigilance into every province of her territory, and extend her dominion over the earth, till it becomes, far more truly than any before, a universal empire." Prof. Whewell, in his Address as President of the Geol. Soc. Feb. 15, 1839. The concluding sentiment referred only to human dominions, civil, or intellectual. I am sure that the learned and estimable speaker is not indifferent to the unearthly empire of Christianity, which God has destined to be the parent of virtue and happiness, knowledge and peace, to all nations.

will be satisfactory to those prepossessed persons; or to others, who take up an opinion at first sight, and are not disposed to go through the course of investigation which is necessary for a proper understanding of the question. I cannot but fear that it must have the fate of the Newtonian Philosophy; and must wait its time, till pious and learned men shall be convinced that their objections are groundless.

I cannot imagine any motive but the excellent one of veneration for the Bible, that can induce a pious mind to feel satisfied with the idea which attributes to the first exercise of creating power, a date so recent as six or seven thousand years ago. Yet we may reasonably ask, *Ought* the mind of a Christian to sit down with passive acquiescence in this persuasion? A commencement of creation unquestionably must have been: and before that point, from eternity, the All-sufficient JEHOVAH was his own universe. But what reason, viewing the subject solely in itself, can we have for assuming that we are living in so early a stage of the flow of time? What objection can we, a race of poor, feeble, sinful creatures, pretend to set up against the idea that the glories of the Creator had been displayed, in diffusing a holy and happy existence through worlds upon worlds, and throughout ages which man cannot number, before he called human kind into existence? If it be said that the "great mystery of godliness," the display of the divine perfections in the work of REDEMPTION, forbids such an extent of our conceptions; I would reply, with humility and deference, that the objector has forgotten the grand attribute of Deity, the basis of all the Divine Perfections,—INFINITY. He is measuring JEHOVAH by a standard applicable only to creatures. —And are not the *purposes* of God, including the glorious plan of salvation to a lost world (Eph. i. 4, 5; iii. 11) from eternity? —To my judgment and feeling, the grandeur of those heavenly counsels is presented to us the more sublimely by the views for which I have been pleading, of the extent, antiquity, and endless duration of the products of God's creative power and provident wisdom.*

* Let the reader turn back to the quotation from Mr. Scrope in page 104.—What materials for reflection lie deep in this sentence of the wise and devout Richard Baxter! "I meddle only with mankind, not with angels. Nor will I curiously inquire whether there were *any other world* of men created and destroyed, before this had being." *Saints' Everlasting Rest;* p. 115, ed. 1688. Thus the mind of this good and great

But, why do you not let these matters alone? Why do you bring them before the christian public, distressing the minds of pious persons, and incurring the danger of shaking the faith of your weaker brethren?

I am bound to acknowledge that my own breast is no stranger to the feelings involved in these queries. Scarcely can I turn out of my heart emotions approaching to envy, at the tranquil state of many of my fellow-christians. Happily ignorant, exempt from perplexities and conflicts, at least on such subjects as this, they spend their blameless lives in the exercises of piety, usefulness to mankind, and all the sweet enjoyments of religion; they go down to the grave in peace, and the angel of death leads their purified spirits to the perfection of heaven.—Would we harass them on their pilgrimage?—Far, far from it!—Alas, the choice is not left with us! These subjects are not allowed to lie in concealment. They are bruited abroad. If Christians can be quiet, infidels will not be so.* "The arrow flieth by day, and the pestilence walketh in darkness." Not only in books of philosophy, but in the periodical journals and common literature of the day, in this country and in others, in Europe and in America, by various phrase, covertly and openly, coarsely and politely, it is proclaimed that Cuvier has supplanted Moses, that Geology has exploded Genesis. There is a class of persons, who understand the scientific side of

man did not absolutely reject the notion of a prior race even of beings like ourselves; though such a notion would have appeared much more in collision with the Scriptures than the admission of creatures quite different from the human. Geology confirms the scriptural doctrine concerning the origin of man, and supplies proofs that man is among the newest productions of the Creator's power, and that our kind had no existence before Adam.

* "The time has come when the whole question must be understood and settled by the friends of Revelation, unless they wish it to be turned to evil account by its enemies." *An Anti-infidel Geologist*, Christ. Observ. May, 1834; p. 313.

I quote, with pleasure and entire assent, the remark of an excellent writer; yet observing that it is applicable only to questions of pure Theology. The case before us is widely different: it is a case in which physical facts compel us to question, not the authority of the Bible, but the justness of certain interpretations and inferences; and our questioning is sustained by the undeniable analogy of language, used much more abundantly in the Bible, upon the most venerable of subjects, the Attributes of the Deity.—Having mentioned some theological difficulties, and the simple facts to which they refer, the author proceeds:—"These things are all plain. With these the humble Christian is content. If, beyond these, perplexities and troubles arise, they are the gratuitous, self-inflicted perplexities and troubles of scholars and philosophers. The plain good man, who simply believes his Bible, who can follow where it leads and pause where it stops, effectually escapes them." Dana's *Letters to Prof. Moses Stuart;* Boston, New England, 1839; p. 31.

the difficulty enough to make out of it an excuse for open infidelity, or secretly cherished scepticism; and thus they are able to pacify their consciences in a contemptuous neglect of the evidence and authority of religion. Do we owe no regard to those persons? Have we no sympathy for them; no consideration for the educational and other unhappy causes of their doubts? Are not their souls as precious as our own? Is not their state, before God and for eternity, as important as ours? Can we prevail upon them to unlearn their knowledge, to stifle the convictions of their judgment, or suppress the avowal of those convictions?—And if we could; if they were to promise silence and to keep the promise; would religion be served thereby?——Examples have not been wanting of complimentary verbiage, with affected solemnity, offered to the christian religion; while the fraternity of concealed unbelievers can look significantly at each other, and mutually build up their self-flattery and pride; as if they were men immeasurably superior to the vulgar, but who, to soothe prejudice, and flatter public opinion, are willing to uphold a style of conventional hypocrisy.

But, can we not throw ourselves into the arms of our brethren in the faith, who, as we have seen, summarily dispose of the whole matter?—We cannot. First; our own convictions stand in the way. The facts cannot be set aside: they are too numerous, too various and independent, and too weighty in their character as grounds of reasoning. Secondly; if we could so put off our reasonable faculties, the great cause would not be relieved. It would be far more deeply injured. The body of scientific men, in every country, would only be confirmed in their hostility, and the more completely discharged from keeping terms with us: while we should be the men that laid Christianity under the feet of its adversaries.*

* "From ill-informed, or too often prejudiced persons, we hear frequent remarks disparaging the inquiries and conclusions of the Geologist, while they allow and applaud the inferences of the Astronomer and the Chemist. They condemn as visionary and presumptuous the results of the one as to the antiquity of strata, and the successive æras of animal organization, the monuments of which are before their eyes; while they revere as unquestionable truths the most marvellous and paradoxical inferences of the other, which refer to subjects utterly beyond the scope of the senses, to periods and distances which transcend our arithmetical powers to conceive, and to processes of nature which exceed our faculties to apprehend.——Yet, when the Geologist contends that the crust of the earth, with its organized productions, has been gradually brought into its present condition, by a series of CREATIVE changes, going on through millions of ages;

Hence arises a motive of the greatest force to quicken our endeavours to diffuse every where just principles for understanding the figurative language of Scripture. We cannot but be affected by the prevalence of ignorance and misconception on this point; and the consequent influence of those misconceptions upon the formation of religious sentiments and their practical results. The eloquent profusion of striking scripture-language, in sermons and treatises and poems, yet without the accompaniment of just caution and correct interpretation, has made many enthusiasts and many infidels; and not a few have rushed from the one extreme to the other. The unexplained ascription of human forms and passions to the Deity leads some to breathe the atmosphere of a piety imaginative and picturesque indeed, but degrading to its glorious Object and nursing most pernicious fancies in its subjects: and it helps forward another class in their injurious conceptions of the attributes and government of God; for these are ideas which they are very ready to accept, as a bolstering up of secret scepticism. In their own minds, they put upon the adorable One a garb of unreasonable, turbulent, and changeful passions; instead of representing him as the Being all whose attributes are PERFECTIONS, fixed and invariable *principles* of rectitude and wisdom. Thus, the pure character and the reasonableness of moral obedience, and the inviolability of the law that requires it, are thrown out of sight; the necessity of a Divine Saviour is therefore hidden from view; the whole economy of redeeming grace is distorted; Christianity is represented as an irrational dream; and the best hopes of man are thrown to the winds. But, how often does a melancholy reaction take place; and the empire of superstition succeeds to that of scorn! Sorrow and desolation, age and death, present themselves; and the miserable victim, "ignorant of God's righteousness," and never having cast the anchor of his soul "within the vail," is overwhelmed with terrors, and flees into the arms of some foolish and delusive scheme, for relief from the

his conclusion is condemned as chimerical and dangerous.——They allow the full claims of the human mind, to assign spaces and periods which transcend the flights of the loftiest imagination:—yet they talk of the arrogance of the Geologist in pretending to maintain that, millions of years ago, the world was going on, governed by the same physical laws which prevail now, and replete with vegetable and animal life in all its varied forms of perfection and adaptation to a state of things, of which the existing order is only one of a series of gradual and regular changes." Prof. Powell's *Connexion;* pp. 67, 69.

scourge of a terrified conscience:—a false relief, to be followed by the bitterest aggravations of disappointment, and the death of hope! To prevent such ruin, let us do all in our power to inculcate just views of the true meaning of scripture-imagery, the unalterable perfections of God, the majesty of his holiness, the riches of his grace, and the exceeding greatness of his power, through faith in Christ, to liberate our souls from sin and wretchedness, and raise them to immortal purity, activity and joy. THIS is "the glorious gospel of the Blessed God;—the truth according to godliness, in hope of eternal life, which God who cannot deceive (ὁ ἀψευδὴς Θεός) has promised before the world began."*

Our religion,—blessed be God!—is not a religion of contrivance and expediency. We want only TRUTH: and we cannot barter it for ease, custom, or fashion.

Is it not then our duty, as honest men and Christians, to make ourselves somewhat more than superficially acquainted with the evidence in this case; and to take some pains in diffusing correct knowledge upon it?

This is the proceeding which I humbly recommend; and to promote which has been the design of these lectures.†

III. I would entreat my friends to consider what are the proper ACCOMPANIMENTS of all human knowledge, if it be sought and

* 1 Tim. i. 11. Tit. i. 1, 2.

† "The subject before us is not one which can be advantageously discussed with the people at large." [Meaning, no doubt, in sermons.] "A wide range of facts and an extensive course of induction are necessary to the satisfactory exhibition of geological truths; and especially to establish their connexion and harmony with the Mosaic history. It is a subject exclusively for the learned, or at least for the studious and the reflecting. But *it can no longer be neglected with safety by those whose province is to illustrate and defend the sacred writings*. The crude, vague, unskilful, and unlearned manner in which it has been too often treated, when treated at all, by those who are to a great extent ignorant of the structure of the globe, or who have never studied it with any efficient attention, can communicate only pain to those friends of the Bible, who are perfectly satisfied, after full examination, that the relation of geology to sacred history is now as little understood, by many theologians and biblical critics, as astronomy was in the time of Galileo. There is but one remedy. *Theologians must study Geology:* or, if they will not or from peculiar circumstances cannot do it, they must be satisfied to receive its demonstrated truths from those who have learned them in the most effectual way, not only in the cabinet, but abroad on the face of nature and in her deep recesses. They will then be convinced, that geology is not an enemy but an ally of revealed religion; that the subject is not to be mastered by mere criticism; that criticism must be applied to facts as well as to words; and that there is, at most, only an apparent incongruity, an incongruity which vanishes before investigation." Dr. Silliman (Prof. Chem. Yale Coll. U. S.) in his App. to a republication of Mr. Bakewell's Geology, near the close; published separately in London, by Mr. J. S. Hodson, with the title, *Consistency of the Discoveries of Modern Geol. with the Sacred Hist.* 1837.

employed in the manner that becomes reasonable and accountable creatures.

Science is the knowledge of truth. Its proper tendency is to augment our desire to obtain higher measures of that possession; and to increase our love to that truth of which it is the image. But all truth is connected with all other truth, by natural alliances numerous and ever multiplying. Physical truth, though the fact is often overlooked, has much in common with moral truth. From a sound acquaintance with the kingdoms of nature, innumerable benefits accrue to the comfort and always extending usefulness of the life that now is: and we thus obtain enlarging convictions of the pernicious consequences of ignorance and false opinions. From the want of knowledge in some branches of science, many a flattering project has been marred, much property has been thrown away, families have been ruined, and the public has been injured. This has been remarkably the case from the want of geological knowledge. Almost incredible might appear the history of disappointments and pecuniary losses which have been produced by this cause, in laying down lines of road, in selecting materials for road-making and stone for building, in making cuttings and tunnels, in sinking for coal, and in the economy of metallic mines. Hence we may derive lessons, by reasonable analogy, to enforce the scriptural precept, in its moral aspects, as well as in every other: "Buy the truth and sell it not." It is a treasure above all price, and nothing can compensate for the loss of it. Ignorance and error, in relation to God, our duty to him and expectations from him, are the causes of unbelief, impenitence, insensibility to the evidences and claims of revealed religion, and all sinful affections and conduct; what the inspired author calls "foolish and pernicious lusts, which drown men in destruction and perdition."* But a mind which ingenuously loves Truth, will "search for it as for hidden treasure;" and will see a beauty in moral and religious truth transcending every other kind of excellence, and connecting itself with the glories of eternity.

Well-conducted studies also tend to promote a right estimation of Evidence universally, a wise discrimination of its various kinds, and the habit of regarding it with integrity and fidelity.

These qualities of mind are congenial with others, which advance

* 1 Tim. vi. 9.

still higher the holy edifice in our minds; such are a profound sense of the universal presence and the infinite perfections of God, veneration and filial love to him, cordial submission to his authority, delight in his precepts, the thankful reception of his gospel, and the repose of the soul in HIM as the ground of its immortal hopes.

So shall we answer the purposes of our existence, and shall be prepared for the momentous changes which are hastening on, and in which we have a never-dying interest. Infinite happiness or infinite woe will be the result of a due regard to these considerations, or a contempt of them. This result for eternity will be the product of our present character, as it is seen by the Omniscient; a product *necessary* by the laws of our intellectual nature, and *just* under the government of eternal rectitude.

God has written the lesson of responsibility and retribution upon the large scale of affinity and sequence, through the whole empire of nature. The felicities of holiness and the punishments of sin, are not arbitrary inflictions, but grow out of the necessary constitutions which the All-wise Sovereign has fixed for the good order of his universe. Hence, it is not less an inevitable certainty, from physical truths and rational evidences, than it is a primary doctrine of the Bible, that "they who hate knowledge and choose not the fear of the Lord, who reject his counsels and despise his reproof, shall eat of the fruit of their own way."*

* Prov. i. 29—31. With this coincide the reasonings of Mr. Babbage, in his chapter "On the Permanent Impressions of our Words and Actions on the Globe we inhabit." Laplace had observed that "the curve described by [the motion of] a single molecule of air or any fluid is subjected to laws as certain as those of the planetary orbits: there is no difference between them, but that which arises from our ignorance." Mr. Babbage pursues the idea, and shews that "these ærial pulses, unseen by the keenest eye, unheard by the acutest ear, unperceived by human senses, are yet demonstrated to exist by human reason.——If man enjoyed a larger command over mathematical analysis, his knowledge of these motions would be more extensive: but a being, possessed of unbounded knowledge of that science, could trace every the minutest consequence of that primary impulse. Such a being, however far exalted above our race, would still be immeasurably below even *our* conception of INFINITE Intelligence.——Whilst the atmosphere we breathe is the ever-living witness of the sentiments we have uttered, the waters and the more solid materials of the globe bear equally enduring testimony of the acts we have committed. If the Almighty stamped on the brow of the first murderer, the indelible and visible mark of his guilt; he has also established laws by which every succeeding criminal is not less irrevocably chained to the testimony of his crime; for every atom of his mortal frame, through whatever changes its several particles may migrate, will still retain, adhering to it through every combination, some movement derived from that very muscular effort by which the crime itself was perpetrated. The soul of the negro whose fettered body, surviving the living charnel-house of his infected prison, was thrown into the

The instruments of his righteousness are in preparation; and, how soon they will be ready for action He knows who created, who sustains, and who governs his own world. But we need not expect a delay till the workings of the atmosphere and the running waters shall have worn down the mountains and washed away the plains to the sea-level. A different point in the course of the agency which God has ordained, may bring on the catastrophe. Let but the deposits at the bottom of the sea, over any particular area, proceed to a certain amount of thickness, and Deity knows, (and he may have disclosed the event and its time to creatures superior to man,) how near we are to the attainment of that point; and upheaving must take place, escape of the fiery liquid below by a volcanic vent may not be permitted, new continents must then be raised from the bed of the sea, and now-existing land must resume its former place at the bottom of the waters. It may be said that this is a slower process than numbers can assign. Be it so: but before this point is reached, the operation of the same constant cause may produce earthquakes and volcanic explosions under the soil of Great Britain or Germany, or the intermediate sea; and in a few moments may send into eternity every human creature, over a wide district. That these countries have not been the seat of such destructive outbursts, within the record of history, or since the creation of man, forms no objection. That they have been so agitated in former periods is among the most certain of facts: and no man can be assured that the renewal of similar events will not take place, at any hour.

I do not advert to these considerations as if religion needed them. Its evidences, its authority, and its motives stand forth full and complete on their own grounds; and a few years, or per-

sea to lighten the ship, that his *christian* master might escape the limited justice at length assigned by civilized man to crimes whose profits had long gilded their atrocity, will need, at the last great day of human account, no living witness of his earthly agony. When man and all his race shall have disappeared from the face of our planet, ask every particle of air still floating over the unpeopled earth, and it will record the cruel mandate of the tyrant. Interrogate every wave which breaks unimpeded on ten thousand desolate shores, and it will give evidence of the last gurgle of the waters which closed over the head of his dying victim, confront the murderer with every corporeal atom of his immolated slave, and in its still quivering movements he will read the prophet's denunciation of the prophet king,—*Thou art the man*." *Ninth Bridgewater Treat.* chap. ix.

But the arm, the tongue, the brain, were but the organism of the *mind;* and for mind with all its machinations God has made equally effective registers: "and the books WILL BE OPENED."

haps a few of our rapidly fleeting days, will bear away each one of us to our personal judgment. But this is one of the lights in which we may view the interest of geological studies. The records of earthquakes and volcanoes, if we contemplated nothing else in this rich field, are the most awfully impressive that visible nature affords. The Christian cannot exclude them from the universal government of God: nor would he, if he could. Physical events have moral relations. Here we see large extents of country, rising, or sinking down, at the slow rate of two or three feet in a century: there, an elevation or a depression of several feet through hundreds of miles, takes place in a few hours. On our own coasts are many examples of ancient sea-beaches, even several in superposition, but far above the highest tide-level of the present day. In places innumerable of the British Isles, the early and secondary and tertiary beds have been upraised, fractured, and pierced through by the melted rocks from below; parts of which, having become solid, as necessarily and speedily they would, form our most magnificent mountains, and other parts have run in lines of many miles in length, filling up the cracks and chasms which the upbursting force had rent. In many parts of the ocean which covers three-fourths of the surface of our globe, new islands have been raised up; some of which have soon sunk down, or have been washed away, leaving dangerous shallows, and others continue to this day and have become the abodes of life and action. The vestiges of ancient volcanoes stand up in their unquestionable demonstration, in countries next to our own. At distances a little greater, we find volcanic vents, either in never-ceasing though temperate action, or at uncertain periods breaking forth in terrible magnificence. Fifty-six years ago, in the island geographically near to us, Iceland, the eruption of the mountain Skáptar Jokul, which was prolonged through two years, dried up rivers and filled their beds, covered valleys of five hundred feet in depth and overflowed their mountain-limits, and spread its lava-torrents over areas of country from seven to fifteen miles in breadth, in length forty to fifty, and in various thickness from one hundred feet to six hundred. Twenty villages were destroyed, and nearly the fifth part of the population perished.

In 1797, the old city Riobamba, in Peru, was destroyed in one day by an earthquake; and, in a few minutes, forty-five thousand human beings were thus awfully sent into eternity.

In 1815, the island of Sumbawa, at the eastern end of Java, was the scene of volcanic devastation to a most dreadful extent. The eruptions began on April 15th, and continued for three months. Great tracts of land were buried under the lava. "Violent whirlwinds carried up men, horses, cattle, and whatever else came within their influence, into the air; tore up the largest trees by the roots, and covered the whole sea with floating timber."* The shocks were felt to the distance of 1000 miles; and the terrible sound of the explosions was heard over a range of 1500. The ashes ejected reached 200 and 300 miles in distance, covering the sea extensively with pumice and cinders to the thickness of two feet, and making the day darker than the thickest night over a wide space in length more than 500 miles. Out of about twelve thousand persons, in two small districts, no more than five or six persons survived; and of the whole population, the number of which is not stated, only twenty-six escaped this awful catastrophe.†

Seven years afterwards, in the same island, an eruption took place of the mountain Galongoon, which, with its deluges of rain and scalding mud, destroyed 114 villages and 4000 persons.

Thus the instruments of change are incessantly at work, in modifying and altering the surface of the planet which the adorable Creator has appointed for our dwelling-place, in this incipient state of being. The examination of the earth affords us an insight into its state and many of the changes through which it has passed, before it assumed its present condition; and spreads before us volumes of evidence that those changes have been produced by the same instrumental causes that we see working at the present moment. The intensity has varied: different states or circumstances have augmented or diminished their resulting forces; but the causality, mediate as well as primary, has been of the same kind; and the variations of intensity have affected but a small portion of the immeasurable system of Jehovah's empire, and have been all the effect of more general laws. Every thing that we can observe and every deduction that we can form, presents the

* Lyell's *Princip. Geol.* vol. ii. p. 200.

† Sir T. S. Raffles's *Hist. of Java*, vol. i. pp. 25—28. "Twenty-six of the people who were at Sumbawa at the time, are the whole of the population who have escaped. From the most particular inquiries I have been able to make, there were certainly not fewer than twelve thousand inhabitants in Tomboro and Pĕkatĕ at the time of the eruption, of whom only five or six survive." Page 28.

glorious unfoldings of beauty and majesty, the progressive triumphs of wisdom and beneficence.

We ought not to omit the observation, that the causes of most extensive operations are and have been the most silent and quiet. The volcano and the earthquake, necessary as their part has been in carrying on the economy of God's physical government, have had to perform a much inferior part compared with the slow and tranquil processes of deposition, consolidation, elevation, crystallization, cleavage, and electric affinities continually acting. Those hidden operations, whose depth and breadth and length were to be the elements of the most important results through a vast futurity, have in all past time been effected, and now are proceeding, in a manner so gradual, so slow, and yet without any needless consumption of time, as to overwhelm our minds with the contemplation, and to impress us with conceptions at once awful and delightful, of the Wisdom, Power, and Goodness, which have connected incalculable numbers of beings and events, stretching through ages to which we are incompetent to apply a measure; so that they all combine with unfailing accuracy, to effectuate the purposes which only Infinite Perfection could form, or when formed could execute.

Whether fiery catastrophes shall take place, local and successive over different regions, or one universal conflagration involving the globe in simultaneous destruction, (improperly so called, for a glorious future will lie beyond,) is probably above the power of human knowledge to determine. How far the prophetic announcements of Scripture import a literal action of fire, or whether they are altogether significant of moral changes, are questions, the resolution of which I presume not to assert.*

IV. There remains another object of my heart's desire, with which if I might be gratified, my prayers would be answered, and my joy be unspeakable. Might I but hope that those sons of science, to whose labours and our obligations for them, so frequent reference has been made, would be persuaded to give to the noblest objects of contemplation, a portion of their attention *correspondent* to that which they have devoted to objects valuable indeed, but infinitely inferior;——happy should I be, beyond expression!

The philosophers, whose names form a wreath of honour to our

* See pages 155—157.

own and other nations, cannot but be objects of regard, with feelings of interest and solicitude to which no words can give full utterance.——Illustrious men; we look up to you with more than respect: we admire and reverence you. Your early acquisitions in mathematics and the exact sciences, in all that could lay the foundation of an enduring edifice; your separation from the frivolity and vice, to the temptations of which you have been exposed; your devotement of youth and manly age, of fortune, health, labour and peril, and severe studies; your generous readiness in giving to the public the fruit of your toils; the debt which physical science owes you; the benefits which you have conferred upon society, for economical and national purposes; the excitement and encouragement which you have so readily given, through wide circles of influence;——all entitle you to our honour and affection.

But these reasons add to the justness and warmth of our wishes, that you would adorn all other excellence with the pearl of greater price. Your penetration into the vastness of space and time, has made you familiar with the sublimest ideas in nature. Those ideas have brought you into a contact, incomparably closer than that of ordinary men, with the ETERNAL and the INFINITE. Is it then possible, that you do not meditate on eternity and infinity, as subjects in which you have the highest interest? The powers of intellect which you so exercise, must have given to you a more than probable conviction, that those powers are not extinguished by the stroke of death. Knowing that not an atom of material existence is destroyed, or even fails to come into beneficial uses; *you* above all men cannot suppose that moral powers and susceptibilities sink into annihilation. Witnesses as ye are to the demonstrations of forecast, wisdom, and design, upon the grandest scale, in the connexions and adjustments of unintelligent matter; and to the disclosures of the same qualities, in forms of still higher magnificence, through all organized nature, as well the dead memorials of ancient life, as the wonders of actual animation;—*you cannot* but see the evidence that an all-presiding MIND exists: nor can you think it reasonable to suppose that HE is not the possessor of all perfections; of all that is lovely and all that is awful. You contemplate the laws and you calculate their results, by which you shew us that the Infinite Being has bound together all the parts of his material universe; that, through their complexity, divine simplicity reigns; and that *one* fundamental law exercises its sovereignty over the mighty whole.——And has it never occurred to you, that the Lord of the world must also love every other kind of *order;* and must rule by fixed laws, in his *highest* domain, *the minds* which he has created? Is it not a reasonable presumption that he has made known his moral laws, to the beings from whom it is right that he should expect gratitude, love, and voluntary obedience? Is it not possible that there may be an intercourse, between the human mind and the glorious Deity? Are there even now, no incipient communings of your spirits with the Infinite Being? No aspirations after a greater good than nature yields? Are there no means of securing the favour of the All-Sufficient, and so of looking forwards to the immortality which awaits you, with something better than vague hopes; with rational joy and confidence?

There are such provisions, made by the Being of supreme goodness on behalf of rational and therefore accountable creatures. Christianity presents them. She opens a portal into the palace of undying purity and happiness, and she invites you to enter.

Astronomers, geologists, and microscopic observers have peculiar facilities for acquiring the most sublime conceptions of the Deity; from their deep, extensive, and accurate acquaintance with his works. Can they gaze at the wondrous mechanism with which they are familiar; can they calculate its workings, based upon the most recondite mathematical truths; can they predict the results on the greatest scale and with infallible certainty;——and yet cherish no admiring and affectionate thoughts of the FORMER? You disclose to the astonished view the animalcules of the living world, or the shells and habitations of those which peopled their proper stations in the long past conditions of creation: you witness their exquisite beauty, their especial adaptations, and the appropriate places which they fill in the ranks of organized being: and you shew us many species, of which millions of the individuals do not weigh a grain: and does not this impress upon you the weakness of scepticism with respect to the doctrines of a Divine Redemption, as if they gave to mankind too much importance in the view of the Almighty God? Your science carries you back to periods of past time, the review of which is overwhelming to even your well-trained understandings: and do you not hence gather a presumption of credibility to the plan arranged from eternity, of holiness and wisdom, for the highest welfare of human beings?

There are indications of a thought latent in some minds, that the Deity cannot be expected to take that notice of the human race, still less of an individual man, which the christian religion affirms. But is it possible that a philosopher, a mathematician, a true student of nature, can entertain such a thought? Accustomed as he is to the demonstrations of wisdom and power which he cannot but call infinite, in the farthest regions of the microscopic world; he must grant that every unit in the aggregate of creation, let it be more minute than can be expressed, has a share as complete in the regards of the Infinite Mind, as if that unit were the universe. Can it be thought unworthy of the Supreme Majesty, or on any ground improbable, or indeed any other than a *necessary* truth, that He should require the affectionate attachment and the zealous obedience of each rational creature; and that he should govern the intelligent world and every being in it, by a system of the purest moral law?——*

Can such men as you be enslaved to the prejudices of little minds?—Can you be satisfied with a knowledge of Christianity, so meagre as to be a parallel to that ignorance on scientific subjects which provokes your pity? When large expatiating and thorough research upon all other objects, are esteemed indispensable and are nobly achieved by you; can you be contented with fragments of knowledge about religion, picked up in childhood, or accidentally and carelessly in the course of life; and which have no coherence, no completeness, no standing upon well-studied proof; which are often indeed nothing but vulgar prejudices?†

Did the religion of Dr. Turner, who so long and meritoriously filled the office of Secretary to the Geological Society, impede his

* See Supplementary Note U.

† O that they would practically and efficiently abrogate the distressing monition of one of the distinguished philosophers of our country!———"There is no subject on which the generality, even of educated and reasoning persons, are less given to reason than on religion. Hence the prevalent disposition (even among those who think deeply, and are perhaps profoundly engaged in philosophical investigations on other subjects,) is to avoid all such examination of religious matters; to adopt nominally the established creed without question; to dismiss all particular distinctions from their thoughts; or, if questioned, to recur to mystery, and repose in the incomprehensibility of the doctrine; maintaining this, too, as in itself the most effectual and legitimate means of cherishing a due and becoming sentiment of religion. And all this grounded upon and vindicated by the favourite and fashionable idea, so grateful to human nature, that religion is altogether a *matter of feeling*." Powell's *Tradition Unveiled;* p. 62.

exertions in the field of philosophy; or in any way depreciate their value? The testimony of his friend Mr. Dale should be inscribed upon the heart of every man of science. "He received the Bible with implicit deference, *not as the word of man, but, as it is in truth, the word of GOD.*—Blameless, excellent as he was, to outward appearance, in every relation of life, he knew that he could not abide the scrutiny of one who looked upon the heart; and he joyfully took refuge in the *comfortable* doctrine of an Almighty Saviour, one *able to save them to the uttermost that come unto God by him.*"

When Dr. Turner knew that death was near, he adverted to the perfect calmness of his pulse, and asked, "What can make it so at such an hour? What, but the power of religion? Who, but the Spirit of God?——I could not have believed (he said,) that I could be happy on my death-bed. I am content my career should close.——The question was put to him by an anxious relative, Is not Christ as good as his word? *Yes,* he faltered, *quite.* And when he had said these words, he fell asleep."*

I cannot but add, that any member of the learned and scientific societies to which Dr. Turner belonged, is doing himself a wrong if he do not read and deeply ponder the Sermon which has furnished these extracts.

In a word: suffer one to entreat you, who puts forth no claim but that of the sincerest regard, and the warmest desire for your enjoying happiness of the most exalted kind and in the most perfect degree. Suffer him to entreat, that you would effectually resolve to yield to religion its rightful place in your minds and your hearts: that you would give the just proportion of your studies to the facts and evidences of Christianity, its doctrines and duties, its promises, its invitations, and its faithful warnings.

"GLORY TO GOD IN THE HIGHEST; ON EARTH, PEACE; AMONG MEN, GOOD WILL!"

Fourth ed. Upon one subject, which has not been made prominent as it ought to have been in the preceding Lectures, I add a few words: the Direct Agency of God in the Achievements of the Human Mind. A consistent believer in Christianity cannot bring this into doubt; but we have far too slight an impression of it. Professed faith in God's

---

* *The Philosopher entering as a Child into the Kingdom of God:* a Sermon preached at the Parish Church of St. Bride, Feb. 27, 1837: on the Death of Edward Turner, M. D., F. R. S. &c. By the Rev. Thomas Dale, M. A. Pp. 24, 28, 29.

PROVIDENCE is commonly a formal and vapid word-currency, standing for some kind of inspection and general government; but by no means letting itself down to the smallest particulars of creatures and events, and producing no holiness in the heart and the life. Atoms and moments are thought to be too inconsiderable for the attention of the Infinite Majesty; and not infrequently men scornfully sneer at the doctrine of a providence really universal, that is, which omits nothing from its view and action. Let a thing existent, or an event occurring, be such that a finite intellect might judge it totally and for all purposes insignificant; such judgment would be not only presumptuous but erroneous, yea, sinfully false. May devout reason pursue the thought! I use it only to awaken the sentiment that, in the physical and mental conformation, and in all the predicates of parental, educational, and every other actuation, there has been a special influence from the Deity. Conjecture, inquiry, experiment, induction, confirmation, application of ascertained truths, all the causes or occasions that have produced science and art, in every degree and form of TRUTH, *have come from* GOD, by his acting upon the susceptibilities of the individual, in a manner distinguishing and specific. Thales, Hippocrates, Plato and Aristotle, Archimedes and Hipparchus, Kepler, Bacon and Galileo, Newton, Leibnitz and Bradley, and the bright galaxy of our own time studded with names for admiration,—all have been the subjects of that communication from ON HIGH of which the Book of Inspiration remarkably speaks. For example: "In thy hand is power and might, and in thy hand it is to make great.—Jehovah spake to Moses,—See, I have called by name Bezaleel, and I have filled him with the Spirit of God, in wisdom and in understanding and in knowledge and in all manner of workmanship, to devise cunning [*i. e.* knowing, such as indicate profound insight,] works.—Unto Solomon—God said,—Behold—I have given thee a wise and understanding heart.—God gave to Solomon wisdom and understanding exceeding much, and largeness of heart, even as the sand which is on the sea-shore;—for he was wiser than all men;—and he spake of trees, from the cedar tree that is in Lebanon even unto the hyssop that springeth out of the wall; he spake also of beasts and of fowl and of creeping things and of fishes.—Doth the ploughman plough all day? Doth he open and break the clods?—Doth he not cast abroad,—and cast in—[the different seeds]?—For his God doth instruct him."*

The imperative lessons from these facts are,—that scientific men are under the strongest obligations to cultivate their rich domain with the most reverential spirit towards Him who has given it to them:—that as, in a natural sense, they are thus privileged to "draw nigh unto God" and as it were "enter into his secret chambers," they, above all men, ought not to satisfy themselves without the exalted, pure, happy, influence of the Almighty Spirit which will transform them into His likeness "in knowledge, righteousness, and the holiness of the truth;" that CHRIST may be "made by God unto them wisdom and righteousness and sanctification and redemption."

O, may this supreme blessedness be granted to all those whom God's distinguished mercy has raised so high!

---

* 1 Chron. xxix. 12; Exod. xxxi. 3; 1 Kings iv. 29—33; Is. xxviii. 26.

SUPPLEMENTARY NOTES.

SUPPLEMENTRAY NOTES.

[A.]

Referred to at pages 7 and 200.

DISSERTATION ON THE LAWS OF ORGANIZED NATURES, INVOLVING THE NECESSITY OF DEATH; AND ON GEOLOGICAL STUDIES IN GENERAL.

In the Congregational Magazine for November, 1837, the inquiry was proposed, under the signature of T. K. "Could there be death, by violent and painful means, before the entrance of sin had deranged the order of a holy world, or had given occasion for bringing into action the instruments of violent death?"

To this, the following answer was returned: and, as it has been made an object of controversial attack by Mr. Mellor Brown, and as it may contribute some further illustration to several of the topics treated in these lectures, I have thought it not unsuitable to be here introduced, omitting a few sentences.

The question of your correspondent, T. K., merits the most serious attention. It forms one, and probably the heaviest, of the two great difficulties which Christians feel in relation to the discoveries and doctrines of modern Geology; the first is the alleged necessity of admitting that God had put forth his creating energy from an era impossible to be even conjectured, but stretching back through immeasurable periods, from the adaptation of the earth, to be the abode of a new race of creatures, with MAN at their head. I have said, *alleged* necessity; because that qualifying term is proper at the outset of an inquiry: but, though I cannot now undertake this part of the discussion, I am bound to profess that there is no doubt in my own mind. I must even go so far as to express my conviction, that it is *perfectly impossible* for any intelligent person to understand the facts of the case, and sit down with any modification of the sentiment which supposes our globe to have been created a few thousand years ago. But it is much to be lamented, that many well-meaning persons have imagined themselves qualified to decide this question, while really unacquainted with *the essential* parts of the argument; having probably derived what they suppose to be a competent measure of knowledge, from a perusal of some one or two books, lofty, and even haughty in assertion, but ignorant, to a degree almost incredible, of the very grounds on which the inquiry must proceed so as to have any reasonable prospect of success. Indeed, Geology, as a *science deduced by the severest logic* from phenomena which, when once fairly ascertained, a man can no more doubt of, (I think I speak not too strongly,) than he can doubt that it is day when he sees the sun, can scarcely be said to have come into existence till within the last thirty or forty years; for it is within such a period that Dr. William Smith's discovery of *characteristic* fossils to each stratum and series of strata, laid a foundation on which many most cautiously *practical* and *reasoning* geologists have built, and from which, by general accordance, the epithet has been applied to him, *the father of Geology*. Yet, at this hour, many excellent persons are reposing upon the belief that one theory is about as good as another, that the primary doctrines which prevail among geologists are nothing but ideal hypotheses, not at all advanced beyond plausible conjectures, mostly at variance with each other, and that, as fast as one theory is set up, it is found to be wrong by some succeeding inquirer; so that, upon the whole, we may rest satisfied that the right theory has not yet been discovered, and that the phenomena are not yet justly understood, nor their real bearings discerned. Of such persons there can be no hope, unless they will take pains in more ways than one, and to a degree which they have not yet dreamed of. It is no wonder that Geology has risen so high within but the last fifteen years, and has attracted to it the most gifted minds in this and other countries: for it is based upon the evidence of sense, in the laborious and protracted examination of mines, mountain-regions, and less dangerous places without number; and it demands, in order to its successful cultivation, an acquaintance with at least the principles of chemistry, electricity, mineralogy, zoology, conchology, comparative anatomy, and (as the papers of Mr. Hopkins and Sir J. F. Herschell have recently shewn) of the sublimest mathematics. Thus Geology maintains relations with the whole sphere of natural knowledge; and, above all, it bears a most important reference to THEOLOGY and BIBLICAL studies, that we may know truth, and maintain it against both well-meaning believers, and ill-meaning unbelievers, and may magnify "the wondrous works of Him that is PERFECT in knowledge."

The question is, how can we admit the existence of animal pain and death, before "sin entered into the world, and death by sin?"

1. The matter of *fact* must be ascertained. Is there evidence, such as cannot be set aside, of such facts as the following? That the *state* of the surface of our globe has been changed by submersion under oceanic or lake water, and frequent elevation and drying, a great number of times, (say 30 to 40;) that *each* of those successive states continued during a vast period, which it would be presumptuous to conjecture, but which might very moderately be taken at many thousands of years; that, in every one of those states, (till, in the descending order, we arrive at the very early strata,) we find the *unquestionable remains* of animals, or their shelly habitations; that these are not huddled together, as if drifted on by a torrent, or thrown into a hole, but are disposed in horizontal, or what was once horizontal, order, spread over large surfaces, often of the same family or tribe, in all stages of their growth, preserving the most delicate parts of their form, and thus shewing that *there* they had quietly *lived* and *died;* that of these humble beings, many are shewn, by the structure of the shell, to have been *carniverous;* that, in some far more recent* members of the *secondary* class of strata, are found the skeletons of *gigantic lizard-formed animals*, with their stomachs remaining under their ribs, and those stomachs still retaining the more solid relics of their food, among which are fish-scales, and bits of bone; and that every stratum has its own *characteristic* animal and vegetable remains, the differing natures of which indicate great and progressive *alterations* in temperature and other circumstances. All these are familiar facts to the geologist. He sees those remains in the midst of hard rocks, yea, often composing the chief substance of those rocks; he digs them out; he sends them to the British and other Museums, or to be preserved in private collections; and there the delicate inhabitants of cities may see them without pains or peril.

We cannot argue against facts. Let us seek the solution of difficulties, in the best way that we can; but let us proceed with modesty and humility, ever ready to confess our weakness and ignorance; thankful for what we may know, submissive in what we cannot know, and confidently relying on the glorious perfections of GOD, when we

* *Recent*, in a geological sense, but if compared with our common measures of time, we confess ourselves unable to give an equation. Untold thousands of years before the adjustment of the earth for the human race, would be no extravagant expression.

cannot follow their unfolding. Are there not, *ought* there not to be, many things in nature, as well as in providence and grace, of which it is our *privilege* to say, "Such knowledge is too wonderful for me; it is high; I cannot attain unto it! His judgments are a great deep:—unsearchable;—past finding out!"

2. It has pleased the Adorable Supreme to give existence to a dependent world, in part spiritual, and in part material. Of the material part of the universe, one great division is insensitive, and consists, so far as we know, of only aggregated and crystallized matter: the other is sensitive, and its structure is *organized;* that is, it is composed of a system, arranged by divine skill, of tubes or cells, in which fluids circulate, the more solid parts being perpetually in motion of receiving and giving, each particle passing on in a course of change, the whole endowed with the mysterious property or functional possession, called *life*, and distributed into a classification of kinds, descending from larger to smaller groups, till we arrive at an individual. The individuals reproduce similar ones: each individual is born, grows, becomes mature, decays, dies; and the dead organic matter is seized upon by appropriated agents; some of which effect a recombination of certain portions with the mineral kingdom; others, being themselves organic and living, both vegetable and animal, take and recombine with their own structure, certain other portions. Thus all living organized beings are maintained in life by the assimilation into themselves of portions of dead organized beings; and this is the universal circle of process in *all material nature* that is endowed with life, vegetable and animal.

3. The law of dissolution, that is death, is therefore *necessary* to organic life. Each individual has its term; then it dies, and enables others to live. Through a vast period, the *species* continues; it at last ceases, but other species of the same genus appear, and enjoy their time of duration. Mightier cycles revolve, during which great changes take place in the temperature and the strata of the globe, and whole *genera* live no more. The life of man, however, does not extend to witness the commencement and the extinction of a single species: yet the period of the human race upon earth has outlived several *species*, some of which obscurely appear in the traditionary history of nations, and one (the dodo) has become extinct within the last two hundred years; and finally, we have not the slightest reason to think that any *genus* has ceased, "since the day that God created man upon the earth."

4. A system of nature, according to which organized creatures should *not die*, would be totally incompatible with the plan which the

Creator has been pleased to establish in this department of his works. But let us try some hypotheses.

(1.) Put the case that there be no death. Upon this supposition, two or three modes are conceivable:

a. Life prolonged without food. But this would be irreconcilable with a system of successive production, nutrition, assimilation, and growth. Such beings would be perpetual possessors of the earth and the waters, in their own persons, without any progeny. Only imagine such a world! Shall we say one, or some number, of each species? Quadruped, bird, reptile, fish, mollusc, zoophyte, insect of every kind, including all those invisible without microscopic aid; each immortal.

b. Life prolonged by vegetable food alone. But this would require a differently constituted vegetable world: for there is no plant on the land or in the sea, which does not nourish myriads of minute insects, which are destroyed in the eating of the plants.

c. Must there be any multiplication by progeny, upon any scheme? Then, either the whole number must be always extremely small, by being kept down in some inconceivable way; or would, after a time, multiply to that degree that there would not be room for them. The land and the waters would be over-filled!

(2.) Let the supposition be, that death take place, but only in the way of natural decay and old age; not by violence, as in becoming the prey of other animals. This seems to be the hypothesis of T. K. or that for which he wishes. But he certainly has not reflected upon the working out of this notion. The debility and decay of age require the nursing and soothing attentions of other individuals of the same species. But, except very imperfectly in a few instances of *quadrumana* and some domesticated animals, nothing appears in the brute creation analogous to the care and tenderness of man for man, in nursing and tending the sick or feeble. Even in the human species, unless where RELIGION breathes its vital influence, that class of duties is miserably attended to. Let your worthy correspondent ask the aid of some judicious physiologist, to assist him in weighing the opposite amounts of suffering, the one by natural and untended decay, the other by an almost instantaneous act of violence by another creature, in the full health and vigour of the devoured animal. He will find the very reverse of the estimation which he appears to have made. Besides, there is some reason to think that the first surprise produces a paralysis, by which the sense of pain is diminished, or wholly extinguished. I am not writing ludicrously; but seriously, as the subject requires.

But Geology furnishes cases of animal life extinguished upon a scale immensely large, by other processes than being devoted to furnish nutriment for other living creatures. The polishing stone called tripoli was till lately thought to be a siliceo-argillaceous rock; but it is now ascertained to be a congeries of microscopic many-chambered shells: and there are rocks of nummulitic limestone, and vast heaps of the shell milliola compressed into solid masses. The able and indefatigable Curator to the Geological Society, Mr. Lonsdale, has discovered microscopic shells in chalk, unutterably numerous. In all these cases, the densely associated and countless millions of once living beings, which inhabited those shells, must have died by the unheaving, out of the sea, of the compact masses consisting of them, and being thus left dry. Was not that as painful a death as if they had supplied food to larger cephalopods? It was probably much slower, and consequently involving more protracted distress. Some approach may be made to an idea of the number of animals thus become the prey of death, by considering the fact that, in a cube of tripoli rock of but one-tenth of an inch, 500 millions of those shells are contained,* each one an exquisitely formed dwelling, comprising several cells, most beautiful in material, and in general structure resembling the existing genus *nautilus*. We might in like manner argue from the mountain limestone, in Yorkshire, Derbyshire, on the banks of the Wye, and in innumerable other places, many miles in extent and hundreds of feet in thickness; and which, without a microscope, any man may see to consist of scarcely any thing beside the skeletons of the many-fingered crinoideal families, and the occasional beds of bivalve and some univalve shells, evidently not brought together by any moving body of water, which would have broken their tender carved-work, and have left them a huddled mass; but, on the contrary, lying together, orderly, and in all ages and degrees of growth.

It is a common supposition that, in the interval between their creation and the fall of man, all animals were gentle, and fed solely upon vegetable productions. Some have proposed the hypothesis that the carnivorous tribes were not created till after the fall, or even after the deluge. This hypothesis seems to lessen the difficulty, but it overlooks the fact that the grasses, leaves, seeds, and fruits, which are the food of the herbivorous races, swarm with insect life. The supposition that the carnivorous animals could at any time have fed upon vegetables, cannot be entertained for a moment, except it were by a person quite ignorant of the anatomical structure of those ani-

* See Supplementary Note G.

mals. Their bones and muscles, their teeth, claws, stomachs, and intestines, *demonstrate* that they were *created* to be nourished solely by animal food. Let it also be considered, that the tribes of *fish*, great and small, with very inconsiderable exceptions, so immensely filling rivers, lakes, and the ocean, are formed by the all-wise Creator to be carnivorous. I have formerly thought that our first parents had never witnessed death, till they beheld with agony the first sacrifice, offered up by divine prescription. But I do not now see the necessity or the probability of such a state of things. Rather, the denunciation in Gen. ii. 17, would seem to imply that they understood *what* the penalty was, in consequence of their having witnessed the pangs of death, in the inferior animals.

5. What, then, is the meaning of Rom. viii. 20—"The creation (ver. 22, all the creation) has been made subject to vanity," &c.? I reply, that here the word (which is used in different senses and under great limitations, as in Col. i. 23; 1 Pet. ii. 13;) denotes the part of the created universe which is immediately related to man, or comes under his influence; and that "vanity" denotes the frustration of high and holy purposes to which that part of the universe is subjected by the wickedness of mankind, ungratefully towards God and cruelly towards sentient animals, abusing the gifts of providence.

6. Still, the question will be proposed, Are we compelled to acquiesce in these conclusions? Might not the deposition of all the strata, their superposition, the imbedding in them of vegetable and animal remains, and their elevation so as to form our present continents and islands, all have taken place in the 1656 years from the fall to the deluge, completed by the powerful action of the diluvial waters!

This is *the question of questions* in relation to Geology. To discuss it fully would require a volume: yet, long as this paper has become, I must offer a few words. There are two classes of men, each of which gives its reply.

The first class consists of those who have heard the word *Geology*, but have been told (often by truly excellent men) that it is a dangerous study, that it impugns the truth of the Scripture records, and that it seeks to betray the unwary into infidelity. Of this class, some have read a little about geological subjects, have heard say a little more, and have eked out the rest by their own conjecture and imagination: and they answer this question *in the affirmative.*

The second class of persons comprises those who have spent thirty, forty, even fifty years in laborious investigation; many of them, having set out with the opinion of the former class; who have personally explored all the most important districts in the British isles, in France, in the Alpine countries, in Germany, and in Eastern and Northern Europe; also, in Asia, North and South America, and many parts of Africa and Australasia; who have endured herculean toils in the field of personal labour; expending large sums of money in their travels for this very object; who have come to geological investigations well prepared by mathematical and chemical science; who have pursued those investigations with untiring perseverance, and with the severest jealousy against precipitate conclusions: and what answer do THEY give? With one mouth they say, No; IT IS IMPOSSIBLE.

There are thirty, or rather more, well-defined *beds*, *layers*, or *strata*, of *different** mineral masses, lying upon each other, so as to form the surface of the globe on which we dwell. These combine themselves, by natural characters, into three or four grand groups. Compare them to a set of books, in 30 or 40 volumes, piled up on their flat sides. No where, indeed, can *the whole* set of the earth's strata be displayed, lying each upon the other, for reasons which will presently appear; and, if it were so at any spot, all the power and art of men could never penetrate through more than one, two, or three of the layers. They are placed one over the other, in a *sure* and *known* order of succession; that is; though in *no* locality are *all* to be found, or (which is saying the same thing conversely) in *every* locality *some* are wanting, the order of position is never violated. Let the letters of the alphabet represent the strata, thus; the TERTIARY, *a*, *b*, *c*, *d*, *e;* the SECONDARY, *i. e.* all from the chalk to the old red sandstone inclusive, *f* to *z;* the PRIMARY, *aa*, *bb*, &c. to *jj:* then observe that any member or several members of the series may be *absent*, for example, *d* or *f*, or *l* or *p;* but *b* is never above *a*, nor *m* above *k*, nor *s* above *q*. When this fact is rightly conceived of, let it be further observed, that the strata do not lie over each other in continuous concentric spheroids, like the coats of an onion; but may rather be compared to a vast number of wafers, of irregular forms, laid on a globe, and patched upon each other in different sets as to thickness, and variously under-passing, out-cropping, and over-lapping. Now, let the mind imagine mighty forces from below, acting upon certain points and along certain lines: then the wafer patches will be raised to all angles, bent, broken, their edges often turned up, so that the edges of lower strata stand in some places over the higher ones which had been thus shat-

* *Different* in mineral composition: for it must be observed, that many a homogeneous stratum of great thickness is itself laminated or stratified, like the leaves of a book or a number of pasteboards closely pressed together.

tered. Further, let the mind conceive of a mass of melted matter, suppose pitch, having lain for some time quietly underneath the lowest of the wafer-patches; then boiling up, bursting forth, and in many places raising the wafers, piercing them, passing through them, and finally hardening in fantastic shapes, and towering over the upheaved and fractured outside. This little play of imagination will present a pretty fair idea of the *real stratification* of the earth's surface, the eruption of the *non-stratified* (granitic and similar) rocks which have boiled up, elevating linear ridges (mountain-ranges) when they could not pierce through, but actually piercing through where their force could overcome the resistance, and when cooled, remaining the magnificent crags and summits of the loftiest mountains. It must also be understood, as a matter of the clearest *sensible demonstration*, that these processes have occurred several times, at various and distant intervals; producing among the strata many varieties of direction, inclination, contortion, cleavage, conformity, and nonconformity in reference to each other. If all the strata could be placed, or, for illustration sake we may say replaced, upon each other, to what thickness or depth would they amount? It is commonly said five miles: Dr. Buckland, who is so eminently qualified to make an estimate, gives his authority to the supposition of ten miles. With respect to the actual surface of the earth, the greatest height from the lowest valley-bottom to the top of the highest mountain, may be taken at five miles. This height, compared to the diameter of the earth, may be fairly represented by the thickness of a *fine* thread laid upon the surface of a twelve-inch globe.

All these things being considered, the inquirer may be able to conceive the appearance of the accessible end, or denuded cross-cut, of a stratum or several strata. The observer sees that the whole has been deposited from water either as a mere precipitate from a mixture, or as separated from chemical solution. Hence, the variety of rocks, siliceous, clayey, limestone, marly, and all these in various compounds. The eye also perceives, in many cases, the lower portion of a stratum to contain pebbles, the waterworn fragments of the older rocks to which they can be traced; higher up, the coarser sandstone; and towards the top, the finer sediment. Moreover, the separations of the distinct strata are often presented to view; the bounding surfaces of the formations.

Now we want a *measure* for the rate of deposition. A *perfect* rule for this is beyond the present reach of science; but there is an ample sufficiency of *ascertained facts*, to prove that *the whole series of deposits has occupied untold ages.* This letter has grown to so alarming a length, that I can only hint at the phenomena which furnish the grounds for this approximate estimate. They are observations upon the rates of deposit, in all kinds and in all circumstances, as it is continually going on in ponds, lakes, river-beds, estuaries, deltas, flat shores, siliceous and limestone springs of water, and conclusions analogical but most powerfully supported, concerning the deposits in the depths of the ocean.

This may give some idea of the processes of observation and reasoning, by which we are brought to the conclusion which I have mentioned; that the whole series of stratifications, which lie upon the *non-stratified* masses of rock, MUST have taken a period of time *immeasurable by mortals*, but which is but a point in comparison with the ETERNITY of the *CREATOR.*—It may be proper also to observe, that it is only in the *newest* and *latest* kinds of formation that any remains of man and his contemporary animals are to be found.

6. By this long but necessary circuit, we are brought to the question of your correspondent. We cannot resist the evidence of facts perceived by ocular demonstration, and every other kind of sensible evidence: and that evidence tells us that the system of organized life which the Creator has established, is *a cycle of production, growth, decay, and death.*

It is easy to shew that this plan of vegetable and animal existence provides for an amount of creatures and their enjoyment, unutterably greater than any scheme imaginable by us, and which should exclude death by carnivorous violence. We ought not to smile at this; nor to affect horror at it: let us examine thoroughly, and judge fairly.

7. But, if even we decline to press this reasonable argument, we have a last resort: "Who art thou, O man, that repliest against God? Shall the thing formed say to Him that formed it, Why hast thou made me thus?"

8. We may now ask, what is the just interpretation of Rom. v. 12. "By one man sin entered into the world, and DEATH BY SIN?" We reply, that it refers to the access and dominion of death *over man*, involving the presupposition that, had not our first parents sinned, they would, on the expiration of their probationary state, have undergone *a physical change different from dying*, which would have translated them into a higher condition of happy existence. This glorious prospect they forfeited, and, as the just penalty of their transgression, sunk down into the condition of the inferior animals, in becoming the prey of temporal or corporal death: but, in relation to their higher capacities, they plunged themselves into the gulf of death in senses infinitely more awful. Thus to Adam and all his

natural descendants, "the *sting* [that which constitutes it a real evil] of death is SIN:" but to the irrational creation this does not apply. They are incapable of moral obedience or disobedience towards God (though they have *resemblances* of both with respect to man, who is to them in the place of God, Gen. i. 26;) and therefore death is not a sting to them, in a spiritual sense, or in any sense inconsistent with the equity, goodness, and wisdom of the divine government.

As your inquiring correspondent calls himself "a beginner in Geological Researches," he will not deem me presuming or rude if I offer a few words of humble advice: and, for brevity sake, I will suppose myself to be addressing a young friend.

1. Do not suppose that a satisfactory knowledge of Geology can be obtained in a short time, or by skimming over a book or two.

2. Necessary prerequisites are a knowledge of chemistry, mineralogy, and natural history, particularly comparative anatomy, conchology, and botany according not only to the Linnæan artificial system, but to the natural arrangement of Dr. Lindley, or some other recent and eminent botanist. A profound intimacy with any one of these branches of science is indeed a work for a man's life; but where there is such a minute acquaintance with any one, a masterly knowledge of the others is easily and delightfully acquired, provided the due appropriation be made of *time* and *diligence*. But a general knowledge of essential principles, taking care that it be ACCURATE *so far as it goes*, may be acquired by pains-taking in the few inestimable years which usually follow a good school education.

3. Go into the field of actual search and observation; sea-cliffs, steep ravine sides, quarries, cuttings through hills for highways, canals, rail-roads, and well-diggings, or any accessible exhibitions of the faces of rocks. The great gravelly plain of London is destitute of good localities of this kind: yet the sand-pits of Woolwich yield a very good lesson. But the West of England, Wales, and the North, are the grand academy for these studies. A person who has made himself familiar with a few *good* instances, will be able, with the aid of books, maps, views, and sections, to form a mental idea of others; which will be in its measure just, though of course far inferior to the impression of the actual objects. Mr. De la Beche's *How to Observe, in Geology*, will be found of great use.

4. Hand-specimens of rocks must be studied. There are many fine collections throughout the kingdom. I may mention Bath, Bristol, Brighton, Norwich, York, Scarborough, Leeds, Newcastle-upon-Tyne, Liverpool, and many other places.

5. For books, without involving the least prejudice against other

valuable works, I take the liberty of recommending the following short list.

Prof. John Phillips's *Guide to Geology;* the last edition, and his *Treatises on Geology* in the seventh edition of the Encyclopædia Britannica, and published separately; Edinb. 1837, and in the Cabinet Cyclopædia. The latter works form excellent illustrations of the preceding.

Mr. Lyell's *Principles of Geology;* 4 vols. 12mo. the fifth edition, 1837. An admirable collection of facts, and which carefully separates facts from hypotheses. Mr. L. makes you acquainted with the former, without urging your assent to the latter.*

Outlines of the Geology of England and Wales; by the Rev. W. D. Conybeare, and the late Mr. W. Phillips; Vol. i. 1822. Unhappily the second volume has never been published: but I have reason to hope that Mr. Conybeare will favour the world with a new work, incorporating, condensing, and completing the volume just mentioned, which is now far behind the actual state of geological science, but it can never lose its value for local descriptions.

De la Beche's *Geological Manual,* 8vo. 1833. Phillips's *Guide* should precede this.

The same author's *Tablet of the Tertiary and Secondary Rocks.*

Viguier and Collon's Tablet, drawn from Alex. Brongniart's *Tableau des Terrains.* Paris.

These two are single sheets of paper upon a synoptic plan, and comprising the essence of many volumes: and the same praise is due to the tablet which forms the first plate in Dr. Buckland's *Bridgewater Treatise;* 2 vols. 8vo. 1836. That work is of the richest interest for Palæontology, the study of organic remains; but a *previous* acquaintance with the mineralogical branch is absolutely necessary, and it did not belong to Dr. Buckland's design and plan to supply that.

A series of exceedingly good systematical papers on Geology and the Minerals, are in the *Penny Magazine,* chiefly during the year 1833: but many since. No. 51, Jan. 19, 1833, contains a little Tablet admirably drawn up, perhaps in imitation of Mr. De la Beche's. Also, in the *Saturday Magazine* for the present year, 1837, a series has commenced of *Familiar Illustrations of Geology.* Two articles have appeared, viz. in Nos. 329 and 344; and they well answer to their title.

* The Elements of Geology, by Mr. Lyell, the second edition, is in two volumes, and should be studied before, and then in collation with, the Principles; of which also say the sixth edition. [1847. Of course, the *latest* editions must be sought.]

A System of Geology, with a Theory of the Earth, and an Explanation of its Connexion with the Sacred Records. By John Macculloch, M. D. F. R. S. 2 vols. 8vo. 1831. This is a work which, for illustration and amplifying comment, should be read both after, and, a second and third time, concurrently with, any of the preceding. Indeed I would say, that Professor Phillips's Guide and this work, would admirably constitute the initial course. Dr. Macculloch was a geologist of a very high order, though he strangely neglected the Palæontological branch, indefatigable in the arduous toils of personal examination in the most interesting regions of Great Britain, an independent thinker, and yet a man who delighted to do homage to the government and the word of God. The work was written in 1821, and therefore some modifications and corrections will accrue, by comparing it *seriatim* with Mr. John Phillips's books. Yet we must confess that it has serious faults of style and manner. It ought also to receive, as a most important supplement or companion, the following posthumous work of the same author; which is indeed a little too prolix, and its arrangement might admit of much improvement, had not death put upon it the sacred seal of inviolability. *Proofs and Illustrations of the Attributes of* God, *from the Facts and Laws of the Physical Universe: being the Foundation of Natural and Revealed Religion.* 3 vols. 1837.

Finally, let me intreat the student to be on his guard against expecting, that a few months of light reading will make him a geologist. The study is indeed one for life; and that general acquaintance with it which a person of liberal education ought to possess, must be acquired with long continued diligence and care, to be minutely accurate, or he will be liable to fall into perpetual and most serious errors. "Those who have taken a narrow view of this great and growing branch of human knowledge, who have satisfied themselves with collecting a few fossil shells, naming a few compound rocks, and constructing a few sections and maps, may possibly be startled at the *mighty circle of perpetual research* in which they are unconsciously engaged."—*Phillips's Encycl. Treatise*, p. 4. J. P. S.

Homerton, Nov. 10, 1837.

Aug. 1839. I cannot resist the transcribing of some paragraphs from an unknown writer in the Christian Observer.

"As one who—has taken great interest in Geology, though no geologist, I beg to offer a few observations upon the idea that the inferior animals were not subject to death before the fall.——Perhaps, the remarks of a mere *christian* observer might, so far as they are of value, be received with less suspicion than those of a professedly scientific man.——I was accustomed to entertain the idea of death having passed generally upon the whole creation, at the fall of man. But, when I heard of the discoveries of geologists, I was led to examine into the foundation of this opinion. I referred to Scripture; but upon examination I found no passage which supports such a notion.——Not finding it declared in Scripture, I began to consider what reason there might be for supposing it; and I was led to the conclusion that there was none. For (setting aside the discoveries of geologists,) which is the most difficult to believe; that the inferior animals had only a limited existence, or that they were created immortal? Immortal! From the iguanodon or mammoth, to the fluttering butterfly or invisible animalcule? A notion which involves a belief of the eternal duration of the earth; unless we are to suppose a series of transmigrations from world to world, as each dissolved.——The belief that death was in the world previous to the fall of Adam, I am aware, *seems at first*, to a christian mind, to destroy the idea of death as a penal consequence of sin. But this difficulty soon vanishes: for, when man saw that he was placed above the inferior animals, not merely in the possession of intellect, but in being honoured with immortality while they were subject to death, he would not only understand *what was meant* by the threatened consequences of sin, but surely would feel the curse as denouncing a deep degradation, to be sunk to the level of that creation over which he was made lord. 'The wages of sin' were 'death;' a curse indeed, since it made him like the beasts that perish in this world, at the same time that it could not deliver the immortal spirit from the eternal wrath of its offended Maker."——J. A. W. in Christian Obs. July, 1839; p. 405.

[B.]

Referred to at page 11.

ON THE EVIDENCE DERIVED FROM ASTRONOMY TO THE EXTENT AND ANTIQUITY OF THE UNIVERSE.

In the Philosophical Transactions for 1800, is a paper by the late Sir William Herschel, upon the *Power of Telescopes to penetrate into Space*, a property distinct from the *magnifying* power. By observations and calculations which appear to have been conducted with the greatest care, and which were corroborated by facts independently and previously ascertained, the space penetrating power of his 40 feet reflector is brought out to be a little more than 191 times that of ordinary natural vision, or extending to more than 300,000 times the distance of Sirius, which on satisfactory grounds is regarded as one of the nearest of the fixed stars. The light by which Sirius is seen by us, moving at its known velocity of 192,000 miles in a second, is at least six years and four months on its passage to our system. By applying his equation, Sir William brought out that the brilliant nebulæ which only his telescope could [*at that time*] reach, are distant from our system by a number of miles, to express which in common arithmetical numeration requires twenty figures, of which the first eight are 11,765,475, the 11 denoting trillions, and the other number billions; the remaining part of the sum being much more than 948 thousand millions. This almost unmanageable number is expressed by Sir William Herschel thus,—"above 11¾ millions of millions of millions of miles!" It follows, that the light by which those bright objects become visible to us, cannot have been less than one million and nine hundred thousand years in its progress.

Yet, when we have strained our minds to contemplate, in the extremely feeble manner to which our faculties are competent, this overwhelming distance, we have no reason to think that we have touched the circumference of the astral sphere; or that we have advanced beyond the threshold of God's creation.

If it be objected that, in accordance with these deductions, we might expect new portions of Jehovah's dominion to be frequently disclosing themselves, stars and clusters of stars "blushing out" on our view, new to us, because their light had now first arrived at our earthly abode; I conceive the following considerations sufficient to meet the objection.

1. The absolute distances of fixed stars and groups from each other, may be such as to require respective intervals of years and even centuries for the light of the more remote objects to reach us; that light arriving successively from each according to the distance.

2. Our case refers to objects which, though self-luminous, are not visible to the naked eye. They may "blush out," even frequently; but men are not capable of being their observers. Only a few of mankind can enjoy, and be qualified to use, such telescopes as those of Sir William Herschel, and his still more accomplished son.

3. Granting the possession of those advantages, the opportunities for observation are too scanty for the construction of a negative argument. Sir William Herschel, in the same paper, says that the number of night-hours, suited to this kind of celestial observation, is

averaged favourably in our climate at one hundred in a year; and that to "sweep,"—to examine as rapidly as is consistent with astronomical attention,—every zone of the heavens, for the two hemispheres, would require eight hundred and eleven of such favourable years. The number of the objects to be observed is great almost beyond conception. Sir W. H. by counting the stars in a definite portion of the field of view, which he observed in one hour, and estimating the rest, concluded that fifty thousand passed under his review in that hour. It is therefore within the scope of probability that new masses of light are achieving their first arrival in parts of our telescopic sphere, frequently, without its being possible for men to be aware of it: and, when any of them come to be discovered, the date of their arrival is unknown.

I draw no argument from the fact that, within the short period of the last two or three centuries, stars have been discovered which earlier catalogues or descriptions had not noticed. The attention, requisite to give certainty in this matter, we cannot assume to have been exercised; and to look for evidence from this quarter would be forgetting that it can exist in the domain of only the greatest telescopic powers.

These views of the antiquity of that vast portion of the Creator's works which Astronomy discloses, may well abate our reluctance to admit the deductions of Geology, concerning the past ages of our planet's existence.

Fourth ed. The argument of this Note may be usefully represented by comparison. The velocity of light is 192,000 miles in a second of time. I borrow the following Table and observations from an interesting paper intitled "Astronomical Transcendentalism," in the *Scottish Congregational Magazine*, Jan. 1847.

"From the Moon, light comes to the earth in				1¼	second.
"	Sun	"	"	8	minutes.
"	Jupiter	"	"	52	"
"	Uranus	"	"	2	hours.
"	a fixed star of the 1st magnitude,			3 to 12	years.
"	"	2d	"	20	"
"	"	3d	"	30	"
"	"	4th	"	45	"
"	"	5th	"	66	"
"	"	6th	"	96	"
"	"	7th	"	180	"
"	"	12th	"	4000	"

"Now, as we see objects by the rays of light passing from those objects to our eye, it follows that we do not perceive the heavenly bodies *as they are* at the moment of our seeing them, but *as they were* at the time the rays of light by which we see them left those bodies. Thus, when we look at the moon, we see her, not as she is at the moment of our beholding her disc, but as she was a second and a quarter before; for instance, we see her, not at the moment of her rising above the horizon, but 1¼ second after she has risen. The sun, also, when he appears to us to have just passed the horizon, has already passed it by 8 minutes. So, in like manner, of the planets and the fixed stars. We see Jupiter, not as he is at the moment of our catching a sight of him, but as he was 52 minutes before. Uranus appears to us, not as he is at the moment of our discovering him, but as he was 2 hours previously. And a star of the 12th magnitude presents itself to our eye, as it was 4000 years ago: so that, suppose such a star to have been annihilated 3000 years back, it would still be visible on the earth's surface for 1000 years to come: or, suppose a star of the same magnitude had been created at the time the Israelites left Egypt, it will not be perceptible on the earth for nearly 700 years from this date" [i. e. till A. D. 2547].

After some striking applications of these truths, the able and ingenious author proceeds:—"Of what use are such speculations? We reply that, besides seeking to awaken—impressive views of the grandeur of creation, and reverential feelings towards HIM who made and who sustains all this wondrous scheme,——they may help us to apprehend, in some degree, what may be the grand conditions of knowledge, in that higher state which, for ransomed man, is to succeed the resurrection."—The whole Essay will richly reward perusal.

May I intreat my young readers to brace themselves up to the acquiring of astronomical knowledge? Let them combine with the facts, above stated, just ideas of the number, magnitudes, distances, and motions of the heavenly bodies. Let them reflect upon such truths as these. Of our earth the circumference is 25,000 miles. The moon, at the distance of 240,000 miles, is less than a fiftieth of the earth's bulk. If the sun were laid upon the earth, the centres corresponding, it would cover the orbit of the moon around the earth, and its circle extend 200,000 miles beyond. Our distance from the sun is 95 millions of miles: that of the planet Herschel [—I abhor and lament the change, to which we have no choice but to submit:—Christians owe no honour to the Grecian idolatry:—] is from the sun twenty times our distance: that of Le Verrier's planet, which we are condemned to call Neptune (three thousand two hundred millions of miles,) about thirty-five times our distance. To travel from the earth to the Herschel, at the rate of 20 miles an hour, would require ten thousand years; but, at a thousand miles an hour, it would take only

200 years. Our solar system is itself moving, at the rate of 35,000 miles an hour, among the fixed stars; and were our system to be annihilated, it would not be missed by an intellect like ours surveying no more than *what we know* of the astral universe. Of that astral universe, the number of stars, within the range of good telescopes, is computed at 100 millions: but, to examine every part of the celestial hemisphere, with due observance, supposing 100 favourable hours each year (a good average for the climate of Britain,) would require 800 years. If, from the most distant part of the heavens, the light has taken two millions of years to come to us,—could we be transported thither,—perhaps we should have advanced to the threshold only of the material creation.

It will interest the ingenuous reader to see two paragraphs from subsequent papers of Sir William Herschel, which, being in the *Philosophical Transactions of the Royal Society*, are accessible to those only who have the opportunity of consulting that voluminous repository of science.

"Hence it follows, that, when we——see an object of the calculated distance at which one of these very remote nebulæ may still be perceived, ... the rays of the light which convey its image to the eye, must have been more than nineteen hundred and ten thousand, that is almost *two millions* of years on their way; and that consequently so many years ago, this object must already have had an existence in the sidereal heavens, in order to send out those rays by which we now perceive it." *Philos. Trans.* for 1802; p. 498.

"——When our gages will no longer resolve the Milky Way into stars, it is not because its nature is ambiguous, but because it is fathomless." *Philos. Trans.* 1818; p. 463. The last contribution, I believe, to Astronomy, from that distinguished man. He died, Aug. 23, 1822, aged 83.

Alexander von Humboldt, in his *Cosmos*, transl. by Mrs. Colonel Sabine, (vol. i. pp. 145, 496; Lond. 1846,) cites the former of the two of these memorable passages, and adds the observation:—"Such events or occurrences—reach us as voices of the past.——We penetrate at once into space and time.——Much [of the phenomena in past periods] may have disappeared even before it became visible to our eyes, and in much the arrangement and order may have varied. ——It is more than probable that the light of the most distant cosmical bodies offers us the oldest sensible evidence of the existence of matter."

I subjoin a recent contribution to this branch of astronomical science, extracted from the "*Etudes d'Astronomie Stellaire*," a Report upon the State of Astral Observation, made to Count Ouvaroff, Min. of Publ. Instr. and Presid. of the Imperial Acad. of Sciences, by Prof. F. G. W. Struve; May 19, 1847. Petersburgh.

Table of the Time required by the different Magnitudes of Stars, for the passage of their respective Emissions of Light to our Sun. The Earth may be safely taken to be the same, as the difference is only a very minute fraction.

MAGNITUDE.		RADII OF THE EARTH'S ORBIT.	JULIAN YEARS, NEGLECTING FRACTIONS.
I.	One whose distance from our sun is	986,000	15
	Another	1,246,000	19
II.	One	1,778,000	28
	Another	2,111,000	33
III.	One	2,725,000	43
	Another	3,151,000	49
IV.	One	3,850,000	60
	Another,	4,375,000	69
V.	One	5,378,000	84
	Another	6,121,000	96
VI.	One	7,616,000	120
	Another	8,746,000	137
	Another	8,100,000	127
VII.	For the distance	14,230,000	224
VIII.	————	24,490,000	386
IX.	————	37,200,000	586
	A star	224,500,000	3541

"And these are SUNS! Vast, central, living fires,
Lords of dependent systems, kings of worlds
That wait as satellites upon their power
And flourish in their smile. Awake, my soul,
And meditate the wonder. Countless suns
Blaze round thee, leading forth their countless worlds!
Worlds, in whose bosoms living things rejoice,
And drink the bliss of being from the fount
Of all-pervading love. What mind can know,
What tongue can utter, all their multitudes?
Thus numberless in numberless abodes!
Known but to THEE, Blest Father! Thine they are,
Thy children and thy care; and none o'erlooked
Of thee. No, not the humblest soul that dwells
Upon the humblest globe that wheels its course
Amid the giant glories of the sky;
Like the mean mote that dances in the beam
Amongst the thousand mirror'd lamps, which fling
Their wasteful splendour from the palace-wall.
None can escape the kindness of thy care;
All compass'd underneath thy spacious wing;
Each fed and guided by THY powerful hand."

Prof. Henry Ware, jun., Cambridge Univ. Massachusetts. For the citation I am indebted to Dr. W. B. Carpenter's *Popular Cyclop.* vol. iv. 1843.

[B b.]

Referred to at page 32.

ON THE THICKNESS OF THE SOLID CRUST OF THE EARTH.

"As for the internal heat of the earth, I am of opinion that it ought not to be considered as an hypothesis, but as a *fact* well grounded on numerous phenomena." Prof. Gustav Bischoff, of Bonn, in Jameson's Journal, Jan. 1841, p. 14.

"All the calculations,—if they can be at all trusted, tend to prove that the earth's crust is not much more, and perhaps less, then *twenty* miles in thickness: and if this be so, the crust may indeed be well compared with a thin sheet of ice over a frozen pool."—Mr. Darwin, in Memoir on the Connexion of certain Volcanic Phenomena in South America, *Geol. Trans.* second ser. vol. v. p. 608, 1840. This able philosopher uses the language of deferential caution from respect to Mr. Parrot, (known for his observations on the Caspian Sea, &c.) but with little or no doubt in his own richly-informed mind. In this interesting Memoir, Mr. Darwin brings much evidence to establish the position, that the crust of the earth rests upon a mass of melted mineral matter, whose undulations, with other modifying causes, produce elevations, earthquakes, and volcanos. He has eminently the talent of simple but graphic description, and luminous deduction. Considering the extent of the field of action, a space, in the instance considered, of little less than 7000 miles,—"and likewise the symmetry of the whole, we shall be deeply impressed with the grandeur of the *one motive power* which, causing the elevation of the continent, has produced, as secondary effects, mountain-chains and volcanos. The same reasons, which led me to the conviction that the train of connected volcanos in Chile and the recently uplifted coast, together more than 800 geographical miles in extent, rested on *a sheet of fluid matter*, are applicable, with nearly equal force, to the areas beneath the other trains." After enumerating several considerations, he continues: "It appears to me that there is little hazard in assuming, that this large portion of the earth's crust floats in a like manner on *a sea of molten rock*. Moreover, when we think of the increasing temperature of the strata, as we penetrate downwards in all parts of the world, and of the certainty that every portion of the surface rests on rocks which have once been liquefied;—when we consider the multitude of points from which fluid rock is annually emitted, and the still greater number of points from which it has been emitted during the few last geological periods inclusive, which, as far as regards the cooling of the rock in the lowest abysses, may probably be considered as one, from the extreme slowness with which heat can escape from such depths;——when we reflect how many and wide areas in all parts of the world are certainly known some to have been rising and others sinking, during the recent æra even to the present day, and do not forget the intimate connexion which has been shown to exist between these movements and the propulsion of liquefied rock to the surface in the volcano;——we are urged to include *the entire globe* in the foregoing hypothesis.——The furthest generalization, which the consideration of the volcanic phenomena appears to lead to, is that *the configuration of the fluid surface of the earth's nucleus is subject to some change,——its cause completely unknown,——its action slow and intermittent*, but irresistible." Pp. 629—631.

But justice to this subject requires it to be stated that Mr. William Hopkins has applied his pre-eminent talents in mathematical analysis to the solution of this problem. Of this laborious investigation he has given the processes and the results, in four papers, communicated to the Royal Society in the years 1838, 1839, and 1842, "On the State of the Interior of the Earth;" and published in the Philos. Trans. of those years. That the entire mass of the earth was originally in a fluid state, and that, by cooling, it has obtained a superficial coating of solidified matter, was first adopted as a result of astronomical considerations, but is now corroborated by the discoveries of geology. It occurred to Mr. H. that an indirect, but sure test of the truth of the hypothesis might be derived from the consideration of the Nutation of the Earth's Axis, a fact arising from the attractions of the sun and the moon, which produce the Precession of the Equinoxes. It is obvious that this nutation must affect the earth differently on the supposition of its being a fluid contained in a solid spheroidal shell, from what it would do if the globe were throughout a solid mass. Equally is it to be expected that differences of result will be produced according as the quantity of the contained fluid is less or greater; that is, as the thickness of the containing crust is greater or less. An indefinite number of conditions is thus presented for selection and investigation. To the immense labour of these operations, Mr. Hopkins applied himself, with his characteristic power and perseverance. Now the amount of the gyratory change constantly produced by the nutation of the pole is astronomically known. But the amount, as deduced from the hypothesis of the earth's being composed of a heterogeneous solid shell inclosing a heterogeneous fluid, will not agree with the actually known amount, unless the ellipticity of the interior surface of the shell were less by a certain quantity than that of the outward surface. Finally, Mr. H. arrives at the conclusion that the thickness of the crust, to answer all the conditions, must be at least equal to one-fourth or one-fifth of the distance from the outer circumference to the centre of the earth; in other words, that the thickness of the solid envelope of the globe cannot be less than 800 or 1000 miles.

Here then is an astounding difference from the conclusion before mentioned, that in which so many eminent and accomplished physicists agree, and of which the evidence appears unexceptionable. But Mr. H. has furnished a mode of conciliation. He supposes that the solidity of the crust is not everywhere the same, but that there are insulated fluid masses, or what may be called vesicles, interspersed through it, containing portions of more fusible matter, and which is actually in a state of fusion, forming subterranean reservoirs or lakes, some of which are distinct, and others communicating by passages of different degrees of openness or obstruction. This he proposes for the explanation of the phenomena of volcanos. We must extend the idea, by supposing an extensive distribution of those fiery lakes, so as to cause the observed ratio of the increase of temperature in the descent of mines.

This investigation has produced another very important result, in *demonstrating that no change has taken place in the direction of the earth's axis*, from the epoch of the formation of the external crust.

Fourth ed.—On this subject, at the sitting of the Paris Academy of Sciences, Dec. 9, 1844, "M. Elie de Beaumont made some observations on a question submitted for consideration, viz. What relation exists between the progressive cooling of the earth and that of its surface? M. de B. thinks that the experiments made by M. Arago, in the gardens of the Observatory at Paris, with thermometers sunk in the earth at various depths, furnish the most essential elements which are necessary for the solution of the problem. According to this solution, the antiquity of the period, when our globe was entirely incandescent, is of a remoteness which defies calculation." *Athenæum*, Dec. 28, 1844; p. 1202.

[C.]

Referred to at page 41.

ON THE NUMBER OF SPECIES IN THE EARLIER FOSSILIFEROUS ROCKS.

THIS proposition, as it stood in the first edition, expressed the doctrine, which till lately was received among geologists, that the organic remains found in the earliest rocks possessing any such remains at all, are "the fewest" in proportionate numbers. But the recent herculean toils of Mr. Murchison have opened new fields of view upon this interesting subject. The proposition is a little altered, that it may be in accordance with the observation of that distinguished geologist; "Another remarkable fact illustrating this point of inquiry is, that although the older fossiliferous strata often contain *vast quantities* of organic remains, the *number of species* is much smaller than in more recent deposits." Silur. Syst. p. 583.

It is interesting to observe the careful and cautious progress of Geology, as in other respects, so in this. Seven years before the publication of Mr. Murchison's work, Sir Henry De la Beche had treated this subject with his characteristic judgment and sagacity. I will cite a few paragraphs, as specimens of the penetration and anticipations of his geological mind, while the facts of the case were not as yet brought clearly to light; and with a wish also to excite my readers to peruse the whole passage. It must be premised that the German term *grauwacke*, now generally disused, must be understood as the same with, or including, the Silurian System.

"Although, when we regard the mass of the grauwacke rocks, we are struck with the *minute proportion* that organic remains bear to the whole, we must still perceive that the atmosphere was capable of supporting vegetation; and the seas of sustaining zoophytes, crinoidea, annulata, conchifera, mollusca, crustacea, and fish. What other creatures existed, we are unable, *from the absence of their remains*, to judge: it may however be by no means unphilosophical to conclude that vegetation did not exist alone on dry land, but that, consistently with the general harmony of nature, it afforded food to terrestrial creatures suited to the circumstances under which they were placed." [Yet no vestiges of such creatures have been found.]——"Whatever the kind of animal life may have been which first appeared on the surface of our planet, we may be certain that it was consistent with the wisdom and design which has always prevailed throughout nature; and that each creature was peculiarly adapted to that situation designed to be occupied by it." *Geological Manual;* third ed. pp. 428, 429; 1833.

I hope I shall not give pain to a very kind friend whose qualifications make him one of the safest authorities, by transcribing a part of a letter with which he has favoured me. The certainty and accuracy of the remarks may be fully relied upon, and their application is extensively important.

"In the *older* fossiliferous rocks, animal life appears in as full a developement with respect to SIZE, as in the existing analogous animals. The zoophagous cephalopods were also of gigantic growth. It does not appear that animal life, at that period, was limited with respect to NUMBER. The lowest Silurian rocks are crowded, in some localities, with organic bodies; and their absence over extensive districts is only a condition in the distribution of testacea, &c. which prevails in our seas. There are many coasts from which a reasoner, who had visited no other, might infer that marine animals are *now* few and small-sized; and, if he were a geologist, he might say, Life is on the decrease!" WILLIAM LONSDALE, ESQ. Sept. 7, 1839.

[On this subject, however, the following statements from men of the highest authority, as to both science and judgment, cannot be disregarded. But a conciliation arises from considering that the actually occurring fossils in the *Protozoic* rocks are no index of those which existed in previous periods of life; for causes of decomposition must have existed to a great extent. Not only countless individuals but vast groups, animal and vegetable, must have been totally obliterated. Mr. Lonsdale's doctrine, with regard to the lowest Silurian, is confirmed by the observations of the geologist of New York, Mr. James Hall, in the *Boston Journal of Nat. Hist.* Jan. 1845, p. 14.]

"One general conclusion becomes very apparent: wherever we meet with rocks admitting of the preservation of organic remains, the number of these decreases as we descend in the series, till we arrive at a period when the physical monuments of the globe bear no trace of organized beings; an abyss which gives no record of life, and which sets a bound to our zoological inquiries." Prof. Sedgwick, at the Plymouth Meeting of the Brit. Assoc. Aug. 3, 1841.

"These remains of life are most plentiful in the upper strata; decrease in number and variety as we proceed downwards; and, by gradual and continual diminution, approach in the lowest to absolute extinction." Mr. Phillips, at the same time and place.

["It is now a truth which I consider as proved, that the *ensemble* of organized beings was RENEWED, not only in the interval of each of the great geological divisions which we have agreed to term Formations, but also at the time of the deposition of *each particular member* of *all* the formations. For example, I think that I can prove that, in the Oolitic formation (at least within the limits of the Swiss Jura) the organic contents of the Lias, those of the Oolitic group properly so called, those of the Oxfordian group, and those of the Portlandian group, (as they occur in Switzerland,) are as different *from each other* as the fossils of the Lias from those of the Keuper [Pœcilitic], or those of the Portlandian beds from those of the Neocomian formation [Greensand]. I also believe very little in the *genetic descent* of living species from those of the various tertiary layers which have been regarded as identical, but which, in my opinion, are specifically distinct. I cannot admit the idea of the *transformation of species* from one formation to another. In advancing these general notions, I do not wish to offer them as inductions drawn from the study of any particular class of animals, (of the fishes, for instance,) and [thence, by mere theoretical analogy,] applied to other classes; but as the results of *direct observation* of very considerable collections of fossils, of different formations, and belonging to different classes of animals, in the investigation of which I have been specially engaged for many years." Prof. Agassiz; *Report to the Brit. Assoc. on the Fossil Fish of the Old Red;* 1842.]

[D.]

Referred to at page 47, but intended to apply to all the Propositions of Lecture II.

SYNOPTIC TABLE OF STRATIFIED FORMATIONS.

In compliance with the desire of many and those unconnected friends, I have compiled a short view of the Strata of the Earth, almost exclusively as they are developed in our own island. But a similarity will apply to every other country, if the comparison be rightly made; for there are few formations known to exist in any part of the globe, which have not their equivalent or representative in Great Britain; excepting some of the numerous and circumscribed Tertiaries of the Continent.

As this attempt represents only the strata, or aqueous deposits, the reader will understand the vast mass of granite and other igneous rocks as lying under the gneiss, the last stratum; and will recollect that, in various forms, it has elevated, pierced through, and surmounted the strata. (See p. 35.) For impressing this lesson, he will not neglect to avail himself of the graphic representations presented in the splendid first plate of Dr. Buckland's Bridgewater Treatise; or De la Beche's Tabular View, which extends only to the Devonian; or the seventh of Dr. Mantell's Wonders of Geology; or the French plate by Viguier and Collon, as an Exposition of Alex. Brongniart's volume, Tableau des Terrains; or Bartlett's Index Geologicus, (Plymouth, 1841,) which gives a lucid view of all the formations, the seats of metals, and the genera and species of fossils, vegetable and animal, properly classified.

I would advise the possessor of this volume to tint the spaces in the strata column with *faint* water-colours. In the Tertiary, apply with judgment alternate bands of yellow and light brown; the crag, fawn colour; the London clay, slight indian-ink; leave the chalk white; the gault, the lias, the Silurian, and the Cumbrian, light purple, varying the hues; the green sands and the mica schist, green, but the latter with streaks of red; the weald, Hastings, and Purbeck, hues of brown; the oolites, [to be pronounced in three syllables, *o-o-lite*,] bands of gamboge and fawn colour; the pœcilitic, [pron. *poikilitic*,] red, mottled with purple, green, and a few white spaces; the coal, &c. curved bands of indian-ink, with brown, and blue; the millstone grit, greenish brown; the limestones, blue; the Devonian, brick-red; the Cambrian, green, mottled with purple; and the gneiss, pink.

Upon so small a scale, the descriptions are necessarily incomplete, but I hope they are not materially erroneous. *All* the Tertiary beds must not be understood as being successionary; for many are mutually equivalents in different districts, for example, the London clay and the Paris gypseous rocks. Indeed, if we regard this class in France, Belgium, up the Rhine, &c. the number is far greater than this small tablet could represent. These equivalent or substitutionary beds may be compared to cakes of dough, dropped irregularly on beds of other kinds of plastic matter, and lying (to speak with some laxity) nearly in the same plane. I can devise no other way of presenting them, in this small space. In selecting *principal* organic remains, there must be difficulty; I can only follow my own opinion, and a candid geologist will not greatly disapprove. Those in italics are pointed out as the more interesting.

The thicknesses cannot possibly be precise. The numbers given must be taken as *probable approximations* to the *greater* thickness of the masses; it being remembered, that, especially in the Tertiary formations, in consequence of depressions and elevations of the underlying strata, considerable differences must exist: and often they thin out towards the edges

The length of the spaces must not be taken as pretending to be upon a scale of proportions; which would be impossible, except with a very much extended sheet.

Class.	*Group or System.*	*Mineralogical Character.*	*Strata.*	*Some principal Locality.*	*Some principal Organic Remains.*
TERTIARY.		Surface-soil.		Every where.	Buried remains of existing species.
		Beds of rivers and lakes.			Existing species, merely preserved.
	Plistocene.	Sea-bottoms, Coral rocks.		Red Sea, Pacific, Australia, &c.	*Corals*, shells, fish-bones; recent.
		Peat, Marles, Travertins.		Britain, Ireland, Holland, Sicily, Scandinavia.	Existing species; some extinct; *incrustations*.
	Pliocene.	Drift, erratic blocks, gravel, mud-deposits, bone-caves.		Europe, America.	Existing species; more extinct. Elephants' teeth and bones. Carnivorous animals.
		Sands, and clays, limes. 300 feet.		Italy.	Shells of existing species; few extinct.
		Sands; the Crag. 60 feet.		Norfolk and Suffolk.	Sea shells and corals, most extinct.
	Miocene.	Sands and Clays. 400 feet.		South-west of France.	Many extinct.
		Sands, clays; fresh water. 60 feet.		Near Paris.	Shells, land and fresh water; most extinct.
	Eocene.	Same, but marine. 100 feet.		Same neighbourhood.	Sea shells, most extinct.
		Sands, gypsum, and marles; fr. water. 200 feet.		Same.	Extinct quadrupeds, birds, reptiles.
		Dark clay, (London,) pyrites, gypsum. 500 feet.		Essex, Kent, Middlesex, Hants.	Extinct quadrupeds, reptiles, plants, *fruits*; and marine remains.
		Fine sands, and clays. 400 feet.		Hants, &c.	Some sea and fresh water shells; extinct quadrupeds.

Class.	*Group or System.*	*Mineralogical Character.*	*Strata.*	*Some principal Locality.*	*Some principal Organic Remains.*
SECONDARY.	Cretaceous.	Chalk, with flints. ——, without flints. 600 feet.		Flamborough Head to Spilsby; north of Norfolk, through Cambridge, Herts, Berks, Wilts, to S. Dorset, Hants, Sussex, Surrey, Kent.	Abundant in marine productions; plants, sponges, corals, families of crinoidea, asterida, *echinida;* shells, bivalve, univalve, *chambered*, in great variety, crustacea, fish, *some reptiles*. Consult Dr. Mantell's Works.
		Green Sand, upper. Galt, bluish clay. Green Sand, lower. 500 feet.		Kent, Sussex, Isle of Wight.	Similar families to the chalk, but generally of different species; *ammonites*, *nautilites*, &c. small *belemnites*.
	Oolitic.	Weald Clay. Hastings sand. Purbeck stone. 900 feet.		Sussex, and spreading into Kent and Hants.	Some land-plants and fresh water shells; *endogenites;* fish; *monstrous lizard-like reptiles.*
		Oolite, upper. Portland Stone. Kimmeridge clay. O. middle. Coralline sandstone. Oxford clay. Forest marble. Kelloway's rock. Bradford clay. O. great. Stonesfield slate, Fuller's earth, &c. O. lower. 2,000 feet.		A narrow waving course, from north of Lynn to Portland. In Northampton, Bedford, Bucks, Oxford, Berks, Wilts, and Dorsetshires. Waving through Yorkshire, Lincoln, Northampton, Gloucester, Wilts, Dorset, Somerset.	*Trees gymnosperm, allied to* zamia*;* numerous shells of various orders, fish. Coralloids, *echinida;* shells, bivalve, and some univ.; crustacea; fish, lizard-formed; *didelphys.* Similar to the other Oolites; but more of cryptogamous land plants; *apiocrinites, trigoniæ, terebratulæ.*
		Lias. 700 feet.		Waving from Tees-mouth, through Notts, Lincoln, Leicester, Northampton, &c. to Dorset.	Very rich in gymnosp. wood, bivalves, ammonites, fish, *lizard-like reptiles, belemnites.*
	Triassic. Permian.	New Red sandstone, upper. Rock salt. Variegated Marle, (Pœcilitic.) Magnesian limestone, and conglomerate. New Red sandstone, lower. 1,000 feet.		Cumberland, Westmorl. and Durham. Yorks. Notts. Leicest. and Lanc. Cheshire, Stafford, Warwick. Vast tract in Russia.	Coniferous wood, and several species of the fern and equisetum tribes; fish; *saurians.*

SECONDARY—(*continued.*)	Carbo-niferous.	Coal, shale, and sandstone, in alternating layers, forming vast concave patches, like a series of irregularly shaped dishes. 3,000 feet.		Parts of South Scotland, Northern Counties of England, some of the Midland, South Wales.	The coal is entirely compressed land-vegetation, chiefly from trees of great size, whose stems, branches, leaves, &c. are abundant in or on the interposed shales and sands. The trees have been euphorbiaceous, coniferous, monocotyledonous, equisetaceous, ferns, lycopodiaceous, &c. Some river bivalve shells. Fish.
		Millstone grit. 700 feet.		Northern Counties, and Derby, Nottingham, &c.	Land-plants, as of the coal. Thin beds of limestone occur, having sea-shells.
		Mountain limestone, with some beds of shale, sandstones, and inferior coal. 1,000 feet.		Northumberland, Durham, Yorkshire, Derby, Monmouth, Glamorgan, Pembroke.	Land-plants, as the coal. Sea remains in great variety and abundance, as *crinoidea*, coralloids, bivalves, (spirifer, leptæna,) univalves, ammonites, and other chambered shells, *trilobites*, fish.
	Old Red Sandstone.	Red and brown sandstones, tile-stones and marles, with equivalent limestones in Devonshire; whence the system is now called Devonian. 10,000 feet, and in Scotland more.		Scotland; Salop, Hereford, Monmouth, South Wales, Somerset, Devon.	*Fish*. In the Devonian beds, the organic remains of the upper part resemble those of the mountain limestone; and the lower, those of the Silurian system. Those in Scotland and Russia are rich in fishes, of extraordinary forms, and often of considerable magnitude.

Class.	*Group or System.*	*Mineralogical Character.*	*Strata.*	*Some principal Locality.*	*Some principal Organic Remains.*
PRIMARY FOSSILIFEROUS.	Upper Silurian.	Ludlow, upper rocks. Sandstone and limestone. ——— lower. Wenlock and Dudley. Sandstone and limes. Horderley and May Hill. Flagstones, sandstones, and limes. Builth, Caradoc, and Llandeilo. Flags, sandstone, and limes. Longmynd and Gwastaden rocks. Siliceous, very hard and quartzy; slates. 10,000 feet, and probably more.		A district varying in breadth, and undulating southerly and westerly from the vale of Llangollen, through portions of Montgomery, Salop, Stafford (an upheaved insulated tract from Dudley to Beacon Hill,) Worcester, Gloucester, Hereford, Monmouth, Radnor, Brecon, Carmarthen, Pembroke.	Fish-fin-bones, *gigantic serpulæ*, coralloids, *crinoidea*, bivalve, and univalve shells of forms increasingly interesting, including many *brachiopoda*, *trilobites* in great number of the various species, *chambered shells*, straight and in variety of curvature, *graptolites*, *annelids*, &c. &c. See Murchison's Silurian System, founded on Geological Researches through the region.
	Lower Silurian. (Cambrian.)	Slate rocks of Plynlymmon, Snowdonia, &c. with dark limestones and sandstones, both fine and conglomerate. 7,000 feet, and more.		Merionethshire, Caernarvonshire, and other parts of North Wales; and in Cornwall.	Two or three species of coralloids (cyathophylla); a few species of *brachiopodous* conchifers, "*the oldest* monuments yet discovered of the creation of living things." See Phillips's Cyclop. Treat. I. 129; and p. 57 of these Lectures. In Cornwall, *Endosiphonites carinatus*.

METAMORPHIC.	Lowest Silurian. (Cumbrian.)	Vast rocks of slates, purple, green, &c. with very hard and fine sandstones, sometimes conglomerate; the lowest group of slates, soft. More than 10,000 feet.		Westmoreland, Cumberland, and a large breadth of South Scotland, from the Lammermuir Hills to the coast of Wigtownshire.	None.
	Mica schist.	Hard rock, consisting of mica and quartz interlaminated. Many thousand feet.		Scotland, south-west from Stonehaven, becoming very broad across Perthshire and Argyleshire to the Mull of Cantire, and the islands of Isla, Jura, &c.	None.
	Gneiss . . .	Gneiss consists of the component parts of granite (quartz, felspar, and mica); fine grained and laminated, so as to present the idea of being the product of granite, abraded, worn, and then deposited from the water, and acted upon by the heat below. Many thousand feet. See Note F, § 2.		Ben Lomond.	None.

The Crystalline Rocks, Granite, Syenite, Porphyry, Greenstone, Trap, &c. *Depth*, various, vast, not assignable.

[E.]

Referred to at page 49.

DISSERTATIONS ON THE VARIETIES OF THE HUMAN SPECIES.

It would be wrong to conceal the difficulties with which this subject is surrounded, however satisfied we may be with the evidence in favour of the descent of all mankind from one original pair of ancestors. The consideration of those difficulties has betrayed some men of eminence in physiological science into the opinion, that there are four or five *races* of the one species. The fact of a revelation from the Supreme Being, as contained in the Israelitish and the Christian Scriptures, is so firmly established by moral evidence, that we can no longer call it into question. We are entitled to regard it as a thing settled, as much as the chief facts of our national history: and the derivation of all men from the single pair created in Eden, plainly appears to be asserted in Scripture, and to form an article of the Christian doctrine. But, independently of that part of the inquiry, it is not too much to say, that the progress made in all the other lines of investigation is constantly removing, or at least abating, the reasons for doubt. For instance; the diversity of those which appear to be the primitive stems in the classification of languages, has seemed quite unaccountable, upon the hypothesis of a common origin. But the believer in revelation may see, in this circumstance, a ground for believing that the just and not less merciful interposition of divine power in the plains of Shinar, inflicted upon the distinct parties, into which the social mass was broken up, such a radical difference in the vocables as extinguished the idea of a previous intercommunity. Upon this very point also, where unassisted research seemed to be baffled, we are met by a fact undeniable, and directly applying to the subject. The affinity of the ancient Egyptians and the Hindoos has been established by the minute and extensively pervading resemblances in tradition, religion, arts, modes of life, and every important characteristic besides, *language excepted.* Yet this exception is most remarkable, and it contradicts all our notions of antecedent probability. Another class of facts is pointed out by the eminent scholar and naturalist to whom I have referred. "An extensive field of inquiry is opened by the observation, that traces exist, among *the most distant* African nations, of ancient connexion with the Egyptians.——The traces of animal-worship, the belief in metempsychosis, circumcision, and a variety of observances recorded by travellers, among the Kafirs, the native people of Madagascar, as well as among tribes in the western parts of Africa, are too extensively diffused, and occur in too many instances, to be attributed to accidental coincidence."*

Anatomical differences are indeed very great, but they all (with an exception which shall be presently mentioned) refer, not to the essential structure of parts, but only to some modifications of *form*. They are, therefore, capable of being accounted for, from the influence of climate, food, mode of life, occupation, and artificial means directly used to alter the figure of parts. Much stress has been laid upon the differing forms of the skull which are held to characterize the Iranian (= Japetic, or Caucasian,) the Mongole, the Negro-African, and the American, varieties, stocks, races, or whatever else they may be called, of the human species. But what is known concerning the methods used to procure the flattened disfiguration of the skull, so frightfully distinguishing some of the American tribes, both ancient and existing, while it accounts for extreme cases of deformity, clearly gives us a principle adequate to resolve the difficulty in many other deviations from a natural shape.

"Cox, in his Travels on the Columbia River, thus describes the method by which the singular flatness and elongation of the skull are produced:—'Immediately after birth, the infant is placed in a kind of oblong cradle, formed like a trough, with moss under it. One end, on which the head reposes, is more elevated than the rest. A padding is then placed on the forehead, with a piece of cedar-bark over it; and, by means of cords passed through small holes on each side of the cradle, the padding is pressed against the head. It is kept in this manner upwards of a year; and the process is not, I believe, attended with much pain. The appearance of the infant, however, while in this state of compression, is frightful; and its little black eyes, forced out by the tightness of the bandages, resemble those of a mouse choked in a trap. When released from this inhuman process, the head is perfectly flattened, and *the upper part of it seldom exceeds an inch in thickness.* It never afterwards recovers its rotundity. They deem this an essential point of beauty.'——" Linnæus Martin's Nat. Hist. of the Mammalia, vol. i. p. 207.

In the American Journal of Science, edited by Dr. Silliman, (the number for April, May, and June, 1840,) is a Review of an important work: "CRANIA AMERICANA; or a Comparative View of the Skulls of various Aboriginal Nations of North and South America: to which is prefixed an Essay on the varieties of the Human Species.

* Dr. Prichard's Researches; ii. 217.

By Sam. Geo. Morton, M. D. Prof. Anat. Pennsylvania Coll. folio, with 78 plates and a Map; Philad. 1839."* From this review I take the following extracts:—

"In Jan. 1839,—[was examined] a full-blooded Chenouk, twenty years old; his head as much distorted by mechanical compression as any skull of his tribe in Dr. Morton's possession. 'He appeared to me [Dr. M.] to possess more mental acuteness than any Indian I had seen: he was communicative, cheerful, and well-mannered.'—In May, 1839, Mr. George Combe, [the Scots phrenologist] met with Thomas Adams,—twenty years old, of the Cloughewalla tribe.—His head had been compressed by the board and cushions in his infancy. The parietal was actually greater than the frontal and occipital diameter. The organs in the superciliary ridge of the forehead were fully developed; the upper part of the forehead was flat and deficient; his organs of language and form were large. He had studied the English language for two years, and spoke it tolerably well. In conversation he was intelligent, ready, and fluent, on all subjects that fell within the scope of the faculties of observation, situated in the superciliary ridge; but dull, unintelligent, and destitute equally of ideas and language, on topics that implied the activity of the reflecting faculties situated in the upper part of the forehead."

Even among ourselves, we daily see remarkable diversities of configuration, affecting both bones and muscles; which have been produced by mode of life, in both passive and active relations, and which give a very distinct character to classes, families, and the inhabitants of particular districts. Among the natives of our own island, and where there can be no doubt of an unmixed English descent, we meet with heads and faces, whose forms, externally at least, approach to the Mongolian, Negro, Hottentot, Patagonian, and Australian; and in the blackest tribes of the heart of Africa, are found heads whose fine proportions might vie with the Circassian and Grecian specimens.

From all that I have been able to learn, (and upon Dr. Prichard's works I rely as my great physiological authority,) it appears to be established that all the diversities of configuration which belong to human beings, may be satisfactorily referred to external agents, (—temperature, from constringing cold to almost insupportable warmth; the peculiar action of the sun's rays independently of mere temperature; conditions of the atmosphere, from great purity to miasmatic; soil; food; occupation; artificial treatment; and possibly causes yet to be discovered;)—*continuing* their influence through

* This article of the Am. Journ. is now republished in Prof. Jameson's Philos. Journ. July, 1840; with high encomium upon Dr. Morton's work, and the Review of it.

many generations; for it is with those nations which have retained the same mode of life unvaried from time immemorial, and in whom therefore the hereditary predisposition has been *sustained*, by the unceasing action of similar causes,—with those nations it is that the greatest deviations are found from the standard human form.* But *what* and *where* is that standard human form? Where is the true ideal of corporal perfection? We have been trained to view it in the Grecian models; but have we demonstration of our being in the right? Men of eminence have conceived that the primitive and model form lies among the BROWN tribes, the intermediate between all extremes. Divergencies from such a centre will lead by a natural gradation to all the varieties of figure and complexion. One of the highest authorities† has published his reasons for regarding the ARABS of the eastern side of the Red Sea as the *primitive race*, the *prototype* of the Human Species. "This interesting people," he writes, "undoubtedly one of the most ancient in the world,——have a physiognomy and character which are quite peculiar, and which distinguishes them generally from all those which appear in other regions of the globe." In his dissections, he found—the brain and nervous substance more dense and firm than in Europeans generally, the brain large, and its circumvolutions more numerous, and furrows deeper,—the heart and arterial system most regular and perfect,—their organs of sense exquisitely acute,—and the same extraordinary characters of perfection conspicuous in the parts performing the functions of nutrition, respiration, and motion,—their size above the average of men in general,—their figure robust and elegant,—their colour *brown*, but *deepest in the face*,‡—their "*intelligence* proportionate to that physical perfection, and without doubt superior, other things being equal," to that of other nations.§

Thus far, then, anatomy and physiology, the characters of language

* This doctrine receives support and illustration from facts detailed in a recent work of great merit, Dr. W. B Carpenter's *Principles of General and Comparative Physiology*, book ii. ch. xiv.

† The Baron de Larrey, surgeon-general to the French army of Egypt in 1798, author of several surgical works held by all in great estimation. *We* may think it equivocal moral honour, that Napoleon Buonaparte bequeathed him 100,000 francs, and designated him *the most virtuous man he had ever known*. But De Larrey's scientific merits none will dispute: and his opportunities for the study of Physical Anthropology were signally advantageous. He has died this month (July, 1842,) at the age of seventy-six.

‡ It deserves to be universally known that they protect the faces of their children and others, when attacked by the small-pox, with a covering of leaf-gold, renewed as occasion requires; and thus *disfiguration* is prevented.

§ De Larrey's Paper for the use of the Scientific Commission proceeding to Algiers; Paris, 1838. Transl. in *Jameson's Philos. Journ.;* Oct. 1838; p. 318.

Third ed.—" It must not be forgotten that, although there are black races and white

and the phenomena of mind, all lead us to conclude in favour of an identity of species, and derivation from one origin. But I must now adduce a fact alluded to at the beginning of this Note. The greater number of mankind, that is, the brown and black varieties, differ from the fair portion who form the minority, not merely in circumstances more or less considerable of *form*, but also in the possession of a distinct peculiarity of structure. The cuticle, or scarf-skin (*epidermis*), is a transparent covering, consisting of several layers, the upper and lower of which are especially distinct. It is derived by secretion from the exquisitely sensible (*true skin, epidermis, cutis, corium.*) Between these is interposed a remarkably soft and slippery *cellular substance*, which is produced so as to line all the open cavities of the body, and performing other most important functions. This is usually called the *mucous membrane*, or *mucous net;* and it has been often said to be the cause of complexion, being white in fair people, dusky in brown, and black with increased solidity in negroes. But this is not the exact state of the facts. The colouring matter is distinct from the membranous tissue, is a substance perfectly of its own kind, and may not improperly be called a *paint*. It is *spread over* the mucous membrane, as a foreign substance having no vital or chemical connexion, but only the union of mechanical contiguity. This paint, shewing itself through the cuticle, is *the cause* of the phenomenon of which we are treating, the diversity of colour in mankind. It is therefore affirmed, that we have here a *new* existing thing, a character, not of form, but of *structure*, found in the darker varieties of men, (for the reddish or copper-coloured have it of their own hue,) but not existing in the white nations: and hence it is positively concluded, that "the two races, the white and the black, form two *essentially* and *specifically* distinct races."* The French physiologist who

races, there are individuals of almost every tint, leading from one of these extremes of colour to the other: although there are races with a facial line nearly vertical, and others with the same line greatly inclined, there are individuals who display every possible degree between these differences. Where then shall we draw the line of separation, if they are not all from a common origin?" Supplements of Griffith, Hamilton Smith, and Pidgeon, to *Cuvier's Anim. Kingd.* vol. i p. 179. The same author adduces the species *hog* (sus scrofa,) in illustration of the fact that single species of other animals, when widely dispersed and domesticated, undergo differences of structure, colour, skeleton, and other particulars, equally great with those which diversify mankind: and he adds, "We are fully warranted in concluding, both from the comparison of man with inferior animals, so far as the inferiority will allow of such comparison, and, beyond that, by comparing him with himself, that the great family of mankind loudly proclaim a descent, at some period or other, from *one common origin*."

* Paper by M. Flourens, from the *Annales des Sciences Naturelles*, tome x., transl. in Jameson's *Philos. Journ.*, Oct. 1839. I do not feel myself at liberty to apply any remedy to his solecism in using his term "races."

has drawn this inference readily admits the essential character of *species* to be the succession of fructiferous individuals; yet he contends for a *specific* distinction of *races:* thus seeming to involve the belief of two or more pairs of first ancestors. His concluding paragraph is; "The fact of the *succession*, therefore, and of the *constant* succession, constitutes alone the unity of the *species*. Thus *unity*, absolute unity, of the human species, and *variety* of its *races*, as a final result, is the general and certain conclusion of all the facts acquired concerning the natural history of man."

The reader will observe the self-contradiction which M. Flourens commits, in asserting both a *specific distinction*, and an absolute *unity* of the *species*. But he might perhaps retreat, by imputing the contradiction to the imperfection of nomenclature.

We cannot indeed affirm it to be an *impossibility* that the Almighty Creator should have seen fit to bring originally into being duplicates, triplicates, or other multiples of pairs, formed so alike that there should be no specific difference between them.* Yet it appears antecedently improbable; and it is unnecessary, for, grant an extension of time not at all prodigious, with the requisite provisions for sustenance, and a sufficient increase of posterity will ensue from a single pair.

All the probabilities of the case (and they amount to a high degree of moral evidence,) seem to warrant our adoption of De Larrey's theory. Let us then take some brunette hue for the normal complexion of the human race; and let all the existing colours be represented by radii from a centre diverging in all directions. The diffe-

* Winer, in the sec. ed. of his *Biblisches Realwörterbuch*, [Dict. of the Civil and Nat. Hist. of the Bible,] refers to Prof. Link's *Urwelt*, [Primitive World,] and says, "He adduces many solid reasons for the derivation of men from one original, *one* species; but he leaves it undecided whether of this species there might not have been created several pairs." Vol. i. p. 25. This venerable naturalist is Henry Frederick Link, M. D. Prof. Medic. in the University of Berlin, and Director of the Botanic Garden. He is the author of several highly esteemed works, in Botany and Natural History generally; and is distinguished as an erudite and elegant scholar. Among his works is (*Die Urwelt und das Alterthum*, &c.) The Primitive World and Antiquity, illustrated by Natural History; 2 vols., Berlin, 1821. We had the gratification of seeing him at the meeting of the British Association at Glasgow, in September, 1840. It is a curious circumstance, which shows that difficulty upon this head was felt at an early period, that in the Targum, a Jewish paraphrase upon the Pentateuch, ascribed, but without sufficient evidence, to Jonathan Ben Uzziel, (a rabbi who lived in the apostolic times,) the passage, Gen. ii. 7, is thus paraphrased—"And Jeja Elohim formed and created man [*Adam*] by two creations, and he collected dust from the habitation of the holy place, and from the four winds of the world; and mixed from all the waters of the world, and created him red, black, and white; and breathed into his nostrils the soul of life, and the soul was in the body of man for a speaking spirit, for the enlightening of the eyes, and for the hearing of the ears."

rences would increase with the distance, and the extremities of the lines, in opposite parts of the periphery, would present contrasts of colour, and of every other deviation produced by the range of causes. I presume not to be a physiologist, but it will not be deemed arrogant in me to ask, May not the alteration of colour in the pigment of the mucous tissue be dependent upon causes analogous to those which change the colour of our hair, from yellow, brown, or black, to a perfect white; while yet the follicles are not absorbed, nor their functions extinguished in the nutrition of the hair? May not that pigment, in one line of alteration, that influenced by augmenting solar heat, be increased in quantity, and be made more intense in its qualities, and so pass through every shade to the deepest black: and, in the opposite direction, sustain a gradual diminution of quantity and strength, tending to ultimate obliteration, (for its existence in fair persons has been questioned, and what may be its minute rudiment can be shewn only by very fine injection,) or at least the loss of colour, and so producing the fairest specimens of the human complexion?* Is it not known that, in mountainous districts of hot countries, the inhabitants of the highest regions are fair, while those of the plains below are extremely dark?

But the gradation supposed, and proved by examples, presents us with shades of *brown* only. We have no instance of a white family or community acquiring the proper *negro* colour, nor of a negro family losing its peculiarity, and becoming of a proper, healthy, North-European white, where there are not intermarriages with fair persons, long continued in the favourable direction.

This, I believe, must be admitted; and another fact, of great importance, must be added to it. The recent explorings of the Egyptian tombs and temples have brought to light pictures of native Egyptians and of men and women of other nations, comprising *negroes*, who are distinguished by their characteristic form of face and their *completely black* colour. Some of these highly interesting representations are proved to be of the age of Joseph and earlier, and some, in which *negro-figures* occur, are of the eighth century after the flood.† Assuming then that the complexion of Noah's

* "Although I cannot demonstrate *rete mucosum* in the European, I think that there must be under the cuticle some colouring matter. How can we otherwise account for the difference between the fair and the swarthy, or for the remarkable peculiarity of the Albino?" Lawrence's *Lect. on Comp. Anat.* seventh ed. p. 189.

† It would be a blameable omission, were I not to recommend to my young readers the devoting of two or three successive days to studying the Egyptian antiquities in the British Museum; and to peruse a work, small in size, but ample in matter, Dr. Cooke Taylor's *Illustrations of the Bible from the Monuments of Egypt;* 1838. See also

family was what I have ventured to suppose, as the normal brown, *there was not time for a negro race to be produced* by the operation of all the causes of change with which we are acquainted. On the other hand, some of the Egyptian figures, particularly those consigned to constant labour under the sun, and (which is very remarkable) persons performing religious ceremonies, are of a brown so deep, as to be almost black.

Is it unreasonable to expect that a more perfect acquaintance with the physiology of the mucous membrane, and particularly in the negro subject, remains yet to be acquired? I look with a feeling almost of impatience, to the publication of Dr. Prichard's third volume of "Researches into the Physical History of Mankind;" in which one cannot doubt that this subject will be discussed.

But, to any upright mind, I appeal, whether, in relation to a subject so complicated, this one difficulty, even should it never be scientifically disposed of, is of sufficient weight to overbalance all the evidences, psychical and moral, (so ably treated in Dr. Prichard's Book ii. ch. ii.) physical, philological,* and historical, which flow together in proof of the *unity* of the human race, by derivation from one ancestry.†

Above all other topics of argument are the melancholy demonstrations that moral depravity has acquired the dominion over all the nations and families of mankind; that there is a mournful consciousness of this, lying deep in every human breast; that we all need a redemption from guilt and misery; and that all the varieties of our race, down to Esquimaux and Hottentots, are capable of receiving that holy happiness, and all its elevation of character, which spring from restoration to God through our Lord Jesus Christ. The whole constitution of revealed grace stands upon the declaration made against the autochthonic‡ folly of the Athenians, the declaration of

Prof. Hengstenberg's *Bücher Moses und Ægypten;* or the Engl. Transl. with Notes by Prof. Robbins, the American Translator, and Dr. Taylor; Edinb. 1845.

* The fundamental principles for applying philological investigation to the question before us, are beautifully illustrated in the same author's "Eastern Origin of the Celtic Nations."

† A great anatomist, who cannot be suspected of prejudice with regard to this question, draws this conclusion from his very extensive induction of facts and reasonings;—"that the *human species*, like that of the cow, sheep, horse, and pig, and others, is SINGLE; and that all the differences which it exhibits, are to be regarded *merely as varieties*." Lawrence on *Comp. Anat.* p. 376.

‡ Imagining themselves to have been derived from no other stock of men, but that the first occupants of Attica sprung out of its soil:—"ut ipsa ex sese suos cives genuisse dicatur, et eorum eadem terra parens, altrix, patria." Cic. pro L. Flacc. 26. It was the popular opinion, but their wiser men disallowed it.

one whom the Omniscient Spirit led into "all the truth" (John xvi. 13) that involves man's highest welfare,—"God, who made the world and all things that are in it,—the Lord of heaven and earth,—who giveth to all, life and breath and all things, *hath made of one blood* every nation of men, to dwell upon the whole face of the earth." (Acts xvii. 24—26.)

But, if we carry our concessions to the very last point,—*if* the progress of investigation should indeed bring out such kinds and degrees of evidence, as shall rightfully turn the scale in favour of the hypothesis that there are several RACES of Mankind, each having originated in a different pair of ancestors,——what would be the consequence to our highest interests, as rational, accountable, and immortal beings? Would our *faith*, the fountain of motives for love and obedience to God, virtuous self-government, and universal justice and kindness,——would this faith, "the substance of things hoped for, the evidence of things not seen,"——sustain any detriment; after, by due meditation and prayer, we had surmounted the first shock? ——Let us survey those consequences.

If the two first inhabitants of Eden were the progenitors, not of all human beings, but only of the race whence sprung the Hebrew family, still it would remain the fact, that *all* were formed by the immediate power of God, and all their circumstances, stated or implied in the scriptures, would remain the same as to moral and practical purposes.

Adam would be "a figure of Him that was to come" the Saviour of mankind; just as Melchizedek, or Moses, or Aaron, or David: the spiritual lesson would be the same.

The sinful character of all the tribes of men, and the individuals composing them, would remain determined by the most abundant and painfully demonstrated proofs, in the history of all times and nations. The way and manner in which moral corruption has thus infected all men, under their several heads of primeval ancestry, would be an inscrutable mystery (—which *it is now ;*—) but the need of divine mercy and the duty to seek it would be the same; the same necessity would exist of a Saviour, a redemption, and a renovation of the internal character by efficacious grace.

That the Saviour was, in his human nature, a descendant of Adam, would not militate against his being a proper Redeemer for all the races of mankind, any more than his being a descendant of Abraham, Judah, and David, at all diminishes his perfection to save us, "sinners of the gentiles."

Some difficulties in the scripture-history would be taken away;

such as—the sons of Adam obtaining wives not their own sisters;—Cain's acquiring instruments of husbandry, which must have been furnished by miracle immediately from God upon the usual supposition;*—his apprehensions of summary punishment, ("—any man that findeth me will slay me;")—his fleeing into another region, of which Josephus so understands the text as to affirm that Cain obtained confederates and became a plunderer and robber, implying the existence of a population beyond his own family;—and his building a "city," a considerable collection of habitations.

The characteristic differences of the great divisions of mankind, physical and intellectual, would create no difficulty in our reasonings: for instance, the mental distinctions laid down by Dr. Morton:—"The Caucasian race; distinguished for the facility with which it attains the highest intellectual endowments. '[Is there no flattery here? Are the effects of centuries of cultivation sufficiently considered?—]' —The Mongolian;—ingenious, imitative, and highly susceptible of cultivation.—The Malay; active and ingenious, and possessing all the habits of a migratory, predaceous, and maritime people.—The American; averse to cultivation, slow in acquiring knowledge, restless, revengeful, fond of war, and wholly destitute of maritime adventure.—The Ethiopian; joyous, flexible, and indolent; the many nations which compose this race presenting a singular diversity of intellectual character, of which the far extreme is the lowest grade of humanity." The hypothesis also will diminish our surprise, but not our sorrow, that many fine nations of men have appeared incapable of being persuaded by all the attempts of wisdom and humanity, as well as the stern demands of want; so that they prefer to perish by inches, rather than to cultivate the soil and adopt those habits of

* "He that speaks of tilling presupposes a great many other arts; and he that speaks of a husbandman presupposes a great many other artificers. But if there was no artificer in those days besides Cain, then certainly Cain was a very busy body. Therefore he digged iron-mines, made furnaces, made his hammers and his anvil" [which implies the previous possession of mighty hammers, &c.] "and other tools to make his ploughshare, sharpened his hatchets—to cut down timber to make his ploughs, &c.—digged the quarry to make his mill to grind;"—From the anonymous book, "Præ-Adamitæ, sive Exercitatio super Rom. v. 12—14; et Systema-Theologicum ex eadem Hypothesi;" published in 1655, in which year there was also an English translation, without any indication of place, from which this citation is taken. The author was Isaac de la Perere, of Bordeaux. On account of this book he was prosecuted by the Inquisition, but found means of escaping, went to Rome having abjured Protestantism, recanted his book, and obtained the protection of Pope Alexander VII. Our countryman, Mr. Edward King, a zealous Christian, in his "Morsels of Criticism," vol. ii. 1800, strenuously maintained the opinion of the plurality of human ancestry. [In 1835, Dr. Thomas Arnold, that superlatively upright and candid man, wrote to Archbishop Whately in terms indicating apprehension that "the physiological question is not yet settled." *Life and Corresp.* vol. i. p. 410.]

civilized life by which they might be preserved; and that thus they appear to have had no share in the divine appointment to "increase and multiply and replenish the earth." See reflections upon this fact, at the close of a very interesting article, entitled "The Red Man," in the Quarterly Review, March 1840. In like manner it would furnish a solution to the question, Why any tribes of men should refuse to fix themselves in climes, warm, fertile, and comfortable, and in which there were no impediments to their stay, and should push on to such countries as Terra del Fuego, where they miserably exist, with scarcely shelter, clothing, and food? Even the purifying and ennobling influence of Christianity, of which the Americans in particular have shewn themselves powerfully susceptible, has not surmounted these difficulties. But allowing to the utmost these confessedly very remarkable disagreements, Dr. Prichard is of opinion that they afford no proof of diversity of origin, and that differences equally great may be pointed out as, not only characterizing individuals, but marking families in the bosom of English society.

With regard to Acts xvii. 26, it cannot be proved that "one blood" necessarily signifies descent from a common ancestry: for, admitting a specific identity, though having proceeded from distinct foci of creation, both the physical and the mental characteristics would be the same in all essential qualities.

Thus, if, contrarily to all reasonable probability, this great question should ever be determined in the way opposite to what we now think the verdict of truth, the highest interests of man will not be affected.

Third edition. Dr. Prichard has now (1841) published the third volume, Part First (523 pages), of his herculean work, the "Researches." This volume is occupied entirely with the Ethnography of Europe, ancient and modern. The physiological characters of those nations are considered, as much in detail as was requisite: but the attention of the author is principally occupied with the intellectual and moral indications of character, and those lines of inquiry involve a large extent of investigation into the history and antiquities of the European nations, their mythology, manners, and early literature. As few men can be thought of as comparable to Dr. Prichard in the united qualifications of glossographic knowledge and natural science, it is the more a reason for gratitude to the Author of every good and perfect gift, who has so richly conferred those talents and the disposition to make an impartial use of them.

But this excellent philosopher has perhaps intermitted his severer labour of the "Researches," for the composition of a work expressly on the subject before us: "The Natural History of Man; comprising Inquiries into the Modifying Influence of Physical and Moral Agencies on the different Tribes of the Human Family:" with a splendid furniture of engravings, and six large charts or maps; 572 pages; 1842. He has travelled through the physiology of the case, in its length and breadth; examining the doctrines of Genus, Species, Variety, and Race, in their application to plants and animals, especially the domesticated. Hence physical principles are established, the application of which is pursued in relation to all the nations and tribes of mankind; for the unwearied enterprises and successful investigations in all the branches of Geography, which have signalized the last thirty years, render it no other than a sober supposition that all the distinctions of the human race are known.

A part of the concluding paragraph will be a fit termination to this Note.

"——We contemplate, among all the diversified tribes who are endowed with reason and speech, the same internal feelings, appetencies, aversions; the same inward convictions, the same sentiments of subjection to invisible powers; and, more or less fully developed, of accountableness or responsibility to unseen avengers of wrong and agents of retributive justice, from whose tribunal men cannot even by death escape. We find every where the same susceptibility, though not always in the same degree of forwardness or ripeness of improvement, of admitting the cultivation of these universal endowments, of opening the eyes of the mind to the more clear and luminous views which CHRISTIANITY unfolds, of becoming moulded to the institutions of religion and of civilized life. In a word, *the same inward and mental nature* is to be recognised in all the races of men. When we compare this fact with the observations which have been heretofore fully established, as to the *specific* instincts and *separate* psychical endowments of all the distinct tribes of sentient beings in the universe, we are entitled to draw confidently the CONCLUSION that *all human races are of one species and one family*."

[Jan. 17, 1846: Capt. T. J. Newbold read a paper to the Asiatic Society describing a number of rude sepulchral monuments, in some western parts of the Indian peninsula, closely resembling the cromlechs and kist-vaens of our Druidical ancestors; he adduces similar remains in Circassia and Tartary; and "he considers that these widely separated vestiges of the same family of the human race, form a strong link in the chain of argument which, independently of holy writ, conducts the migration of the human race from one central point throughout all the world, and carries us back to the remote period when 'the whole earth was of one family and one speech.'" *Athenæum*, Jan. 24, 1846.

"——We have suffered habits of theory to mislead us. We must find new and more comprehensive distinctions; or allow that locality, more or less of exposure to climate, idleness, severe labour, quality of food, abundant or scanty or hard fare, have greater influence on those [distinctions] which really exist than we have yet been willing to allow." *Rev.* of Horatio Hale's Ethnography and Philol. of U. S. Exploring Exped. in the *Athenæum*, Feb. 27, 1847.]

[May, 1847. Dr. Prichard has now completed his great work, the *Researches*, by the publication of the fifth volume. It contains the investigation of the Malayan, Polynesian, Australian, and American nations: and the result of the whole is a FINAL CONFIRMATION of the conclusion just cited.]

[Jan. 1848. The inquiry into the Origin, Dispersion, and Connexion of Nations is now pursued in a manner demanding much gratitude to Him from whom "all good counsels and right works proceed," and esteem for those learned and indefatigable persons in our own and other countries to whom we are indebted for laborious investigations in this which well claims to be a distinct science, Ethnology. The *Ethnological Society*, formed in 1843, has produced auspicious results. The last Anniversary Address (June, 1847,) by Dr. Prichard, is of deep interest. It is on "The Relations of Ethnology to other Branches of Knowledge." Its concluding paragraph, upon "the bearing of facts on the great question of the unity or diversity of human families," is —— "that the farther we explore the various paths of inquiry which lie open to our researches, the greater reason do we find for believing that no insurmountable line of separation exists between the now diversified races of men; and the greater the probability, judging from such data as we possess, that all mankind are descended from one family." *Jameson's Edinb. Philos. Journ.*, Oct. 1847, p. 335.

To conclude on this important subject, we may well repose on the final judgment of one who, without injustice to any philosopher, may be regarded as personally the man of superlative qualifications for the investigation. (See *Edinb. Rev.* Jan. 1848, p. 172.)

"The general view of nature which I have endeavoured to present would be incomplete, were I to close it without attempting to trace, by a few characteristic traits, a corresponding sketch of MAN, viewed in respect to physical gradations, to the geographical distribution of contemporaneous types, to the influences which terrestrial forces exercise on him, and to the reciprocal but less powerful action which he in turn exerts on them. Subject, though in a less degree than plants and animals, to the circumstances of the soil and the meteorological conditions of the atmosphere, and escaping from the control of natural influences by the activity of mind and the progressive advance of intelligence, as well as by a marvellous flexibility of organization which adapts itself to every climate, Man forms every where an essential portion of the life which animates the globe.——Whilst attention was exclusively directed to the extremes of colour and of form, the result of the first vivid impressions derived from the senses was a tendency to view these differences as characteristics, not of mere varieties, but of originally distinct species. The permanence of certain types in the midst of the most opposite influences, especially of climate, appeared to favour this view, notwithstanding the shortness of the time to which the historical evidence applied. But, in my opinion, *more powerful reasons lend their weight to the other side of the question, and corroborate the* UNITY *of the human race.* I refer to the many intermediate gradations of the tint of the skin and the form of the skull, which have been made known to us by the rapid progress of geographical science in modern times; to the analogies derived from the history of varieties, both domesticated and wild; and to the positive observations collected, respecting the limits of fecundity in hybrids. The greater part of the supposed contrasts, to which so much weight was formerly assigned, have disappeared before the laborious investigations of Tiedemann on the brain of negroes and of Europeans, and the anatomical researches of Vrolik and Weber on the form of the pelvis. When we take a general view of the dark-coloured African nations, on which the work of Prichard has thrown so much light, and when we compare them with the natives of the Australasian Islands, and with the Papuas and Alfourous (Harafores, Endamenes,) we see that a black tint of skin, woolly hair, and negro features, are by no means invariably associated." Alex. von Humboldt; *Cosmos*, the translation of Mrs. Colonel Sabine; vol. i. pp. 350—352.

That distinguished master of physical science then quotes a passage from "one of the greatest anatomists of our age, Johannes Müller, in his—*Physiologie des Menschen*;"—which brings out the conclusion, that "the different races of mankind are forms or varieties of a single species."

[F.]

Referred to at pages 55 *and* 159.

DISSERTATION ON THE REASONS FOR ASSIGNING A VERY HIGH ANTIQUITY TO THE EARTH.

The evidence of geological phenomena constrains us to the belief that our earth has existed, has been the seat of life, and has undergone many changes of its surface, through periods of time utterly beyond human power to assign. That evidence is of distinct and independent kinds, chiefly derived from the appearance of stratification and the remains of animal and vegetable life: and, to at least the most of those who have taken pains to become competently acquainted with its nature and variety, it produces the effect of an overpowering ocular and tangible demonstration. At the same time, there is extreme difficulty in communicating such a knowledge of the facts, to persons who have not the sensible perceptions upon which it rests. I have therefore felt it to be necessary, in the preceding lectures, to rest my repeated assertions in reference to this object upon authority; pleading that the authority is of a kind sufficient to be the ground of certainty, on account of the moral and intellectual character of the witnesses, their scientific qualifications, their opportunities for investigation upon the largest scale, their original prepossession against this conclusion, and finally their number and diversity as to country, party, religious denomination, and other circumstances which are rational guarantees against prejudice. But this is not sufficient to satisfy all. Some of our friends persist in rejecting the conclusion, resting chiefly upon the fact of its denial by persons, who, though very few in number, possess some geological knowledge and opportunities for personal observation. The difficulty is perhaps increased, and advantage is given to the objector from the fact that our most distinguished philosophers, avowedly and much to their honour, decline the task of laying down any common measure between geological time and our ordinary enumerations of years and centuries. The best writers abound in general expressions; such as, "immense periods of time,—undefined—yet countless—ages,—a duration to which we dare not assign a boundary,—a work infinitely slow, a space of time from the contemplation of which the mind shrinks; a long succession of monuments, each of which may have required a thousand ages for its elaboration;—successions of events, where the language of nature signifies millions of years:—it is evident that no greater folly can be committed, than to think to serve the cause of truth by contracting the long periods of Geology into the compass of a few thousand years."*

Opponents have not been backward to take notice of this style of expression, and to make use of it for their own purposes. In so doing, they act a very uncandid and unreasonable part: but we can administer no remedy to them, so long as they persist in refusing to provide themselves with the requisite preliminary knowledge, and to examine the question with far more diligence and patience, and I may add christian honour too, than they appear to have yet exercised.

We readily acknowledge that the problem, *to represent geological by astronomical time*, is of the greatest difficulty; perhaps it is utterly beyond human power to resolve, in the present state of our being.† Some approximation is all that we venture to hope for. It is self-evident that the application of any continuous measure of time, analogous to our common periods of multiples and products, is utterly out of the question. It would be the height of absurdity to imagine it: for each one of the phenomena whose aggregate forms the whole case, must have occupied its own particular portion of time destitute of any rule of conformity to others. In the formation of strata, each process (transportation, deposition, consolidation, elevation, and subsidence; to be followed by a renewal of similar actions under new conditions; and that several times repeated;) might occupy a duration different from that of the corresponding process in every other stratum or system of strata. Yet this does not set aside the reality of a prevailing analogy; nor does it destroy the evidence of a general conclusion from a multitude of particular facts, each one of which must have required, for its consummation, a very long period; we may in most cases say, immensely long. This will appear, if we consider a few of those facts.

1. The remains of human beings and of any vestiges of the arts

* Mantell's *Wonders of Geology*, i. p. 6. ii. 247. Macculloch's *Geol.* i. 455, 473. Sedgwick *on the Studies of Cambridge*, p. 26. Lyell's *Principles*, i. 117. Phillips's *Treatise in the Encycl. Brit.* p. 293. Similar passages might be quoted indefinitely.

† In 1834, the Council of the Royal Society announced the prize of one of the Royal Medals, the gift of the Sovereign, to the author of the best paper, to be entitled "Contributions towards a system of Geological Chronology, founded on the Examinations of Fossil Remains and their attendant phenomena." The period for such communication was fixed to expire in June, 1837. It did so expire, without producing the result required. "The Geologists of England," remarks Prof. Phillips, "gave a fair proof that hypotheses were out of fashion, when they declined to compete for the medal." *Treat. on Geol.* (in Cabinet Cyclop.) vol. i. p. 245.

and operations of man, are discovered only upon or in those surfaces and earthy masses which are demonstrably posterior to all regular geological deposits; and under circumstances indicating the human species to have been among *the most* recent products of the Creator's power. Disinterments of human bones have often occurred, with articles characteristic of an age, one third, and in the Egyptian relics one half, of the period back to the creation of man; but these are all in the superficial soil, or in situations accessible from it. In peat produced by the growth of mosses, and in the areas of felled or submerged forests, the bones and utensils of men are found; and the remains of recent animals. The limestones which are continually formed by the deposition of the fine particles previously dissolved in water, coral formations close to sea-shores, and sand and mud drifted into hollows, would readily involve human remains; so that it is rather a subject of surprise that instances like that of the Gaudaloupe skeleton, and fragments of pottery in travertin, are not abundant. It seems impossible to avoid the conclusion that such would have been the case, if human beings had existed in any of the geological formations, previous to the most recent surface. In clefts and cavities of the older rocks, which have been upheaved and subsequently shattered and laid bare, men have taken refuge, or their bodies have been buried; but the access to those hollow places, and the various matters which have fallen or been carried into them, are always of a recent character. In some countries, vast quantities of mud brought down by mighty rivers and occasional floods, have buried the persons and habitations of men; and the same result has been produced by terrible and sudden subsidences of land, and slips on mountain-sides. The strata of mud and sand which have necessarily been forming in the waters, ever since the present distribution of sea and land was arranged by the power and wisdom of the Most High, have been receiving, for at least three thousand years, the bodies and the property of men, in wrecks without number; and many of the substances so sunk in the deep, when encased as they sooner or later must be, are indestructible till the internal fires shall prey upon them. Consequently if ever those strata be upheaved, and come to be quarried by the men of a future age, what astonishing disclosures will be laid open to their view!

But nothing of this kind is brought to light in the stratification of the earth, below the habitable surface, or that which it is demonstrable has been recently detached from it: while those strata contain the most astonishing multitudes of animal populations; not excluding the order (Quadrumàna) which approaches nearest to the human form, for fossil bones of at least two large species of the monkey tribe were discovered in 1836, in the lower part of the Himalayan mountains. Other remains of that order have recently been found in France, in Brazil, and but this summer (1839) in an apparently London-clay formation, near Woodbridge. Yet in no formation that can be called stratified, even of the newest Tertiary beds, has any thing human been discovered. Not in the mass of fine loam which covers 3000 square miles of surface in the valley of the Rhine, and it is often more than 200 feet in thickness; nor in the Norfolk crag, nor in our own London clay, often far more than 300 feet in depth; nor in the alternations of freshwater and seawater beds down to the chalk; nor in the chalk itself or any earlier formation. This is surely going low enough: and it demands to be considered on the one hand, that the formations above the chalk occupy a small proportion of distance which would be perpendicular, if all the strata could be restored to strict horizontality; in comparison with the total amount of the lower stratified rocks, scarcely one thirtieth part; and, on the other, that Mr. Babbage, referring probably to these Tertiary or supracretaceous beds, but certainly never intending to go farther, regards it as a truth supported by irresistible evidence, "——that the formation even of those strata which are nearest the surface, must have occupied vast periods, probably *millions* of years."*

I am sensible of the delicacy and danger of venturing upon this ground; but I will do no more than touch it. It will be going as far as in reason we can be desired to do, if we take the general surface, with the drifts of sand and gravel, and whatever masses of clay or loam may be fairly deemed of equal age with an average of those drifts; and regard them as representing the period from the creation of man. That period, according to the usually received chronology, is a little more than 5840 years; according to the late Dr. Hales's system, it is about 7250. Now the average thickness of this superficial accretion is perfectly inconsiderable, compared with the formations composing what is commonly called the Tertiary series. If we were to say that each of those formations, in number six or seven, should be considered as requiring for its production some such term as we have mentioned, we should be presuming upon a really contracted scale. The probability is that several of those formations, if not each one, must have singly required a length of time equal at least to our present period: consequently the product would be from forty to fifty thousand years. But the whole bearing of the evidence,

* *Ninth Bridgewater Treatise;* p 79.

upon considering its component parts, goes to mark that conclusion as not furnishing a period sufficiently long for a probable computation of the processes which it involves. Each stratum and each group of strata has its limits in extent; each was deposited and otherwise affected under its own special circumstances; to each, correspondents or equivalents are generally found upon other areas; in each case, the mechanical and chemical circumstances of production and alteration, recognisable in their results, carry plain evidences of very great periods of time for their action: but one formation cannot give law or precedent to another, and to reduce those periods, or any one of them, to the ordinary measures of time, is beyond our reach, simply because the duration of human experience and observation is too short to furnish a standard.

Recently (June, 1840,) surprise has been excited by a statement, in some of the Paris and London papers, that a large part of the body of an infant, (head, trunk, and the commencement of the shoulder-bone,) and this, not the skeleton, but the full form, had been found petrified in silex, in a quarry near Brussels. That city stands upon a formation equivalent to that of the London basin, and consisting of sand and gravel, siliceous grits often passing into flint, and friable limestones. Mr. Lonsdale, with his characteristic urbanity, has shewn me a good drawing of this alleged petrifaction. It requires some fancy to make out a resemblance to the human form. The thing itself is, however, nothing but a large flint-concretion, such as are common in our upper chalk. I have seen many of those flint-masses which bear an equally good resemblance to portions of animals; and I remember one especially, which presented a far closer likeness to the head of a lamb. This story would not be worth noticing, but that serious consequences may have been drawn from it, by persons who, perhaps, did not think of asking, whether a conversion of *the soft parts* of an animal into flint, or any other mineral substance, had ever been heard of in the records of natural history.

About twenty-five years ago, at St. Louis in the state of Missouri, on the worn limestone bed of the river Mississippi, near the brink, were discovered two human footmarks, a right and a left, having the appearance of having been impressed on the limestone, now exceedingly compact, hard, and polished, by a person standing with naked feet and expanded toes, characteristic of the tribes which never used shoes, when that limestone was in a condition of mud sufficiently soft to receive an exact impression, and yet sufficiently hard to prevent the feet from sinking more than one-sixth of an inch, thus preserving a level surface. No other footmarks or human impressions exist: so that, if these were made in the manner just described, the person must have stepped once on the yielding surface, and then, in some way, have been completely withdrawn; a supposition not easy to realize. The rock is (*not sandstone*, as some cause of error had led Dr. Mantell to suppose, *Wond. Geol.* vol. i. p. 76,) but a fine crinoidal limestone, corresponding to our Mountain Limestone of the Carboniferous series. The mass of stone was dug out in 1819, weighing above a ton, and it is now in the possession of David Dale Owen, M. D. Of this slab, which of necessity excited very great interest, so long as it was thought by any to be a genuine impression, that gentleman has given an ample history and description, with an engraving, in the American Journal of Science, July 1842, pp. 14—32. The result of the investigation is a conviction, that the marks are artificial, sculptured within the last two or three centuries, in the style of that minute and patient labour which the natives of many uncivilized countries are wont to bestow in the carving of stones and wood.

2. The whole series of strata, from the earliest of them to the present surface of the globe, exhibits a body of evidence in favour of our doctrine. Every stratum consists of a mass of earthy matters which once formed the substance of rocks on elevated land: partially excepting the limestones, for a reason to be presently mentioned. Those portions of the rocks have been separated from their parent masses, worn down, comminuted, transported often to great distances by the force of water, deposited, consolidated, elevated, and hardened. Operations of this kind have been repeated many times, homogeneously and heterogeneously as to the mineralogical constitution of the masses; but the thickness, the lamination, the joints and cleavage, and the imbedded remains of animal and vegetable beings, cannot be contemplated with due attention, without producing a conviction stronger than words can express, of periods of time amazing and overwhelming to the mind. The most prominent instances may be mentioned, and we will begin with the earliest.

The first appearance of stratification is in the rock called Gneiss. This is composed of the same materials as Granite, on the irregular outline of which it rests. But, whereas in Granite the component ingredients are not only distinct but preserve their crystalline figure, in Gneiss they are indeed perfectly distinguishable, but their edges and corners are rounded off, and their disposition with regard to each other may be called an arrangement lengthwise and leaf-like. Now, this is precisely that state which would be produced by an action upon the granitic surface, whether unaltered or somewhat disintegrated, of wearing-off, removal, rolling about, diffusion in water, subsiding by its own weight, settlement at the bottom, and finally disposition by the straight direction of a current: in a word, it is that state which those materials would necessarily acquire, in the way of being worn and arranged by water working upon them, through a long space of time; also being further acted upon by the heat transmitted from below. But, *how long* was *that portion of time*, it would be too daring to conjecture. We know, from the ordinary way of such a process, which, in many cases, can be observed and watched, that it would be *extremely* slow. The trituration, depositing and permanent fixation of a very few inches, would be a liberal allowance for a hundred years. What then is the average thickness of the gneissic rocks, in Scotland, Ireland, and other countries where they have been brought up to view? On account of the intervention of other rocks, they cannot be sufficiently explored, and therefore surveys fall short of the full amount as to magnitude; but enough is exposed to demonstrate an exceedingly great thickness. Professor Phillips, one of the most cautious of geologists, says, "We may believe it to exceed many thousand yards."*

Over the Gneiss, come the beds of Mica Schist, and Slates, to a great amount as to number, and whose thickness is unknown from the causes mentioned, but certainly very great. If we should venture to estimate the united thickness of this class, added to the gneissic, at three or even four miles, we could not be charged with exaggeration. These are the Cumbrian and Cambrian series; and their mode of formation is proved, by the most striking characters, to have been the same as that of the Gneiss, modified by the increase and progressive composition of the materials. The number of strata and their sub-divisions is very great. Consequently, the periods of alternating action and comparative repose must have been numerous. Could the reader with his own eyes contemplate the finest exhibitions of them in the precipices of Scotland, Cumberland, and Wales, he would be convinced of the imperfection and poverty of verbal description; and he could scarcely fail to receive the sensible demonstration of indescribable time, as necessary for these mighty operations of the omnipresent Deity. He would see a new beauty in the words of inspired devotion, "Great is the Lord, and greatly to be praised; and his greatness is unsearchable. I will speak of the glorious honour of thy majesty, and of thy wondrous works;—the might of thy terrible acts."† These Slate-rocks bear evidence of having

* *Treatise* (Cabinet Cyclop.) vol. i. p. 117.

† Ps. cxlv.

been subjected to intense heat, after their deposition; so that their constitution is *metamorphic*, that is, original sediment altered by fire, producing high incandescence, close coherence, partial fusion, and penetration by both injection and sublimation. This point of geological theory was illustrated by the Rev. David Williams and Professor Sedgwick, at the Plymouth Meeting of the British Association, July 30, 1841. See the Report, in the Athenæum, No. 720, p. 627.

Upon this class of rocks, an author distinguished for the extent of his labours in actual examination, the late Dr. Macculloch, remarks: "The thickness of these strata we know to be enormous.—These depths are discovered by geological observations and inferences:—— that they extend to many miles was also proved.——We have every reason to know, from what is now taking place on our own earth, that the accumulation of materials at the bottom of the ocean, is a work *infinitely slow.* We are sure that such an accumulation as should produce the primary strata, as we now see them, must have occupied a space, from the contemplation of which the mind shrinks."*

It would be with a continued application of similar observations, if we were to pursue our upward course through the numerous beds of siliceous, slaty, and limestone aggregates to which the name *Silurian System* is given by that distinguished geologist who has devoted seven years of toil and study, with unsparing expense, to their investigation. He has thus supplied some connecting links, the absence of which had created difficulties and perplexing inquiries, between the primary strata and the old red sandstone, now better called the Devonian System:† and has poured a stream of light generally upon British, or justly speaking European, and still more extensive, stratification. Their united thickness is about a mile and a half; but the numeration of all the beds, between which a boundary of separation is discernible, would probably exceed human power: who, then, can calculate the periods of their derivation from the older formations, their deposition, their elevations and *small* distortions; their convulsions, penetrations, and alterations of the adjoining rocks, by *frequent*

* *Syst. Geol.* vol. i. pp. 472, 473.

† *Third ed.* Mr. Conybeare has remarked that the term "Devonian" savours too much of localism, and would involve something of solecism when applied to the Old Red in Herefordshire, Scotland, and Ireland: and he proposes the word *Episilurian*, that is, *over the Silurian.* Brit. Assoc. ref. above.—But a similar objection might be made to *Silurian*, as too local and national, and the same kinds of formation occur largely in Russia and other countries. Yet it is better to submit to some imperfections and incongruities in nomenclature, than to be making frequent alterations. A temperate middle course should be observed.

outbursts from the fiery liquid below, and other movements, till they were brought to their existing condition?* It would seem perfectly impossible for any person, but moderately acquainted with the visible phenomena of volcanic regions, to escape the impression that myriads of ages must have been occupied in the production of these formations, before the creation of man and the adaptation of the earth's surface for his abode. In short, the Silurian System of formations contains within itself a compendious body of instruction, examples, and demonstrations of Geological truths.†

Evidence to the same effect would accumulate upon us to a vast amount, in examining the Old Red Sandstone, a remarkable deposit several thousand feet in thickness, found in some parts of Great Britain, more abundantly in Ireland, and either in resemblance or in equivalence in many foreign regions. Next we come to the Mountain Limestone, consisting almost entirely of the shells and coralline productions of sea animals, often a thousand and more feet in thickness. In this and other Limestone the imbedding part is not, as in other strata, a sediment from mere watery mixture, but the deposit from solution of Carbonate of Lime in water. This formation is frequently more or less interposed among the beds of coal, composed of compressed vegetable matter, underlaid and overlaid with shales and sandstones in every variety; often effecting a thickness of three thousand feet. The New Red Sandstone, comprising many most interesting varieties of strata, each involving great changes of condition in the modes of formation, advances us about another thousand feet.

Other changes, implying probably some alteration in the disposition

* Let the impartial inquirer study Mr. Murchison's *Silurian System*, particularly chapters xvi. xix. xl. xlii.

† Will my reader accept of a little specimen?—"Coupling the preceding observations with what has been said concerning the Trap rocks, and the dislocations of Coalbrook Dale and the Clee Hills, it may be affirmed that this district in Shropshire furnishes proofs of the *alternate play and repose* of volcanic action during very long periods. These evidences demonstrate,

"1. That volcanic Grits were formed during the deposition of the Lower Silurian strata.

"2. That the Upper Silurian rocks and Old Red Sandstone were accumulated tranquilly, without a trace of contemporaneous eruptions.

"3. That, after their consolidation, the last-mentioned deposits were dismembered, and set upon their edges, by vast outbursts of intrusive Trap.

"4. That the Carboniferous System was deposited after the older strata had been upheaved.

"5. That subsequent dislocations, including some of the most violent with which we are acquainted, took place after the accumulation of the Coal Measures and the Lower New Red Sandstone." Murchison, vol. i. p. 235.

and consequently the action of the fiery gulph below,* marked the next great system, or series of rocks, to which, by a convenient extension of meaning, the term Oolitic has been given. Its general thickness can be little less than half a mile. It is filled with the most convincing proofs of deposition from sea-water, both shallow and deep, the mingled waters of river-mouths, and perhaps even fresh water of rivers and lakes; affording indications that the depositions, in many varieties, both contemporaneous and successive, were carried on through a very long period.

We arrive, in ascending, at the great masses of chalk, and its accompaniments of peculiar clays and sands; to the thickness of a thousand feet or more. Though the lines of stratification are not here so visible as in the underlying formations, the evidence of deposition from watery mixture, and of very interesting effects from molecular and chemical attractions, is so clear as to be irresistible. In our country, and in some others, the Chalk formation, like the Old Red Sandstone at the other end of an immense series, may have been thought to form a kind of resting-place, a term to mark the total cessation of one order of things, and the commencement of another upon a different plan; but it would be a fallacy to suppose so. No formation of stratified material is continuous over the whole globe. Both the Old Red and the Chalk are of limited extent; and, where they do exist, there is not always an abruptness in the succession, below or above. In the Eastern Alps, Professor Sedgwick and Mr. Murchison have demonstrated a large series of a peculiar Limestone and other formations, making, in part at least, a transition from the highest chalk-beds to the commencement of the Tertiary series;† according to the usual and convenient nomenclature. Also beds occur near Maestricht, which hold the same intermediate position. But whether or not these fill up the interval between the Secondary and Tertiary Series of formations (for it is a mere dispute of words, to which of the two they should be assigned), does not affect the argument respecting time. If geologists have not yet arrived at a complete acquaintance with the formations that effect the passage

* "We have recently seen two of our first philosophers (Babbage and Herschel) maintaining that, a central heat being granted, the *necessary* result of the increment of fresh matter in one part and its abstraction in another (as is now taking place), must produce such variations in the conducting media, that the result would be the gradual elevation of some parts of the earth's surface, and the depression of others." Murchison i. 576. The statements referred to are letters of Sir John Herschel to Mr. Lyell, in the *Proceedings of the Geological Society*, May 17, 1837, and Jan. 31, 1838; and the *Ninth Bridgewater Treatise*, pp. 225—247.

† *Trans. Geol. Soc.* Second Series, vol. iii. pp. 301—420.

from the Chalk to the Sands and Clays commonly esteemed the lowest of the Tertiaries; if, from well ascertained discoveries in countries not yet explored, it should turn out that some bed or beds of distinct character are to be intercalated; it will be so much of addition to the time necessary for these formations,—their being deposited at the bottom of great waters, obtaining their fossil inhabitants, being raised up, dried, hardened; and these processes being probably several times repeated. The whole lapse of time, for so small a part of stratification as this, is astonishing; to our faculties, in the present state, it is immense.

Our last stage of ascent comprehends that Tertiary Series; a succession of beds, Clays, Sands, and Limes, variously intermixed occupying a thickness of some six or eight hundred feet, and reaching up to the ground which we tread in our London basin; but in neighbouring districts there are two or three later formations. Stratification, generally undisturbed, though in some places strikingly otherwise, as in the Isle of Wight, is here marked in characters impossible to be mistaken. When we have mounted to the most recent of those later formations, immediately below the soil on which we tread, we find enormous masses of gravel and other transported materials; demonstrated by their position to have been rolled along by mighty currents, subsequently to all the lower formations. They are sometimes spread out upon extensive horizontal areas; but sometimes, from local causes, heaped tumultuously together. If the reader will refer to what was advanced in Lect. V. upon the distribution of Drift, he will perhaps see reason to conclude that this operation cannot be assigned to an epoch later than what I venture to call the *Adamic creation;* but, as it was of different ages, much of it must, in all probability, have preceded that date.

Let me intreat a thoughtful person to meditate on the succession, which we have thus rapidly and imperfectly reviewed. Let him represent to himself a series of earthy materials, for the most part dried and consolidated into hard rock, proved by the plainest evidence of the senses to have been sediments from mixture in water; carrying in their texture and accompaniments the equally manifest proofs of quiet, gradual and slow deposition; altered at different and long distant times, by forces urging from below, often and perhaps usually of very slow and gradual action, but frequently by the intrusion of melted rock driven up with tremendous violence; and that the united thickness of the whole cannot be less than five miles, but certainly, in extensive ranges, approaching to the double of that estimate. Let him ask, in each case, *whence* were those earthy materials derived.

He will find, that they have been worn away from the surfaces of antecedent and now underlying rocks and dry land. Let him then reflect upon the time requisite for this repetition of operations so prodigious, producing a series of many terms, requiring intervals of both repose and action, to which it is difficult for the imagination to soar. And let him consider, whether he can conceive the possibility of those results having been effected, in less periods of duration than such as bid defiance to our poor chronology.

But, still it may be asked, Can you give no sensible idea whatever, to assist our conceptions? Is there nothing in nature that may serve as a standard of approximation? Is this vague language of magnitude and duration all that you can afford? Why then may we not compress the whole succession of stratifications, into a space of six or seven thousand years. At least you are bound to demonstrate that the lower numbers are inapplicable; that the position of the ordinary chronology is undoubtedly too short. Is there no plain fact that may measure some defined part of the series; and set at rest this part of the question, the negation of short time?

I will derive an answer from an assiduous, sagacious and eminently qualified observer; a most extensive labourer in the field of practical Geology; and a zealous friend of revealed religion.

"Let us contemplate *Time* as it relates to the CREATOR, not to ourselves, and we shall be no longer alarmed at that which the history of the earth demands.——Every stratum of rock is the work of time, often of far more than we choose to contemplate; while, from what we see, we can approximate to that which we know not how to measure. He who can measure and number the strata from the first to the last, is prepared to solve this question as it relates to the intervals of repose; but of those only: not to those of the revolutions. Let him ascertain the time required to produce a stratum of a given depth; let him seek it in the increase of colonies of shell-fishes, in deposits of peat, and in the earthy deposits of seas and lakes: and he has found a multiplier, not to disclose" [*i. e.* entirely and precisely] "the truth, but to aid his imagination.——*Who indeed can sum this series?*——The data are not in our power; yet we can aid conjectures.

"The great tract of peat, near Stirling, has demanded two thousand years;* for its registry is preserved by the Roman works below it. It is but a single bed of coal:—shall we multiply it by 100? ——We shall not exceed,—far from it,—did we allow 200,000

*He puts a round number. It is 1760 years since the Romans invaded Scotland. But the difference is inconsiderable in this argument.

years for the production of the coal-series of Newcastle, with all its rocky strata.* A Scottish lake does not shoal" [*i. e.* deposit mud or marl to remain at the bottom,] "at the rate of half a foot in a century; and that country presents a vertical depth of far more than 3,000 feet, in the single series of the oldest sandstone. No sound geologist will accuse a computer of exceeding, if he allows 600,000 years for the production of *this series alone.*——And yet, what are the coal-deposits, and what the oldest sandstone, compared to the entire mass of the strata?——

"If these views of the powers and the results of geological investigation are alarming to feeble minds, they tend to exalt that science in the estimation of those who neither fear to seek TRUTH, nor dread it when found."†

I do not take upon me to affirm that these numbers are incontrovertibly correct; but let it not be forgotten that they proceed from one of the most experienced and indefatigable of studious observers and practical labourers in this field, besides that he was an avowed and warm friend of revelation. If my advice should have the effect of inducing any of my young friends to read his Description of the Highlands and Western Isles of Scotland, in four volumes; his Geological Classification of Rocks, (though the Classification, in the present advancement of discovery, requires considerable correction,) and his posthumous three volumes on the Attributes of GOD, as proved and illustrated by the Physical Universe;—I am sure that they will not blame me. Yet it must not be forgotten that he did not live to acquire a proper knowledge of Palæontology.

3. There is a fact which may be made intelligible to an uninstructed person, or even to a child. In those stratified rocks which are of a sandy constitution, it is common to find pebbles, from the size of coriander-seeds to that of birds' eggs, and much larger. These bear demonstrative evidence of having been derived from more ancient rocks, by fracture and detachment, long rolling on a hard bottom under water, dispersed through the loose sand of a deposit, subsiding to the lower part if a tolerably free motion were permitted, and then consolidated. To this portion of a sandy formation, whose parts are thus agglutinated, the appropriate term *conglomerate* is given. Let the Old Red Sandstone be our example.—In many places the upper part of this vast formation is of a closer grain, shewing that it was produced by the last and finest deposits of clayey and

* The reader will observe that the author is speaking of the Newcastle coal-strata alone; not including the subsequent formations up to the present condition of the earth.

† Macculloch's *System of Geology;* vol. i. pp. 506, 507.

sandy mud, tinged, as the whole is, with oxides and carbonates of iron, usually red, but often of other hues. But frequently the lower portions, sometimes dispersed heaps, and sometimes the entire formation, consist of vast masses of conglomerate, the pebbles being composed of quartz, granite, or some other of the earliest kinds; and thus shewing the previous rocks, from whose destruction they have been composed. Let any person first acquire a conception of the extent of this formation, and of its depth, often many hundreds and sometimes two or three thousand feet; (but such a conception can scarcely be formed without actual inspection;*) then let him attempt to follow out the processes which the clearest evidence of our senses shews to have taken place: and, let him be reluctant and sceptical to the utmost that he can, he cannot avoid the impression that ages innumerable must have rolled over the world, in the making of this single formation.

4. In the texture of the early stratified rocks, to which the abundant evidence leads us to ascribe a vast antiquity, pieces of granitic rocks are often found, of such forms as shew that they had been broken off from the crystallized formations: for, if they had come from the injection of newly-formed granite, the marks of elevation and intrusion in a fused state would not have been wanting. Hence, it is plain that the parent rock, in any case, existed before the formation of the derivative.

5. The earliest slate rocks, like all other strata, must have been originally deposited in a position horizontal or nearly so. By subsequent movements, not one but evidently many, they have been raised to all elevations, and bent to the utmost extent of contortion: as is shewn by the lines of stratification. But there is another kind of division, first brought to light by Professor Sedgwick; that of lines of cleavage and intersecting joints, or called by a general term, structural or divisional planes. These are productive of signal benefit to the arts and convenience of men: but they involve profound geological and mathematical researches, and their causes can be explored only by going into the deepest night of terrestrial antiquity. Those who are the best qualified to form an opinion, impute this structure to an agency (—call it electric, galvanic, magnetic, or chemical,—) connected with the grand and mysterious operations of the terrestrial magnetism, operating upon a scale of magnitude and distance which we cannot graduate, and requiring a proportionate vastness of time for its taking effect; probably the same agency that reigns in

* The most convenient localities for us are in Herefordshire and Monmouthshire.

the wonderful processes of crystallization, from points of invisible minuteness to formations of indefinable greatness:—or some parts of these phenomena may be imputed to the slow action of the heat from below, producing a general and regular contraction of the argillaceous formations:—or the cause may be sought in the change of cohesion in masses becoming solid from a state of fluidity. The contraction mentioned is founded upon a known property of argillaceous earth: all these causes act quite independently of the stratification: the jointed structure is found to affect the crystalline rocks also: the stratification contains in itself the evidence of having required periods, impossible indeed to be determined by any assignment of figures, but to which, judging from all approximating evidence, our cycles of time afford none but a totally defective measure of comparison. This branch of investigation is indeed one of extreme difficulty; and with which I acknowledge myself to possess but a very imperfect acquaintance. The expectation is with good reason indulged, that both the learned Professor just mentioned, and another ornament of the same University, Mr. Hopkins, who has long employed his rare mathematical powers upon the class of problems to which this belongs, will confer upon the whole subject important elucidations, and open its further connexions with the most recondite parts of geological science.*—But the impression which the general view of the phenomena makes upon me, is that of an unspeakable addition to the reasons for Mr. Scrope's exclamation,—"*Time! Time!*—Geology compels us to make unlimited drafts upon antiquity!"

It is established by such evidence as places the fact beyond contradiction, that by far the larger part, more probably the whole, of the dry land, not excepting the highest mountains, has been raised out of the bed of the sea. There is also evidence that the process of elevation is extremely slow. The general proof accrues from the ancient beaches, now far above the highest sea-level, which abound on almost all bold coasts. But a favourable concurrence of circumstances has brought the elevation of an extensive portion of the Scandinavian peninsula, within the range of measurement; and three feet in a century have been well established. Now there are successions of such ancient sea-beaches, in several of the glens of Scotland, at heights

* See Prof. Sedgwick's Remarks on the Structure of large Mineral Masses, in the *Trans. Geol. Soc.* Second Ser. vol. iii. p. 461. Mr. Hopkins's Mem. in the *Trans. Philos. Soc.* Cambr. vol. vi.; and the brief Sketch of his communication to the Geol. Section of the British Assoc. at Bristol, in the Report for 1836; *Trans. Sect.* p. 78. Prof. Whewell's brief but most interesting summary of the problems which Mr. Hopkins has proposed, and the results to which he has already arrived, in his *Presidential Address to the Geological Society*, Feb. 15, 1839; p. 40.

of eight, ten, twelve hundred feet, and more, above the present sea-level. Mr. Darwin has shewn, by a series of very probable arguments, that these have been all produced by the regular action of the ocean-waters upon rocky shores, and the no less regular rising of the land, in its bodily mass, over large areas, and with that extreme slowness of which we have so many proofs. Applying then the example of Sweden to the case before us, we bring out a period of *thirty thousand* years, from the lowest and of course the latest elevation to the formation of the present shore; and from the time of the highest elevation, the period is more than *eighty thousand* years. But a period remains to be added to this, for the interval before that highest beach was raised and while the upper part of the mountains was slowly rising out of the waters: for this prior period, no rule or approximation of estimate is known.*

I must cease; or I had intended to push my argument farther, and to ask some reflection to be bestowed upon the crystalline rocks.—Can any man imagine that granite was created in its characteristic state, a composition of visibly and palpably distinct materials, scarcely mixed, only put loosely together?——It would be almost as reasonable to affirm that the stomachs of the first animals were created with bitten and masticated fragments of the appropriate food in them.——Whence came the quartz, the mica, and the felspar; each a rock of separate existence?—Whence, the schorl, the augite, the steatite, and other interminglings?——Must we not pursue them to their chemical decomposition? Can we stop short of believing that the original act of creation produced the *few primordial elements*, by the combinations of which all mineral and all organized matters have been formed?—Then we have gone back to the fathomless abyss of ages of ages.—But this unutterable period!—Compared with the INFINITE existence, with the ETERNITY of GOD,——it sinks to a moment.——

"Combining in our survey, then, the whole range of deposits, from the most recent to the most ancient group, how striking a succession do they present!—So various, yet so uniform! so vast, yet so connected!———In thus tracing back to the most remote periods in the physical history of our continents, *one system of operations* as the *means* by which [so] many complex formations have been successively produced, the mind becomes impressed with the singleness of nature's laws; and, in this respect at least, Geology is hardly inferior in simplicity to Astronomy.———Need we recapitulate those curious

* Mr. Maclaren's Paper on the Parallel Roads of Glen Roy; in Prof. Jameson's *Philos. Journ.* Edinb. Oct. 1839; p. 395. See an additional remark at the end of this Supplementary Note.

changes in the lithological character of the deposits effected by igneous action? Or endeavour to arouse the mind to a sense of the greatness of those powers, whatever they may have been, which produced the *symmetrical jointed structure* of mountains, and carried countless lines of *parallel cleavage* throughout regions of slaty rocks, in spite as it were of the original forms of the strata?"*

Thus far I have endeavoured to reason from the mineralogical character of stratified masses, not so much from their constitution or composition individually, as from their position above and below each other. I have continually endeavoured to leave out the consideration of Organic Remains, though it was impossible to do so entirely. But it appeared probable that, for general readers, the method of surveying the two lines of evidence apart, might be the more favourable to a correct apprehension of the whole. We must, therefore, now direct our attention to the attractive department of Geology, to which the name of Palæontology has been appropriated.

In all the terrene formations till we reach the very early ones, we are met by the remains of creatures which once had life, and were furnished by their Creator with the means of performing functions and enjoying life, to the extent of their capacities. In some of the strata, the number is comparatively small, but in the greater part it is very considerable.

The first systems of stratification, gneiss, mica schist, and so on to the lower part of the Cambrian beds, supply no vestiges of vegetable or animal life. But it would be unwarrantable to affirm absolutely that living creatures had no place in the waters which once covered those rocks, and from which they were deposited; for the heat propagated from below, through the substance of the granitic masses, and which has given a partially fused and crystalline character to the gneissic, would be effectual to dissipate all organized matter, had such existed before the high temperature was produced.

In a citation before given from Professor Phillips† we have contemplated a sketch of the forms of organic life from the earliest appearance in the slate-mountains of North Wales and Cornwall, to those of the present creation. To have the mind duly impressed by a view at all approaching to completeness of the little that is known, the study of many geological works, a familiar acquaintance with collections, and an actual inspection of the rocks themselves, are, if not necessary, yet highly desirable. The first and second of these means are all that many studious persons can command; but for them

* Murchison; *Silur. Syst.* i. 574.

† Pages 57—59.

let us be thankful, and by the use of them we may acquire the qualifications which are indispensable for enjoying the survey of nature upon a grand scale, whenever it may be put into our power.

The earliest appearances of life are two or three species of zoophytes, and casts (that is, impressions in mineral matter remaining after the organized substance has been dissolved and washed away,) of several species of shells which have been discovered* in the slate-rocks just mentioned. The structure of those shells shews that their inhabitants stood higher in the scale of organization than our cockles and oysters. But we should not be warranted in supposing that these, should we call them twenty or thirty species, were the whole amount of the kinds of living creatures at that remote era. It is a wonder that any have escaped total obliteration. Besides these few corallines and hard shells, there might be many species of many animal orders, the remains of which have been entirely decomposed and absorbed. The fossils referred to are arranged along the surfaces of deposit, in such positions and regularity as shew that the animals lived and died on the spots which have preserved their remains. An indication is thus afforded of the lapse of time, which is very impressive. An area of soft clay at the bottom of a primeval ocean was deposited, and received its living tenants with their shelly habitations; from their first creation growing up to the preservation of individual life, increasing and multiplying their kinds, and generation succeeding generation till the species becomes extinct. Though perfect knowledge is not possessed, yet there are reasons for believing that the duration of life to testacean individuals of the present races is several years. But who can state the *proportion* which the average length of life to the individual mollusc or conchifer, bears to the duration appointed by the Creator to the species? Take any one of the six or seven thousand known recent species. Let it be a Buccinum, of which 120 species are ascertained, (one of which is the commonly known *whelk*;) or a Cypræa, comprising about as many, (a well-known species is on almost every mantel-piece, the *tiger-cowry*;) or an Ostrea (*oyster*), of which 130 species are described. We have reason to think that the individuals have a natural life of at least six or seven years; but we have no reason to suppose that any one species has died out, since the Adamic creation. May we then, for the sake of an illustrative argument, take the duration of testacean species, one with another, at 1000 times the life of the individual? May we say, 6000 years?—We are dealing very liberally with our opponents.—— Yet, in ex-

* By the late Rev. John Josiah Conybeare, the Rev. Prof. Sedgwick, and Prof. Phillips.

amining the vertical evidences of the cessations of the fossil species, marks are found of an entire change in the forms of animal life; we find such cessations and changes to have occurred MANY times, in the thickness of but a few hundred feet of these slate-rocks. But the homogeneous, or nearly homogeneous deposit consists of many thousand feet; and it is only one of several, perhaps four, great formations which constitute this early system.

But when we rise to the Silurian formations, we find a long succession of strata many thousand feet in thickness, and imbedding not fewer than 375 species belonging to the animal kingdom; corallines, encrinites, analogues of crab and lobster, bivalve and univalve shells, and the skeletons and detached bones of fish.

The Old Red Sandstone, now called by a preferable name, the Devonian system, had been thought to be almost destitute of organic remains; but recent researches, particularly in Scotland, have brought to light numerous and highly interesting bones and skeletons of fishes: but none of them are such as belong to the present order of creation. They are all of species, and even genera, not now existing; and the same observation is to be made with respect to the fishes which occur more abundantly in a very thick and extensive formation which comes much later in the geological series, the New Red Sandstone, and especially that which is usually considered as one of its subordinate parts, the Magnesian Limestone.

Between these two great yet very distinct and distant Red Sandstone formations, there is, in many parts of Wales, England, and Scotland, the Mountain Limestone, usually 900 and more feet in thickness, and which consists of nothing else than the remains of coralline and testaceous animals compressed into masses of stone, hard and compact, often many miles in length and breadth. Over that, and in many of the same localities, we have the coal-strata, consisting entirely of compressed plants, with their sandstones, shales, and iron-stones, full of land vegetables, and presenting some fresh-water shells and fishes.

Above these, we are in the New Red just mentioned; 2000 feet of marl, clay, sand-rock, conglomerates, sulphate of lime, rock-salt, and magnesian lime-stone; red of all hues, white and variegated: much less, in our country, replenished with the vestiges of living creatures, than the preceding or the succeeding formations; yet not destitute of them. In the equivalent rocks of Germany and France, organic remains are more frequent.

In one of the members of this formation, the first known appearance of reptile life presents itself, in several species of lizard-like animals. But in the beds which come next in the ascending order, the Lias, we are met by other and very different species, of the same family, of appalling size, power, and armature,* besides other orders; and through all the Oolitic strata, we find remains, in great variety and abundance; above fifty of plants; of the animal classes a number of species and forms of organization, which may well fill us with astonishment, from the zoophytes upwards, but as yet (so far as is known) only, as it were, just touching upon the mammifers. Neither, amidst the crowds of other animals, till we have risen over all the sandy, clayey, and chalk formations, do we find any further appearances of that class. The thousands of species, through whose periods we have thus in idea been passing, are all different from any in the now existing creation, though possessing generic and family analogies: and yet (with the remarkable and contested† exception just hinted at, the Stonesfield fossil, and see p. 57,) no mammiferous animals. When we have risen above the chalk, we discover in the shell-fish a small beginning of existing species; and, in the subsequent formations, the proportion increases till all the older species have successively become extinct, and the land, the fresh waters, and the ocean, come to be occupied by the present edition of creation. But many deposits and very long periods, from the chalk upwards, have existed, till mammiferous animals are found (the various *theria* of several regions); and they are all exceedingly different from living species or even genera. Finally, in the formations immediately preceding our own, we find animals falling into existing genera, but specifically different; and, as they gradually cease, our present species succeed to their places.

This sketch, hasty and imperfect as it is, demonstrates a series of changes in organic nature, adapted to the variations in temperature, atmospheric constitution, and mineral composition, which, upon inde-

* The reader should not fail, if he can, to inspect the specimens which are in the Long Gallery of the British Museum: the figures, by Mr. Hawkins, who collected the most of those specimens and chiseled them out of the rock; (see the note at page 68;) and the reduced figures in Dr. Buckland's Bridgewater Treatise, with his admirable enucleations of the structure and habits of the animals.

† Some eminent anatomists are of opinion that the few bones in question (only two or three broken jaws, upon which the greatest men in this department have put forth their utmost powers of discrimination) belonged not to a mammal, but to a small reptile, of the lizard or iguana family, and to which those naturalists give the generic name of *amphitherium*. *Sec. ed.* Yet Mr. Owen's repeated examinations, in which his exquisite familiarity with Comparative Anatomy has been aided by microscopic observation of the interior structure of teeth, have confirmed the belief of Dr. Buckland and other distinguished men, that the animal was a small mammal, of a kind analogous to the opossum.

pendent grounds, we have reason to believe did take place. The perfections of the Creator are conspicuous in all this wondrous course of change. We see unity of purpose, harmony of means and adaptations, and infinite variety in modes of developement. "O Lord, how manifold are thy works! In wisdom hast thou made them all. The earth is full of thy riches: so is this great and wide sea." (Ps. civ. 24.)

Upon this argument one might expatiate without limit; but I leave it to my studious and impartial readers, persuaded that, in proportion to their mental cultivation and their assiduity in pursuing these interesting objects of research, will be their conviction of the immeasurable antiquity of our earth, and the whole created system—immeasurable, indeed, but *only so to our feeble faculties:* compared with the *prior eternity* of JEHOVAH, it sinks into a short period.—ETERNITY!—How awakening is the thought, that each of us is born for a duration to which that word can be applied; and that it depends upon ourselves, in the present stage of our existence, whether it shall be an eternity of dignity and happiness unspeakable, or of the most appalling degradation, and misery, and despair!

There is one class to which, in this argument, the appeal may be made with peculiar force of evidence; the students of Conchology. Their elegant science makes them familiar with probably seven thousand species of creatures, the inhabitants chiefly of the waters, in whose forms and organic provisions, and in their shelly habitations, the wisdom and goodness of the Creator are displayed with striking beauty. Of those species, the conchologist finds not one in the former strata of the earth's crust, except with a rapidly decreasing proportion, in the most recent formations:*—he finds not one living species in the chalk and the older systems. Yet he perceives identities of genera, but decreasing; and, where the genera are different, there is the relation of analogy; all exhibiting the presiding energy of the one Mind, with the admirable adaptations of every circumstance in the organization to conditions of temperature and the gaseous

* In the newest strata of our country, certain parts of Norfolk and Suffolk, and the basin of the Thames, Mr. Lyell has determined the existence of 90 to 95 in the hundred of such species as now live; the same proportion as in the most recent beds of Sicily. (Charlesworth's *Mag. Nat. Hist.* July 1839, p. 327. Lyell's *Princ.* iii. 369, 370, 373, fifth ed. not repeated in the sixth, as Mr. Lyell proposes a separate work on the Tertiary formations; but a summary on this subject is in vol. i 244-5. *Elements*, p. 284—290.) In the nearest older formations, the proportion of number runs from 70 to 40; the Norfolk Crag, Red, 30; Coralline, 19; and in older beds diminishing to 26, 17, and finally about three: till, in the Chalk, crowded with conchological as well as other remains, all existing species are found to have ceased.

composition of the atmosphere. The fossil conchologist finds above four thousand kinds, which have had their respective periods of existence; I speak not of the individuals, but of the species or races, to each of which, from the analogy of living nature, we must assign some thousands of years. He sees those species at length ceasing: even whole genera going out of existence; and others occupying the vacancies, *always adapted* to altered conditions of the earth and the waters. "This fact has now been verified, in almost all parts of the globe; and has led to a conviction, that at successive periods of the past, the same area of land and water has been inhabited by species of animals and plants as distinct as those which now people the antipodes, or which now coexist in the arctic, temperate, and tropical zones. It appears, that from the remotest periods there has been ever a coming in of new organic forms, and an extinction of those which preexisted on the earth; some species having endured for a longer, others for a shorter time; but none having ever reappeared, after once dying out." (Lyell's Elements, p. 275.) "General and particular results all agree in demonstrating that the physical conditions of the ancient ocean must have been very different, in some respects, from what obtain at present; and that these conditions were subject to great variation during the very long periods which elapsed in the formation of the crust of the earth. In the course of these changes, whole groups of animals perished; others were created, to perish in their turn; and these operations were many times repeated, *not only before* the present races of animals *were formed*, but even *before* the relative *numbers* in the leading groups *approximated* to the proportions which appear in the actual sea." (Phillips's Geol. in Cabinet Cyclop. vol. i. p. 84.)

Other distinct arguments might be adduced in support of our position, the immense antiquity of the earth; but they will present themselves frequently and powerfully to the attentive student, in his patient explorings for geological truth. This note is too long already. Yet I thankfully avail myself of support to its design from the eloquent address of the Rev. William Vernon Harcourt, as President of the British Association, at the meeting of this year (1839,) at Birmingham.

"No one, I think, can doubt that those who condemned the Copernican system were justified in conceiving that the Scriptures speak of the earth as fixed, and the sun as the moving body. Every one will allow also that this language is ill adapted to the scientific truths of Astronomy. We see the folly of any attempt, on this point, to interpret the laws of nature by the expressions of Scripture; and *what* is the *ground* of our judgment? We are not all competent to judge between the theory of Copernicus and those which preceded it; but we determine against the seeming evidence of our senses, and against the letter of Scripture; because we know that competent persons have examined and decided the physical question. Now, gentlemen, in Geology *we are arrived at the self-same point;* that is to say, a vast body of the best informed naturalists have examined, by all the various lights of science, and by undeniable methods of investigation, the STRUCTURE OF THE EARTH: and, however they may differ on less certain points, they will agree in this: that *the earth exhibits a succession of stratification, and a series of imbedded fossils, which cannot be supposed to have been so stratified and so imbedded in six days, in a year, or in two thousand years, without supposing* also such numerous, such confused and promiscuous violations of the laws and analogies of the universe, as would confound, not the science of Geology alone, but all the principles of Natural Theology. Here then is another point of discordance; and in this case [also] the discordance lies between the language of Scripture and the truths of science.—

—"Who then would expect to find in Genesis the chronology or sequence of creation? Who can think that he upholds the authority of Scripture by literal constructions of such a history; by concluding from them that the earth was clothed with trees and flowers before the sun was created, or that the great work was measured by six rotations of the earth upon her axis! It scarcely needed the evidence of physical or geological science, to teach us that such a mode of interpreting the sacred writings is utterly unsound. When the same author speaks of man as 'created in the image of God,' every one perceives that this is one of the boldest figures which language can produce.* And in what but a figurative light can we view the 'days' of creation? What *can* we find in such a description but this truth, that the six grand classes of natural phenomena were, all and each, distinct acts of divine power, and proceeded from the fiat of a single Creator?

"——All the conclusions of human science coincide with Revealed Religion; and none more remarkably than that which has been so falsely termed irreligious Geology: for as Astronomy shews the unity of the Creator through the immensity of space, so does Geology,

* It perhaps did not occur to the accomplished President, that we have divine authority for understanding that expression as signifying the intellectual capacities and moral excellence with which man was endowed, Eph. iv. 24; Col. iii. 10. Also the connexion of the original passage (Gen. i. 26—28) conducts us to the idea, that this "image of God" was intended to signify the dominion over the lower creatures conferred upon mankind.

along the track of unnumbered ages, and through the successive births of beings; still finding in all, the uniform design of the same almighty power, and the varied fruits of the same unexhausted goodness.—" *Report of the Ninth Meeting of the British Association;* page 18—20, also, in the *Athenæum*, Aug. 31, 1839.

Upon this noble generalization, I cannot refuse to cite one passage more from the christian philosopher of New England, so frequently mentioned with respect in the preceding pages.

"Nor ought it to be forgotten, that these very principles and deductions of Geology, that have excited so much of alarm and opposition among some friends of religion, and so much of premature and groundless exultation among its enemies, have nevertheless, when taken in connexion with Astronomy, developed and established a LAW of God's natural government of the Universe, *grand beyond all others known to man*, and undiscovered or only dimly seen by the great minds of other generations. I refer to the fact, that *perpetual* CHANGE *is made the grand conservative and controlling principle of the universe.* Men have always seen and felt this instability in respect to every thing on earth; and they have regarded it as a defect, rather than as a wise law of the natural world. But they now find it to be equally true of suns and planets as of plants and animals. 'Perpetual change, perpetual progression, increase and diminution, appear to be the rules of the material world, and to prevail without exception.' (Prof. Whewell's *Bridgewater Treat.* p. 158.) And this very instability is the great secret of the permanence and constancy of nature's operations, and of the adaptation of the external world to the wants and happiness of organized beings. It is 'a principle superior to those grand rules which we have been accustomed to regard as constituting exclusively the laws of nature; from the security, which we see in it, beyond the longest and apparently most perfect periodical movements of our solar system.' (Cordier, *sur la Temp. de l'Intérieure de la Terre;* p. 84.) In fine, it is probably the most splendid display of the divine skill which the universe can furnish." Hitchcock's *Geol. of Massachusetts;* p. 251.

The importance of the subject of this Dissertation supersedes any apology for its length. But, in relation to that subject, I am under an obligation, the feeling of which is a pleasure: and thus is rendered more incumbent the duty of acknowledging it. The Rev. Professor SEDGWICK, whose liberality of mind and heart is the fit accompaniment of his scientific eminence, has favoured me with communications on this vital point, and with permission to use them as I might think fit. But I cannot adorn myself with another's robe; I cannot incorporate his matter into my own, without a sense of doing wrong. Yet to deprive the reader of the satisfaction to be derived from the information and reasoning of so high an authority,* I should feel to be an inexcusable offence. It is also proper to mention that the Professor's letter was written by him in haste, under the urgency of University engagements, and when setting out on his geological tour this summer in France, Belgium, and other countries.

"——The fossils demonstrate the time to have been *long*, though we cannot say *how* long. Thus we have generation after generation of shell-fish, that have lived and died on the spots where we find them; very often *demonstrating* the lapse of *many years* for a few perpendicular inches of deposit. In some beds, we have large cold-blooded reptiles, creatures of long life. In others we have traces of ancient forests, and enormous fossil trees, with concentric rings of structure marking the years of growth. Phænomena of this kind are repeated again and again: so that we have three or four distinct systems of deposit, each formed at a distinct period of time, and each characterized by its peculiar fossils. Coeval with the Tertiary masses, we have enormous lacustrine deposits; sometimes made up of very fine thin laminæ, marking slow tranquil deposits. Among those laminæ we can find sometimes the leaf-sheddings and the insects of successive seasons. Among them also we find almost mountain-masses of the *Indusiæ tubulatæ*† and other sheddings of insects, year after year. Again, streams of ancient lava alternate with some of these lacustrine Tertiary deposits.

* To geologists it is unnecessary; but to many otherwise well-informed persons, it will be gratifying to know the terms in which Prof. Whewell has adverted to the merits of his friend and colleague. "The classification of the rocks of this portion of our island [the Cambrian] to which Prof. Sedgwick has been led,——is the fruit of the vigorous and obstinate struggles of many years, to mould into system a portion of Geology which appeared almost too refractory for the philosopher's hand: and which Prof. Sedgwick grappled with the more resolutely, in proportion as others shrank away from the task, perplexed and wearied.——A series of formations distinguished and reduced to order by [his] indefatigable exertions and wide views.——It has been necessary to employ and improve all the best methods of geological investigation."——He has traced "the geographical continuity of the strata, almost mile by mile, from Cape Wrath to the Land's End." *Presid. Addr. Geol. Soc.* 1839; p. 25.

† These are cylindrical cases formed for its habitation by a six-legged insect-larva, which inhabits ponds and small streams, creeping at the bottom. The cases are constructed of small portions of leaves and stalks laid and finely joined together, agglutinated by a secretion of the insect, lined with a silky fibrous matter, and defended on the outside by small substances of a harder texture made to adhere by the insect's gluten, such as minute bits of wood or bark, grains of sand and *very small shells*. When it quits the larva state, it comes out a brownish, four-winged, moth-like insect. Reaumur calls them *butterfly-flies*. They are seen in clouds about ponds on summer evenings. The generic name is *Phryganea,* but there are many species in England and other countries.

"In Central France, a great stream of lava caps the lacustrine limestone. At a *subsequent period*, the waters have excavated deep valleys, cutting down into the lacustrine rock marble, many hundred feet: and at a newer epoch, anterior to the authentic history of Europe, new craters have opened, and fresh streams of lava have run down the existing valleys. Even in the Tertiary period, we have thus a series of demonstrative proofs of a long succession of physical events, *each* of which required a long lapse of ages for its elaboration.

"Again; as we pass downwards from the bottom Tertiary beds to the Chalk, we instantly find new types of organic life. The old species, which exist in millions of individuals in the upper beds, disappear: and new species are found in the Chalk immediately below. This facts indicates a long lapse of time. Had the chalk and upper beds been formed simultaneously at the same period," [as the supporters of the diluvial theory represent,] "their organic remains must have been more or less mixed: but *they are not.* Again; at the base of the Tertiary deposits resting on the Chalk, we often find great masses of conglomerate, or shingle, made up of Chalk-flints rolled by water. These separate the chalk from the overlying beds; and many of the rolled flints contain certain petrified *Chalk*-fossils. Now every such fossil proves the following points:

"1. There was a time when the organic body was alive at the bottom of the sea.

"2. It was afterwards imbedded in the cretaceous deposit.

"3. It became petrified: a very slow process.

"4. The Chalk was, by some change of marine currents, washed away, or degraded" [*i. e.* worn away under the atmosphere by the weather and casualties, a process slow almost beyond description,] "and the solid flints and fossils" [thus detached from their imbeddings,] "were rolled into shingles.

"5. Afterwards, these shingles were covered up, and buried under Tertiary deposits.

"In this way of interpretation, a section of *a few perpendicular feet* indicates a LONG lapse of time: and the co-ordinate fact of the

An excellent figure of the *Phryganea rhombica*, a common English species, (which the author has forgotten to say is the size of life,) is in Lyell, vol. iv. p. 153.(1) In that place, Mr. L. has given an account of one instance of the rocky limestone-masses here alluded to by Prof. Sedgwick, with beautiful figures. The cases are studded over with small water-snail shells, like those of *Paludinæ*, or Linnæus's *Helices viviparæ.* Often ten or twelve of these well-loaded cases are packed up, as it were, yet not broken, within the compass of a cubic inch.

(1) *Fifth ed.* and *Elem. sec. ed.* vol. i. p. 373.

entire change of organic types between the beds above and those below, falls in with the preceding inference, and shews the lapse of time to have been VERY LONG. [—But who can say, *how* long? Many thousands of years sink into a trifling period, for the passing through of these processes.——]

"If I travel in Greece, I may find monuments of ancient art perhaps under the foundations of a Turkish house. If I compared these works of art with those of the present day, I should be convinced at once (quite independently of history,) that they belonged to a different epoch in the annals of the human race. These changes are partly due to the progress of civilization, the caprice of man's will, and other moral causes; still, however, subordinate to certain laws. In the geological case, the total change in organic forms has been brought about by the slow operation of physical causes, *not under the control of man*. But he can *observe* them; and, because they are LAWS, that is, have *the impress* of MIND upon them, he can *interpret* them. Those who argue against you as some of your opponents do, not only deprive man of his intellectual privilege, but strip the GOD of nature of his honour."

See pp. 291 and 294. "The Old Red Sandstone often appears as a new conglomerate, of great thickness, separating the old slate-rocks from the Mountain Limestone. But, even in this form and without fossils, it demonstrates that the older strata were solid and perfected before the existence of the Mountain Limestone." [Recent investigations have found it to be rich in fossils, of the most peculiar and instructive character. See the close of this Note.]

"Again; there was a *total* change in the inhabitants of the sea, between the Limestone-beds and Coral-reefs of the Silurian and Cambrian period, and the time when the Mountain Limestone was deposited. Hence, we should conclude that there was a *very long* lapse of time, between the period of the highest Silurian beds and the period of the Mountain Limestone. This inference is confirmed by very modern discoveries. In Scotland, in the country examined by Mr. Murchison [the Silurian region], and above all in North and South Devon, the Old Red Sandstone contains innumerable regular beds, with fossils which have lived and died where we find them; that is, in the same *relative* situation, as of course they [with the entire sea-bottom mass in which had been their habitation,] had been lifted bodily out of the sea by elevatory forces. Subordinate to it are lines upon lines of old Coral-reefs and other calcareous masses, full of organic structures, and indicating most emphatically long periods of time. The organic types [in this Old Red] are of an *intermediate* character, between the types of the Silurian and Cambrian and the types of the Mountain Limestone.

"Every thing indicates a very long and very slow progression:—one creation flourishing and performing its part, and gradually dying off as it has so performed its part; and another actual creation of *new* beings, *not derived as progeny* from the former, gradually taking its place; and again this new creation succeeded by *a third.*—Nothing *per saltum;* all according to law and order: all bearing the impress of MIND, a great dominant *will*, at the bidding of which all parts of nature have their peculiar movements, their periods of revolution, their rise and fall."

"These alternations of Limestone beds [see above, page 289,] full of fossils (shells and zoophytes), prove the slow progression of the series. Each Limestone bed must have taken a long time for its formation, *yet many* of them *alternate with beds of Coal.* There are regular shell-beds in the Coal-strata, stretching scores of miles. These shells often have both valves united, like common living muscles on the sea-shore; and [thus it is shewn that they] have not been transported. They prove that a few inches of strata required a time equal to the lives of several generations of these muscles.—Many of the fossil-plants appear not to have drifted from the spots where they grew; and we have enormous trees, with rings of growth marking their great age: all in the Coal-fields. Yet all the plants are absolutely of *extinct* species, though of a structure that allows a botanist to reason on their habits. The God of nature is 'without variableness or shadow of turning.' Different species were created to suit different conditions of the earth, air, and sea: but the organs of life were the same; and of their modes of growth, nutrition, reproduction, &c. &c. animal or vegetable, we can reason as well as if we saw them. For there are *great dominant laws* of organic life which mark ONE MIND; the very Mind that made us, and has given us eyes to see, and souls in part able to comprehend the great Master-Mind himself, and his ways of working out his will. To deny us the power of drawing inferences from God's laws, is to strip us of the best thing left us in our fallen state, and all creation of its glory.

"In passing through the New Red Sandstone to the Oolitic series of formations, again there is a *complete change* in *all* the forms of organic life; and there is the same proof of a very long lapse of time, that we have in descending from the Tertiary to the Chalk, or in passing [by ascending] from the Silurian to the Carboniferous epoch.

"In the superficial gravel containing rolled blocks of stone, coming from vast distances, we find bones of the elephant, rhinoceros, hippopotamus, &c. &c. of *extinct* species, mingled with bones of mammals of known species; but not a single fragment of a human bone, or a single trace of any human work. Some have referred this gravel to the Noachian Deluge. It cannot be of any newer date: but the safest way is to draw no conclusions not founded on physical evidence; and, as different regions have been elevated at different periods, it seems probable that there must have been many periods for the formation of gravel, some, at least, *long anterior* to that *last act of creation*, by which, a fit habitation being at length prepared for him, MAN and a new creation of beings were called into existence by that Hand which had ordained and regulated all the previous movements."

The inquirer will do well to study Dr. Grant's (Prof. Compar. Anat. Univ. Coll. Lond.) General View of the Characters and the Distribution of the Extinct Animals; in the *British Scientific Annual*, edited by Dr. Thomson, for 1839, pp. 22—281. I cite the concluding paragraph.

"The unity of the plan of organization, and the regular succession of animal forms, point out a *beginning* of this great kingdom on the surface of our globe, although the earliest stages of its developement may now be effaced; and the continuity of the series through all geological epochs, and the *gradual transitions* which *connect* the species of one formation with those of the next in succession, distinctly indicate that they form the parts of one creation, and not the heterogeneous remnants of successive kingdoms begun and destroyed: so that, while they present the best records of the changes which the surface of the globe has undergone, they likewise afford the best testimony of the recent origin of the present crust of our planet, and of all its organic inhabitants."

The observant reader will perceive that, in Dr. Grant's application of the word *creation*, he differs in phrase only, not in doctrine, from the Professors Sedgwick and Phillips.

Third ed. A geological work has appeared, small in size, unpretending in spirit and manner, its contents the conscientious and accurate narration of fact, its style the beautiful simplicity of truth, and altogether possessing for a rational reader an interest superior to that of a novel:—*The Old Red Sandstone;* by Hugh Miller; Edinb. 1841. Were I to express my sense of the value of the book and the genius and talent of its author, I should seem to be a flatterer. In his boyhood, the author began his untaught and independent course of exploration, upon his native soil, the Old Red of Caithness; and his sagacity of penetration and sound faculty of induction have enabled him to draw forth a luminous picture of God's wonderful works through the—"onward and ascending march, the stages [of which] are slow, but the tread is stately; and, to Him who has commanded and who overlooks it, a thousand years are but as a single day, and a single day as a thousand years." Page 269.

Mr. Miller sets before us many demonstrations, striking and even overwhelming, of the *incalculable periods* indicated by the stratifications of his district, and the living creatures which, in the succession of origin, duration, and extinction have characterized the formations. I cannot indulge in citations, but I intreat the possessor of these "New Walks in an Old Field," to study, in their connexions, pages 113, 127, 223, 227, 228, 241, 260, and 269. The book concludes thus: "—How well——to be enabled to look forward to the coming of a new heaven and a new earth, not in terror but in hope; to be encouraged to believe in the system of unending progression, but to entertain no fear of the degradation or deposition of man! The adorable MONARCH of the future, with all its unsummed perfection, has already passed into the heavens, flesh of our flesh, and bone of our bone; and Enoch and Elijah are there with HIM, fit representatives of that dominant race which no other race shall ever supplant or succeed, and to whose onward and upward march the deep echoes of eternity shall never cease to respond." Page 275.

At the Glasgow Meeting of the British Association, Dr. Buckland said that "he had never been so much astonished in his life, by the powers of any man, as he had been by the geological descriptions of Mr. Miller.——That wonderful man described these objects with a felicity which made him ashamed of the comparative meagreness and poverty of his own descriptions in the Bridgewater Treatise, which had cost him hours and days of labour. He would give his right hand to possess such powers of description as this man; and, if it pleased Providence to spare his useful life, he, if any one, would certainly render the science attractive and popular, and do *equal service to* THEOLOGY *and to Geology.*"

Treating upon the Devonian formation, Mr. Richardson observes, that it has been "described with so much ability and eloquence by the Scottish historian of this deposit, that we must refer to the graphic and highly interesting publication of Mr. Hugh Miller,——which combines the instruction of a work of science with the fascination of a romance, and the ability of a writer of the very highest genius." *Geology for Beginners*, p. 466.

I cannot but add the following passage, from the American Journal of Science, by Prof. Silliman and his son Mr. Benjamin Silliman; July, 1842, page 199.

"In our turn, we take leave to add, that this admirable work, the production of a man who obtained his geological knowledge while working day by day as a labourer in a quarry of the Old Red Sandstone in the north-east part of Scotland, evinces talent of the highest order, a deep and healthful moral feeling, a perfect command of the finest language, and a beautiful union of philosophy and poetry. No geologist can peruse this volume without instruction and delight. It affords an admirable synopsis of the formations between the granitic schists and the coal-measures, and indeed embraces an enlarged and highly philosophical view of the science, and of its relation to the Creator."

A remarkable pamphlet has been recently published, which has a strong claim upon the attention of both geologists and scripture-students; *A Catechetical Illustration of the First Chapter of Genesis*; by William Whyte, Latin Master in Watson's Hospital. 9 pages, Edinburgh, 1842. The object is to shew that the creation and subsequent history of the earth's strata, and of the vegetable and animal tribes which have had their periods and have become extinct, through countless ages, is represented, in the simple Hebrew style in Gen. i. 2—25;——that the operations themselves are the ordinary course of the works of God, from the beginning, and still constantly proceeding, (thus acquiescing in a chief principle of Mr. Lyell's works;)——and that "the only peculiarity in all the narrative,"——is "the creation of a new species, MAN;"——and that the scenes of the operations are the various *portions* of the earth's surface, which are thus prepared and suited for the habitation of vegetable and animal tribes, either already in other regions enjoying life, or expressly called into life, that is *created*, in order to the occupation of a newly prepared region.——To say the least of this little work, it is a striking example of the extent to which learned and pious men may depart from the commonly received interpretation of the beginning of Genesis.

Fourth ed. At the twelfth meeting of the British Association,

(Manchester, 1842,) Prof. Agassiz presented a Report, comprehensive yet exact and specific, of the Fossil Fishes of the Devonian system; in which he involves a just tribute to the originality, the scientific proceeding, and the remarkable success of Hugh Miller, and the late accomplished, liberal, and amiable Lady Gordon Cumming. Very few years have elapsed since it was believed that this formation (then usually called the Old Red) was nearly destitute of organic remains. Now, are determined, in Scotland alone, besides two or three in Wales, at least *twenty* genera, spreading out into about *fifty* species, of Fish; whose configuration is of the most remarkable, and even astonishing kind. (See Lyell's *Elem.* sec. ed. vol. ii. ch. xxv.; Ansted's *Geol.* 1844; vol. i. ch. x.) Over an area of Russia more extensive than the whole of Great Britain and Ireland, in beds identical with our Old Red, or equivalent to it, Sir Rod. Murchison and his associates have exhumed in abundance the Fishes of Scotland, and the shells of South Devon.

To the evidence on this subject, the following may be added:—

Mr. Lyell, with his lady, the participant in his scientific zeal, made a tour in the United States, and the British possessions of North America, in 1841-2; of which he has given a narrative in two volumes, rich in interest, picturesque, literary, and politico-economical, as well as geological. The investigations connected with the river-bed and the falls of the Niagara were fully carried out. I cannot condense into a few paragraphs his luminous descriptions and reasonings, concise as his style is. Of even general readers, every person that can, should read the work. It must suffice to say that, calculated upon rigidly cautious grounds of evidence, the river cuts back the edge of the precipice over which it falls, at the mean rate of one foot annually. The distance which it has had thus to wear away, from the place of its very probably ascertained ancient precipitation, is seven miles. The process of erosion may and even must have varied, sometimes being retarded, and sometimes accelerated; but, as Mr. Lyell's estimate is but a third of Mr. Bakewell's, it is the less likely to *exceed* the truth. The result is, that this process has occupied 35,000 years. Yet this is one of the superficial, and, in comparison of innumerable others, recent operations on the face of the earth.

After enucleating, with his characteristic penetration and precision, the changes which, upon the soil of this geographical district, must have preceded the process, Mr. L. proceeds.

"The principal events enumerated in the above retrospect, comprising the submergence and re-emergence of the Canadian lake-district and valley of the St. Lawrence, the deposition of fresh-water strata, and the gradual erosion of a ravine seven miles long, are all so modern in the earth's history as to belong to a period when the marine, the fluviatile, and the terrestrial shells were the same or nearly the same as those now living. Yet if we fix our thoughts on *any one portion* of this period,—on the lapse of time, for example, required for the recession of the Niagara from the escarpment to the Falls,—how immeasurably great will its duration appear in comparison with the sum of years to which the annals of the human race are limited!

"But, however much we may enlarge our ideas of the time which has elapsed since the Niagara first began to drain the waters of the upper lakes, we have seen that this period was one only of a series, all belonging to the present geological epoch.——If such events can take place, while the zoology of the earth remains almost stationary and unaltered, what ages may not be comprehended in those successive tertiary periods during which the flora and fauna of the globe have been almost entirely changed! Yet, how subordinate a place in the long calendar of geological chronology do the successive tertiary periods themselves occupy! How much more enormous a duration must we assign to many antecedent revolutions of the earth and its inhabitants! *No analogy can be found in the natural world* to the immense scale of these divisions of past time, unless we contemplate the celestial spaces which have been measured by the astronomer. Some of these within the limits of the solar system, as, for example, the orbits of the planets, are reckoned by hundreds of millions of miles, which the imagination in vain endeavours to grasp. Yet one of these spaces, such as the diameter of the earth's orbit, is regarded as a mere unit, a mere infinitesimal fraction of the distance which separates our sun from the nearest star. By pursuing still further the same investigations, we learn that there are luminous clouds, scarcely distinguishable by the naked eye, but resolvable by the telescope into clusters of stars which are so much more remote, that the interval between our sun and Sirius may be but a fraction of this larger distance. To regions of space of this higher order, in point of magnitude, we may probably compare such an interval of time as that which divides the human epoch from the origin of the coralline limestone over which the Niagara is precipitated at the Falls. Many have been the successive revolutions in organic life, and many the vicissitudes in the physical geography of the globe, and often has sea been converted into land, and land into sea, *since that rock was formed.* The Alps, the Pyrenees, the Himalaya, have not only begun to exist as lofty mountain chains, but the solid materials of which they are composed have been slowly elaborated beneath the sea, within the stupendous interval of ages here alluded to.

"The geologist may muse and speculate on these events, until, filled with awe and admiration, he forgets the presence of the mighty cataract itself, and no longer sees the rapid motion of its waters, nor hears their sound, as they fall into the deep abyss. But, whenever his thoughts are recalled to the present, the tone of his mind, the sensations awakened in his soul, will be found to be in perfect harmony with the grandeur and beauty of the glorious scene which surrounds him."—*Travels in N. America*, vol. i. p. 50—53; 1845.

At the meeting of the British Association at Southampton, in September, 1846, Mr. Lyell delivered a discourse, marked by his characteristic comprehensiveness and perspicuity, upon the *Delta of the Mississippi*, a narrow promontory projecting into the Gulf of Mexico. This is known to have been and still to be increasing and advancing, from the constant action of the river in bearing down mud and other matter of deposit. Observation and comparison, made during more than one hundred years, had directed attention to the progress of deposit, and the consequent gain of land advancing into the sea. But never before had the requisite talents, the result of science and experience, been employed for the resolution of the question. Mr. Lyell had the concurrent investigation, and assent to his conclusions, of several American men of science. The conclusion of the whole is, that the alluvial plain from which the portion of land projects, with that portion itself, after making great deductions to satisfy the most excessive caution, has required *more than one hundred thousand years.* Yet the operations effected in that period are insignificant, geologically considered, when viewed in connexion with the underlying deposits. Mr. Lyell concluded with the sentiment, that "the further we extend our researches into the wonders of creation in time and space, the more do we exalt, refine, and elevate our conceptions of the Divine Artificer of the universe." See the Athenæum, Sept. 26, 1846; p. 992.

Among the delightful occurrences which indicate the wide diffusion and rapid progress of scientific observation, we may mention a monthly publication, the "Journal of the Indian Archipelago," which commenced at Singapore in July last. Its introductory article comprises a view of the geological phenomena, presented, in characters so plain that "he may run who readeth" them, by the formations and manifest succession of the tract from the loftiest mountain-ridge on the globe (yet, like the Alps, comparatively recent), the Himalaya, over the plain of Bengal, to the innumerable islands, isles, and islets, all along till beyond the last east meridian. In this series of beauty and awful grandeur are displayed the movements of elevation and depression, whether gradual or sudden, eruption, denudation, dislocation, coral workings, and the wondrous variety of plutonic and volcanic forces. He who, with some intelligence of the matter, surveys the sketch, must be overwhelmed with the idea of incessant action, rising out of illimitable antiquity, and perpetuated to the present moment.

Addition to the Note at p. 299.—In Jameson's *Edinb. Journal*, Oct. 1847, is a memoir by the able geologist, Mr. David Milne, giving the results of long, laborious, and accurate explorings of these so-called Parallel Roads. The proof seems to be complete, that they are not *sea*-beaches, but beaches of ancient *lakes*, which remained at different levels, after the successive elevations of the district, the water having been pent up by the mountain sides, till drained off by subsequent geological changes; the processes of which, with their causes and concomitants, must have been extremely slow. This advance of discovery does not affect my reasoning, except as it gives augmented strength to the evidence of immense antiquity. A similar augmentation will also accrue from another hypothesis, advanced by Sir George S. Mackenzie, in the same *Journal*, Jan. 1848.

[G.]

Referred to at pages 67 *and* 244.

ON THE FOSSIL ANIMALCULES.

It is not in my power to say whence I derived this estimate. Perhaps it was given from a general recollection of information in different scientific works. I therefore lay before my readers an extract from a paper of Dr. Ehrenberg himself, shewing that, while the numbers in one description of fossil-masses fall short of my statement, those belonging to another are the double of what I have given.

" The *Polirschiefer* [Polishing Slate] of Bilin in Bohemia occupies a surface of great extent, probably the site of an ancient lake, and forms slaty strata of fourteen feet in thickness, consisting almost entirely of an aggregation of the siliceous shields of *Gaillonella distans*." (Dr. Buckland's Supplementary Notes to his *Bridgewater Treatise*; p. 17, or continuously 610—613.)

I have used, above, the general term *shells;* but *shields* is the more appropriate word, or *cuirasses*, as Dr. Buckland also calls them. They are most beautiful armature-coverings, sometimes of a single plate, sometimes double; formed of the purest quartz or rock-crystal, and therefore perfectly transparent.

The *Raseneisen*, which might be translated *Iron-clod*, is a mass of fine earthy matter, strongly tinged with ochre, the peroxide of iron; probably the same, or nearly so, as what we call Bog Iron Ore; or not unlike the mud of our common chalybeate springs, compressed and dried.

The *Gaillonella distans* is one of the species of the genus *G.* of which some idea may be formed by comparing it to a piece of candied Angelica;* but imagination is baffled in attempting to conceive of its diminutive size, as an extract will shew which shall follow in this Note.

Whoever has the opportunity should not fail to use it, for inspecting the superb German work, *The Infusorial Animalcules, as Perfect Organizations; a Glimpse into the Deeper Organic Life of Nature:* by Dr. Christian Godfrey Ehrenberg. Leipzig, 1838. It is an imperial folio, giving ample accounts of the families, genera, and species of this astonishing region of the animal kingdom. The accompanying Atlas consists of sixty-four plates, of which the drawing, engraving, and colouring are models of beauty. Each plate contains many figures, magnified of course many hundreds and even thousands of times, and all presenting 722 species. The forms of these minute creatures are prodigiously varied, and their organization richly diversified and complicated. Some of them resemble the *infusoria* exhibited by the hydro-oxygen microscope; but many species are extremely different. They are globular, or almost so, wheel-shaped, boat-shaped, legume-formed, pear-shaped, funnel-shaped, and poly-

* A figure is given of two species, in Mr. Lyell's *Elements*, page 52; and in his *Principles*, vol. iii. p. 271 (6th ed.) the *G. ferruginea*, whose shields, composed of silex and iron, constitute the substance of Bog Iron Ore. The Noble President of the Royal Society has made felicitous discoveries of many-chambered shells (Spirolinites,) of several species, in the chalk flints: of which figures are given by Dr. Mantell, *Wond. Geol.* vol. i. p. 322. Other naturalists have successfully pursued this line of microscopic inquiry. In particular the Rev J. B. Reade, F.R.S., who has devoted his powers of research to this empire of wonders; "an investigation which," he justly observes, "no right-minded man will prosecute, without directing his thoughts to Him who, of old, 'turned the hard rock into a standing water, and the flint-stone into a springing well.'" Some of these interesting communications from Mr. Reade may be consulted in the *Seventh Report of the British Assoc.* (Liverpool, 1837;) in the *Annals of Nat. Hist.* Nov. 1838; and with figures and a comprehensive summary in the *Wond. Geol.* vol. i. and ii. and the Appendix. See also communications from Ehrenberg, Meyen, Kersten, and Mr. Richard Taylor; and extracts from Professors Whewell and Rymer Jones, on this subject, in *Ann. Nat. Hist.* 1838 and 1839.

parious in a variety of forms. Many are of brilliant hues, green, yellow, blue, crimson, and fainter colours; and often perfectly transparent, so that not only the mouth, ciliary fringes, and numerous organs of progress and prehension are seen, but the internal organs, such as the œsophagus, the stomach and appendages, and canals, with their inosculations.* Ehrenberg "has discovered in them muscles, intestines, teeth, different kinds of glands, eyes, nerves, and organs of reproduction. He finds that some are born alive, others produced by eggs, and some multiplied by spontaneous divisions of their bodies into two or more distinct animals." (Buckl. i. 446.)

Having given these as preliminary explications, I proceed to the citation from "Remarks on the Real Occurrence of Fossil Infusoria, and their Extensive Diffusion; by Prof. Ehrenberg: read in the Royal Academy of Sciences, Berlin, July 7, 1836." Translated by Mr. W. Francis, and published in Mr. Richard Taylor's *Scientific Memoirs*, vol. i. p. 400—413.

"The size of a single one of these Infusoria, which form the Polirschiefer, amounts, upon an average and in the greater part, to $\frac{1}{288}$ of a line, which equals $\frac{1}{6}$ of the thickness of a human hair, reckoning its average size at $\frac{1}{48}$ of a line. The globule of the human blood, considered at $\frac{1}{300}$, is not much smaller. The blood globules of a frog are twice as large as one of these animalcules. As the Polirschiefer of Bilin is slaty, but without cavities, these animalcules lie closely compressed. In round numbers, about twenty-three millions of animals would make up a cubic line, and would in fact be contained in it. There are 1728 cubic lines in a cubic inch; and therefore a cubic inch would contain, on an average, about 41,000 millions of these animals. On weighing a cubic inch of this mass, I found it to be about 220 grains. Of the 41,000 millions of animals, 187 millions go to a grain; or, the siliceous shield of each animalcule weighs about $\frac{1}{187}$ millionth part of a grain.

"The animalcules of the Raseneisen are only $\frac{1}{1000}$ of a line in diameter; or the $\frac{1}{21}$ part of the thickness of a human hair, $\frac{1}{3}$ of the diameter of a globule of the human blood, $\frac{1}{8}$ of the blood globule of a frog. A cubic line of such animal Iron-ochre would thus, in the same relation, contain one thousand millions; one cubic inch, one billion; and one cube of nine feet diameter, one trillion, of living beings."

But I cannot so forget the obligations of reason and truth as to

* A compendious work, including the most essential parts of Ehrenberg's costly volume, has been published by Mr. Andrew Prichard, *A History of Infusoria, Living and Fossil*; London, 1841: with twelve plates, containing 531 objects beautifully engraved and in their proper colours.

end this Note without requesting my reader to do this subject the justice of reading the impressive passage, which cannot be too well known, the comparison of the moral argument from the telescope and that from the microscope, in Dr. Chalmers's *Discourses on the Christian Revelation, viewed in Connexion with the Modern Astronomy;* p. 112—116. Yet, lest the book should not be at hand, I will quote a few lines.

"——The one led me to see a system in every star: the other leads me to see a world in every atom. The one taught me, that this mighty globe, with the whole burden of its people and of its countries, is but a grain of sand on the high field of immensity. The other teaches me, that every grain of sand may harbour within it the tribes and the families of a busy population. The one told me of the insignificance of the world I tread upon. The other redeems it from all its insignificance; for it tells me that, in the leaves of every forest, and in the flowers of every garden, and in the waters of every rivulet, there are worlds teeming with life, and numberless as are the glories of the firmament. The one has suggested to me that, beyond and above all that is visible to man, there may lie fields of creation which sweep immeasurably along, and carry the impress of the Almighty's hand to the remotest scenes of the universe. The other suggests to me that, within and beyond all that minuteness which the aided eye of man has been able to explore, there may be a region of invisibles; and that, could we draw aside the mysterious curtain which shrouds it from our senses, we might there see a theatre of as many wonders as Astronomy has unfolded, a universe within the compass of a point so small as to elude all the powers of the microscope, but where the wonder-working God finds room for the exercise of all his attributes, where he can raise another mechanism of worlds, and fill and animate them all with the evidences of his glory."

Fourth ed. An interesting appendage to this Note will be the following paper, for which I am indebted to a work valuable for both science and general literature, the *Bibliothèque Universelle Genève;* new series, vol. xxxi. p. 197; 1841.

"*Summary View* of the Inferences to be drawn from the Facts observed by Prof. Ehrenberg upon the Infusorial Animalcules.

"1. The greater number of microscopical animalcules are endowed with a complex organization.

"2. They form, in their structure, two very distinct classes.

"3. Their geographical distribution over the globe follows the same laws as those which govern other animals.

"4. They impart particular colourings to large masses of water;

and, by the light which they emit, they occasion specific varieties of phosphorescence in the sea.

"5. By their accumulation in a living state, they often form what might be called animated earthy masses. As forty-one thousand millions of individuals may often be ascertained in a cubic inch of substance, their absolute number must certainly be greater than that of all other animals taken together. It is even probable that, in their collective volume, they exceed that of all other animated beings.

"6. They possess the greatest power of production that exists in organic nature. A single individual can, in a few hours, procreate many millions of beings like itself.

"7. These animalcules form, by means of their siliceous coverings, earthy masses, stones, and rocks. Those substances then become the components of many natural and artificial products, as glass, floating bricks which were manufactured by the ancients, polishing earths (tripoli, ochre, &c.), manures, alimentary earths as the fossil flour [*Bergmehl*] used in the north [as a partial substitute for food in some of the barren districts of Sweden and Lapland], which fill the stomach without injuring it. Sometimes these minute creatures are injurious, by vitiating the water, killing the fish in ponds, and producing miasms [in marshes which have no sufficient drainage:] yet it has not been proved that the plague, cholera, and other contagious diseases are to be attributed to them, as some have maintained.

"8. So far as observation has penetrated, these animalcules appear never to sleep.

"9. They exist in the bodies of men and other animals.

"10. They are themselves infested with still more minute parasitical animalcules, which live in their insides; and these also have parasites which can be observed.

"11. They are in general affected by external agents, in ways very similar to what the superior classes of animals are susceptible of.

"12. As they are extremely light, the gentlest breath of air raises them, and floats them off into the atmosphere.

"13. Some of these animalcules are capable of remarkable changes in their form, but within certain limits to both the constancy and variations, so that the entire combination of phenomena can be referred to precise organic laws.

"14. Their organization is comparatively very powerful, as is especially manifested in the strength of their teeth and other instruments of mastication. They appear also to have the same organs of sense as other animals.

"15, Observation of these microscopic beings has led to more exact definitions of what constitutes an animal, and distinguishes it from a vegetable; thus leading to a more perfect knowledge of the organic systems which are wanting to plants.

"16. The complication of the organization of the microscopic animalcules would alone serve to refute the theories and ill-made observations which have ascribed to them a spontaneous generation from brute matter. "I. M."

I solicit particularly my readers' attention to the last position.

This indefatigable explorer has subsequently applied his talent as a microscopist to the mud and sand accumulated at the mouths of great rivers, and driven, by the under-flow of the salt water, in the direction contrary to the descending (lighter and therefore superior) current of the fresh water, to great distances up the rivers. He has thus examined the fine deposits of the Elbe up to eighty English miles from its mouth; also of the beds and plains of the Weser, the Ems, the Mersey, the Liffey, and the same must hold universally. These districts, forming the rich soils of the great river valleys from their mouths to a vast extent upwards and on each side, contain immense quantities of marine animalcules, fresh and in all stages of dissolution, which have most probably been killed by the mixing of the fresh with the sea water. The proportion in mass of these animal accumulations, near Hamburgh, is at least one-twentieth of the soil.

It is thus proved, that millions of the acres which minister the most largely to human sustenance, owe their fertility, not merely to the washings of animal and vegetable matter from the higher grounds, but to the large intermixture of once living beings, whose very existence is a recent discovery, which cannot be seen individually without a high microscopical power, and which have formed, in even many of the still existing species, immeasurable masses of earthy and rocky matter, from the oolite, the chalk, and all through the tertiary periods, countless ages before the creation of the race for which God was thus providing. The same lesson is taught us by the unfathomably more distant date of the coal formation, and the universal diffusion of lime and iron. That great Being thus teaches us, that mere words of admiration are vapid and worthless, and that true piety is shewn in the imitation of his beneficence.

The discoveries of unwearied microscopists have also established another truth, the *wide geographical range* of many species. From analogy, the same must be inferred of others; and not improbably the conclusion may be extended to the whole class of *Microzoa.* Conglomerations of them, accumulated undoubtedly through millennaries, are ascertained to compose immense banks on the shores and the bottoms of the seas; and these, when upheaved by geological causes, have been solidified into mountains. There is good reason for the belief that all chalk, and we may add all other calcareous masses, are nothing but the corpses and habitations of these infinitesimally minute creatures. This fact, with regard to other rocks which had never been suspected to be any thing but mineral masses, has been mentioned in these Lectures, p. 67.—I cite another excellent authority.

"It is a remarkable fact, that Ehrenberg detected in the *chalk* and *chalk-marls* from Oran in Africa, Caltanisetta in Sicily, and certain parts of Greece, no less than fifty-seven species, which are *identical* with existing animalcules at Cuxhaven and other localities in the North Sea; making good the opinion entertained by geologists, that, in the higher classes of fossil organic remains, *no representative exists* on the earth, but, in the lower, the identity of many species is perfectly established.—By the aid of the microscope, we have been enabled to discover the *universality* of these creatures, for the same are met with in the polar as are found in the tropical seas, and those of both regions can be proved to have existed at the earliest dawn of this world's existence." [Mr. Quekett probably means the earliest organic system of our planet.] "—A striking proof of the important part which these minute organisms were created to perform in the deposition of materials for the earth's surface, and how, by these imperceptible agents, such gigantic consequences have resulted." [These facts] "stamp upon reflecting minds that no creature, even the most minute, is formed without special purposes; and that the least in size of all, by [means of] the organization given to them by the great Architect of the universe, have been employed to carry out his unfathomable intentions." Mr. Edwin J. Quekett, in *Lond. Physiol. Journ.* Feb. 1844, p. 145.

Connected with this subject is a striking exemplification of the Divine prospective benignity in the constitution of nature. It is, indeed, only one out of the instances innumerable which investigation brings to light, to an extent ever augmenting even in the present state;—how much more is reserved for the disclosures of the holy heaven! I derive it from a valuable article in the Edinburgh Review, (Oct. 1847,) on *Holland, its Rural Economy;* p. 424.

"—— In the waters of the river, but especially in those of the sea, there exist vast numbers of minute microscopic animalcules, called by Ehrenberg *Infusorial Animals;* which are fitted to live, each class *in its own special element only*, and which therefore die in myriads where the sweet and the salt waters mingle. It is almost incredible,—how densely the water is sometimes peopled by these creatures, how rapidly they multiply, in what countless numbers they exist. Their skeletons and envelopes, consisting of calcareous and siliceous matter extracted from the water, are almost imperishable. They commix with the mud of the river; and, *with it*, they come to form the deposits of slime that fill up the channels, raise the growing islands, or add to the belt of most fertile land which increases seaward where the waters are still. As the tide advances up its channel, the waters of the river spread and flow over the surface; so that, far up the stream, where the upper waters are still sweet, the salt or brackish under-current carries the living things which float in it to certain death, and leaves their bodies behind it to add to the accumulating mud. The extensive mutual surfaces of river and sea-water which in this way are made to meet, insure a more rapid destruction of infusorial life than could in almost any other way be brought about.

"Experiment has shown that, as far up as the tide reaches, the so-called alluvial deposit in and along the channel of the river abounds with the remains of these marine animalcules; while above the reach of the tide none of them are to be found. In the Elbe they are seen as far as eighty miles above its mouth. About Cuxhaven and Gluckstadt, which are nearly forty miles from the open sea, their siliceous and calcareous skeletons form from $\frac{1}{4}$ to $\frac{1}{3}$ of the mass of the fresh mud, exclusive of the sand; while, farther up the river, they amount to about $\frac{1}{2}$ of this quantity. In the Rhine, the Scheldt, the Mersey, the Liffey, the Thames, the Forth, the Humber, and the Wash, the same form of deposit goes on: so that, in the mouths of all tidal rivers, there are to be superadded to the mechanical debris brought down by the upper waters, the more rich and fertilizing animal spoils which the sea thus wonderfully incorporates into the growing deltas and the banks of rising mud. And thus it is seen that river-islands encroach upon the ocean, not merely in proportion to the solid matters held in suspension by the descending water, but in proportion also to the richness of the sea in microscopic forms of life, and to the volume of fresh water which the river can bring to mingle with it."

[G g.]

Referred to at page 85.

ON THE PEBBLES.

In the constitution of these common objects, the despised pebbles of our plains and the shingle of our coasts, there is much that deserves attention. They consist very extensively of the fragments of the older rocks, chiefly the igneous, called primary; and these often include distinct masses of very pure silex, both amorphous and crystallized, from which the detached and rolled fragments become pebbles of jasper and chalcedony. In many of these, and in the Flint nodules which characterize the Upper Chalk, there are recondite wonders, not only of deep intrinsic interest, but carrying us back to the view of a degree of heat affecting the ancient surface of our globe, so high as to be immensely beyond the capacity of the vegetables and animals of the present creation ever to have sustained. That heat must have been such as, combined with the pressure of an atmosphere, probably of carbonic acid gas, and that made heavier by enormous condensation, enabled the waters to hold in solution a quantity of pure siliceous earth, so great as to have furnished the masses of pebbles (chert, flint, jasper, and agate,) which so abound in many countries. It has long been observed that many varieties of chalcedony (called moss-agates, mocha-stones, and perhaps by other names,) shew substances imbedded and beautifully spread out, as if suspended in a fluid, or like the finer sea-weeds (*algæ* and *confervæ*) as delicately displayed in a lady's album or *hortus siccus*. These, after making all reasonable deduction for mineral infiltrations, are indubitably organized bodies; and which, with some exceptions from the insect tribes, were referred to the Confervæ, or other cryptogamic plants. See a Memoir, with beautiful coloured plates, by the late Dr. Mac Culloch, in the *Geol. Transact.* first series, vol. ii.

But the recent investigations of a distinguished Geologist and Microscopist, Mr. James Scott Bowerbank, have thrown a satisfactory light upon the constitution of the many species and varieties of the well-known substance Sponge, have established its claim to belong to the animal kingdom, and have detected numerous instances of spongeous bodies, *in the fossil state*, *and always imbedded in flints*, *agates*, *or other siliceous stones*. Now sponges (and in some degree other Porifera, as the Alcyoniums,) have in their internal structure minute aggregations of silica, generally in the shape of needles or darts, and therefore called *spicula*. There is a manner of action, we presume to call it a *law*, which may be named *homogeneous attraction;* the result of which, in the waters of a former state of the globe, was that these phytozoic bodies attracted around their own substance the silica dissolved in the hot waters, bringing it more or less gradually, and often it would appear most rapidly, into the solid state; in these masses they themselves being enclosed. This subject has been illustrated by Mr. Bowerbank, in various Memoirs, published in the Geological and Microscopical Societies' *Transactions and Proceedings*, the *Annals and Magazine of Natural History*, and the *Microscopical Journal;* in the years 1841 and 1842, and subsequently.

The inference to Geological theory from these facts is a strengthening of the general argument for believing in a high antiquity of the earth; from its having existed and been the abode of organized creatures, whilst it was under conditions incompatible with the life of its present inhabitants.

A similar fact we have which, though not bearing in the same way on the estimate of past time, is highly interesting as a proof of the abundant solution of silica, in the heated waters of a former terrestrial condition. This is the Marquis of Northampton's discovery of microscopic shells of the nautilaceous family, in the heart of flint-pebbles. See the preceding Note.

[H.]

Referred to at page 91.

ON ANCIENT GLACIERS AND THEIR EFFECTS.

At the time when the second edition of this book was published, Dr. Lewis Agassiz was exploring the northern mountains and valleys of our island, and applying the hypothesis which he had built upon the foundations of MM. Venetz and De Charpentier, of the presence of extensive glaciers, and their action in glazing and marking the surfaces of rocks, and in the transport and arranged deposition of pebbles, bowlders, and masses of stone retaining the edges and angles, thus shewing that they had not been much if at all rolled. He detailed many of his observations and opinions to the Geological Section of the British Association, at Glasgow, in September 1840. Similar communications he also made to the Geological Society of London.

In the same year he extended his laborious researches, aided and in great part accompanied by Dr. Buckland, Mr. Lyell, Mr. Charles Maclaren, and other eminent Geologists, in Scotland, the north of England, and some parts of Ireland; applying the principles which he had derived from the study of his native Alps. In the autumn he published at Neuchâtel his interesting work, *Etudes sur les Glaciers;* with an Atlas of magnificent plates, executed with rigid accuracy as well as beauty. Most or all of our great authorities gave their approbation to his theory, to some extent; on the degree however of that extent, they varied. All viewed their frank and pleasing visitor with honour and esteem; all admired his extensive and minute knowledge, his indefatigable laboriousness, his prompt and lively talents in communication, and his ability in supporting his doctrines. Without presumption, I trust, it may be said that those doctrines and their application will stand the test of time to a considerable extent, but not so far as the distinguished man carries them. Many rock-surfaces, polished, scored, or grooved, and many arcuated aggregations of travelled stones, are well proved to be in such conditions as authorize the belief, that glaciers had formerly existed in the higher latitudes of the British Isles, producing similar results to those now observed in the Alps; and that an elevation of climatic temperature, immediately preceding the creation of the present tribes of nature, obliterated the cause and left us the effects.

A chief temptation of accomplished yet sanguine minds is the pushing too far of a good principle: and this temptation finds scarcely any where more scope and occasion than in relation to Geology. It can scarcely be doubted that Agassiz has rested too much upon the simple glacial action, the dry movement; and has not sufficiently introduced the evidences of the same action urged by torrents and tides. The principal Geologists of the continent, including Switzerland, have the most severely impugned this theory: and, in our country and America, its claims are a good deal limited; yet with great liberality to its talented advocate.

Mr. Charles Maclaren of Edinburgh is the author of a compendious summary of Dr. Agassiz's volume and his other communications on this subject: *The Glacial Theory of Prof. Agassiz ;—being an Outline of the Facts and Arguments adduced by him to prove that a Sheet of Ice enveloped the Northern Parts of the Globe at a recent Geological Epoch.* Edinb. 1841. But this small treatise is not a mere analysis or abridgment of the *Etudes ;* it contains judicious observations upon the theory, and a testing application of it to geological phenomena in the neighbourhood of Edinburgh. The author observes, "These very original and ingenious speculations of Professor Agassiz must be held for the present to be under trial. They have been deduced from a limited number of facts, observed by himself and others, and skilfully generalized; but they cannot be considered as fully established till they have been brought to the test of observation in distant parts of the world, and under a great variety of circumstances. Supposing the theory to be substantially sound, the magnitude of the consequences it involves will undoubtedly bring objections to light, which may render modifications necessary, both in its principles and its details. In the mean time, it assists us in resolving some difficulties. It contributes, in a greater or less extent, to explain the dispersion of erratic blocks, the bizarre situations they occasionally occupy, the banks of clay and gravel found on the sides and at the mouths of valleys, the *striæ*, polishing, and grooving, observed on the surface of rocks *in situ*, and of large stones in the till" [a Scottish term for superficial deposits of clay, sand, and gravel;] "and it promises to throw light on what is at present a very obscure subject, the origin of the older and new alluvium." Page 38.

Professor Hitchcock urges the necessity of taking a larger account of aqueous power, and judges it "extremely probable that all the phenomena of what has been called Diluvial Action, are the result of the joint agency of ice and water; the water resulting from the melting of the ice." *Elementary Geology*, sec. ed. p. 192.

More recently, Dr. Hitchcock says—"It will need important modifications—I doubt whether any one [of the American Geologists] is ready to adopt the unmodified glacier theory of Agassiz; although doubtless many will admire the ingenuity and indomitable perseverance of that distinguished naturalist, and thank him for the great light which his labours have cast upon the phenomena of drift. *Amer. Journ. of Science;* Oct. 1842, page 398.

All must regard Mr. Murchison as peculiarly qualified to hold the balances, and mark the preponderance of argument, on any geological question. In addition to his great attainments in geological knowledge, his tact in judging of facts and opinions, and his practical skill in exploring and observing, he has, in the two years 1840 and 1841, travelled over large tracts in the northern part of the Russian Empire, both European and Asiatic, employing his practised eye and patience, expressly for the advancement of this branch of natural science. In his Discourse as President of the Geological Society, delivered February 18, 1842, he has discussed the Glacial Theory at considerable length. I select a few extracts, the briefest possible in consistence with the requisite perspicuity.

"— The Glacier Theory, as *extended* by its author, in proving too much, may be said to destroy itself. Let it be limited to such effects as are fairly deducible from the Alpine phænomena so clearly described by Agassiz, and we must admire in it a *vera causa* of exceeding interest. But, once pass the bounds of legitimate induction from that *vera causa*, and try to force the many and highly diversified superficial phænomena of the surface of the globe into direct agreement with evidences of the action of ice under the atmosphere; and you will be driven forward, like the ingenious author of the theory, so to apply it to vast tracts of the globe, as, in the end, to conduct you to the belief that not only both the northern and southern hemispheres, but even *quasi* tropical regions, were shut up during a long period in an icy mantle."——[Unless framing hypothesis upon hypothesis,] "we also build up former mountains of *infinitely greater altitude* than any which now exist, we have no adequate centres for the construction of the enormous glaciers which imagination must create in many regions to account for the phænomena.—The observations of M. Böhtling—(a young Russian naturalist of great promise, but, alas! prematurely carried to the grave,—) give the—result, upon a very grand scale—in the Northern territories of Russia;—that the Scandinavian mountains, as a whole, had produced exactly the same detrital result as the Alps, having poured off their detritus in all directions *from a common centre*, the northern chain differing only from that of central Europe by the much wider range to which its blocks and boulders were transmitted.

"My own belief—[is]—that by far the greatest quantity of boulders, gravel, and clay distributed over our plains, and occupying the sides of our estuaries and river banks, was accumulated *beneath the waters* of former days. Throughout large tracts of England, we can demonstrate this to have been the case, by the collocation of marine shells of existing species with far-transported materials.—Wide researches, during the last two years, have strongly confirmed [these] my early views.

"——Dr. Buckland abandons, to a great extent, the theory of Agassiz, and admits fully the effects of water as well as of ice, to account for many of the long disputed phænomena.

"——We cannot quit the glacial subject without avowing our obligations to Venetz, Charpentier, and Agassiz, and above all to the last, for having brought the agency of ice more directly into consideration as a *vera causa*, to explain many phænomena on the surface.—He was the first person who roused our attention to the effects produced by the bottom of an advancing glacier: and, if geologists should eventually be led to believe that certain parallel scratches and *striæ* on the rocks were, in some instances, due to glaciers moving *overland*, but in many other cases were produced by icebergs, we must remember that the fertile mind of Agassiz has afforded us the chief means of experimentally solving the problem."

In the Edinburgh Review, No. 151, April 1842, is an article which enters both comprehensively and deeply into this subject, and discusses it with consummate ability. It carries strong presumptive evidence of having proceeded from Professor Forbes. Though published after the delivery of Mr. Murchison's Presidential Address, it was probably written before it, and certainly without any knowledge of the contents of that Address. It will richly reward the being diligently studied. Its concluding paragraph is,—"To maintain the Glacier Theory still requires some confidence, some courage. We have not dissembled its difficulties. But, by presenting it as we have endeavoured to view it, with unprejudiced eyes, as fully entitled to rank among *geological probabilities*, we place it on its most defensible ground, and we venture to predict, at least abroad, a speedy reaction in its favour. Its evidences are such as must be *seen*, and carefully studied without prejudice, in order to be appreciated; and such evidences, though often required to be sought for, and difficultly to be found, are not less conclusive when attained. We have constructed a formidable panoply out of the missiles of its adversaries:—will they not yield to their own weapons? If they pronounce the theory imperfect, we acknowledge it; but we may safely challenge them to produce a better or less improbable one, from amongst those already proposed. If they have a new one, we are ready to consider it."

Yet the arguments, objections, replies, and renewed examinations, on this fruitful subject, are not exhausted. Ample and able disquisitions have been published during the years 1841 and 1842, in the Proceedings and Transactions of the Geological Society, the Philosophical Magazine, the Bibliothèque Universelle of Geneva, other French and German scientific journals, and the Edinburgh New Philosophical Journal, by Professor Agassiz himself, the late Mr. Bowman, Sir George Mackenzie, Mr. Darwin, Professor Brown, Professor Forbes, and others. The general result seems to be, that the Glacier Theory cannot be accepted to the extent for which Agassiz pleads; and that, besides other modifications, floating icebergs must be regarded as, no less than the sliding of glaciers on dry land, essential to the solution of the interesting and complicated problem.

The subject was discussed at great length, at the Third Annual Meeting of the Association of American Geologists and Naturalists,

April 25 to 30, 1842, at Boston; upon papers by Prof. Hitchcock, and Mr. Couthouy, and in the oral communications of Mr. Lyell (whose scientific zeal and liberality has led him to cross the Atlantic, and devote a year and a half to the geological exploration of large districts in the United States, thus accomplishing the wish expressed with no less ardour than judgment in one of our national periodicals, *Edinb. Rev.* vol. lxix. p. 440), Professors Silliman and H. D. Rogers, and others.

The prevalent opinion appeared to be favourable to the course of sentiment above cited from Mr. Murchison; with which however it was scarcely possible that the writers and speakers could be acquainted.

[I.]

Referred to at page 102.

PROGRESS OF CHRISTIAN PIETY IN THE VOLCANIC DISTRICT OF THE PUY DE DOME.

As the design of these Lectures is to serve the highest interests of mankind, I need no apology for introducing some parts of a letter, which has appeared in some of the public papers of London and Paris. The writer was a well known and highly respected clergyman of the English Church, who died lately (January, 1844). His veracity is unquestionable, and his narrative cannot fail to give pleasure so those who are the best friends of mankind and sincere disciples of Christ.

"Amongst the hills of Auvergne and in the Department of the Puy de Dome, is situated the town of Thiers. It is celebrated for its picturesque position, being planted on the steep declivities of rocks and mountains, which are adorned with chesnut-trees, walnuts, oaks, and other striking ornaments of the forest. In front, and at no great distance, is the pyramidal Puy de Dome, with the whole chain of mountains of Mont d'Or and the Cantal; beneath them is the beautiful plain of Clermont, with the silver stream of the Dore winding its way through the midst, and all around the rugged peaks and deep dark mountain ravines stand in striking contrast with sloping hills clothed with vines and corn-fields. The population of this town, computed at 15,000, is almost entirely employed in the manufacture of cutlery. One universal sound, the hammer clinking on the anvil, and the file rasping on the vice, continually strikes the ear *in every* *street*, and no other noise has disturbed, from time immemorial, the dull uniformity of Thiers. During the terrible convulsions of the Revolution and the Empire, this place, indeed, as all others in France, had to deplore its youth sacrificed in foreign fields; and the monotony of human life was then arrested by the news of some falling by the lake of Mantua, others at the walls of Saragossa, and others on the plains of Germany.* But the regrets of such calamities have long since ceased to agitate the hearts of survivors, and nothing seems to occupy attention but to partake of food, to labour for its acquisition, and to die. About two years ago, however, the quiet of the scene was disturbed by a most novel occurrence. The report was circulated, 'There are Protestants arrived at Thiers; they are selling Bibles; they are praying, reading, conversing at the Boullet.' This intelligence acted like an electric shock on the somnolent population. Out rushed no less, it is asserted, than 2000 persons towards the place, where one of the *colporteurs* of the Geneva Society was explaining in his simple manner the great truths of the Gospel. So furious was the mob, such their threats, their gesticulations, and their spirit, that the most serious consequences were apprehended. Not only had the colporteur to escape with the utmost haste by a way removed from the tumult, but even the *commissaire de police* and the *gens d'armes* had to interfere most promptly to prevent evil. The riot of this day will ever be a memorable fact in the history of Thiers!

"It might have been supposed that truth, meeting with such opposition on its first arrival, would have retired in dismay from the whole region; but such an opinion would have been most erroneous. It has pleased the God of mercy to pour out his Holy Spirit so remarkably on this place, that a considerable number of persons are not only reading with attention the Holy Scriptures, and affording good hopes of eventual conversion, but an infant church of Protestant Christians has been already formed; and at the first sacrament, no less than twenty-seven persons, all of them, in the judgment of charity, sincerely seeking eternal salvation, were partakers.

"I have been residing in the midst of this little flock about a fortnight, and I am deeply affected with admiration at the work of divine grace which is here exhibited. Eighteen months ago the very name of Protestant was scarcely known in the neighbourhood, no right views of Christ and his salvation were in existence, the grossest superstitions of popery and the most reckless infidelity divided the territory between them; in short, a moral midnight brooded over the

* "It is positively asserted, that no less than 150 young men, belonging to a single and small quarter of the town, perished in ten or fifteen years."

whole population: now a religious impression has been produced of the most extensive character; not a family, perhaps, can be found, which has not conversed, and thought, and felt, either favourably or unfavourably, on this great subject. Up to this hour the Protestant labours are the theme of universal and perpetual conversation. To my own observation, the twenty-seven communicants above mentioned, and several others, have been 'brought from darkness to light, and from the power of Satan unto God;' and it is known to God alone how far eventually the blessings of the Gospel will be diffused in this region.

"It is most interesting to mark the new converts, to observe their diligent study of the Bible, some of them even in old age beginning to read, that they may peruse the sacred pages; to listen to them singing delightfully the praises of God, in the beautiful hymns and tunes of our Geneva brethren; to hear with what simplicity and unction they lead the prayers of the congregation when invited to do so; and, above all, to notice that 'where sin abounded, grace doth much more abound.' The habitual deportment of the converts is highly consistent; the world cannot reproach them with ill-conduct; some of their number, who had been notorious for drunkenness and other sins, are now eminent examples of temperance and holiness; and 'the peace of God which passeth all understanding,' reigns over the whole Church. I was exceedingly struck with the expression of countenance of many persons amongst them. There is a calm, solid happiness portrayed on their features, which no principle, no ideas, no events, however prosperous in life, nothing but the assurance of eternal glory, through the sacrifice of Christ our Redeemer, could ever produce.

"John Hartley."

"*Thiers, Puy de Dome, August 5th*, 1839."

[K.]

Referred to at page 106.

An objection to these reasonings from the extinct volcanoes of Auvergne has been advanced in the Quarterly Review, vol. lxxiv. p. 295; 1844. It is grounded upon one of the numerous Epistles of Caius Sollius Apollinaris Sidonius (the correct order of his names, often mistaken), who was Bishop of Clermont, in Auvergne, from

472 to 487. In that epistle, addressed to Mamertus, the Bishop of Vienne, he describes phænomena which had taken place, some fifteen years previously. Allusions also are adduced from one of the homilies of Avitus, the successor of Mamertus, of which the date is about another fifteen years later. From those writers are drawn accounts evidently exaggerated of *terrifying prodigies* driving the inhabitants out of the city of Vienne, *noises underground, earthquakes, and fires bursting out, buildings thrown down, and their ruins covered with a mountainous mass of ashes, animals fleeing into the city for protection,* combined with the efficacy of relics and the *bishop's saintly presence* and *processions*, as affording preservation and deliverance. Now, be it observed that Vienne is a hundred miles from the extinct volcanoes; that Sidonius says not a word about *that region*, his own residence; that he is a remarkably extravagant and bombastic writer, strongly inclined to turn the poetical into the historical (—he represents Homer as an *historian,—G. J. Vossius de Histor. Latin.* 1651, p. 515 :—) and that he, Mamertus, and Avitus were credulous devotees of superstition. Hence, we could not rely upon the accuracy of his statements, if even they did refer to the tract of country in question; and we are compelled to regard his testimony as irrelevant.

Mr. Lyell has examined these allegations, with his characteristic acuteness and fairness, in a lecture at the Royal Institution in April last; and he adds,—"Although the epistle proves Sidonius to have had a fair share of the credulity of his age, in respect to both miracles wrought in favour of a contemporary saint and the efficacy of relics, it would be unfair to charge him with a belief in the occurrence of a volcanic eruption at or near the site of the city of Vienne, which the investigation of the ablest government surveyors, to whom the construction of a Geological Map of France has been intrusted, has entirely disproved. There are, in fact, no monuments of volcanoes, ancient or modern, in Dauphiny," [Mr. L. must include the Viennois;] "and, if there had been, they would not throw light on the date of the eruptions in Auvergne." Reported in the Athenæum, May 15, 1847. My readers will study the article with great advantage. They will find much further evidence of the antiquity of the Auvergne volcanoes, an antiquity immeasurable when compared with our historical periods, yet small in its relation to the anterior geological formations.

[L.]

Referred to at pages 112 *and* 202.

ON THE LONGEVITY OF TREES.

This is a subject of great interest. There are species which, in this respect, strongly attract our attention. The tree, called in our version an oak, but we have reason to believe that it was the terebinth,* under which Joshua deposited the ratification of the covenant made by his countrymen, was probably the very tree made memorable by events in the life of Abraham and that of Jacob. Our English oak attains to the age of a thousand years, and instances have been ascertained of one thousand five hundred.† To the yew more than two thousand, even above three thousand years are on good grounds attributed.‡ But there are other trees possessing a higher longevity, and individuals of which have been ascertained to go back from our times to dates long prior to the Noachian deluge. Of the Baobab (*Adansonia digitata*,) a tree of stupendous magnitude§ growing in

* Pistacia terebinthus; *elon*, unhappily rendered *plain* in Gen. xii. 6, and other places.

† Prof. Henslow's *Princip. of Descr. and Physiol. Botany*; p. 248: 1835.

‡ Ib. p. 245; and a paper, by the lamented John Eddowes Bowman, Esq. (who died, after three days' illness occasioned by inadvertent exposure to cold, Dec. 4, 1841,) on the Yew, in *Charlesworth's Magazine* for 1837; in which the admirable methods of obtaining sections for determining the age of trees, without injuring them materially, are clearly described. That paper was read, in an abridged form, at the meeting of the British Association at Bristol, August 1836; where it excited great interest.—With regard to the application of the trephine-saw to such tree-trunks as those here mentioned, it may be apprehended that to penetrate to the heart, 14 or 15 feet, and to extract the cylinder, are hopelessly beyond the power of art. I reply, that the ingenuity of British engineers has overcome greater apparent difficulties than these; and that a cylinder of 12 inches, should none longer be obtained, would supply very good data for a safe inference, considering the other known parts of the case.

§ Called by Dr. Lindley, "the largest tree in the world;——the trunk has been found with a diameter of 30 feet." *Nat. Syst. Bot.* sec. ed p. 94. The traveller M. Russeger, in the interior of Africa, as far as 10° N. L., saw "Adansonias measuring 56 feet in circumference,——exciting the astonishment of the beholder." Charlesworth's *Mag. Nat. Hist.* Feb. 1838, p. 108. *Second ed.* "The first account of this tree occurs in Cadamosto's Travels (Ramusio, col. 1, f. 118, 6,) to this purport. The Venetian navigator, Cadamosto, by command of the Portuguese Prince Henry in 1456, visited the Cape Verd Islands and the western coast of Africa. There he discovered the monstrous Baobab, whose trunk was 17 ells [about 30 English feet] in diameter. Adanson (*Familles des Plantes*, tome i. p. 216,) estimates the age of this tree upon a ground which does not appear perfectly secure, since he fancied that there were letters cut in the bark which indicated the 14th century; whereas those regions had not been visited at that time. [This is not absolutely certain; some Genoese or other vessel might have been driven so far to

Senegal and other parts of Africa within the tropics, one specimen has been subjected to the process which scientific men of the first ability have invented, and the age has been brought out to be 5232 years, and there is every reason to expect many centuries of further life to this tree and its congenerates. A still higher antiquity is claimed for the Taxodium (*Cypressus disticha*), an American tree, which attains the height of seventy feet and a circumference of thirty. It is stated by Professor Henslow to possess a longevity of 4000 to about 6000 years. One now growing in the churchyard of Santa Maria de Tesla, near Oaxaca in Mexico, and which was observed as a tree of wondrous magnitude by the Spanish conquerors of that country, is affirmed by M. De Candolle to "go back certainly to the origin of the present state of the world; an epoch," he says, "of which it is the most indisputable monument."* With regard to the period that has flowed since the creation of man, the christian world generally consents to use Archbishop Usher's system, because to depart from it would perplex us in our ordinary reading; yet most educated men are aware that the evidence runs in favour of a longer period. Perhaps no man has laboured on this subject with greater assiduity than the late Dr. Wm. Hales, in his Analysis of Ancient Chronology. According to him, we are now in the 7250th year from the creation; and the 4994th from the deluge.

Now the physical argument is, that the flood could not be universal, because these trees exhibit an age which, for the Baobab, goes

the south, and its crew never return, from being wrecked.] But it is the fact that he ascertained one of these trees to be the individual which Thevet observed in 1555; and it was 6 feet in diameter. Now Adanson calculates that this tree must have been, in Thevet's time, from 3 to 4 feet in diameter, and that consequently the increase in 200 years must have been from 2 to 3 feet. Hence he reasons that a tree of this species would acquire a diameter of 10 feet in 550 years; in 1050, 14 feet; in 2800, 20 feet; and 30 feet in 5150 years. As there are now trees of 27 feet in diameter, they must have an age of 4280 years.——Of this tree we know only one species, [called by the natives] the Baobab, or Ape's bread tree; or [the appellation very properly given by Europeans,] Adansonia digitata. It is the stoutest tree in the world, though it has not a very remarkable height. Its diameter is 25 to 27 feet. Adanson saw some which were from 75 to 78 feet in circumference. Barrow [Sir John?] saw a specimen at St. Jago, 56 feet in circumference and 80 feet high. The magnitude of the tree is effected not so much by the trunk as by the branches, for they grow to be 50 or 60 feet in length. In their spreading around they bend towards the earth, and so each tree forms a wood, or a monstrous foliage, of 150 feet in diameter. The usual height is 60 to 70 feet." Sprengel, Prof. Bot. at Halle, cited in Ersch and Grube's *Encyclop.* Leipz. 1818.

* "Il remonte certainement à l'origine du monde actuel. C'est le monument le plus irrécusable d'une époque sur laquelle l'opinion des savans n'est pas entièrement fixée." *Bibliothèque Universelle; Sciences;* Geneva, vol. xlvi. p. 393; 1831. He probably alludes to the difficulties of Chronology, arising from the discrepancies of the Hebrew text, the Samaritan, the Septuagint, Josephus, &c.

upon the common chronology to 1045 years before the date of the deluge; and, according to Hales, to 238 years: and, for the Taxodium, each of these numbers is increased by some centuries.

Will it be contended that these trees might live, submersed in water for near 300 days? Certainly it is impossible to try the experiment: but all analogy, all physiological reasoning from the functions of vegetable life, decide in the negative, and determine that elephants and oxen and men might live so long under water, almost as well as dicotyledonous trees.

Mr. Rhind meets the argument by questioning its premises. He affirms that, "in tropical regions, some dicotyledonous plants never shew indications of annular circles at all, while many have them very irregular; while it is far from improbable that some species may produce more than one woody circle in a year."*—The assertion, upon irregularity, is indeed true; but in such a manner as rather to bear against Mr. R.'s conclusion; for, when irregularity exists, it is in the way of weakness and deficiency. In a feeble tree or an unfavourable season, a layer may be unusually thin and even with difficulty discernible: so that, in careful counting, a ring or two might be omitted, *diminishing* the estimate by so many years.

The late Mr. De Candolle, whom all revere as one of the princes of Botanical science,† has expressed himself upon this point in the clearest and strongest manner. He shews at considerable length that there is not a law of nature on whose invariable validity we may with greater confidence rely, than in this instance. All that is wanted is ability and care in making the observation. Any variations that may occur are in the earliest stages of growth; afterwards the greatest regularity is established as to number of layers, though extraordinary

* *Age of the Earth;* p. 120.

† *Third ed.* This eminent naturalist, distinguished for his benevolence and his amiable delight in communicating, especially to young inquirers, out of the rich stores of his knowledge, died on Sept. 9, 1841, aged 64. As a memorial of justice, and an excitement to imitation, I transcribe a part of Dr. Roget's eulogy. "The activity and powers of De Candolle's mind were displayed in a multitude of objects of public utility, the furtherance of which ever called forth in him the most lively interest; whether it was the improvement of Agriculture, the cultivation of the Fine Arts, the advancement of Public Instruction, the diffusion of Education, or amelioration of the Legislative Code. Feeling deeply of what vast importance to the welfare of mankind it is, that sound principles of Political Economy should be extensively promulgated and well understood by all ranks of men, De Candolle never failed to develope and enforce those principles, in his lectures and popular discourses, as well as in his official Agricultural Reports. On these subjects, and especially with respect to the immense advantages which would accrue to the community from the *unrestricted freedom of commerce*, his views were those of the most enlightened policy, and exhibited a sagacity in advance of the times in which he lived." *Address to the Royal Society*, Nov. 30, 1841.

coldness or dryness of a season prevents the usual degree of thickness in the formation of the layer for that year.* In young trees the liability to error leads to an excess of calculation, but the tendency is the reverse in the more advanced stages of growth.

Sec. ed. It is incumbent on me to state that the late Sir J. E. Smith objected to some part of this reasoning; and that Dr. Lindley has written upon it the following important passage.

"Each zone of the vascular system of an exogenous stem being the result of a single year's growth, it should follow that, to count the zones apparent in a transverse section is sufficient to determine the age of the individual under examination; and further that, as there is not much difference in the average depth of the zones in very old trees, a certain rate of growth being ascertained to be peculiar to particular species, the examination of a mere fragment of a tree, the diameter of which is known, should suffice to enable the botanist to judge with considerable accuracy of the age of the individual to which it belonged. It is true, indeed, that the zones become less and less deep as a tree advances in age; that, in cold seasons, or after transplantation, or in consequence of any causes that may have impeded its growth, the formation of wood is so imperfect as scarcely to form a perceptible zone: yet De Candolle has endeavoured to show in an able paper *Sur la Longévité des Arbres*, that the general accuracy of calculations is not much affected by such accidents, occasional interruptions to growth being scarcely appreciable in the average of many years. This is possibly true in European trees, and in those of other cold or temperate regions in which the seasons are distinctly marked. In such, the zones are not only separated with tolerable precision, but do not vary much in annual dimensions. But, in many hot countries, the difference between the growing season, and that of rest, if any occur, is so small that the zones are as it were confounded, and the observer finds himself incapable of distinguishing with exactness the formation of one year from that of another. In the wood of Guaiacum, Phlomis fruticosa, Metrosiderus polymorpha, and many other Myrtaceæ, for instance, the zones are extremely indistinct: in some Bauhinias, they are formed with great irregularity: and in Stauntonia latifolia, some kinds of Ficus, certain species of Aristolochia (as A. labiosa,) and many other plants,

* *Biblioth. Univ. Sciences;* vol. xlvii. p. 49, &c. 1831. Mr. Darwin records his own observation confirmatory of this fact. *Voyages of the Adventure and Beagle*, vol. iii. p. 157. Mr. Babbage has also given us an instructive example of reasoning upon our very subject, from this law of the vegetable economy, in his *Ninth Bridgewater Treatise*, p. 256—264.

they are so confounded that there is not the slightest trace of annual separation. It is also to be remarked, that in Zamias we seldom find more than two or three zones of wood, whatever may be the age of the individual; and yet it appears from Eckton's observations, that a zamia with a trunk only four or five feet high can scarcely be less than 200 or 300 years old.*

"With regard to judging of the age of a tree by the inspection of a fragment, the diameter of the stem being known, a little reflection will show that this is to be done with great caution, and that it is liable to excessive error. If, indeed, the zones upon both sides of a tree were always of the same or nearly the same thickness, much error would not perhaps attend such an investigation. But it happens that, from various causes, there is often a great difference between the growth of the two sides; and consequently that a fragment taken from either side must necessarily lead to the falsest inferences. [Prof. Lindley then gives examples.]————When we hear of the Baobab trees of Senegal being 5150 years old as computed by Adanson; and the Taxodium distichum still more aged, according to the ingenious calculations of Alphonse (?) De Candolle; it is impossible to avoid suspecting that some such error as that just explained has vitiated their conclusions." *Introd. to Botany;* p. 94—96. Third ed. 1839.

It would be absurdly presumptuous in me to maintain with positiveness any opinion upon a question which thus divides the most profoundly scientific Botanists in the world. I may however acknowledge myself unable to perceive that the suspicion just mentioned is unavoidable. The vast size and structure of the trees referred to would seem likely to protect them completely from atmospheric or any other external causes, by which weakness or material irregularity could be induced so as to affect the woody deposits on one side of the trunk more than on the opposite. It appears also, from Dr. Lindley's statements, that, though the liability to error may run in either direction, yet that the incompleteness of the data is *far more likely* to affect the result by bringing out *too short* a period than one that exceeds the reality.

But, in this age of universal exertion, it must be hoped that some of the many scientific travellers, who are labouring for the service of mankind, will set about the determining of this question, by the best possible examination of the trees, in their places of growth. To saw one through, or to cut it down, manual labour would be ineffectual;

* "According to Decaisne (*Comptes Rendus*, v. 393,) the zones of wood, in Menispermaceæ, each result from the growth of several years."

and it may be long before the requisite European machinery will be transported into those regions. But it is not too sanguine to expect, that Mr. Bowman's method of taking out cylinders on opposite sides of the tree, by means of a circular saw like a surgeon's trephine, will be applied; and this will give results so complete that it would be idle scepticism to doubt them.

It should also be observed, that Mr. Bowman, after many observations and experiments, arrived at a general conclusion that M. de Candolle's calculations tended, and would even of necessity operate, to make *old* trees seem younger than they really are; and consequently, in the cases before us, to bring out a result *short of the truth.*

Third ed. Since the publication of the former editions, a work has commenced, anonymous indeed, but bearing in a very high degree the indications of accurate knowledge, independent research, and fine judgment; the *Popular Cyclopædia of Natural Science.* Its plan comprehends the most important branches of Natural History, and to a certain extent Natural Philosophy, and it will have the advantage of proceeding all from one mind. Two volumes, in small octavo, are published; the first on *Vegetable Physiology*, 1841; the second on *Systematic Botany*, 1842. It is greatly to be desired that the remaining parts of the series should be given to the world as speedily as may consist with the sustaining of its manifest superiority. In the first of those volumes a passage occurs which I feel it a duty to cite, not only as a step leading to further knowledge, but as due in justice to Mr. Rhind; see page 338.

" There are some trees of tropical climates, which completely lose their leaves two or three times in every year, appearing as bare as in winter; and these are speedily replaced by a new crop. It is *probable* (though it has not been *certainly ascertained*) that, in such trees, a new woody layer would be formed by every crop of leaves." Vol. i. p. 189.

Upon this subject, seeking information where I believed it might most safely be had, I applied to a friend in whose researches and ability of judgment I could place full confidence, Dr. William B. Carpenter, the author, besides many valuable contributions to medical science, of two works which confer singular advantage upon the student; *The Principles of General and Comparative Physiology*, 1841; and *The Principles of Human Physiology*, 1842.

To my application Dr. Carpenter courteously replied:—" In regard to the question you put to me, I have much pleasure in stating my opinion.——All our knowledge of the formation of *wood* leads us to refer it to an action of the *leaves;* and we know that, when a tree loses its leaves, the formation is checked. In this country, we find *one* new layer added every year; and this corresponds with the annual renewal of the leaves. I am not aware of any evidence which leads to the belief that the layers are annual *in themselves:* all that we can say is, that they are so in those trees of which the renewal of the leaves is annual. Now, that many trees renew their leaves two or even three times a year in tropical climates, is a fact which I have myself ascertained by inquiry in the West Indies, where I spent a few months some years ago. I saw a tamarind tree come out into full leaf, within six weeks after it had been entirely bared by the deciduation of the previous crop; and I was told that this happened three times in a year, or five times in two years. Now I cannot myself imagine but that the interruption must have been marked in the stem by a *distinct line*, in each of these instances.—I have in my possession sections of wood, *of this country*, in which a *very thin* ring intervenes between the ordinary annual layers; a ring so thin that no degree of unfavourableness of the season could account for it, supposing it to be of a year's growth." [Dr. Carpenter alludes to the phænomenon occasionally observed in this country, in a mild winter, especially after a remarkably dry summer, that some trees put forth leaves and blossoms, and bear fruit, though not well ripened. Usually, in such cases, the powers of the tree exhibit signs of exhaustion in the following year.—] "For the word *years*, in the ordinary statement, I should be inclined to read *epochs* of vegetation." July 26, 1841.

Yet I cannot but question whether the *hard-wooded* trees, of which remarkable species exist in hot climates, do not, in the periods of leafing, form exceptions to the rule of my accomplished friend.

Few of those who may read this book can consult the Genevese periodical work, *La Bibliothèque Universelle;* and therefore I do not hesitate to conclude this Note with another citation from A. P. De Candolle's papers.

——"I have reason to believe that there now exist in our countries, [Switzerland, France, England, &c.] oaks of fifteen to sixteen centuries old.——Of all European trees, the yew appears to me to be that which attains the greatest age. [—Examples are given whence the author concludes that, through its first period of 150 years, the yew increases a little *more* than a line, *i. e.* one-tenth of an inch, a year, and, in the next period of 100 years, a little *less* than a line.—] If then, for very old yews, we take the mean of one line a year, it is probable that we are below the truth, and that, in reckoning the number of their years of age as equal to that of their lines of diameter, we make them younger than they are. Now I have become acquainted with the measurements of four celebrated yews in England. That of Fountain Abbey, near Ripon in Yorkshire, of which we have historical notices in 1133, was, according to Pennant, in 1770, 1214 lines in diameter, which will give above twelve hundred years of age. That in the churchyard of Crowhurst, Surrey, is stated by Evelyn, in 1660, to be 1287 lines of diameter. If still standing, as I am informed it is, the age will be fourteen centuries and a half. That of Fotheringall in Scotland had, in 1770, a diameter of 2588 lines, and its age is consequently 25 to 26 centuries. That in the churchyard of Braburn in Kent had, in 1660, a diameter of 2880 lines; if then it be still in existence, it must have reached three thousand years.

"——I [am anxious to] call the attention of travellers to the massive trees which have very hard wood; such as the Mahogany, which commonly attains to seven feet in diameter; the Courbaril of the Antilles, said to reach twenty feet of diameter, and which is so hard that we must admit of an extreme slowness in its growth; the different kinds of trees known under the name of *iron-wood;*——&c.——But above all, I would recommend the verification of the accounts of the Taxodium (*Cupressus disticha* of Linnæus) of Mexico. Is this vast tree of Chapultepec, which is said to attain a circumference of 117 feet and ten inches, really one tree, or a union of several?——I earnestly recommend a new examination of this gigantic tree, perhaps the most ancient vegetable on the globe.——" *Biblioth. Univ. Sciences;* vol. xlvii. p. 65—67.

In *The Phytologist* for January 1843, is an interesting account of the *Adansonia*, embodying almost all the existing information concerning it, by Mr. George Luxford: with a strikingly picturesque figure of *the tree*, and figures of its leaves, flowers, and fruits. *The Phytologist* and its companion the *Zoologist* are publications both very cheap and highly valuable to the students of nature.

Fourth ed. Our idea of the tree is aided by two sentences in Sir James Ross's admirable work, *Voyage of Research and Discovery in the Southern and Polar Regions in* 1839—43; 2 vols. 1847. "Not far from the town [Port Praya, Madeira] we saw a fine specimen of the gigantic tropical tree of Africa, the Baobab (*Adansonia digitata*). Its short, pear-shaped trunk, not more than ten feet high, exceeded 38 feet in circumference, and at this period its fruit was forming." Vol. I. p. 11. No doubt this is a *young* tree: perhaps but two or three centuries old!?

[M.]

Referred to at page 152.

UPON DR. YOUNG'S SCRIPTURAL GEOLOGY.

In perusing this book, I have been not a little grieved at the sight which it presents of a pious and amiable man, struggling to give credit and currency to opinions which, to my full conviction, cannot be supported by evidence; but the advocacy of which is likely to mislead some, and to confirm the sceptical prejudices of others. It appears a duty to offer a few observations; but to go over the whole ground which he has opened, would require a treatise of considerable length. Erroneous statements and fallacious arguments can seldom be duly examined, and refuted satisfactorily, without much expenditure of time and labour. I shall select what appear the principal parts of the argument.

A layer of oyster-shells, with the valves separated, and exhibiting other marks of water transport, is found in the Whitby lias, extending for many miles along the coast, and ten or twelve into the interior; and Dr. Y. lays this instance as a principal foundation for the inference of a diluvial origin to shelly beds generally; and he extends his conclusion to vertebrated animals. (p. 15.) Yet he says not a word upon a fact, of which he seems to have had a glimpse a dozen years ago,* that beds occur of a peculiar valve, which all confess to be a stranger to the present condition of the seas, *Gryphœa incurva*, presenting the clearest evidence that the shells had never been drifted, and that the countless individuals lie, as family groups, in their native seats;—and that these beds may be traced, in the same geological position, from Whitby northward to the mouth of the Tees, and southward to the lias of Dorsetshire, and further appearing on the western coasts of Scotland, and again extensively in Germany and in France. If the worthy author could make so much of his seam of disparted oyster-shells, washed over a small piece of land, what ought he not to have concluded from the case of the opposite character, and covering an area a thousand times more extensive?

In like manner, because it is probable that some, or let us say even a large proportion, of the coal-beds, and their sandy and shaly accom-

* *Geol. Survey of the Yorkshire Coast*, p. 242. After briefly describing the species, Dr. Y. says, "Numbers are often found clustering together." This I call a *glimpse* of the truth. It deserved to have been followed out.

paniments, have been the results of transportation, he reasons as if *all* the coal had been formed in this manner. (pp. 10, 14.) But there are eminent geologists, who attribute only the smaller proportion of coal formations to this mode of origin; and conceive that the greater masses have been derived from trees of vast size and close contiguity, submerged in their native seats, without being removed from their place of growth, and marking their scarcely disturbed prostration by the well-known impressions, on the shale-roofs and bottoms of their most delicate parts, which would have been greatly defaced or quite obliterated by even a little tossing and drifting. Detached pieces of trunks do indeed occur, whose denuded and broken state suggests a derivation from neighbouring high land, and whose forms and position prove them to have been accidental intruders; but the idea of masses of such vegetation as composes the coal-beds having floated from different quarters, and then, which must have been of necessity, *irregularly and confusedly heaped together*, appears to be absolutely irreconcileable with the facts exhibited in the impressions of the plants upon the shale, just now mentioned. My kind readers will give themselves pleasure and do justice to the argument, by consulting the specimens of this kind in most of the Museums of Natural History, which happily are multiplied in our country. An excellent suite is in the Adelaide Gallery, presented by my young friend, Mr. Edward Charlesworth, a gentleman whose devotedness to Natural History from his very childhood has produced important results, and promises more. For this purpose, I cannot but also wish that studious attention were given to the accurate and beautiful figures in the Fossil Flora of Great Britain, by Dr. Lindley and Mr. William Hutton; and in Mr. Artis's Antediluvian Phytology.—"That any considerable part of the plants which formed the beds of coal were drifted at all, appears—to be highly improbable: that they should have been brought by equatorial currents from the regions of the tropics, is perfectly chimerical." *Fossil Flora*, vol. ii. pref. p. xxi. In the same splendid work, an accumulation of facts is brought in proof of this doctrine, and to illustrate the alternations of material in the coal measures, a circumstance on which Dr. Y. lays great stress, (p. 11,) but which those eminent naturalists account for in a way which his objections do not touch. *Foss. Flor.* vol. iii. pp. 28—35. On the other hand, Prof. Phillips deems it "the most probable view, that the plants forming coal were, with the arenaceous and argillaceous substances, swept into the sea by inundations from the land, and subsided into strata on the bed of the sea." *Treatise in Cabinet Cyclop.* vol. i. p. 160. But it is important to consider that this must have been from *neighbouring* land, probably clusters of islands overgrown by succulent trees of exceedingly great magnitude, *resembling* families chiefly cryptogamic, which now exist in only small species, except in hot climates, and which we have great reason to think must have flourished in an atmosphere essentially different from that which is necessary to animal life, under the existing system of creation; all of which conditions will agree with Mr. Phillips's hypothesis, understanding a very small distance of removal by the flooding off. On the contrary, Dr. Y.'s object is to establish that all this vegetation had grown in the sixteen or seventeen centuries before the deluge, and that the coal-beds are due to its being floated away and deposited by the diluvial waters; and his whole reasoning seems to imply the transport from considerable distances. This is the object for which he proposes his theory. But apart from all the reasons furnished by the phenomena of stratification and animal remains, those naturalists whom all reason binds us to regard as the best qualified to form a correct judgment, draw the opposite conclusion. "That the face of the globe has successively undergone *total changes*, at *different remote epochs, is now a fact beyond all dispute;* as also that, long anterior to the creation of man, this world was inhabited by races of animals *to which no parallels are now to be found;* and those animals themselves made their appearance, *after the lapse of ages*, during which no warm-blooded creatures had an existence. It has been further remarked by zoologists, that the animals which first appeared in these latitudes were analogous to such as now inhabit tropical climates exclusively; and that it was only at a period immediately antecedent to the creation of the human race, that species similar to those of the existing æra began to appear in northern latitudes. *Similar peculiarities* have been also found to mark the *vegetation* of correspondent periods." *Foss. Flor.* vol. i. pref. ix. x.

I annex a passage from a high American authority:—"Coal, being peculiarly limited in its local relations, and often contained in basins, it seems probable that it generally arose from local circumstances, with all its attendant and alternating strata of shales, sandstones, limestones, clays, iron ores, pudding-stones, &c., and, as these depositions are often repeated several times in the same coal-basin, and the mines are occasionally worked to a great depth, (even to 1200 feet, in some places in England,) it is plain that no sudden and transient event, like the deluge, could have produced such deposits, although it might bury wood and trees, which, in the course of time, might approximate to the condition of lignite, or bituminized, or partially mineralized, wood, which is often found under circumstances indicating a diluvian origin." Prof. Silliman's *Outline of Geology*, p. 122.*

The phenomena of the coal-formations have been ably argued by Mr. Murchison, in a series of considerations, which prove both the intensity of action and the long succession of periods that are marked in the structure and alterations of the crust of the earth. "How have the coal-fields been rendered accessible to man's use? Have we not shewn that many have been forced to the surface by volcanic action; and that some have assumed a basin shape, in consequence of their margins having been thrown into that form by a number of violent upcasts of the subjacent solid masses, which, wrenched from their original position, now converge towards a common centre?" Silur. Syst. i. 574.

Our respected author appears not seldom to fall into the besetting error of controversialists, misapprehension of the opinions which he opposes, or of some part of their relations. For example; he seems to think it a fatal objection to the doctrines generally held by geologists, that the Tertiary Strata "occupy but a small space in the crust of the earth, yet three or four ages have been assigned to them;" that "the whole Tertiary Strata cover but a small portion of the face of our globe, and each of the four sections" [the Eocene, the Miocene, the older Pliocene, and the more recent Pliocene] "can claim but a

* *Third ed.* A remarkable instance of this phenomenon has been communicated to the Royal Society, (in a letter read April 1, 1841,) by Mr. Mac Cormick, one of the band of scientific men whom Her Majesty's enlightened and judicious government had sent upon the Antarctic expedition under Capt. James Ross. It is a description of Kerguelen's Land, two very small islands with a few islets, at so high a latitude as must, in that hemisphere, ensure perpetual storms and cold, producing no vegetation above lichens, mosses, and a few grasses and water-plants. "From its sterility," says Capt. Cook, "I should with great propriety call it the *Island of Desolation*, but that I would not rob M. de Kerguelen of the honour of its bearing his name." These isles are masses of basaltic rock, with *fossilized wood* imbedded in it, and *coal* beds or seams overlaid by it. Thus there is evidence that the locality was once an extent of dry land on which grew large trees, that the climate must have been much warmer than in its present condition, that submurgence took place, and then pressure under stratified deposits, that such a succession was effected at least once, perhaps oftener, and that, at last, an outburst of melted rock from the fiery gulf below elevated, shattered, enwrapped, and overtopped the whole.

Fourth ed. The best and most recent account, historical and descriptive, is given in Sir James Clark Ross's interesting volumes, *Voyage of Discovery and Research in the Southern and Antarctic Regions;* chap. iv. Mr. Mac Cormick, who gives the geological descriptions, says: "The most remarkable geological feature in the island is the occurrence of fossil-wood and coal; and, what is still more extraordinary, imbedded in the igneous rocks. The wood, which for the most part is highly silicified, is found inclosed in the basalt, whilst the coal crops out in ravines, in close contact with the overlying porphyritic and amygdaloidal greenstone." Vol. i. p. 74. "The numerous seams of coal vary in thickness from a few inches to four feet." P. 71.

few patches; yet to these patches a whole age is assigned!" (Pp. 19, 20.) On the scale of reason, this is much the kind of argument which infidels employ, when they object to Christianity that it is not universal. Does our objector suppose that topographical extent is a measure of duration? Is it not of the very essence of the case, that these "patches" (which, be it remarked, cover thousands of square miles in Europe, Asia, and America,) should occupy the situations which, by the laws of nature, belong to them? They consist of the wearings away and washings down of older rocks, derived from the elevations and projections of innumerable eras; and they must of necessity have been received and retained in the intervening hollows. This is one of the most striking instances of the Creator's wisdom and goodness; that, by a series of slow operations, effected according to the known laws and methods of physical action, diversified results are brought to pass which are in the highest degree beneficial to the animated tribes and preeminently to the race of man. The very processes are marked with the indications of very long periods of time, which (if I may express my humble opinion) our imaginations are more in danger of unduly contracting than of immoderately extending.

Yet, after all, Dr. Young makes a surrender of the chief position; and therefore all the other parts of the field are fairly debateable without mutual prejudice, however we may feel convinced that he has unhappily undertaken the defence of posts which cannot be maintained. He says, "Many are of opinion, that as, without contradicting Scripture, we may believe in the existence of numerous planetary worlds, all furnished with their respective inhabitants; so also we may be allowed to think that numerous creations might exist on our globe, long before the creation recorded by Moses; the sacred pages making no mention of the one, any more than of the other. To a certain extent, this may be conceded. I agree with my learned friend Dr. Buckland, that the narrative of Moses does not necessarily preclude the supposition, that the materials of our globe might preexist under another form, and that this world may have been constructed out of the wreck and ruins of a former creation." (Pp. 40, 41.) Yet under the reservation clause "to a certain extent," he attempts to render this concession of little value. He is willing to admit of a previous condition of the earth, provided it may be a state of darkness and confusion, devoid of life and beauty. He thinks that, how the supposition of "a goodly world——can be reconciled with the scripture narrative, it is difficult to conceive." May we not reasonably ask, Why should this be difficult? The scripture narrative relates (according to our views of its meaning) an adjustment of a suitable district of our globe for the reception of a new order of creation; and, to make this known in the manner best adapted to the comprehension of the early ages of mankind and to the religious benefit of all generations, was the gracious intention of that page in the records of revelation. I am unable to perceive any inconsistency in this with the belief that the bountiful Creator had before made ample use of this part of his works, to be one of innumerable other seats of life, intelligence, and happiness. Rather should I think that we might regard this arrangement as *a case included* under the grand proposition, "By faith we understand that the worlds were arranged [κατηρτίσθαι τοὺς αἰῶνας, which might be rendered, *the vast periods adjusted*,] by the word of God, to the effect that the objects seen [τὰ βλεπόμενα] did not come into existence out of those which are manifested."*

Dr. Young's mode of reasoning about stratification appears to me surprising. From a partial, trivial, and much exaggerated case which he alleges, of the action of the waves on a soft sea-beach, he draws conclusions extravagantly large. A few feet or yards of sand and marl may be washed down by a flood, or torn off by a storm; and almost immediately afterwards redeposited in sorted forms: and this occurrence which, in the very conditions of the case, can take place only on a small scale, he applies unlimitedly by simple multiplication, and infers thirty feet of strata in a day, and nine hundred in a month. But he takes no notice of the extremely slow rate of deposit, in those circumstances which constitute the general course of nature; and which is demonstrated by facts innumerable in estuaries, in deltas, or in fresh-water lakes.

He exhibits the crude impertinence of a few foreign sophists, whose day in this respect is past, representing the succession of organized beings as becoming gradually more complete and perfect, so as to indicate an improvement by practice in the Creator's skill; and he notices not the fact that all the great geologists repudiate such a notion with abhorrence, and give physical evidence of its falsehood.

With respect to this subject, it should not be forgotten that, on account of the perishable substance of their structure, many species of both animal and vegetable creatures must have failed to perpetuate any memorials of themselves, in all the periods of the earth's antiquity. The more profoundly anatomical investigations are carried on, the more abundantly is it evinced that, within the range of the

* Heb. xi. 3. I have ventured to give the closest translation.

animal remains presented even in the earliest fossiliferous strata, the remark will hold, as a general truth, which has been made by eminently qualified judges, in relation to the vegetable kingdom:—"The result of this investigation is well worthy of attention. It shows that, so far from 'a gradual perfection of organization having been going on from the remotest period, till the latest geological epoch,' [the words of an able adverse writer,] some of the *most perfect* forms of each of the three great classes of the vegetable kingdom were among the very first created; and that, either the more simple plants of each class did not appear till our own æra, or that no trace of them at an earlier period has been preserved." Lindley and Hutton's *Fossil Flora;* vol. i. pref. p. xix.

It would appear almost incredible that Dr. Y. should say, "Fishes, zoophytes, ammonites, belemnites, terebratulæ, &c., occur in almost every portion of them [the secondary strata]; but those in the inferior strata have as much similarity to the living races as those in the superior." P. 9. An assertion full of extreme inaccuracies! Can he, for example, push out of sight a most remarkable circumstance in the caudal prolongation of the back-bone, which distinguishes all the fish of the Magnesian limestone and the earlier formations from the subsequent; and from almost all existing species? This, and many other striking peculiarities in the fossil ichthyology, were discovered by the distinguished investigator, M. Agassiz. See Lyell's *Elements*, p. 417. And who ever heard of ammonites or belemnites of "living races?"

I thankfully avail myself of the authority (—can there be a higher?—) and testimony of Mr. Murchison. "—The fossils of the Silurian system here represented, and amounting in all to about 350 species, are, with the exception of a very few (chiefly doubtful casts), essentially distinct from any of the numerous and well-defined fossils of the Carboniferous System; and further, that the Old Red Sandstone which separates these two systems is also characterised by fossils peculiar to it.——Having for a series of years collected fossils from every stratum of the Silurian rocks, throughout a large region, in which the stratigraphical order is clear, I now present the results. Professor Phillips had previously completed a valuable monograph of the organic remains of the Carboniferous System; [in his *Illustrations of the Geology of Yorkshire;* vol. ii. 1836.] If the naturalist will compare the figures in these, the only two works yet published upon the older fossiliferous rocks, which combine geological description with zoological proofs, he will at once see the truth of my position.

"Beginning with the *vertebrata;* Are not the fishes of the Old Red Sandstone as distinct from the Carboniferous System on the one hand, as from those of the Silurian on the other? M. Agassiz has pronounced that they are so.

"Are any of the *crustaceans*, so numerous and well-defined throughout the Silurian rocks, found also in the Carboniferous strata? I venture to reply, not one.

"Are not the remarkable *cephalopodous mollusca*, the *Phragmoceras*, and certain forms of *Lituites*, peculiar to the older system?

"Is there one species of the *Crinoidea* figured in this work, known in the Carboniferous strata?

"Has the *Serpuloides longissimum*, or have those singular bodies the *Graptolites*, or, in short, any zoophytes of the Silurian System, been detected in the well-examined Carboniferous rocks?

"And, in regard to the *corals*, which are so abundant that they absolutely form large reefs, is not Mr. Lonsdale, who has assiduously compared multitudes of specimens from both systems, of opinion that there is not more than one species common to the two epochs?—

"Such evidences are—additional supports of the important truth which Geology has already established; that *each great period of change, during which the surface of the planet was essentially modified, was also marked by the successive production and obliteration of certain races.*" *Silur. Syst.* pp. 581, 582.

With astonishment I read in Dr. Y., "The general conformity of the strata and their undisturbed succession, indicate that they must have been deposited about the same æra." P. 23. He admits indeed of some exceptions, but he confines them to the elevating force of "volcanic agency." One might almost fancy that the worthy author had never fixed his eyes upon any rocks but those of his own Yorkshire coast, and that he had explored even them but cursorily. That all strata were at their origin deposited horizontally, or nearly so, is not the question. But, is it possible for him to be ignorant of the instances innumerable, in almost all parts of the world, where the formations of the secondary series, and many even of the third, follow with most remarkable disconformity? How often a deposit has been laid, long after the underlying one has been raised and bent and broken? The Sections published in the Geological Society's Transactions, and innumerable other works of unquestionable authority, furnish the most ample proofs of the contrary to Dr. Y.'s assertion.

If possible, I am still more surprised to read, "The breaks, or faults, in the strata affect the whole mass of rocks, in almost every instance where they occur; instead of being limited by the boundaries of particular formations." P. 24. So far as, in a subject including many and various conditions, one can lay down general positions, I must say that what he affirms is not the fact, and what he denies, and builds largely upon his denial, is the fact.

It is painful to me to remark thus upon the writing of a very estimable friend; and to be obliged to acknowledge that to me his book appears to abound in misconceptions of the sentiments of others, and wrong imputations to them, in assertions positively made, but often hazardous or decidedly erroneous, in narrow investigation and defective induction, and in too rapid conclusions from imperfect premises. I should not, however, have brought forward these observations, which might be considerably extended, but for this reason; Dr. Young's character as a Christian and a minister of the Gospel, gives weight and currency to his opinions, and some persons have not failed to display his authority as if it were a sufficient refutation of the doctrines commonly maintained by geologists.

Fourth ed. Returning to the part of the preceding Note which respects the Coal-formations, I now add that Mr. E. W. Binney, than whom few persons can be better qualified, from scientific knowledge and extensive observation, to give an opinion upon this subject, has published a Disquisition *On the Origin of Coal;* in the "*Memoirs of the Lit. and Philos. Society of Manchester*," vol. viii. and reprinted separately, 1847. He examines the subject minutely and comprehensively, and arrives at the following principal conclusions; that the vegetable matter now forming coal had grown in vast *marine* swamps, subjected to a series of *subsidences* with long intervals of repose; that the trees and perhaps smaller plants were submerged under *tranquil* water, in the places of their growth; and that very inconsiderable portions, if any, of the beds are owing to drifting.

[N.]

Referred to at page 158.

ON THE COMPARISON OF THE EGYPTIAN AND THE MOSAICAL COSMOGONIES.

In Mr. Lyell's Principles of Geology, Book I. chap. ii. under the title "Oriental Cosmogony," he has given ample and interesting descriptions of the doctrines held by the ancient Hindoos and Egyptians, and those brought from the east into Greece and Italy by Pythagoras, concerning the changes which the surface of our globe has undergone. Now, as every reader knows that, under the name *Oriental*, the documents of the Hebrew Scriptures cannot but be included, the expectation is raised (I might say almost necessarily) that some direct and specific notice will be taken of the Mosaic Cosmogony. This expectation is strengthened by the fact, that certain writers of the German antibiblical school have maintained that Moses derived his materials for the commencement of the Pentateuch, from Egyptian sources. From these considerations I cannot but fear that the total silence upon what most readers will think the chiefly interesting branch of the subject, will be construed into the inference, that the author deemed the Hebrew account to be no more than a human production, and to be justly thrown into the same class with the allegorical, mythological, or fabulous traditions of the grossest idolaters. It would have been happy and signally beneficial, if Mr. Lyell had pointed out the differences between the Egyptian and the Phœnician Cosmogonies, and the simple, beautiful, and majestic description of the Hebrew Genesis; and if, which he might have briefly done without entering into philological discussions, he had said that the *Scripture account* of the creation is susceptible of a fair interpretation, in perfect consistency with the facts disclosed by Geological research.

With respect to the identity or similarity alleged by the critics just adverted to, I may remark that it is assumed by them in a way little better than a gross begging of the question. Because Moses was educated as the adopted son of an Egyptian princess, and must therefore, they say, have been instructed in all the histories, traditions, and doctrines of the Egyptian priests; as also the first martyr testifies concerning him, that he "was educated [ἐπαιδεύθη] in all the wisdom of the Egyptians;" and because Simplicius (a Greek philosopher of the sixth century, zealously adherent to the expiring cause of heathenism,) calls the relation of Moses concerning the origin of the universe, "a certain mythic tradition, drawn from the Egyptian Mythi;" the inference is boldly drawn that he made that tradition the basis of his narrative, simplifying and accommodating it to his fundamental doctrines, the unity of God, and the creation by him and dependence upon him of all other existences. But, if we look at the earliest authorities that we have, (and they are 1400 years later than Moses,) Diodorus Siculus and Plutarch, we find but a scanty resemblance; and so much as does obscurely appear, suggests the idea of being a far removed and adulterated cast of traditions, derived from that primeval fountain of knowledge, which had flowed down to Moses in its original purity. The passage of Diodorus, (who was an industrious compiler rather than an independent historian or judicious collector,) which, in the opinion of the best critical philosophers, details the Egyptian doctrines, is the following. "Concerning the race of all men, and the things which have been effected in the parts of the habitable earth subjected to our knowledge, so far as is possible in relation to objects so ancient, we shall write accurately, beginning with the earliest times. With regard then to the first production of men, two opinions have been proposed by the most distinguished inquirers into nature and history. One party, assuming the world to be without beginning and to be incapable of destruction, maintain that the human race has existed from eternity, having never had a commencement of child-bearing. The other party, supposing the world to have had a beginning and to be destructible, affirm that mankind, like the other parts of the universe, had a first production, in fixed periods of time." [This is the Egyptian theory.] "They suppose that, at the original constitution of all things, heaven and earth possessed one uniform appearance, their respective natures being mixed up together. But, after this, the material substances [σώματα] separating from each other, the world" [evidently meaning the solid earth, as distinguished from the atmosphere,] "took the entire constitution which is now seen in it, and the air acquired a perpetual motion. Hence, on the one hand, the fiery part of the air ran into one mass in the higher regions of the atmosphere, its nature being such as would be borne upwards on account of its lightness; from which cause also both the sun and the remaining multitude of the stars became involved in the universal rotation: and, on the other hand, the earthy and dark miry part, combining with the moist substances, sunk down to the lowest situation, in consequence of their weight. This mass then being compressed within itself and continually rolled round, from the watery portions was produced the sea, and from the more solid the land, which was as yet clayey and quite soft. By the heat of the sun acting upon this earthy body, it first received consolidation; and afterwards fermentation taking place on the surface, in consequence of the heat, some of the moist matter swelled up into bubbles in many places, and around them putrescent pieces were produced inclosed in thin membranes. Such an effect is, even in the present condition of the earth, sometimes brought to our view, in bogs, and such low places as are continually turned into marshes by the irruption of water; when, while the ground is cooled, the air suddenly becomes very hot, not being with sufficient rapidity susceptible of the change of temperature. In this way, those moist spots became, by means of the heat, impregnated with animal life [τινὰ τῶν ὑγρῶν—ζωογονουμένων]; receiving nutriment by night out of the mist which fell from the surrounding air, and being made firm and strong by the heat in the day-time. At last, these embryos [κυοφορούμενα] having acquired their full growth and the enveloping membranes being dried up and bursten, all the various forms of animals were brought forth. Of these, those kinds which had partaken of the greatest heating went away to the higher regions, becoming birds: those which retained the earthy constitution were reckoned into the order of creeping animals, and the other kinds which live upon the earth: those which had gotten the greater abundance of a moist nature, ran together to the place of the same watery constitution, and these are called swimmers. The earth being thus continually more and more dried and hardened, by the heat of the sun and the action of the winds, in the end became incapable of procreating the larger animals; and consequently henceforth all the kinds of animated beings were produced by sexual union with each other."

Here, in some manuscripts, a pretty long paragraph follows, intended to confirm the preceding statements, by affirming that the Egyptians down to the present time produce instances of such generation, in that, after an abundant overflow of the Nile, when it has subsided and the sun has acted upon the putrescent surface, an innumerable multitude of mice is brought forth out of the mud. But this passage, though no doubt very ancient, the best critics reject as spurious; its matter is however taken, almost word for word, from a subsequent part of the same book. The historian then proceeds:

"And such are the declarations which we have received concerning the first production of all things; [ἡ πρώτη τῶν ὅλων γένεσις.] The human creatures produced from this beginning, are said to have existed in a way of life disorderly and brute-like; wandering dispersed over the verdant plains, and for food seizing upon the plants which they found most agreeable to the taste, and the spontaneous fruits of the trees. Being attacked by wild beasts, they were taught by the sense of mutual advantage to aid each other; and, being driven by fear to associate, they learned, by slow degrees, to understand one another."——Diod. Sic. lib. i. cap. vii. viii.

The next authority appealed to by the German antibiblicists, is Plutarch's Treatise on Isis and Osiris. But the reference must have been handed from writer to writer, in the hope that readers would seldom take the trouble of examining it. That tedious treatise consists almost entirely of ridiculous and disgusting tales concerning Osiris and Isis, Typhon, Horus, Anubis, and their cognates: and these the moralist declares to be utterly worthless and contemptible, unless regarded as fables, and as he interprets them in a variety of physical, historical, and moral significations. I can discover but two short passages, in which there are any ideas of a cosmogony that could, in even a slight degree, be imagined to possess affinity to the Mosaic narrative. That the reader may judge, I will cite them.

"He who is God is the originating principle" [ἀρχὴ ὁ θεός· yet I fear, Plutarch took the term generally, and without a clear recognition of the Only God:—] "but every originating principle, by its productive power, multiplies that which issues from itself: and the idea of multiplication we usually denote by the numeral *three;* as when we use" [the phrases of Homer] "*Thrice happy!* and *Fetters indeed thrice so many numberless wrap all around him.* [Odyss. vii. 340.] Unless it were the fact that the ancients by such expressions meaned literally the number *three:* since the natural quality of moisture, being the beginning and producing principle [ἀρχὴ καὶ γένεσις] of all things from the beginning, made the three primary bodies, earth, air, and fire."——"One might suppose that the Egyptians were peculiarly fond of comparing the nature of the universe to the most beautiful of triangles," [a right angled one:]——"one line the male,——another the female,——and the hypothenuse the offspring of both: and so, Osiris is to be considered as the beginning, Isis as the principle of reception, and Horus as the complete effect."—Then follow some allegorizings of the numbers, three, four, and five; and of the Egyptian names of Horus and Isis; summed up by saying——"The matter of the world is full, and is composed of the good, the pure, and the well-arranged. It is probable also that Hesiod entertained the same views of producing principles [ἀρχαί·] making the primary existences [τὰ πρῶτα πάντα] to be chaos and earth and tartarus, and love; since, of these names, we may understand that of the earth to belong to Isis, that of love to Osiris, that of Tartarus to Typhon; for chaos seems to be put under the whole [or, the universe, [τὸ πᾶν,] as space and place." Plutarchi *Moralia;* ed. Wyttenbach, vol. ii. pp. 497, 532.

Diodorus the Sicilian flourished about 50 years B. C. Plutarch, more than a century later. All the value of their statement depends therefore upon the authencity of their sources, which are unknown, though no doubt, mediately or immediately, they were from Egypt: but they are far too late to have the stamp of authority, and we well know that, many centuries before, the ancient learning of the Egyptians had been metamorphosed into fables and allegories. Diogenes Laertius, Porphyry, and Macrobius, who lived still later, have only repeated less completely what we have already.

I have written this long and tiresome note, that my readers may determine for themselves, whether the allegation is not devoid of all evidence and probability, that the Mosaic narrative was an offshoot of the Egyptian mythology: the one shining in the most beautiful and majestic simplicity; the other, artificial, low and paltry, absurd and degrading. Much more reasonable appears the supposition, that the traditions which came from the family of Noah, in the line of the Mizraim (a plural name), were the ground-work upon which the Egyptian priests, after the prevalence of polytheism, built up their system of perversion and disguise.

[O.]

Referred to at page 158.

ON SOME PASSAGES IN MR. LYELL'S PRINCIPLES OF GEOLOGY.

THE allusion here is to some remarks upon Mr. Lyell's chapter v. of book i. published in the Christian Observer, April 1834; p. 200. It is in no captious spirit, but with sincere respect and solicitude, that I would ask this eminently gifted man, why, in his beautiful chapter (the viiith of book iii.) on the Introduction, Extinction, and Vicissitudes of Species, he has made so slight mention of the Almighty Creator? He has not said indeed, or implied, that a new species has ever, in the world's history, come into being without God as its cause; but it is painful to see the semblance of reserve on so soul-stirring a theme. He speaks of "admiration—strongly excited, when we contemplate the powers of insect life, in the *creation* of which *nature* has been so prodigal."—Nature?—Creation? O, why did not his heart grow warm within him, and bound with joy, at the opportunity of doing some homage to the GOD of glorious majesty?

Sec. ed. It would have afforded me great pleasure to have cancelled the whole of the preceding Note. But my best reflection induces me to let it remain, with a slight alteration, because its silent withdrawal would have left an unwelcome impression without correction; and I could scarcely have made intelligible the expression of satisfaction and gratitude that, in the sixth edition, Mr. Lyell has in this place put "the Author of Nature:" because also that I could not have expressed my concern at having given pain to the mind of this distinguished philosopher; since he cannot admit the justice of the censure involved, and he must feel it to be unwarrantably severe and presumptuous to insinuate against him, a christian and a member of the Church of England, a design of covertly assailing the evidences of Revealed Religion. Indeed I cannot charge myself with having made such an insinuation; my expressions having imported only the *sorrow of heart* which I did and still do feel, that his reserve in one respect and his expressions in another were likely to *be laid hold of by a too numerous class of persons* who wish to live without piety and religious self-government, and to whom it is a great object of desire to shake off the authority of Christianity by abrading its evidences. To have it in their power to plead either the concession or the reserve of such a man as Mr. Lyell, is an advantage which ought not to be given them; for their cause, standing opposed to the clearest moral evidence, to the highest interests of mankind, the purest blessings of the present state, and our noblest expectations in the future, is not entitled to such a benefit.——Upon the substitution, unhappily so frequent with authors on natural science, of the word *Nature* for *the God of nature*, I am desirous of putting the best possible construction, (yet I beg attention to the Note at page 74;) especially if authors and readers would take care not to forget the exposition of the term which Lamarck himself has given:—"An order of things constituted by the Supreme Being, and subject to laws which are the expressions of his will." This definition is complete and satisfactory. See the *Addenda* to these Notes.

On the other hand, we ought not to pass with slight disapprobation, the practice of making references to the Deity with a frequency and hastiness which border upon familiarity, and tend to produce either presumption or hypocritical affectation.

With respect to the paper in the Christian Observer, (excellent in its *spirit* and *design*, though I am compelled, by what appears to me evidence, to think its writer greatly in error,) I fear that Mr. Lyell never saw it. What he had expressed in the unguarded manner which "laid him open to painful imputations" was, I am assured, intended to apply to the heathen and popish pretences to miracles, and to the numerous forms of vulgar superstition.

Upon the general subject of these observations it would be unjust in me not to point out that, in the chapter (III. viii.) which stirred up my painful feelings, the author explicitly calls us to observe the beneficent care of "Providence" which has "put causes in operation" for checking the destruction to men and many animal and vegetable species, from the natural multiplication of Lepidopterous larvæ. I will also take out of their connexion (the limits of this note not permitting fuller citations) a few clauses which *I take blame to myself for not having observed, as I ought to have done*, before publishing the first edition.—" In no scientific works in our language can more eloquent passages be found, concerning the fitness, harmony, and grandeur of all the parts of creation, than in those of Playfair. They are evidently the unaffected expressions of a mind which contemplated the study of nature as best calculated to elevate our conceptions of the attributes of the First Cause."—Referring to certain cosmological hypotheses, Mr. L. observes, " they had not the smallest foundation, either in Scripture or in common sense."—" When the Author of nature created an animal or a plant, all the possible circumstances in which its descendants are destined to live, are foreseen, and an organization conferred upon it" conformable to the design.—" If the Author of nature had not been prodigal of these numerous contrivances,—&c. . . if He had not ordained that the fluctuations of the animate and inanimate creation should be in perfect harmony with each other,—" &c. " In whatever direction we pursue our researches, whether in time or space, we discover every where clear proofs of a Creative Intelligence, and of his foresight, wisdom, and power."—" To assume that the evidence of the beginning or end of so vast a scheme lies within the reach of our philosophical inquiries, or even of our speculations, appears to be inconsistent with a just estimate of the relations which subsist between the finite powers of man, and the attributes of an Infinite and Eternal Being."—" The geologist can bring new and original arguments from fossil remains, to bear on that part of Natural Theology which seeks to extend and exalt our conceptions of the Intelligence, Power, Wisdom and Unity of design manifested in the creation.——We can prove that man had a beginning, and that all the species now contemporary with man, and many others which preceded, had also a beginning: consequently, the present state of the organic world has not gone on from all eternity, as some philosophers had maintained.——Why should we expect to find any resting place for our thoughts, or hope to assign a limit to the periods of past time, throughout which it has pleased an Omnipotent and Eternal Being to manifest his creative power?" Principles B. I. ch. iv. vol. i. p. 102; B. III. ch. ii. III. 30; B. III. ch. x. III. 209; B. III. ch. xviii. III. 406. Presidential Address to the Geol. Soc. 1837, in Proceed. vol. ii. p. 523. The references in this volume to Mr. Lyell's *Princip. Geol.* were adjusted to the sixth edition, as soon as it became practicable, for a part of this book was printed before that was published: but, to facilitate reference to the former editions, the Book and Chapter are also mentioned; which yet may not always answer, because some of the Chapters are transposed or are new.

Third ed. With peculiar pleasure I have read Professor Silliman's observations on the character and labours of Mr. Lyell, in his *Address to the Association of American Geologists and Naturalists*, at Boston, April 24, 1842. From it, I quote the following paragraph.

"To him more than to any other or all other writers on Geology, we owe our recovery from the illusions of dreams and visions regarding imaginary powers supposed formerly to exist; but to have become exhausted or greatly enfeebled or even extinct in modern times. He has proved to us that the powers of nature are the same now that they have ever been; that, except the act of creation, and the first outbreak of the new-born elements and energies, there was nothing in the geological laws of former ages different from the present; and that the causes now in operation, acting with greater or less intensity, are sufficient to produce the effects of earlier epochs.

[P.]

Referred to at page 183.

SENTIMENTS OF THE ELDER ROSENMUELLER, BISHOP BIRD SUMNER, AND THE REV. DR. CONYBEARE, DEAN OF LLANDAFF, ON THE INITIAL PORTION OF THE BOOK OF GENESIS.

The following extracts are valuable and interesting, as they shew the impression made upon the mind of an able Bible critic, the elder Rosenmüller, at a time when geological researches were little known, and when Werner, at the age of 25, was just beginning his career. He was far from the opinion which his son promulgated, fifteen years after, treading in the steps of Simplicius (in the sixth century), and Hetzel, Hase, and others in our own times, that Moses derived his history of the creation from the Egyptians. Whatever resemblance may be assumed or supposed, it is much more rationally accounted for, by supposing that the Egyptian and Phœnician traditions had flowed from a common source, the family of Noah; and that Moses, under the direction of divine inspiration, placed at the commencement of his great work the very written documents of primeval men which had descended in the Abrahamic line, and which were *the genuine records* whence the other traditions had been derived.

"The enemies of religion act a very inequitable part when they require of us such explications of all chronological and historical difficulties, as should leave no portion of doubt remaining. Can it surprise any man that, in the most ancient of all writings, many things should be obscure to us, who live in times so extremely remote?——In consequence of the great advances which have been made in modern times, in Hebrew and Greek philology and the languages and antiquities of the east, no small number of dark and difficult passages have been satisfactorily elucidated, so as to make it perfectly clear that most objections have been engendered by ignorance.——Every good writer must be presumed to speak according to the custom of the men among whom he lived, and their common use of language.——I shall not meddle with the question, whether the contents of the beginning of Genesis were by God revealed immediately to Moses; or that he derived them from more ancient records.——The style, and the entire manner of the description, involve evidence of the highest antiquity. At every step we perceive proofs of that extreme simplicity which must have been the character of our race in its very infancy. With respect to divine subjects, in particular, the first step of human knowledge must undoubtedly have consisted in conceptions of God derived from our own nature; ascribing to the Deity the same properties and perfections which men perceived in themselves, but in modes and degrees infinitely more perfect. Upon this principle are founded the representations of God which are given in the books of Moses, and many other parts of the Old Testament. Indeed this is, in my judgment, a very plain argument, not only of the genuineness and truth of those books, but of their DIVINE origin: seeing that they present to us a method of description concerning God and divine things, perfectly suited to the capacity of men in the earliest times, and yet the most sublime, and when fairly and candidly interpreted, in perfect accordance with spiritual truth. The scoffers at revealed religion, philosophers as they please to call themselves, betray an almost unpardonable ignorance, when they make stumbling-blocks out of those constantly occurring expressions of the Old Testament which speak of the Deity [*anthropopathicis locutionibus*] in language borrowed from human properties and actions. What can be a grosser absurdity, and even folly, than to require that Moses and the prophets should have spoken of divine truths, in the very infancy of the human race, according to the philosophy of Descartes, Newton, or Wolf?—

"In the beginning God created this universe; the heavens and the earth. But, with respect to this earthly globe, it was not at once the abode of men and animals, as it is now: but there was a period during which it was utterly destitute of such a furniture of things as it now possesses: it did not enjoy the light of the sun, and it was completely covered with water. Whether, at its first being brought into being, it possessed a constitution like that of comets,* being consequently uninhabitable; or whether it was reduced into its actual state, after a vast space of time, by some kind of universal inundation of water, with the concurrence of other causes both natural and extraordinary; cannot be with certainty determined from the Mosaic narrative. But this detracts nothing from the truth and dignity of the narrative. It never was in the mind or intention of Moses, to unfold physical causes, of which he was most probably ignorant, and which it was no part or object of his divine commission to make known. Nor could the Israelites, for whose immediate benefit this history was intended, have comprehended such matters: for who can suppose that they knew anything of the nature of comets, or the planetary constitution of the earth?" J. G. Rosenmülleri *Antiquissima Telluris Historia, à Mose Gen.* 1° *descripta;* Ulm, 1776; pp. 6, 10, 11, 12, 71.

It is with peculiar pleasure that I copy the following passages of the learned and pious Bishop of Chester; and they are the more estimable as they were written before 1814, at a time when geological facts and doctrines were less accurately known than they are at present.

"—Any curious information as to the structure of the earth ought still less to be expected, by any one acquainted with the general character of the Mosaic records. There is nothing in them, either to gratify the curiosity or *repress the researches* of mankind, when brought, in the progress of cultivation, to calculate the motions of the heavenly bodies, or speculate on the formation of the globe. The expressions of Moses are evidently *accommodated* to the first and familiar notions derived from the sensible appearances of the earth and heavens; and the absurdity of supposing that the literal interpretation of terms in Scripture ought to *interfere with the advancement* of philosophical inquiry, would have been as generally forgotten as renounced, if the oppressors of Galileo had not found a place in history.——No rational naturalist would attempt to describe, either from the brief description in Genesis or otherwise, the process by which our system was brought from confusion into a regular and habitable state. No rational theologian will direct his hostility against any theory which, acknowledging

* One cannot but observe here the working of a sagacious mind, and the approach which it makes, though on principles purely conjectural, to the Nebular Hypothesis.

the agency of the Creator, only attempts to point out the secondary instruments he has employed." Dr. Bird Sumner on the Records of Creation; vol. i. pp. 270, 283.

Let us hear another distinguished clergyman.

"As to the first point [the antiquity of the earth,]—not the mere theoretical views of geologists alone, but the conclusions which appear, by the most cogent logical necessity, to result from the phenomena of the structure of the earth's surface, and the variety and order of the very numerous successive series of organic remains imbedded in the strata, do undoubtedly appear to require periods of very considerable duration; and to indicate that very many ages had elapsed before (—"the diapason closing full in man,"—) a new exertion of the Creative Energy made, in its own image, a being of higher intellectual and moral capacities, as the head of its other terrestrial works. Now the evidence of geological phenomena most satisfactorily agrees with the scriptural record, in assigning to this last great event a very recent epoch: and it is surely very valuable as an independent testimony to this most important fact, which clearly involves the necessary admission of an interference with the previous order of nature, by a new and direct exertion of creative power, and therefore strikes at once at the root of every sceptical argument against MIRACLES. It is surely nowise inconsistent with the fullest reception of revelation, to maintain that it professedly confines itself to the exposition of the dispensations of the great Creator, as they concern his final intellectual creation; that, in a word, the Bible is exclusively *the history of the dealings of God towards men.*" The Rev. W. D. Conybeare, now (1847) Dean of Landaff; in the *Chr. Obs.* May 1834, p. 308.

[Q.]

Referring to page 185.

EXTRACTS FROM PROFESSORS WISEMAN AND HITCHCOCK, ON THE REFERENCE OF THE MOSAICAL RECORDS TO GEOLOGICAL TRUTHS.

"THE modern geologist must and gladly will acknowledge the accuracy of the statement, that, after all things were made, the earth must have been in a state of chaotic confusion; in other words, that the elements, which later were to combine in the present arrangement of the globe, must have been totally disturbed and probably in a state of conflicting action. What the duration of this anarchy was, what peculiar features it presented, whether it was one course of unmodified disorder, or was interrupted by intervals of peace and quiet, of vegetable and animal existence, the Scripture has concealed from our knowledge; while it has said nothing to discourage such investigation as may lead us to any specific hypothesis regarding it. Nay, it would seem as though that indefinite period had been purposely mentioned, to leave scope for the meditation and the imagination of man." Wiseman's *Connexion of Science and Rev. Relig.* vol. i. p. 295.

"So far then from finding, in the facts and conclusions of Geology, any objections to the Mosaic records, I find in them a striking evidence of the benevolence of the Deity. For, during the long period above spoken of, the globe was evidently preparing for the residence of MAN and the other animals that now inhabit it. Before their creation, its temperature was too high, and its surface too liable to be broken up by volcanoes, and drenched by deluges, to be a secure and happy abode for the more perfect races of animals that now inhabit it. But it was adapted to the nature and habits of such animals as we now find entombed in the rocks. The overflowing benevolence of the Deity, therefore, led him to place such beings upon it; and thus to communicate a vast amount of happiness, which seems to be a grand object in all his plans and operations. The vegetables that existed in those early periods have been converted, in the course of time, into the various species of coal now dug from the bowels of the earth; while the remains of the animals of those times have become changed into limestone. Even those violent volcanic agencies by which the successive races of plants and animals have been suddenly destroyed, have probably introduced into the upper part of the earth's crust, various metallic veins very important to human happiness. And in all this, we see indications of that same benevolent foresight and care for supplying the wants of his creatures, to which our daily—experience of God's goodness testifies." Hitchcock's *Geol. of Massachusetts;* p. 250.

Prof. Hitchcock having adduced strong evidence to prove that an extensive denudation has, at some time, taken place in the New Red Sandstone on the Connecticut river, proceeds to say: "The immense period requisite to wear away such a mass of rock as this theory supposes to have once occupied the whole valley of the Connecticut, will seem to most minds the strongest objection against its adoption: I mean, supposing it to have been effected by such causes as are operating at present. But this is not a solitary example, in which geological phenomena indicate the operation of existing causes, through periods of duration *inconceivably long*. We may, in this case indeed, as I have already shown, suppose the occurrence of numerous deluges in the earlier periods of our globe. Still, even with the aid of such catastrophes, the work must have been immensely protracted. And why should we hesitate to admit the existence of our globe through periods as long as geological researches require; since the sacred record does not declare the time of its original creation; and since such a view of its antiquity enlarges our ideas of the operations of the Deity in respect to duration, as much as Astronomy does in regard to space? Instead of bringing us into collision with Moses, it seems to me that Geology furnishes us with some of the grandest conceptions of the Divine attributes and plans to be found in the whole circle of human knowledge." Ib. p. 226.

[R.]

Referred to at pages 188 *and* 196.

ON THE SOLUTION OF DIFFICULTIES RESPECTING THE MOSAIC NARRATIVE PROPOSED BY PROFESSOR BADEN POWELL.

THE learned Savilian professor, in his "Supplement to Tradition Unveiled," has honoured me by making some observations on the interpretation of the Mosaic narrative, which I have endeavoured to support. This he has done in a spirit so generous and kind, as to merit my warmest thanks. But he would be one of the last men in the world to allow that personal esteem should obstruct the freedom of discussion. I am sure, therefore, of having his cordial approbation of an attempt to survey and compare the two modes of understanding this portion of the sacred writings.

I. There is no controversy between us as to the divine authority of the book of Genesis. Whether it was entirely and originally written by Moses, the unimpeachably faithful narrator of truth, and consequently of the divine communications, and other facts on which revealed truth must rest;* or whether it consists, in a great measure, of more ancient documents, running back to the earliest periods of human history, of which, I think, there is evidence (see p. 140); we hold that the book of Genesis is a part of "the Holy Scripture;"

* See pp. 138, 140.

that "the Old Testament is not contrary to the New;" and that "it is not lawful so to expound one place of Scripture, that it be repugnant to another." (39 Articles, 6, 7, 20.) To quote the clear and decisive words of Galileo, (see p. 184,) "It is therefore the duty of competent and diligent expositors, to bring forth, in every instance, *the true* meaning, and to explain the ground and reason of their having been expressed in the words which are presented to us." The Reverend Professor has also avowed his resolution (and I am equally bound as a christian minister,) to "be ready, with all faithful diligence, to banish and drive away" [*propulsare et amoliri*, certainly by no means except those of fair argument and kind dispositions,*] "all erroneous and strange doctrines, contrary to God's word." (*Ordin. Presb.*)

II. The difference between Mr. Powell and me appears to lie in this chief point: that I regard *the true meaning* of the narrative, elicited not by "hardly strained" wire-drawing of old words, or any sort of "critical refinement," but by the fair rules of interpretation, to be really in accordance with natural truth; while he considers the two as *insuperably discrepant*, *palpably contradictory;* and that, therefore, "this magnificent composition" was "not intended for an historical narrative, not designed for literal history," but is constructed of "the most sublime and unrivalled imagery—the language of figure and poetry—mythic poetry." *Connex. of Natural and Div. Truth*, pp. 250—260; *Suppl. to Trad. Unv.* p. 36.

III. In opposition, therefore, to any littleness of mind, which would torture the phraseology of the sacred narrative, gloss over some difficulties, and evade others by vague general remarks, the Professor thinks it *impossible* that "any reader of ordinary sense, not prepossessed in favour of a theory, can understand the description (whether in the shorter form of the Decalogue, or the more expanded of Genesis,) considered *simply as to its terms*, otherwise than as presenting a magnificent picture of Almighty power, and embodying the representation of one, original, entire, simple, universal act of Divine interposition, at once and for the first time framing and calling into being and operation, out of previous universal darkness and confusion, the heavenly bodies, as well as the earth, and all the races of organized beings upon it, in the actual progressive stages assigned to the six days specially described as literally such."

* Here I cannot but entreat my reader to study the cogent reasoning of my candid and noble-minded remarker, in *Tradition Unveiled*, pp. 49—53; and the recent volume of Archbishop Whately, (a work which every thinking man should read,) *Essays on some of the Dangers to Christian Faith*, pp. 154—220.

IV. With irresistible force of reasoning, the Professor remonstrates against the notion that Moses, or any other inspired writer, could have known in his own mind, or could have ever intended to convey, or even have imagined, those significations and applications of words, which men have excogitated, in order to *make* this primitive document speak the language of modern philosophy. In truth, a charge of moral delinquency is involved in the supposition that a divinely inspired writer should wrap up his meaning in expressions which all men of plain sense and honest minds would understand in one way, while he had the intention of their being understood in a sense quite different, covertly and enigmatically conveying notions which would not be elicited till above three thousand years had rolled away.

V. I submit a few observations, though in them it may be necessary again to introduce sentiments brought forward in former pages.

(i.) The Holy Scriptures contain the records, historically deduced, of the wise and gracious methods which God has employed for remedying the greatest evils which could have befallen his intelligent creation, *ignorance* and *sin*, the causes of untold *misery*. The revelation given in the Bible was therefore intended and adapted for the universal use and benefit of mankind, in all countries and all times,

(ii.) Like all the other works of God, known to us, this grand design has been and is carried on in the way of *gradual disclosure;* improving at every step in the comprehension of matter and the clearness of exhibition. May I be allowed to refer to remarks on this characteristic feature of the plan of Revelation, in "Scripture Testim. to the Messiah," vol. i. p. 218; ii. 413, 415; third ed. Also, we ought to observe the great deficiencies of *doctrinal* knowledge obvious in the Old Testament, especially the infrequency and obscurity of reference to a future life, and the low feeling and errors, to our minds most revolting, which had undisputed possession of the Israelitish opinion upon some of the most important points of *practical morality;* as with regard to marriage and divorce, retaliation, the usages of war, the manner of treating captives, the dreadful massacres, and the permission of the master-evil, war itself. Can any disciple of Christ avoid being convinced that these provisions and concessions are irreconcilably contrary to the doctrines, the precepts, *the very spirit and genius* of Christianity? Yet Christianity does not abjure Mosaism. "The law was not against the promises of God," but subsidiary and preparatory to their accomplishment; "our schoolmaster, to bring us to Christ; having a shadow of good things to come." See also observations on the *progressive* character of Revelation, in the Second

Disc. p. i. of Dr. Davison's *Warburton Lecture on Prophecy*, Oxf. 1839; a volume which will richly reward its diligent study.

(iii.) The vehicle of this series of communications has, of evident necessity, been human language, including *any of the modes* which have been employed among men as signs of ideas; consequently, symbols, significant actions, and figurative language. That this way of giving expression to thought, by a great variety of analogical representations drawn from objects of sense, was employed to make known divine and spiritual objects, was amply shown in Lecture VII.

(iv.) It may well be supposed, it seems even to be a necessary result of the preceding positions, that the best and holiest men under the patriarchial and the Mosaic dispensations, not excepting those who were the inspired messengers of the Divine will, would have been *unable to unfold and expound* their own sayings and writings. Our Lord affirms the superiority of John his forerunner above all the prophets, and yet pronounces "the least in the kingdom of heaven,"—the gospel dispensation,—to be "greater than he," and, consequently, than they; referring, probably, to the clearness and fulness of divine knowledge possessed by the ordinary class of Christians, if they be such, not in name merely, but in heart and practice. The apostle Peter describes the prophets themselves, (by whom "the Spirit of Christ testified beforehand" the sufferings and the subsequent glories which were to belong to him,) as "inquiring and searching" into those subjects, evidently under great deficiencies of both the knowledge itself, and the understanding needful for building upon it.

(v.) I must, therefore, disclaim the supposition, that "the narrative in Genesis is *intended* to describe" any series of phenomena anticipative of modern discovery in astronomy, or geology, or any other branch of knowledge; and "that this is what *Moses* really *intended* to say." Might I be indulged with a flight of imagination, and suppose myself in the heavenly state, and permitted to ask, "Faithful prophet! when you gave forth your account of the creation, what was your own belief and understanding? What did you know, what did you intend to convey, concerning the antiquity and extent of the universe; concerning the heavenly bodies, their number, order, magnitudes, motions, and distances; concerning light and air, land and water, plants and animals? Had you any idea of the natural knowledge which would be acquired, under the leading and blessing of Jehovah Elohim, thirty-three centuries after you?" He would reply, "Most certainly not. In all those things I partook of the general knowledge of my contemporaries. I knew no more of the philosophical realities of nature, than I did of the most abstract spirituality of God, when I spoke of Him as looking, seeking, trying, learning, improving in knowledge, repenting, grieving, changing his mind, coming and going, and having the bodily organization of a man. If questions ever rose in my mind upon these subjects, I remembered my ignorance and weakness, and I said, with duteous humility, Behold, God is great, and I know him not; with God is terrible majesty: touching the Almighty, I cannot find him out.* God spake to me mouth to mouth, even apparently, and not in dark speeches; and the similitude of the Lord I did behold.† I spoke and wrote, as I was moved by the Holy Ghost.‡ I wrote the things which I was directed to write; but I could not have made a comment upon them."

(vi.) But as we believe this narrative to have come, immediately or mediately, from the "Father of lights," the ultimate inquiry arises, and by far the most important, What did He *design* us to understand by it? What was the *intention* of the Author of inspiration?

Of one thing we are certain; His design was not to teach error. But we also know that *his modes* of teaching are not bound to any prescribed model: he exercised the sovereignty of his wisdom in this, as in every other part of His rectoral system. And we further know that, in all the Mosaic writings, the perfections, purposes, and acts of Deity are represented in language which, though of the lowest condescension, yet is not arbitrary; for the usage rests upon a common principle, *analogy*, and it is, therefore, capable of being *explained* upon sure grounds.

Justice to my estimable remarker requires that we should hear his answer to this question.

"Many eminent divines have even admitted that current opinions and prejudices, though erroneous, might yet be adopted, and turned into a vehicle of moral and religious instruction to those to whom they were habitual, without derogation to the inspired authority of the teacher.§ On such a ground we might certainly be permitted to re-

* The reader will perceive that, in presuming to form this speech, I have put into the mouth of Moses words taken from Elihu; because I know not of any expressions in the Pentateuch that convey the same sentiments so free from anthropomorphism. This appears to yield an argument against the hypothesis that Moses was the author, or even translator, of the book of Job.

† Numb. xii. 8. This remarkable passage is couched in the same anthropomorphitic expressions upon which we have had to bestow attention, and which stands at its highest degree in the writings of Moses; but the sentiment manifestly is, that the communications of divine knowledge and precept were made to him in a more immediate manner than had been granted to any other person.

‡ 2 Pet. i. 21.

§ Relinquishing instances less clear, the following may be mentioned as indubitable

gard the first chapter of Genesis,* as embodying what were the commonly received ideas among the Jews, borrowed, perhaps, from some poetical cosmogony, and which Moses was *inspired* to *adapt* and *apply* to the ends of religious instruction; to the assertion of the majesty, power, and unity of the Creator, and the prohibition of the worship of the false gods, especially of those animals and other material objects which were peculiarly pointed out as being merely the creatures of the true God; and this, doubtless, in a more particular enumeration, because *they* were especially the objects of that idolatrous worship into which the Israelites were so prone to relapse. The entire description being thus divested of the attributes of a real history, the concluding portion of it (the account of the solemnization of the seventh day as the sabbath) is, of course, equally divested of an historical character; and thus cannot be understood as referring to any primæval institution; and can, therefore, only be regarded as having been designed for the more powerful enforcement of that institution among the Jews. And this, indeed, would be no more than accords with the opinion of many of the most approved commentators, who, on quite independent critical and theological grounds, have regarded the passage (Gen. ii. 3) conveying that institution, as correctly to be understood in a proleptical or anticipatory sense." (*Connex. Nat. and Div. Truth*, p. 257.)

This is the hypothesis, taking the whole connected description, "as couched in the language of *mythic poetry*," yet "not laid down dog-

examples of our Lord and his apostles acting in this manner; that is, for the sake of arguing with men upon their own principles, conceding for the moment some assumption of the opponent, though by no means really admitting it. Matt. v. 19, the Pharisaical division of God's commandments into greater and less—a notion very likely to lead into theological and practical error upon the obligations of religion; ib. 22, referring to the processes of the Jewish law-courts; xii. 27, seeming to admit the pretences of the Jewish exorcists, though they were fraudulent and very pernicious; ib. 43, alluding to the ignorant and superstitious tales of the Jews, about evil spirits haunting lonely and hot sandy deserts, and prowling about to find springs of water; (see in Apocrypha, Tobit viii. 3, and Baruch iv. 35, derived from a gross misinterpretation of Isaiah xiii. 21; xx. 23;) not correcting the error concerning the nature of the Messiah's kingdom, but giving it a turn to a just application, which, at the time, was not likely to be understood; Luke xxii. 30, quite in the style of those common errors, but which our Lord disarmed of their danger, by converting them to a purpose of spiritual truth, to be afterwards disclosed; Gal. iv. 24, " which things are allegorized," (unhappily in the English version rendered *allegory*,) according to a favourite practice of the Jews. We may add, from the Old Testament, the dominion which the Most High exercises over the invisible world represented by a picture, or parable, formed from the scenes of an Asiatic sovereign's court; Job i. and ii. and 1 Kings xxii. 19—23. J. P. S.

* With the first three verses of chap. ii. See the much-needed instructions of the Archbishop of Dublin, on the evils arising from the preposterous subdivision of the Bible into chapters and verses—*Dangers to Faith*, pp. 225—235. J. P. S.

matically, but simply suggested." I offer the following remarks, also begging the reader to refer to page 136.

1. We have before pointed out that, in this narrative, there is a measure of the anthropomorphitic style; pp. 169, 195.

2. The style of speaking used here with regard to natural objects, is similar to that which has been exemplified from other parts of the Old Testament, describing natural phenomena, (pp. 174—182,) and which might be illustrated by many other examples. The whole may be considered as constituting the nomenclature of the natural philosophy of the Hebrews. It is evidently the expression of what were the universally received opinions concerning the sun, moon, and stars, the earth, the seas, and the atmosphere, motion and the results of motion; and every person moderately informed on natural subjects is perfectly aware that those opinions were widely erroneous. Yet this mode of expression enters largely into the descriptive parts of the Bible. Being a part of the current language of the Israelites, it was used, by Divine condescension, as the vehicle for the conveyance of spiritual truth; and this principle of condescension we have found to reign throughout the whole domain of revelation.

3. Our duty, then, is to draw the line of distinction between the imperfect vehicle, and the treasure which it carries. This can be effected only by intelligence and consideration. We must urge the fire; the foreign matter, necessary as a flux, will separate, and the gold will remain at the bottom of the crucible. The process will probably be as follows. In the clauses which attribute human forms, affections, and infirmities to the Deity, we drop all that is human, all that savours of defect or limitation; and that which remains is the pure truth of the Divine perfections, and their actings. We remove the idea of the Deity's speaking, giving commands to air, land, and water, and pronouncing blessings upon the fishes and the birds; his watching the subsequent proceeding, as if he were uncertain of its success; and then, after finding the result to be according to the intention, declaring his satisfaction. "God saw that it was good. God saw every thing that he had made, and, behold, it was very good." We renounce all pretension to the finding of astronomical correctness, in relation to the heavenly bodies; plainly perceiving them to be set forth merely as luminaries, and notaries of time to men. We take up the classification of plants and animals, not as an arrangement making the smallest claim to either completeness or accuracy, but as that which followed the notions of the time. We withdraw the attributing of repose to HIM who "fainteth not, neither

is weary," (Is. xl. 28,) though the expressions carry the unequivocal implication of previous fatigue.*

We have therefore made these subtractions; but *what* have we subtracted? Nothing but form and mode; the substance of the things remains untouched. Then our great question is, WHAT is that substance? *This is the point* at issue between me and my respected opponent. In his view, it is the assertion of the Unity and the Infinite Perfections of God the Creator, and the prohibition of idolatry; in mine, it annexes the further declarations, that, whatever number of creations may have been, each had its point of commencement, and some one was preeminent, as having been strictly "in the beginning," the first in the order of time, and *generically* comprehending the principle or germ of all following; and that the part of the world to which man is immediately allied, and which alone would be understood by the writer and original readers of this composition, did, in six natural days, pass through a series of changes, effected, immediately and mediately, by the Divine power, and here described in the phraseology of the people and the time.†

Upon the hypothesis of the learned Professor, "the entire description is divested of the attributes of a real history;" "was *not intended*

* Learned and pious commentators are often careful to assure us that the intention of the expression is not that of rest after weariness, but merely that of cessation from action. This is their assertion; but it has no support of evidence. The word occurs in the Pentateuch many times, indubitably denoting the repose of men and cattle after the week's labour; and that the same idea is ascribed to the Creator, is determined by Exod. xxxi. 17, "In six days the Lord made heaven and earth, and on the seventh day he rested, and was refreshed." Besides, the resort is itself fallacious; for it would be contrary to theological truth to suppose that the Infinite Being ever ceases from action. Perfect and unremitted ACTIVITY is included in the necessary attributes of the Divine Nature. It was a maxim of the old divines, that conservation is a continued creation. "My Father worketh hitherto, and I work." John v. 17.

† It may be objected that I commit a fallacy in laying down these two predicates, since the terms of verse 4th are manifestly intended to comprehend all the heavenly bodies. I reply, that the mention of them is *only such* as arises from their relation to man, to furnish light, and to be indications for agricultural and social life. Even to the eat of the sun no reference is made—the most vital of its influences; for it would be absurd to expect any notice of the mechanism of the solar system; yet, upon the hypotheses of some persons, this was the most to be expected, as being of the highest possible importance, more essential to life than even light. It is also worthy of observation that, in the places of Scripture (about twelve) in which any mention occurs of this part of the sun's influence, it is generally under the idea of physical evil, from the excess of heat. This was quite natural in such countries as Palestine and Arabia, admitting the style of writing to have been what I plead for; but quite unnatural upon the principles of those who ascribe philosophical accuracy to the language of the Bible. I am aware of only two places in which a beneficial influence is attributed to the sun's heat, Job viii. 16, Ps. xix. 6; and it is not clear that the first of these does not refer to the withering and burning action, and the second to the penetrating power of excessive heat, as sometimes painful.

for an HISTORICAL *narrative;*" "cannot have been designed for literal history;" and, "taken as a whole, it may be understood as couched in the language of *mythic poetry.*"

A few observations arise.

(1.) Mr. Powell does not deny, or question, but expressly affirms the sacred character and divine authority of this scriptural portion. He regards it "as embodying commonly received ideas, which Moses *was* INSPIRED *to adapt and apply* to the ends of religious instruction." (*Connex.* p. 257.) I request that this fact may be particularly observed with reference to the remarks in Lect. VI. pp. 136—138.

(2.) Though he has unfortunately, as it appears to me, adopted the term "mythic poetry," he must not be understood as symbolizing with the men who have filled Germany, and, in a considerable degree, other countries, with their parade of *mythi.*

All nations have had their traditions of events preceding history, adorning their respective countries and remote ancestors with gods and heroes, and deeds of wonder. A word (*μῦθος*) which at first signified any interesting speech, came to be applied to these national stories, in the common use of the Greeks.* Sixty to seventy years ago, Heyne led the van to a generalizing of the fact, in a manner so broad, as to *imply* a rejection of all the primeval revelations from the Deity—the first links in the unbroken chain which led down to the "grace and truth by Jesus Christ." Soon he found eager followers among his countrymen, always dying of thirst for *τὶ καινότερον.* Schelling, Eichorn, Gabler, Bauer, and a multitudinous host at their heels, betook themselves to the trumpeting abroad that, as the old Egyptians and Persians, Greeks and Romans, Celts, Goths, and Scandinavians, had their stories of heroic times—their *mythi*, so, beyond a doubt, the ancient Hebrews had. Learning and fancy—aye, talent and genius, too—ran mad. Parallels were found in Grecian fable to all the chief facts in the Old Testament history. Hardened in impiety, and drunken with self-flattery, these adventurers pushed on, till they dreamed they had stormed the citadel, had exploded either the death or the resurrection of Jesus, (it mattered not which;) and so had only to sit down on the ruins of human hope, and proclaim the reign of antisupernaturalism, soon to be followed by nominal pantheism and real atheism. "*Mythi*," said they, "are historical tales [sagen] concerning the most ancient history of the earth and of

* Σοφία δὲ
Κλέπτει παράγοισα ΜΥΘΟΙΣ.
"And wisdom with her *mythi*, gently beguiles."
Pind. Nem. vii. 33.

men, particularly of single tribes or nations, united with conjectures and theories in the garb of histories, upon cosmogony and geogony, the physical causes of things, and the objects of sense, all worked up into the miraculous, and by degrees dressed out in a variety of ways."* Another of the same school is pleased to say, "Every system of religion which professes to be derived from a supernatural and immediate revelation of the Deity, was enrapt in mythic representations."†

I feel no little pleasure in saying, that not only am I persuaded that my excellent opponent (—— shall I call him ?—or rather, fellow-helper in the attempt to elucidate a confessedly difficult part of Scripture,)—is not to be involved in these representations. Far, very far from it. He maintains the INSPIRATION of the narrative, and, of course, the DIVINE COMMISSION of Moses, its author or editor. Neither can I give up to the disguised infidel party, the long-ago deceased Alexander Geddes, the learned, nobly upright, and richly instructive man, notwithstanding eccentricities much to be lamented,—who wrote thus upon the passage before us. "I believe it to be a most beautiful *mythos*, or philosophical fiction, contrived with great wisdom, dressed up in the garb of real history, adapted to the shallow intellects of a rude barbarous nation, and perfectly well calculated for the great and good purposes for which it was contrived; namely, to establish the belief of One Supreme God and Creator, in opposition to the various and wild systems of idolatry which then prevailed; and to enforce the observance of a periodical day, to be chiefly devoted to the service of that Creator, and the solacing repose of his creatures." He then enlarges upon the propriety and convincing power of introducing in this manner the created beings, which the narrative particularizes, as they were those which the Israelites had seen to be the especial objects of the Egyptian idolatry:—and he adds,—"This hypothesis of a mere poetical mythos, historically adapted to the senses and intellects of a rude unphilosophical people, will remove every obstacle, obviate every objection, and repel every sarcasm; whether it come from a Celsus or Porphyry, a Julian or a Frederic, a Boulanger or a Bolingbroke." (*Transl. of the Bible*, vol. i. *Critical Remarks:* in-

* (*Hebraische Mythologie, u. s. f.*) *Hebrew Mythology of the Old and New Testament*, by Geo. Laur. Bauer, Prof. of Logic (!) and Oriental Languages in the Univ. of Altdorf, [afterwards at Heidelberg,] 2 vols. Leipzig, 1802, vol. i. p. 3. He died in 1806.

† "Quævis religionis doctrina, a supernaturali et immediata quadam numinis revelatione repetita, mythis involuta fuit." Wegscheider, *Instit. Theol.* cap. i. § 8. Halle, 1829.

serted also in Rees's Cyclopædia, art. *Creation;* and in Mason Good's *Life of Geddes*, p. 344.)

(3.) The capital point in question is thus ably displayed. After touching upon other proposed elucidations of Gen. i., the Professor proceeds:—"To this list we have now to add the interpretations just stated," [that of these pages,] "differing in its details indeed, but still founded upon the like critical distinctions, put forth as what Moses intended to say. Now, as in referring to those former instances, so in the present, I enter into no question, whether the word rendered 'create' may not more properly be translated 'mould' or 'arrange;' whether 'light' signify illumination from one source or another; whether 'darkness' means the absence of light, or only a partial obscuration. With all these, and the like questions, I have no concern. Let the whole narrative, taken together, be read through by any *unbiassed* person of common capacity and the most ordinary degree of taste and feeling; and let him be asked, I do not say whether the ordinary acceptation of every word be rigidly correct; but whether the ENTIRE IMPRESSION *of its tenor* be not something wholly at variance with all such laboured verbal criticisms; whether the matchless sublimity of the whole representation, when simply received, be not such as to leave on the mind little less than a sense of disgust, when we hear attempts thus made to refine away all that is most majestic in its imagery, as well as most strikingly appropriate to the particular object for which it was designed. It is only necessary once to read the comment along with the simple text, to feel the former equally at variance with common sense and correct taste." (*Suppl. to Trad. Unveiled*, p. 33.)

Let me be heard in reply.

(*a*.) There are some oversights in the sketch of particulars held forth as characters of my "critical distinctions," if they must be so called. I do not stop to point them out: if the reader please, he can compare them with the passages alluded to. For further explanation, I beg recurrence to a former part of this note, and to page 139.

(*b*.) I cannot perceive that the impression of grandeur and sublimity, upon readers of taste and feeling, is weakened, or that common sense is shocked, when in reading this document we believe that those to whom it was first given understood it *according to their own ideas* of the forms and motions and extent of the universe; ideas suited to the infancy of the human race. To perceive its magnificence, to enjoy its picturesque beauty, am I obliged to fly to one or other extreme; to take it, either as in every part literally true, or as merely a visionary tablet?

(*c.*) Much more should I conceive that the feelings of admiration at what is great and sublime, are enhanced by superadding those of *love and reverence for* TRUTH; and that those feelings would be repressed and broken, to a most distressing degree, by the notion intruding, that this unique composition, this model of unrivalled simplicity, the product of *Divine inspiration*, the portal to the temple, the beginning of those writings by which Infinite Benevolence is enlightening us and guiding us to eternity;—that this composition possesses *no historical truth*, and is only a mythus, a parable, a fable! Let me intreat my excellent remarker to consider in his own impartial manner, what would have been the effect upon an ingenuous Hebrew child, of being told that the reason given, in the name of God himself, "for the more powerful enforcement" of the sabbatic institution, represented no true fact, and therefore was only an instructive parable.

(*d.*) I can imagine no reason why we should be warned off from this plot of sacred ground, and prohibited to apply to it the same means of understanding and interpreting which we do to all ancient writings, and in particular to the Scriptures. This is all that I have done; and the reasons are, at every step, laid open to the reader.

(*e.*) That a description which is immediately adapted to the confined knowledge of a rude people, should yet, without any enigmatical device, but when only analysed and impartially expounded, be found not contradictory to the discoveries of the most advanced age;—surely may be regarded as not unworthy of the Author of knowledge, and as even what it would be natural to anticipate in any documents of written revelation. Some such position as this is the correlate of the great duty of "searching the Scriptures." The greatest theological mind (*ὡς ἐμοὶ δοκεῖ*) of modern times wrote, nearly a century ago, "The Scriptures, in all their parts, were made for the use of the Church here on earth; and it seems reasonable to suppose that God will, by degrees, unveil their meaning to his Church. It [the meaning] was made mysterious, in many places having great difficulties; that his people might have exercise for their pious wisdom and study, and that his Church might make progress in the understanding of it; as the philosophical world makes progress in the understanding of the book of nature, and in the unfolding of its mysteries." (Pres. Jonath. Edwards.) The divinely designed relation of the more advanced parts of revelation to the early and imperfect, requires us to generalize the axiom, which one of the ornaments of Oriel has propounded with regard to the Mosaic ritual: "Its 'dumb elements' are made animated and eloquent, when the Truth comes to act upon them with its light. They are like the statue, which had its chords wrought within, but was mute till the morning sun struck upon them." (Davison *on Proph.* p. 139.)

(*f.*) If any want of judgment, taste, or feeling attach to the considering of the first sentence in this narrative as an independent proposition, this defect has belonged to others before me, or they have closely approached to it; ancients and moderns, Christian fathers, Roman Catholics and Protestants, Churchmen and Dissenters, divines and philosophers. (See pp. 130—133; Rees's Cyclop. Art. *Creation;* Good's *Life of Geddes*, pp. 333, 345.) I must own that, to my conception, the grandeur and sublimity are increased by this insulation of the sentence. The eminent Bible-scholar and orthodox divine, Seiler, distinguishes the text in this manner; and he was a man of no common judgment and taste in literature. (*Grössere Biblische Erbauungsbuch*, i. 3.)

(*g.*) The Professor has said,—"The sure monuments which we derive from the study of organic remains, disclose to us evidences of a series of gradual changes and repeated creative processes, going on without any one sudden universal intervention or creation of the existing world out of the ruins of a former." (*Connex.* p. 254.) Now, I cannot perceive that the language of Gen. i. is inconsistent with this view. The first verse, "the general proposition," affirms that *there was a beginning*, "an epoch, a point in the flow of infinite duration, when the whole of the dependent world, or *whatever portion of it first had existence*, was brought into being,—by the will, wisdom, and power of the One and Only God." (P. 185 of this book.) The Professor, when he speaks of "*creative* processes," unquestionably understands interventions of the Deity, direct acts of power essentially different from any kind of generative evolutions. Why, then, may not the recited occurrences of the six days have been such a series, extending over that portion of the earth's surface in which man, with his appropriate attendance of organized creatures, was to receive "life and breath, and all things" from his Creator?—I can perceive in this no infringement of common sense, no invasion of taste, no sacrifice of the beautiful, or frittering away of the sublime. The proposition remains, that there is One Universal Creator, whatever may have been the periods of time, or parts of space, or spots on our earth, in which it has pleased him thus to "manifest forth his glory."

Professor Powell has referred, with high but merited encomium, to the Address of the Rev. W. Vernon Harcourt, (mentioned in the Notes at pp. 196 and 305,) as maintaining, "in its grand principles," the view which he had given. In this edition, I have enlarged the previous quotation from that address, so as to include the passage alluded to. (See Supplementary Note F, p. 305.) The reader may see in that extract, that Mr. Harcourt appears to have been directing his discourse chiefly to the confutation of such as imagine that they find time enough for the successive stratifications and the imbedded fossils, in the six days, or in a year, or in two thousand years; probably referring to those who regard the duration of Noah's deluge, or the antediluvian period, as adequate for the purpose. He considers the *days* as a figurative expression, denoting six classes of phenomena, each class being an act of the Creator's power. This is not a total denial of historical truth in the narrative: it is *interpretation*, and it is giving an *exposition* to the words. It seems very different from regarding the six days as fiction and fable, the machinery of mythic poetry. A definite signification is assigned to the days: each day denotes a *class;* and each class is an *act*. This is what I do not understand. That a class of phenomena should be an act, seems incongruous: but, no doubt, the intention was to signify the effect of acts of power. It would not be easy to make the classification supposed, for there are at least ten distinct objects, or groups of objects enumerated in the text. But, be that as it might, the proposed explication refers to certain actual facts, assumed to have taken place separately and successively. I think it lies open to the principle of Mr. Powell's objection, as much as mine does. Mr. W. Harcourt supposes each day to signify an act, inadvertently confounding the idea of *time* with the ideas of *space and motion*. My supposition is, that, in making fit and suitable the portion of the earth designed for the original seat of the human family, the Creator was pleased to distribute the operations into six successive and properly connected daily portions; having the wisest reasons for this arrangement. This involves no perplexity about time requisite for chemical or electric action, or any developement whatever of second causes: for, admitting and maintaining their action, the principal object to be considered is the *creative* cause, which we all, I trust, agree to be the immediate action of the Deity. The *mode* of such action must be inconceivable by us: but we are sure that it can be no other than worthy of Infinite Perfection; and that, whether the causal act be instantaneous, or through any succession of moments, it is the best adapted to the end, and infallibly efficient of that end. Upon the distribution of operations, and the dramatic style of narration (found in Herodotus, Homer, and all archaic compositions,) in which this "excellency of the power" is expressed, see pp. 192 and 195.

Notwithstanding Mr. Harcourt's flood of splendid eloquence, and the acclamations which it instantaneously drew from the vast auditory, —(of which, how many were qualified to judge, and that in a moment, upon a question of Biblical philology?)—I must confess my conviction that his *argument* failed. He adduced passages from the book of Job, those cited in p. 176 of this volume, with others, for a literal understanding of which no person contends; he observed that "here we have the first account of the Creation of the World, proceeding, as it were, from the mouth of the CREATOR himself;" and then his reasoning was that, since this *must* be taken as entirely figurative, we are authorized and bound to understand figuratively the description in "that other most ancient book"—the Genesis. That I may not deprive the argument of any measure of its force, I annex the passages additional to those already in my pages, and a few lines of the impassioned appeal which followed.

"——It speaks of Him 'who hangeth the earth upon nothing,' who 'maketh a weight for the winds, and weigheth the waters by measure.'——In that book, I say, we have the first account of the creation of the world, proceeding as it were from the mouth of the Creator himself. 'The Lord answered Job out of the whirlwind, and said, Where wast thou, when I laid the foundations of the earth? Declare, if thou hast understanding. Who hath laid the measures thereof, if thou knowest? Or who hath stretched the line upon it? Whereupon are the foundations thereof fastened? Or who laid the corner-stone thereof; when the morning stars sang together, and all the sons of God shouted for joy? Or who shut up the sea with doors, when it brake forth as if it had issued from the womb? When I made the cloud the garment thereof, and thick darkness a swaddling band for it; and brake up for it my decreed place, and set bars and doors, and said, Hither shalt thou come, but no further; and here shall thy proud waves be stayed." (Job xxxviii.) Take, then, these 'thoughts that breathe, and words that burn;' and compress them, if you can, into some true or some fanciful system of science. Teach us where to find 'the house wherein darkness dwelleth,' to 'bind the sweet influences of the Pleiades, or loose the bands of Orion.' Explain to us, with respect to one of God's creatures, what the natural process is, by which he 'drinketh up a river and hasteth not;' and of another, how 'his breath kindleth coals, and a flame goeth out of his mouth.'—Then take credit to yourself for vindicating the truth of Scripture: and, when you have thus illustrated a composition by the side of which, *till you touched it*, the images of Homer and Pindar seem but as prose, go on; instruct us how to interpret that other most ancient book, recorded, it has been thought, by the very same hand."—

Now the fallacy, into which the deservedly honoured philosopher had fallen, lies plainly in his having overlooked the change of meaning in one of his terms. All agree that *metaphors* are not to be understood literally; and, that these passages in the book of Job are metaphors, is evident. The conclusion then, with regard to them, is good. But, in applying this to the verse of Genesis, he has *assumed* what cannot be granted him; sliding in a change of his middle term. The middle term, in the valid syllogism, is *metaphorical language;* but, in the second case, it is *the phraseology repeated six times in Gen.* i.—"And it was evening, and it was morning, day the first,—second," &c. It was necessary to have proved that *this* phraseology is metaphorical: but the orator *has not so proved*, nor do I think that he would assert it, or that he can for a moment hesitate to admit that the phraseology is the plainest enunciation of a bare fact. It occurs in a composition which, grand and sublime as it is, especially in its commencement, is not given in poetical diction or form, but in simple prose. He also slides in another idea, evidently with the intention of strengthening his argument; that Moses was the writer of the book of Job: a conjecture of some biblicists, but destitute of evidence, and opposed by a great amount of reasons.—Yet let us not forget that the observance of critical and cold precision is not to be required, in the ardour of public speaking, on such an occasion and before an audience of three thousand lovers of science.

(*h.*) It is impossible to separate a consistent faith in the divine origin and authority of the Christian religion, from a reception of Moses as a messenger of God, especially accredited by miraculous evidence, that he might be the founder of a peculiar dispensation which should be the rudiment of Christianity. Jesus Christ recognised Moses in this light, (Matt. v. 17, 18; Luke i. 27; John v. 46, 47; vii. 19;) and we have, in a speech and the epistles of the apostle Paul, references to this very initial part of the book of Genesis, in such expressions as seem to imply the *historical* sense, and can, by no fair means of interpretation or of analogical argument, be made compatible with a *mythic* character. "Turn from these vanities unto the living God, who made heaven and earth, and the sea, and all things that are therein." (Acts xiv. 15.) "God,—commanded the light to shine out of darkness." (2 Cor. iv. 6.) Allusions to the terms of this narrative, so far as respects the high endowments with which man was invested upon his creation, occur in Eph. iv. 24, and Col. iii. 17.

Upon all these grounds I indulge the hope that the views which, from my opinion of their being true, I have put forth in this volume, are not a following in the wake of arbitrary interpretation, contrivance to serve a purpose, shifting and changing as exigencies arise, attributing to Moses or other men of old, knowledge which they could not possess, secret meanings, and equivocal phrases. I trust that I have adduced sufficient evidence that the design of Divine Revelation was higher and greater than to teach physical philosophy; while yet its declarations are misunderstood, if their fair interpretation be conceived to contradict natural truth.

In another work of Professor Powell's, for which, in my humble opinion, *the whole nation* is under no little obligation to him,* he has the following paragraph.

"—— There is one point to which it may be perhaps thought I am going quite out of my way to allude; yet it strikes me as one which must, in the present age, force itself more and more on our attention: —*In what light are we to teach children to view the Old Testament account of the Creation*, whether in Genesis or in the Decalogue? Are they to be early habituated to take it in its literal sense, and to hold it *historically* true as an article of faith? And then, when they afterwards come to hear (as we must expect all educated persons will), the facts of the case elicited by geological research, so wholly at variance with the reception of it *as history*, are they to be left exposed to the inferences of the sceptic, and the attacks which the advocates of infidelity will not fail to found on the contradiction? Are they to be thus made the victims of a timid prejudice, and weak dread of meeting the question fairly?"

My friends, especially those of my own religious connexions, who have so long and assiduously laboured in the benevolent work of educating the poor, (though this is a question which belongs equally to all orders of society,) will not think it irrelevant to the designs of the Congregational Lecture, that I intreat their most serious consideration to this question. Either we must trample upon the conclusion to which the men have come, who have had the best means of judging, of all countries and classes, with scarcely an exception; and thus be accessory to the fearful state of minds which Mr. Powell has set before us: or we must so modify our catechetical and other instructions as to prevent the collision *between faith and reason*, as our adversaries

* *State Education, considered with respect to Prevalent Misconceptions on Religious Grounds.* 1840, p. 29.

would not fail to call it. My own conviction is, that we ought to say, in the shortest and plainest manner, that this description was written for the use of those who could not have the knowledge which God has since enabled men to attain, and that it referred only to such parts of the Creator's works as those persons were acquainted with. [With this view, I especially recommend Mr. Whyte's *Catechetical Illustration*, mentioned at p. 314.]

Surely also, it is proper to set before our children and congregations that, in the Fourth Commandment, the clause is given as a *reason* for the sabbatic rest, viz. that even the Creator was fatigued and needed repose; *explaining to them the principle* of condescension to the minds of uncultivated men, so abundantly appearing in the earlier parts of the Old Testament: also that, in the repetition of the Ten Commandments, given forty years after in a written form, Moses *omitted this reason*, and introduced another, not as a part of the Commandment, but as a gloss or comment, founded upon the feeling of equitable sympathy: Deut. v. 15. Above all, we should take the requisite pains to make them understand that the unspeakable privilege of the christian Lord's *day*, and the duty of observing it, stand, not upon the Israelitish positive law of the seventh-day-sabbath, but upon *moral* reasons, analogical and inferential, arising from the primary facts of Christianity, and the benefits to piety and morality of this inestimable weekly season.

"——— Si quid novisti rectius istis,
Candidus imperti,———"

[S.]

Referred to at pages 189 *and* 192.

ON THE DUTY OF THESE INVESTIGATIONS, AND IN VINDICATION OF DR. BUCKLAND.

The following letter was courteously admitted into the "Magazine of Popular Science," more than three years ago. It was intended to obviate some remarks, in a Review of Dr. Buckland's Treatise, which the writer thought to be of an unhappy tendency. It is republished here, in the hope of its being useful partly as giving a short view of some principal sentiments maintained in this volume, partly for the sake of representing the importance of the discussion, and partly also to call attention to the interpretation of Gen. i. 2, which is maintained in these lectures, and for the suggestion of which I am under obligation to the Rev. Baden Powell.

Sir,—With cordial approbation of the design and the general execution of your article, in the last month, upon Dr. Buckland's Bridgewater Treatise, I request your candid indulgence of some brief remarks.

[Some of your] observations appear to me capable of being misunderstood, or of being construed injuriously in various ways to the interests of both science and religion. The tendency of those observations appears to be, First, to assume (or at least to warrant the assumption) that the Holy Scriptures contain allegations and implications with respect to the natural history of our earth, which are contradicted and disproved by the demonstrations of modern Geology; and, Secondly, that it is the duty of a philosopher to abstain from any discussion of this discrepancy, and from any inquiry whether it be real or only apparent; as if it were said, Let these two branches of knowledge be kept far away from each other: let philosophers and geologists pursue their own course, and let theology and religion practise their own duties, and watch over their own interests; but let neither interfere with the other; let no inquiry ever be made whether they are in accordance or in opposition.

This short way of dismissing the matter has, indeed, been adopted by some eminent men; but I appeal, Sir, to your impartial reflection, whether it is not *absurd* and *impracticable.*

1. It is *absurd.* TRUTH throughout her whole domain, illimitable as is its extent, is one in principle, and harmonious in details. It is no other than the having our conceptions in accordance with the reality of things. And *Truth in expression* (= veracity) is the adapting of our language, written or spoken, to the honest utterance of our conceptions. A mere child, if he will reflect a moment, perceives that a proposition cannot be true and false, under the same circumstances; unless there be some artifice practised in the use of terms. An assertion cannot be true in theology, and false in geology, or any department whatever of scientific knowledge; nor inversely. It really is an insult to men's understandings, to admit indirectly, that there are affirmations or doctrines in the records of revealed religion, which are disproved by the clearest evidence of science; and then to proscribe investigation, with a solemn pretence of mysteries not to be inquired into, an hypocritical tone of reverence for sacred things. The veil is transparent; no man can be deceived by it: but it is lamentable that any should attempt to deceive by it. We greatly wrong the interests of knowledge, and prejudice our own improve-

ment, when we but *seem* to admit that theology is an insulated portion of science, which may be safely pursued by itself, and which yields no advantages to other departments. True theology, on the contrary, attracts to itself, illustrates, and harmonizes all other knowledge. It is the science which relates to the Author and Preserver of the whole dependent universe; whatever may be known concerning HIM, for the noblest purposes of intellectual improvement, of personal virtue, and of diffusive happiness. It is formed by strict induction from the works and the word of God; natural notices, and positive revelation. It is the friend of all science; it appropriates all truth; it holds fellowship with no error.

2. It is *impracticable.* This kind of ban upon a reasonable, an inevitable query, is never submitted to by any person of sound understanding. Either he receives the assumption,—and, as its consequence, he rejects covertly or openly the truth and authority of the Bible; or he searches out the matter fairly and fully, and then he learns that the assumption is false.

Is it then the fact, that such fair and impartial inquiry will bring out this result? Is it, after all, an erroneous assumption, that the declarations of Scripture and the sensible demonstrations of geological science, pointedly contradict each other? Does not the Bible teach that the moment of the Supreme Being's first putting forth his creating power, was only about six thousand years ago? And do not the undeniable phenomena of stratification, and other facts, demonstrate that our globe (to say nothing of the rest of the solar system, and the astral universe,) has existed, has passed through countless changes, such as are continually in progress, and others of a more intense character, which rational estimation must suppose to have required a period for their production so vast as to fill us with astonishment,—which no calculator ventures to lay down,—which probably amounts to millions and millions of years?

Fully admitting the assumptions in the last query, I deny that of the preceding one.

It is to be lamented that the common habits of expression nourish the opinion, that the authority of Scripture maintains the commencement of dependent nature to have been as has been stated: and it is scarcely less to be lamented that theories have been propounded for conciliating the facts of nature and the Scripture narrative, which rest upon either a defective acquaintance with those facts, or a disregard to the plain use of language in that narrative. Of the former kind are the schemes for finding the time requisite for the terrene formations, in the period from the creation of the first man, to the

Noachian Deluge; of the latter, those which interpret the *days* of successive operation, laid down in the primeval record, as if they were indefinite periods.

It will appear evident to any one who will reflect upon the case, that the records of revelation must have been written in the phraseology and idioms of the people and the age to which they were given; or they would have been unintelligible. Upon this principle we account for the manner in which natural phenomena are currently described; and for the expressions which impute to the Infinite Spirit the form, the organs, and the mental affections of a human being; and various other characteristics of the parabolic style of the Hebrew Scriptures. Such language was a condescension to the infirmities of mortals, and best adapted to the instruction of the general mass of mankind: but it is self-evident that it must be interpreted in a manner congruous with the perfect attributes of the Deity, and the reality of things.

A philological survey of the initial section of the Bible (Gen. i. 1, to ii. 3,) brings out the result:—

i. That the first sentence is a simple, independent, all-comprehending axiom, to this effect—that *matter* elementary or combined, aggregated only or organized, and *dependent sentient and intellectual beings*, have not existed from eternity, either in self-continuity or succession, but had a *beginning;* that their beginning took place by the all-powerful will of One Being, the Self-existent, Independent, and Infinite in all perfections; and that the date of that beginning is not made known.

ii. That, at a recent epoch, our planet was brought into a state of disorganization, detritus, or ruin, (perhaps we have no perfectly appropriate term,) from a former condition.*

iii. That it pleased the Almighty, Wise, and Benevolent Supreme, out of that state of ruin, to adjust the surface of the earth to its now existing condition; partly by the operation of the mechanical and chemical causes (what we usually call *Laws of Nature*), which Him-

* I beg that this position may be understood in the way which the preceding Lectures explain. Prof. Powell's volume awakened my closer attention and directed my mind to what I regard as the more accurate interpretation of this verse, and which is therefore maintained in these Lectures. Referring to the preceding paper, of which he speaks in kind and courteous terms, he has represented me as conceiving "that *the beginning means* an indefinitely long period, during which the successive formations recognised by Geology may have taken place." *Connex. of Nat. and Div. Truth;* p. 297. But I am persuaded that this representation arose from oversight. My intention was to apply that word, not to a period, but to the *first term* of a period, the *commencement* of a series of operations; and that therefore the verb *created* is to be understood *sensu prægnanti*, as the Hebrew grammarians say.

self had established; and partly, that is, whenever it was necessary, by His own creative power, or other immediate intervention; the whole extending through the period of six natural days.

It has been indeed maintained, that the conjunction *and*, with which the next sentence begins, connects the succeeding matter with the preceding, so as to forbid the intercalating of any considerable space of time. To this we reply, that the Hebrew conjunction, agreeably to the simplicity of ancient languages, expresses an annexation of subject or a continuation of speech, in any mode whatever, remote as well as proximate. For denoting such different modes of annexation, the Greek and other languages have a variety of particles; but their use is in Hebrew compensated by the shades of meaning which the tone in oral speech, and the connexion in writing, could supply. To go no further than the first two leaves of the Hebrew Bible, we find this copula rendered in our authorized version, by *thus*, *but*, *now*, and *also*.

This interpretation is what I have been labouring to diffuse for more than thirty years, in private and in public, by preaching, by academical lecturing, and by printing. But it is not my interpretation, though I believe that I originally derived it from the sole study of the Bible-text. Clemens of Alexandria, Origen, Basil, Chrysostom, and Augustine, among the fathers (though not in a truly philosophical way, which was not to be expected), departed from the vulgar notion: and some judicious interpreters of the sixteenth and seventeenth centuries have done the same, in particular, Bishop Patrick and Dr. David Jennings. Of modern Scripture critics I say nothing; for prejudice, justly or unjustly, may lie against them. Not that the question is to be settled by human authority. Our only appeal for decision is to the Bible itself, fairly interpreted. But the mention of venerable names may be useful, to allay the apprehensions of some good persons, who only hear obscurely of these subjects, and have not the means of forming an independent judgment on solid grounds.

I, therefore, with many, feel greatly obliged to Dr. Buckland for having come in aid of this, which I believe to be, *the true sense and meaning* of the sacred writers. I am framing no hypotheses in Geology; I only plead that *the ground is clear*, and that the dictates of Scripture *interpose no bar* to observations and reasonings upon the mineralogical constitution of the earth, and the remains of organized creatures which its strata disclose. If those investigations should lead us to attribute to the earth, and to the other planetary and astral spheres, an antiquity which millions or ten thousand millions of years might fail to represent, *the divine records forbid not their deduction.* Let but the geologist maintain what his science so loudly proclaims, that the universe around us has been formed, at whatever epoch, or through whatever succession of epochs, to us unknown, by the power and wisdom of an Almighty First Cause. Let him but reject the absurdities of pre-existent matter, of an eternal succession of finite beings, of formations without a former, laws without a lawgiver, and nature without a God. Let him but admit that man is but of yesterday, and that the design of revelation is to train him to the noblest purity and happiness in the immortal enjoyment of his Creator's beneficence; and he will find the doctrines of the Bible not an impediment, but his aid and his joy.

I have written much more than I anticipated, and I will tax your indulgence no longer; otherwise, confirmation and illustration might be brought from various passages of Scripture, and it would plainly appear that a just interpretation of the idioms of the Hebrew language, marked with archaic simplicity, would show them to be susceptible of an unforced accommodation to philosophical truth; just as, in every modern language, phrases of current parlance, which, literally taken, would be absurd, are continually used by the masters of science as well as by common men. In such cases, error is neither given nor taken, and to affect philosophical precision would be miserable pedantry. This general principle may, I humbly think, be satisfactorily applied to the account of the Noachian Deluge, and to the obviating of some of its difficulties, though others will probably remain as a proper test of our disposition to rely implicitly on the infinite wisdom, goodness, and power of the glorious Author and Preserver of all things; "in whose hand are the deep places of the earth, and the strength of the hills is His also." J. P. S.

Dec. 10, 1836.

[T.]

Referring to page 207.

ON MOUNT ARARAT.

M. Eugene Boré was sent by the French Academy of Inscriptions and Belles Lettres, on an oriental expedition for literary and scientific purposes. He has lately sent home from Persia a Report upon Chaldæa and its ancient and modern inhabitants. It has been published in the *Révue Française*, vol. xii.; and a large extract is given in the *Sémeur* of Oct. 2, 1839. From this article, which contains much philological and historical information, I extract a few sentences, tending to support the idea that the resting-place of the ark was in some less elevated part of the great mountain region to which the name of Ararat was anciently given.

"The Chaldeans inhabited the mountains whose extended chain over Mossoul, Diarbekir, Van, and Suleïmania, covers the country with its innumerable ramifications. Secluded there and intrenched as in an impregnable fortress, they have constantly maintained themselves in their independence and wild liberty, which they have ever prized above every other enjoyment. Those mountains anciently bore the names of the Gorduian [Gordyæan?], Carduian, or Cardou.—The Syriac Version of the Old Testament does not say that the ark rested upon Mount Ararat, but on the top of mount Cardou.* On the place here pointed out by tradition, the early Christians built the edifice which they called the Monastery of the Ark; in which they kept up an annual commemoration of the patriarch with his family coming out of the ark. The Mahommedan dervishes to the present day maintain in this place a perpetually burning lamp, in an oratory. —The mountains Cardou, Macis as called by the Armenians, and Ararat, are only links of the immense chain of the Taurus."

[U.]

Referred to at page 234.

THE GEOLOGICAL SOCIETY VINDICATED FROM MISREPRESENTATIONS.

In a recent publication, "The Stranger's Intellectual Guide to London, for 1839–40," an account is given of the Geological Society; and in it occurs the following passage.

"The meetings of the Geological Society are perhaps the most

* The Syriac has *Cardu*, the Arabic *Carda;* but the difference is not essential, as every one acquainted with the Shemitic languages must know. The bearing of this evidence is to support the opinions that the name *Ararat* in the Hebrew text was intended to comprehend the whole mountainous district; and that the ark rested in some part of the lower, but yet hilly, region which lies eastward, and is called in Arrowsmith's maps, *Karadaugh.* The Latin Vulgate renders *Ararat* by *Armenia.*

popularly interesting to their attendants of any in town, and each member having the opportunity of admitting two visitors, the capacious meeting-room is generally well filled. The principal interest of these meetings is however derived from the discussions which arise after the papers are read, and which sometimes do not assume a very scientific character. Geology is not generally popular with the public and has not as yet sufficient claims to make it so, the opinions of its advocates being split into party theories, and the papers that are read before the Society giving rise to discussion neither the most rational nor acceptable. What is wanted in the reason is made up for in the jocularity of the discussions, and sallies of wit usurp the place of the grave deliberations of science; what is wanted in argument made up from deductions from close investigation, is met with in the sophistry of the forum or debating-room. Sometimes it is to be lamented that these discussions take a different character, being directed against the fundamentals of revealed religion, and have a tendency to subvert those doctrines which are the basis of our modern civilization. From these circumstances the Society takes especial care that their proceedings shall not be reported: the attendance of every person from whom these might emanate being carefully excluded from the meetings. Their own reports indeed appear carefully worded, and supplied by their own secretaries, in the Literary Gazette and the Athenæum, but in these accounts all allusion to their discussions is avoided. In these respects the Geological Society does not court the freedom of public discussion, which, through the medium of the press, is allowed by every other Society in the metropolis."—Pp. 77, 78.

It may be requisite to assure the reader that this paragraph is copied with literal accuracy. The writer's representation of the general character of Geology may be very safely left to itself, as an instance of the ancient practice not yet become uncommon, that persons "speak evil of the things which they understand not." But it contains insinuations and assertions which call for attention: and I should think myself wanting in the observance of moral duty, were I to neglect the opportunity afforded by the publication of this volume, of bearing testimony to truth, and so of counteracting injurious representations. To any candid thinker it must appear an unreasonable expectation, that any person that pleases should be allowed to take notes of the papers, conversations, and discussions of any scientific or literary institution, and to publish them. No Society of respectability and honour would submit to such an intrusion. Besides other obvious objections, this one immediately presents itself; the contingency, not to call it a certainty, that mistakes and misrepresentations would be committed, and those often of the most serious import, even by well-intentioned reporters.

The impropriety of this complaint is however a small thing, in comparison with other parts of the passage. The writer does not say, that some instance may have occurred, or even more than one, in which a speaker had uttered sentiments irreconcileable to reason or piety. The reflection would then have arisen, that no society to whose objects unreserved discussion is essential, could prevent such an occurrence, or ought to be held answerable for it, unless it had manifested approbation, or at least connivance. I do not say this as an apology for any known fact, for I have never heard of such an occurrence. But the writer evidently strives to produce the impression that scientific investigation is not the chief object of the Society's meetings, that it is made only a mask for the effecting of other purposes, that the most momentous truths of religion are assailed with scoffs, in the guise of witticism and sophistry as the substitute for argument, that infidel and immoral principles are bandied about, and that the Society gives encouragement and protection to such a course of proceeding.

I feel it my duty to declare that, to the best and utmost of my knowledge, these accusations are *contrary to truth* and *exceedingly unjust.* My great affliction, extreme deafness, restricts my advantage, in attending the meetings of the Geological Society, almost entirely to the inspection of the specimens, sections, and figures. Yet I am a constant attendant: and, if infidel or otherwise irreligious and immoral sentiments were propounded by any of the speakers, I am not unprovided with the means of receiving information; and those means would not have been ineffectual. I am well assured that, even if in any *long past* time it may have happened that opinions or insinuations have been broached, of the character which this author alleges, the blame has rested on the offending person, and could, upon no principle of equity, have been imputed to the Society: and, from my own knowledge, I am persuaded that, were such a thing to occur, it would be met by a strong expression of disapprobation from the chair and by the general sense of the meeting. But I can go farther. I have sought information from some of the oldest, most active, and most influential Fellows of the Society: and upon good authority I am enabled to say that the accusations are *not true.* One of those gentlemen, whose means of knowledge are ample to a degree that few men can obtain, has written to me: "I can fully bear testimony to the entire correctness of what is stated in your Note, in contradiction of the calumnious assertions with regard to the discussions at the Geological Society.—I can truly say that no discussions or observations hostile to Revealed Religion, or treating it with levity, have ever been heard by me at the Society's meetings; nor do I believe that in so large and respectable an assembly, generally attended and often presided over by Ministers of religion, any such would be for a moment attempted or permitted."

The abstracts of papers read in the Society are printed for the use of its members, under the title of *Proceedings;* and brief statements, with the approbation of the Society, are sent to the two journals mentioned, by a gentleman in whose ability and accuracy the fullest confidence may be placed. By this method, the public is furnished with correct information, instead of being left to the reports of incompetent persons, which could scarcely be any other than defective and misrepresenting.

Sec. ed. This testimony is confirmed by one of the brightest ornaments of the Society, who has written thus, Nov. 16, 1839. "——I was greatly surprised at your extract [from the book referred to in this Note,] for its shameless untruth. During more than twenty years I have been a member of the Geological Society, and very frequently have attended its meetings; and I never once heard an expression directed against the fundamentals of religion, nor would any sneer at Revealed Truth be tolerated for one instant. And what does this vituperative author mean, when he says that our Society 'does not court the freedom of public discussion which is allowed by every other society in the metropolis?' These words at least prove that ignorance and malevolence often go together. The other chartered philosophical Societies of London, so far as I know them, have no discussion or debate upon the Memoirs submitted to them. Our debates are the exception, not the rule; and I am certain we do right in excluding reporters, who would mangle what we now say in the utmost confidence of a mutual good understanding.——"

ADDENDA.

In addition to the observations which conviction of duty and, I must say, painful feeling, led me to make in pp. 74 and 358 upon the common practice of seeming to deify Nature, I beg attention to some remarkable passages from the Chevalier de Lamarck, (who died a few years ago, at the age of near 90,) to whose talents as a zoologist and a botanist, every person does homage, but whose doctrine of the production of all the species of organized beings, from "appetency," and in the way of "progressive developement," it may be hoped has not many adherents. May it answer good purposes, as an admonitory specimen of the hallucinations in highly gifted minds!—Mr. Lyell felt it necessary, after giving a lucid exposition of that hypothesis, to assure his readers that his sketch was "no exaggerated picture." *Princip.* iii. 22. B. iii. ch. 1.

It is no wonder that Lamarck has been charged with atheism. But, unless we impute to him hypocrisy and fraud, (for which I believe that no just ground could be laid,) great regard is due to both his arguments and the language in which he clothes them, upon the *absurdity* of identifying Nature with God.

I first avail myself of Mr. Lyell's summary. "Nature—is not an intelligence, nor the Deity; but a delegated power,—a mere instrument,—a piece of mechanism acting by necessity,—an order of things constituted by the Supreme Being, and subject to laws which are the expressions of his will. This Nature is *obliged* to proceed gradually in all her operations."

The following passages are from the celebrated work, "*Histoire Naturelle des Animaux sans Vertèbres;*" 8 vols. Paris, 1815—1822.

"In all that belongs to nature, every thing is connected, every thing is dependent, every thing is the result of a common plan, followed constantly, but varied infinitely in its parts and details." Vol. i. Introd. p. 259.

"Man, having acquired sufficient knowledge to elevate himself to the SUPREME BEING, by reflection, aided by the observations of nature or by any other methods, this grand sentiment has become the stay of his hope, and has inspired him with religious feelings, and directed him to the duties which they enjoin." P. 298.

"——That intelligent and infinite power which has brought into existence all the physical beings that we observe." P. 305.

"The different bodies" [elementary, or components of the organized—?] "that we are acquainted with,—shewing themselves to be (according to all appearance) the same, in all times and with the same qualities or faculties, must be as old as *nature* herself, and must have derived their existence from the same cause which gave nature hers." P. 308.

Nature is, "in one word, a power which itself exists only by the will of a power which is superior and infinite, and which, as being the founder, is really *the author* of all that proceeds from it, that is, of all that exists." P. 311.

"The physical universe will subsist as it is, so long as the will of its SUBLIME AUTHOR shall permit." P. 316.

Fourth ed. Upon this subject I gladly offer to the benefit of those upon whom my remarks may have seemed to verge on severity, a passage from HERDER, "the great man,—the citizen, the philosopher, the poet,—all whose endeavours were characterized by the purest and noblest humanity." (*Menzel.*)

"Let no man distress himself for this reason or any approach to it, that I sometimes make a personified use of the name of Nature. Nature is no independent being; but GOD is ALL, in his works. My desire at least was, that I might not, by too frequent use, in which I might fail to maintain its sanctity, misuse the most holy name; which no one deserving to be called a rational creature should utter without the deepest reverence. Let the man, to whom the word Nature, as employed by many writers of our age, has become unmeaning and low, put mentally in its place THE ALMIGHTY POWER, WISDOM, AND GOODNESS; and in his soul worship that INVISIBLE BEING to whom no language of earth can give the right and full name." *Ideen zur Philosophie der Geschichte der Menschen; Vorrede*, p. 16. Carlsruhe, 1790.

The following remarks of the eminent Palæontologist, Agassiz, have a striking interest. They refer to the succession of the forms of animal life in the fossiliferous strata, through periods *incalculably* VAST. Let the reader compare with p. 192 the supplementary Note F. "The progressive concatenation [*enchaînement*] of the four classes of Vertebrata is a fact which, in all respects and in a manner very remarkable, consists with the uniform and parallel developement of all the classes of Invertebrata. The gradation of the Vertebrata is even the more remarkable as it is joined on immediately to the introduction of the human species [*à la venue de l'homme,*] whom we may regard as not only the term but also the object [*but*] of all this developement." *Poissons Fossiles;* p. xix.

On this final page, I copy the prayer with which BACON begins and concludes his "Instauratio Magna;" beseeching all my readers to join me in its sincere aspiration.

"—— Si quid profecerimus, non alia sane ratio nobis viam aperuit quam vera et legitima spiritus humani humiliatio. ——— Quamobrem, ——— ad Deum Patrem, Deum Verbum, Deum Spiritum, preces fundimus humillimas et ardentissimas, ut humani generis ærumnarum memores et peregrinationis istius vitæ in qua dies paucos et malos terimus, novis suis eleemosynis per manus nostras familiam humanam dotare dignetur. Atque illud insuper supplices rogamus, ne humana divinis officiant; neve ex reseratione viarum sensus et accensione majore luminis naturalis, aliquid incredulitatis animis nostris erga divina mysteria oboriatur; sed potius, ut ab intellectu puro a phantasiis et vanitate repurgato et divinis oraculis nihilominus subdito et prorsus dedititio, fidei dentur quæ fidei sunt: postremo, ut scientiæ veneno a serpente infuso quo animus humanus tumet et inflatur deposito, nec altum sapiamus nec ultra sobrium, sed veritatem in charitate colamus."

INDEX.

Adanson, Michael, the eminent naturalist, on the Baobab tree, 336.

Agassiz, Prof.; his hypothesis of an ancient low temperature of the northern hemisphere, 54. On the fishes of the Old Red Sandstone, 315. On the glaciers, 327. On the gradations of fossil animal species, 393.

Agency, Divine, in intellectual greatness, 235.

American aborigines; their moulding infants' skulls, 271.

Animalcules, fossil, 67, 318.

Animals: what kinds provided for in the ark, 109, 201, 206. Estimated number of existing species, 110.

Annihilation of any thing, an unfounded opinion, 154.

Antediluvian hypothesis, and objections to it, 142.

Antiquity of the Earth, 53, 159, 284.

Arabs, proposed as the standard human figure, 273.

Ararat, mount, 207, 387.

Asia, districts of; their low level, 207.

Astronomy, its alliance with geology, 11. Evidence from, to the immense antiquity of creation, 252.

Athenians; their popular notion of their own origin, 277.

Auvergne, volcanic region of, 102, 309, 334. Christian piety in that district, 332. Erroneous statements from Sidonius, 334.

Babbage, Charles, Esq.; on the supposed contradiction of Geology and the Bible, 8. On the antiquity of the earth, 55, 81, 287. On the Mosaic account of the creation, 134. On the responsibility of man, and its eternal consequences, 227. On the mechanical effect of the central heat, 293. On the rings of growth in fossil-trees, 339.

Baily, Francis; the late eminent astronomer, 33.

Baxter, Richard; on the possibility of an antecedent world, 221.

Biblicus Delvinus, an anonymous writer on Geology, 152.

Binney, E. W., Esq.; on the origin of coal, 352.

Blumenbach, John Fred., Prof. Physiol. Götting.; his belief of the unity of the human species, 49.

Botany recommended as the beginning of studies in Natural History, 218.

Bowman, J. E., Esq.; on the longevity of trees, 336.

Brown, Rev. J. Mellor; his strictures on the author of this book, 7. His charges against Geology, 127. His fallacious and pernicious reasonings, 132.

Buckland, Rev. William, D.D., Dean of Westminster; on the connexion of sciences, 3. His Bridgewater Treatise recommended, 27, 117, 250, 303, 382. On valleys of denudation, 83. On diluvial formations, 94. On supposed concessions, 116. On "the Sentence of Death," 200. On microscopic shells, 318.

Burnet, Dr. Thomas; his Theory of the Earth, 29.

Cæsar, his notice of country round Clermont in the Puy de Dome, 106.

Calvin, on the right and duty of examination, 115. On Genesis, i. 126. On Rom. viii. 21, 155.

Carniverous animals; designed by the Creator, 199. Their use, 67. Their existence in all periods of life upon the earth, 241, 244.

Carpenter, W. B., M. D., his Principles of Physiology, 384. On the woody layers, 341.

Cause, the Supreme; 16, 26, 185, 232, 299, 303, 311, 317, 321, 359, 368, 393.

Chalk formation, 293, 309.

Chalmers, Rev. Dr.; his application of the doctrine of chances, 14. On the antiquity of the earth, 23, 196. On the disclosures by the microscope, compared with telescopic discoveries, 321.

Change, perpetual, in the universe, 26, 230.

Chaos, universal, not admitted, 56, 186, 190.

Characterism of rocks and organic remains, 43.

Charlesworth, Edw., Esq.; his Magazine of Natural History, on the early efforts of William Smith, 43. His merits as a naturalist, 345.

Christian Observer; on the futility of anti-geological objections, 129, 144, 151, 160. On the duty of studying the great questions in Geology, 222. On the law of death, 251.

Christianity not necessarily committed to the belief of only one race of men, 278.

Chronology; systems of Usher, and Hales, and Wallace, 142, 336. Geological, its difficulties, 285.

Cleavage and joints, 297.
Coal formations, 295, 311, 342, 345, 349, 352.
Cockburn, Dr. Wm., Dean of York; his Letter to Prof. Buckland, 149.
Cold and heat, extreme; ability of men to bear, 50.
Cole, Rev. Henry; his writings against Geology, 118.
Conchology; its peculiar interest, and relation to Geology, 304.
Conybeare, late Rev. John Josias; his discovery of the Snowdon early fossil-casts, 301.
———, Rev. W. D., D.D, Dean of Llandaff; on ascertained geological facts, 19. His description of the subsidences near Lyme, 39. His and Mr. William Phillips's Outlines of English Geology recommended, 250. On the moral tendency of Geology, 362.
Copernican system; opposed by divines, both Roman Catholic and Protestant, 176, 178.
Coral Reefs, 47.
Cosmogony; the Egyptian system of, compared with the Mosaic, 353.
Creation not universal at any one point of time, 49. The Mosaic account, 52, 134, 141, 167, 180, 185, 189, 368, 372, 380, 385. Not proceeding from any single centre, 63. The Adamic: conceived to relate only to one region of the earth, 190, 192. Successive operations, 191, 193. The heavenly bodies, 193. The animal structure, 195. The human female, *ib.* Vegetable life, 191. Animals, 191. Statement in the fourth commandment, 186. No intrinsic reason for supposing the recent commencement of creation, 221.
Cumbrian and Cambrian rocks, 290.
Cuvier, Baron George; hint of his geological views, 24. On the Deluge, 78. His sagacity and anticipations in relation to Geology, 79, 81. On Dr. Buckland's researches in bone-caves, 83. His geological character, 82. His death and general character, 80.
Dana, Rev. Dr.; on Scripture difficulties, 222.
Darwin, Charles, Esq.; on the South American shingle formation, 87, 102. On the longevity of trees, 339. On elevations of land, 298. On the crust of the earth, 258.
Davison, Rev. Dr.: his Discourses on Prophecy referred to, 368, 377.
Death; necessary in a system of organic life, 65, 197, 199, 242. Demonstrated geologically, 68, 241, 251. Attaching o the infra-human animals, while man remained innocent, 198, 251. How man before the fall was exempted from death, 199.
De Candolle, Augustin Pyramus, Prof. Genev.; on vegetable regions, 48. On the longevity of trees, 336, 340.
De la Beche, Sir Henry Thomas; his works recommended, 27. On drift in Jamaica, 101. On the organic remains in the earlier fossiliferous rocks, 262.
De Larrey on the human prototype, 273, 275.
Deluge, 69, its moral reason, 69, 84. Scripture Narrative, 70, 107. Its date, 142. The fact evinced by history and national traditions, 71. Its relation to geological considerations, 72, 76, 78, 82, 83, 95, 97, 99, 100, 106, 108, 109, 112. Not extending over the whole globe, 102, 106, 109. Summary of arguments against the common opinion, 200. Examination of the terms in which it is described, 203, 212.
Denudation, 41. An instructive instance, 364.
Deshayes M., on the separate groups of fossil animals, 59, 100.
Devonian system of formations, (Old Red Sandstone,) 291, 296, 302, 309, 313.
Didelphys Bucklandi, 58. Controversy upon, 303.
Diodorus Siculus, on the Egyptian mythi, 353.
Districts, animal, 47, 65; botanical, 48.
D'Orbigny, on the Geology of S. America, 51.
Drift, or diluvium, 85, 312. Extensive, 85. Of different ages, 86, 312. Silurian, 88. North British, 88. Eastern, 89. North European, 91. North American, 92. In Jamaica, 101 Patagonian, *ib.* Extensively produced by currents at the bottom of the ocean, *ib.*
Earth; importance of its Natural History, 26. Extent of our acquaintance with its structure, 22. Elevation and fracturing, 30, 37. Advantages of such dislocations, 29. Interior constitution, 32, 130, 228. Specific gravity, 33. Thickness of its crust, 32, 258. Primary condition, 189. Constancy of its axis, 260. Meanings of the term in the Hebrew Scriptures, 189. Its immense antiquity, 53, 55, 84, 129, 160, 221, 239, 247, 284.
Edinburgh Review; on successions of creatures and geological disclosure, 82. Its excellent articles on James Hutton, Buckland, and Lyell, 36. On Cuvier, 82.
Edwards, Pres., on progressive knowledge of the Scriptures, 376
Ehrenberg, Prof. Berl., on the microscopic animalcules, 318. Summary of his discoveries, by I. M. of Geneva, 321. More recent researches, 323.
Elevation of land, 36, 209, 228, 246, 293, 364.
Erratic blocks; *see* Drift.
Evidence, sensible, 13. Moral, *ib.* To be faithfully followed, 15, 226.
Fairholme, George, Esq.; his writings on Geology, 145.
Fathers, the early Christian writers: their general repugnance to physical researches, 176. Upon the interpretation of Genesis i. 124, 386.
Fichte, John Gottl.; on the first human beings, 167.
Fitton, William Henry, M.D.; his "Geology of Hastings," recommended, 28.
Fleming, Rev. Dr. John; on the speedy obliteration of traces of the Deluge, 77.
Flourens, (Secr. Acad. Sc. Par.) on human races, 274.

Forbes, Edw. Prof.; on the former climate of Britain, 53.
Francis, G. W., Esq.; his Botanical works recommended, 218.
Galileo; observations upon his case, 176. His views of Bible interpretation, 184.
Geddes, Dr. Alex. on Genesis i. 127, 374.
Genesis, the sacred book; comprises several distinct compositions, 140. Illustrations of its commencing portion, 121, 124, 141, 150, 168, 171, 174, 180, 185, 193, 196.
Geological Society vindicated from misrepresentation, 388.
Geological time, not as yet reducible to our common measures, 103, 247, 285, 287, 291, 295, 298, 301, 303, 307.
Geologists, distinguished; their credibility, 5. Instances of their fidelity to evidence, 85. Charges against them repelled, 120, 128, 133, 388.
Geology; its nature as a study, its objects and design, 1. Relation to other branches of science, 6, 18. Intention and value, 2, 12, 18, 219, 226. Prerequisites for the study, 3. Objections against, 6. Apparent discrepance with the Scriptures, 6, 52, 116, 245. Wrongfulness and injurious effect of such an opinion, 7, 9, 20, 128, 133, 384. Comprehension of our knowledge, respecting, 32, 50. Vindicated against ignorant and assuming misrepresentation, 120, 128, 159, 224. Especial importance of this study to Christian ministers, 225. Recommendations with respect to it, 27, 249. Its moral tendency, 1, 309, 312, 313, 364, 387.
Gifts, extraordinary; in the Apostolic Churches, 114.
Gisborne, Rev. Thomas, Preb. Durham: his "Considerations on Modern Theories of Geology," 149.
Glacier Theory, 327.
Gneissic rocks, 289.
God; his necessary perfections, 17, 163, 231, 299. Represented in scripture by condescending imagery, 165, 183. To be acknowledged in all scientific pursuits, 74, 233, 312. Our knowledge of the Deity rests upon analogy, 163. That analogy is in various forms, 165, 168, 172.
Granitic rocks, 33, 289.
Grant, Rob. E., M.D., Prof.; on the plan of creation, 312.
Greenough, George B., Esq.; his Geological Map, 28. His change of sentiment with regard to the Deluge, 99.
Harcourt, Rev. William Vernon; his vindication of Geology, 196, 305, 377.
Harris, John, D.D.; his "Præ-Adamite Earth, recommended, 28.
Hartley, Rev. John; on the moral state of Thiers, in the Puy de Dome, 332.
Hawkins, Thomas, Esq.; on the Ichthyosauri and Plesiosauri, 68, 303.
Heat, internal of the earth; 32, 35, 130, 228.
Hebrew language; well understood, 136. Its conjunctive prefix, 188. Idioms for a great and indefinite number, 179.
Henslow, Rev. Prof.; on vegetable regions, 49. On the longevity of trees, 336.
Herschel, Sir William; on celestial distances, 252. On the number of heavenly bodies, 253.
Herschel, Sir John Wm. Fred.; On the harmony of truth, 15. On Mr. Lyell's "Principles of Geology," 158. On the necessity of Mathematics to Natural Philosophy, 216. On the working of the earth's internal heat, 293.
Hitchcock, Rev. Edw., L.L.D., Prof.; on the ignorance and unfairness of distinguished opponents of Geology, 21. His "Elementary Geology," recommended, 28. His judgment of Fairholme, Kirby, and Granville Penn, 20, 146. On deluges and drift, 100. On the grand law of the world, 307. On the relation of Geology to the Divine Government, 364.
Hopkins, William, Esq.; his application of the highest mathematics to geological investigation, 18, 259, 298.
Human petrifaction of Brussels, a mistake, 288.
Human species, varieties of, 270.
Hutton, James, M.D.; his merits in Geology, 36.
Hutton, William, Esq., of Newcastle-upon-Tyne; joint author with Prof. Lindley of the "Fossil Flora," 345.
Iceland; the seat of tremendous volcanic action, 229.
Induction; cautious, at length successful, 40.
Jameson, Robert, Esq., Prof.; on the non-existence of vestiges of the Deluge, 77.
Jarchi, Rabbi, Solom., on Gen. i. 127, 201.
Java; volcanic eruptions of awful violence in that island, 230.
Jennings, Rev. Dr. David; on the Mosaic description of the Creation, 126.
Job, scripture poetical book of; passages of emphatic sublimity, 164, 174, 176.
Joshua; the sun and the moon standing still, 110.
Judæa; its advantages as a country, 25.
Kennedy's Scripture Chronology, on the Mosaic account of the heavenly bodies, 186.
King, Edward, Esq.; on the time of creation, 127. On the primary ancestry of mankind, 279.
Knowledge, human; its imperfection, 216.
Lactantius ridicules the idea of the sphericity of the earth, 176.
Lamarck, M., on the application of the word *Nature*, 358, 392.
Lawrence, John, Esq.; on the *rete mucosum*, 276. On the unity of the human species, 277.
Leibnitz; his scientific anticipations, 75.
Life, animal; earliest appearance of, 57, 300.
Light, before the Adamic Creation, 60. Periods of its transmission, 254, 257.
Lightfoot, Dr., on 2 Pet. iii. 155.
Lindley, Dr. and Prof.; his recommendation of Botanical studies and works to promote them, 218. His admonition to young botanists, 218. His and Mr. W. Hutton's "Fossil Flora," 345, 350. On the formation of Coal, 346. On the *Adan-*

sonia digitata (Baobab) 336. On the relative antiquity of organic remains, 346, 349.
Link, Prof., on the unity of the human species, 275.
London, University of; its requirements for matriculation, 217.
Longevity of trees, 112, 336.
Lonsdale, William, Esq.; his discoveries of fossil microscopic shells, 244. On the number and magnitude of the early fossils, 262.
Luther; on the right and duty of independent inquiry, 115. His exposition of the Mosaic narrative of the Creation, 122. His sound judgment and moderation; and vindication of rational inquiry, *ib.*
Lyell, Charles, jun. Esq.; his works recommended, 27, 158, 250, 319. Dr. Silliman's eulogy, 360. On the deposit of the Ganges, 46. On the earth's susceptibility of conflagration, 155. Remarks on his "Principles of Geology," 158, 352, 357. On the proportions of fossils and recent shells, 304. On successions of species, *ib.* Travels in North America, 100, 315. On the Niagara, *ib.* On the Delta of the Mississippi, 317. On the errors drawn from Sidonius, 335.
Mac Combie, (1842,) on the physical state of our first parents before the fall, 197.
Macculloch, John, M.D.; his works recommended, 251, 296. On the early strata, 291. On the immensity of the geological periods, 296.
Maclaren, Charles, Esq; his Geology of Fifeshire and the Lothians, 28, 55, 153. On the ancient beaches of Glen Roy, 299.
Man; only one species, 49, 270. Belongs to the most recent epoch of creation, 286, 312, 364.
Mantell, G. Algernon, Esq., L.L.D; his geological works recommended, 27, 187, 319.
Microscopic fossil animalcules, 67, 318.
Miller, Hugh; his illustrations of Drift, 90. On the old red sand stone, 313.
Mines; the deepest, 28.
Miracles; not to be rashly assumed, 60, 62, 106, 111, 113. Their nature, 62. Their design, propriety, and importance, 62. Supported by argument from Geology, 364.
Morton, Dr.; on skulls of American nations, 270.
Moses; his fidelity and divine mission inseparable from Christianity, 138, 140, 211, 361, 365, 368, 374, 380, 382. His manner of conveying divine truths, 171, 189, 194, 195, 370, 375, 376.
Motion; constant, but regulated, 26, 223, 230.
Mountains; the highest, 27, 112.
Mucous membrane of the human skin, 274.
Murchison, Sir Roderick Impey; his works recommended, 28. On successive creations, 50. His eulogium on Cuvier, 80. Illustrations of Drift, 91. On the organic remains of the early fossiliferous systems, 261. On the moral impression from geological phænomena, 189, 299. On the succession of fossils, 350. His "Silurian System," 261, 292, 300, 347.
Mythic hypothesis of the German Anti-supernaturalists, 372.
Mythology; Egyptian, 352.
Nature; on using the term as a substitute for the Deity, 74, 358, 392.
Neander, Aug. Prof. Berl.; on the errors of anthropomorphism, 173.
Nebular hypothesis; Prof. Nichol upon, 187.*
Northampton, Marquis of; his miscroscopic discoveries, 319.
Obligation, moral, 18, 227.
Oolitic formations, 303.
Organic remains, 41, 44, 57.
————, in the strata of the earth, 41, 241, 242, 261, 292, 300, 304, 308, 310, 349, 351, 393.
Owen, Dr. John; on 2 Pet. iii. 155.
——, Prof. Richard, M.D.; his researches, in fossil anatomy, 303.
Patrick, Bishop; on Genesis i. 126.
Penn, Granville, Esq.; his theories, 145.
Perère; his Præ-Adamites, 279.
Phillips, Prof. John; his works recommended, 27, 250. His geological map, 35. On the unbroken series of creations, 51. On the coal-beds, 345. On the gneiss, 290. On changes of species, 305.
Philosophy; ignorant declamation against, 123.
Phryganeæ; their habits, 308.
Phrygia, volcanic region of, 105.
Plutarch; on the Egyptian mythology, 355.
Poole, the commentator; on the Deluge, 209.
Population, antediluvian; not great, 205. Its seat, 207, 209.
Powell, Rev. Prof.; his belief of a religious spirit in philosophers, 37. His hypothesis on the Mosaic earliest records, 135, 137, 365. His valuable contributions to theology, 135. His remonstrance to objectors against the long periods established by Geology, 224. His protest against formal and traditional religion, 234. The author's obligation to him, 385. On explaining the fourth commandment, 381, His works on Tradition and Education. recommended, 135, 381.
Prichard, James Cowles, M. D; on animal regions, 48. On the unity of the human species, 49, 270, 280, 282. His inclination of opinion on the Deluge, 210. On affinities of remote nations, 270, 282. His "Natural History of Man," 281.
Prideaux, Bishop; on 2 Pet. iii., 155.
Puy de Dome; *see* Auvergne.

* To that Note, page 187, add:—For the more extensive information, and other rich treasures of Stellar and Solar Astronomy, consult Sir JOHN HERSCHEL's magnificent work, which presents 73 accurate and beautiful figures of nebulæ,—"Results of Astronomical Observations made during the years 1834, 5, 6, 7, 8, at the Cape of Good Hope; being the completion of a Telescopic Survey of the whole surface of the Visible Heavens, commenced in 1825:" royal quarto, 472 pages, London, 1847.

Quadrumanous fossil remains, 286.
Quarterly Review, on the volcanic region of Auvergne, 103, 334.
Quekett, Edwin J., Esq., on the Infusoria, 324.
Raffles, Sir T. S.; his account of volcanic devastation in Sumbawa, 230.
Reade, Rev. Joseph Bancroft; on the microscopic animalcules, 319.
Red Sandstone, Old; *see* Devonian.
Red Sandstone New; 292, 302.
Redemption; its importance and glory, 63.
Redford, Rev. Dr.; on the antiquity of creation, 127.
Regions of animal and vegetable nature; fossil, 45. Recent, 48, 64.
Religion; its necessary connexion with Theology, 10. The dignity and happiness of man, 114, 214. Its pure nature, 225. Its attractions, 233, 236.
Responsibility, 227, 234.
Revelation; its evidence, 11, 18. Its necessity, 24. Harmonious with science, yet using the then current style, 11, 136, 166, 172, 175, 179, 183, 194, 203, 213. Its style and illustrations adapted to the capacities of men, 172. Its employment of imagery derived from human nature, to represent the Deity, 165. Finally completed by Christianity, 183. Necessity of studying, with serious application, 225, 234.
Rhind, Mr. William; on the age of the earth, 153. His opinion upon vegetable structure, 338.
Richardson's (G. F., Esq.) "Geology for Beginners," recommended, 28.
Rocks; pyrogenous, 32, 299. Stratified, 34; *see* Stratification.
Roget, P. Mark, M.D.; on using the term *Nature*, 74.
Romaine, Rev. W.; on the manner in which the Deity is revealed, 212.
Rosenmüller, the elder; on the Mosaic records, 360.
Ross, Sir James Clarke; his Antarctic Voyage; and on the Baobab, 343. On the coal of Kerguelen's Island, 347.
Russeger, on the Baobab, 336.
Science; connexions of, 3, 5. Duty of cultivating, 214; by personal effort, 216. Its benefits, 226. Its tendency to religion, 304.
Scientific men; their advantages and responsibility, 233. Their high motives to piety, 234.
Scripture; the genuine sense to be sought, 18, 163, 172, 212, 384. Dissonance with Geology, only in superficial appearance, 52, 116, 212, 305. Not designed to convey philosophical knowledge, 138, 194, 361. Its certain truth, 163. Its condescending manner, 165. Its style with regard to natural objects, 173, 178, 180, 182, 193, 195, 305. Its manner and style in describing the Deity, 168, 172, 211. Injurious effects of not justly interpreting its figurative language, 224, 362.
Scrope, C. Poulett, Esq.; on the geological phænomena of Central France, 104. On the antiquity of the earth, 298.
Sea, depth of, 27.
Sea-beaches, 87, 298.
Sedgwick, Rev. Prof.; on the opponents of Geology, 21, 308. On its general character and interest, 22, 220. On diluvium and deluges, 96, 309. On Mr. Lyell's principal work, 158. On the misunderstanding of the figurative language of Scripture, 183. On symmetrical divisions of early rocks, 298. Observations in the Alps, 293. The author's obligations to him, 307. On the evidence of the earth's antiquity, *ib.*
Sediment, deposited by water, 46, 290, 293, 296, 347.
Sheppard, John, Esq.; his lecture on Fossil Osteology, and other works, recommended, 154.
Silliman, Benj. M.D., Prof. Yale College; on the duty of christian ministers to become acquainted with Geology, 225. On Coal-formations, 347.
Silurian System of rocks, 291, 292, 302, 350.
Smith, Dr. William; his services to Geology, 42.
Somerville, Mrs; on the distribution of plants, 65.
Species of animal remains; their range, 44. Number and proportion, 41, 44, 261, 304. Different regions, 45, 48. Vertical penetration, 47. Position, *ib.*
Species, human; varieties of, 270. Model race, 273. Characteristic differences, 279.
Sprengel, Kurt, M D., distinguished for his extraordinary attainments in classical and oriental learning, and in natural science;—his account of the Adansonia, 336.
Stillingfleet, Bishop; on the Deluge, 209.
Stonesfield fossil, 57, 303.
Strabo's opinions on some geological phænomena, 73.
Stratification; 30, 34, 38, 39, 246, 289, 294, 297, 309. Order, 30, 43, 160. Disposition and Texture, 34. Influenced by heat, 35. Erroneous reasoning upon, 347, 351.
Strickland and Hamilton, on the extinct volcanoes of Western Phrygia, 105.
Struve, F. G. W., Prof. Univ. of Poltawa; on the transmission of the stellar light, 257.
Subsidence, 37. At Axmouth, &c. 39.
Sumner, Dr. John Bird, Bishop of Chester; on concessions mutually of Geology and Biblical Science, 117. On the relation of the Mosaic records to Geology, 363.
Swainson, William, Esq.; on animal regions, 48.
Targum of Uzziel; on the creation of Man, 275.
Taylor, Rich, Esq.; Scientific Memoirs, 320.
——, Dr. W. C.; on the Egyptian antiquities, 276.
Tertiary strata; their constitution and extent, 294, 347. Their organic remains, 309.
Theology; its mental and practical nature, 10. Its alliances with all knowledge, and its harmony with sound philosophy, 383.

Time; its reference to Geology, 53, 55, 158, 285, 295, 298, 299, 302, 305, 309, 313, 314, 364.
Truth; scientific and religious, ever consistent, 18, 19. Its nature and various aspects, 13.
Turner, Edward, M.D.; his merits in geological and other science; his character, and his death, 235.
—— Sharon, Esq.; his observations on geological subjects, 150.
Universal geological formations; not admitted, 48.
Universe; dependent, 17. Distinction from the INDEPENDENT CAUSE, *ib.*
Vegetation; simple primitive distribution, 191.
Volcanic action, 29, 31, 32, 228.
Volcanoes of Auvergne, &c., 102.
Von Schouw; on vegetable regions, 49.
Wardlaw, Rev. Dr.; on the antiquity of Creation, 127.
Ware, Prof. Henry; on the Astral Universe, 257.
Water, fresh and salt, effects of, 111.
Watson, Rev. Richard; on the Mosaic descriptions, 211.
Whately, Dr., Archbishop of Dublin; recommendation of his works, 366, 370.
Whewell, Rev. Prof., D.D.; his general character of Geology, 220. On the law of change throughout the dependent universe, 307. On the labours and merits of Professor Sedgwick, 308.
Whyte; on the beginning of Genesis, 314.
Wilks, Rev. Samuel Charles; on geological doctrines, 144. His Poem, "The Fossil Shell," 151.
Wiseman, Dr., Rom. Cath. Bish.; on the opinions of the Fathers upon Genesis i., 125. On geological doctrines generally, 156. On the previous condition of the earth, 363.
Young, Rev. Dr. George; his geological opinions, 152. On universal expressions, 205. Observations on his book, "Scriptural Geology," 343.

THE END.

ROBERT E. PETERSON,

BOOKSELLER AND PUBLISHER,

N. W. CORNER OF FIFTH AND ARCH STREETS,

PHILADELPHIA,

Invites attention to the following valuable works, just published:

THE RELATION BETWEEN THE

HOLY SCRIPTURES

AND SOME PARTS OF

GEOLOGICAL SCIENCE.

By Rev. JOHN PYE SMITH, D. D., L. L. D., F. R. S., & F. G. S., Divinity Tutor in the Protestant Dissenting College at Homerton, Member of the Philological, Ethnological, Microscopical, and Palæontological Societies; and Honorary Member of the Natural History Society of Devon and Cornwall, and of the Washington, U. S. National Institute for the Promotion of Science: from the fourth London edition, greatly enlarged.
Octavo, cloth, $1,50.

From the English Papers.

Devoted to the truths of Revelation no less than to those of science, and regarding them both as proceeding from the same Divine source, he (the Author) will allow of no compromise, distortion or subterfuge, with respect to either.—*Annals and Magazine of Natural History.*

It places the justly esteemed author in the very first rank of scientific and philosophical theologians, and has already procured the enrolmeut of his name among the members of two of the most learned societies in Great Britain.—*Lancaster Guardian.*

From the Charleston Medical Journal and Review, Vol. 5, May 1850, No. 3, page 341. Foot-note to Letter to Rev. John Bachman, D. D., on the Question of Hybridity in Animals considered in reference to the Unity of the Human Species. By Samuel George Morton, M. D., Penna. and Edinb.—I regard this (Relation between Scripture and Geology, by the Rev. J. Pye Smith, L. L. D., 4th edition,) among the most instructive volumes that has issued from the press since the revival of letters, and for this reason—that it constitutes a link between Religion and Natural Science—studies which have hitherto been as isolated as if they were incompatible with each other. Mr. Robert E. Peterson, of Philadelphia, has the work in Press, and will shortly publish it in a style not inferior to the English Edition.

THE PRINCIPAL PROPHECIES AND TYPES

OF THE OLD TESTAMENT,

WITH THEIR FULFILMENT; ARRANGED IN THE VERY WORDS OF SCRIPTURE, FOR THE USE OF SUNDAY SCHOOLS.

BY THE REV. BENJAMIN DORR, D. D.,

RECTOR OF CHRIST CHURCH, PHILADELPHIA.

"The testimony of Jesus is the Spirit of Prophecy."—REV. XIX. 10.

The design of this work is to store the minds of the young with the principal texts of the Old Testament which relate to the coming and offices of our Redeemer, together with such passages of the New Testament as show their fulfilment. It was prepared for the Sunday Schools and Bible Classes connected with the parish under the author's charge. The manner of using it has been to give out as many verses as could be conveniently committed to memory at one time, and make these the subject of instruction and examination by the teachers in their respective classes. The same lesson is repeated each Sunday in the month; and on the last Sunday afternoon, when the children are catechized by the Rector, "openly in the church," they are questioned on the lesson of the preceding Sundays, and such explanations and illustrations are given, as time will permit, or as the subject may require.

After many years trial of this mode of Biblical instruction, connected with the catechising of the young in the presence of the congregation, the author has found it highly beneficial in his own parish, and he doubts not that most parochial ministers would find it equally useful in theirs.

He indulges the hope, at least, that this arrangement of the Prophecies and Types, relative to the Messiah, will be a help to Teachers in their endeavours to lead the lambs of Christ's fold to those good pastures and those well-springs of salvation, where they may be so nourished up in all virtue and godliness, that, "when the Chief Shepherd shall appear, they may receive a crown of glory that fadeth not away."—*Preface.*

Philadelphia, June 22, 1850.

From the Banner of the Cross, August 3, 1850.

THE PRINCIPAL PROPHECIES AND TYPES OF THE OLD TESTAMENT, WITH THEIR FULFILLMENT.—The author of this little work seems to have the happy faculty, no mean one, of giving us just such books as we want for the Church's use. He does not seem to be moved by the mere love of authorship, that worst form of self-love, but he bestows his labor upon a work to meet some want in the Church. Every Teacher must have felt the need of some assistant in this department of Biblical instruction. We speak now of those plainer Prophecies whose fulfillment is a clear exposition of their meaning. Herein, the Word of God must be "its own interpreter." And in this just view it is presented by the author of this little work. The Principal Prophecies and Types are given in one column, and then in another their fulfillment is presented in the language of the inspired writers. This best of expositions is not diluted or confused with needless comment or labored disquisitions. The Teacher, with very little trouble, can add all that is necessary, such as the time elapsing between the prophecy and its fulfillment, &c. The book is addressed "to the Superintendents and Teachers of Sunday Schools and Bible Classes." It is in a form and of a size well suited to its design.

From the Christian Chronicle, July 31, 1850.

THE PRINCIPAL PROPHECIES AND TYPES OF THE OLD TESTAMENT, WITH THEIR FULFILLMENT.—This is a small cheap book of about 75 pages, got up for the use of Sunday Schools by Dr. Beniamin Dorr, of this city. It will throw much light on many obscure passages, and will he found exceedingly valuable to the pupils of Sabbath Schools.

THE CHURCHMAN'S MANUAL,

BY THE

REV. BENJAMIN DORR, D. D.,

RECTOR OF CHRIST CHURCH, PHILADELPHIA.

THIRD EDITION, REVISED AND ENLARGED.

12mo., cloth, 75.

I do not hesitate to say that it will fully sustain the title which it bears, and deserves to be in *the hands of every Churchman.* As a family book for the instruction of Christian households in "the principles of the doctrine of Christ"—as a parish and Sunday school library book for the engagement and edification of the young—as a tractate to be put into the hands of all who are inquiring for "the truth as it is in Jesus"—as a guide to "the Gospel in the Church," so that all may read, so plain that all must understand it—thoroughly scriptural, practical, spiritual,—I commend it to the widest circulation, and implore for it the blessing of the Lord.

GEORGE W. DOANE,
Bishop of the Diocess of New Jersey.

From the Sunday School Visitor,

This excellent volume seems to unite all suffrages in its approval. Dr. Dorr has clearly shown in reference to the Protestant Episcopal Church that her doctrines are evangelical, her ministry apostolic, and her worship primitive and scriptural. The work before us is written in a truly Christian spirit. It can give offence to no one who feels a real desire to inquire after the truth as it is in Jesus.

From the Utica Gospel Messenger.

The prevailing excellence of Mr. Dorr's manual consists, as we think, in the distinct and unequivocal manner in which his several subjects are presented. They are brought forward under the following divisions:

Doctrines of the Church; Ministry of the Church; Worship of the Church; With an appendix containing three chapters *on Bowing at the name of Jesus; on Christ's descent into Hell; on the word "Catholic" in the Creed.*

We say to our readers get the book. Use it as a family volume, and let the young especially study and understand it. Every Churchman—ay, every one who desires to know what the Church is, should have one.

From the Episcopal Recorder.

It will be found a work of an interesting and useful character for those who are inquiring into the peculiar claims and characteristics of the Episcopal Church. It is compiled in a Christian and excellent temper.

From the Protestant Episcopalian—by late Rev. J. W. James.

Church people, and inquirers about our Zion, if they take this book and steadily peruse it, will find themselves frequently saying, "this is the very thing we wanted." To embrace all these subjects in a book of its size, it was necessary to study condensation and brevity; the author has done this and more: he has not indulged himself in spinning theories, in rounding sentences; but has evidently designed to explain and to instruct.

It may be safely and profitably put into the hands of any whose hearts are just becoming sensible of religious duties. We should be very much pleased if we could present a copy to every acquaintance we have.

From the Charleston Gospel Messenger.

Among the many excellent books, which leave all without excuse who choose to continue in ignorance of our Church, we know of none more likely than this, to answer the end designed by its author, of giving "some such compendious views of the doctrines, ministry, and worship of the Church" as may be "put into the hands of those who have neither time nor inclination to read voluminous works, that they may see at once what the Church has taught on these subjects." To such persons, and indeed to every one who would meet with the truth well expressed, and in few words, this manual may be warmly commended.

THE HISTORY

OF A

POCKET PRAYER BOOK,

WRITTEN BY ITSELF.

BY THE

REV. BENJAMIN, DORR, D. D.,

RECTOR OF CHRIST CHURCH, PHILADELPHIA.

THIRD EDITION, REVISED AND ENLARGED.

16mo, cloth, 50 cts.

From the Banner of the Cross—by Bp. Doane, under the name of "A Country Parson."

In taking up this little volume, after several editions, now greatly enlarged and materially improved, we seem to be looking into the face of a dear old friend. We set out with him again on his eventful journey, in all confidence that he will bring us out at the right place, and well satisfied that if the road be longer than it was, we shall only have so much more of his pleasant and instructive company. We really do not know a little volume so well fitted to go out with our missionaries into "the new countries," or to follow the faithful pastor in his daily round in any of our established parishes, urban or rural; and for young people—we have tried it on our own—it is scarcely less interesting, and a sight more profitable than Robinson Crusoe. It is a striking peculiarity, and a strong recommendation of this little volume, that though woven together with a thin, a graceful thread of fiction, the staple is all facts—the characters, those of the author's acquaintances, parishioners and friends, and the incidents mostly such as have really occurred in his own eventful pilgrimage. Such we know to have been, among many others, "the Union Church" and "the Lay reading," the visits to the Oneida Indians, first in the State of New York, and then at Green Bay, and the conversation with the good lady, who did not think she had such a naughty thing in her house as a book written by a Churchman, when nearly all the volumes in her library were such. The case of the Congregational minister, who found the Prayer Book "just the thing" to furnish his extempore prayers, is familiar to all who have read Dr. Chandler's interesting life of Dr. Johnson. To all who know any thing of our domestic missions, the names of Davenport, Phelps, and "Father Nash" will be as "household words." And many a time and oft have we sat delighted at the feet of that venerated mother in Israel, now with God, whose Saturday school (still flourishing in kindred hands and a kindred heart,) forms the charm of the fifteenth chapter. The author has enjoyed singular opportunities of acquaintance with the Church in all places and under all vicissitudes, and possesses a happy talent for relating what he has seen and turning it to good account. Simplicity, earnestness and devotion are blended in his little book with good taste and sound practical sense. To many it will be instructive, interesting to all. It deserves the widest circulation, and wherever it goes, will subserve the best interests of truth and piety.

From the North American and Gazette, July 29, 1850.

Dr. Dorr's Works.—An accident has delayed our notice of the two well known works by the Rev. Dr. Dorr,—*The Churchman's Manual*, and *The History of a Pocket Prayer Book*,—of both which, revised and enlarged by the author, a third edition has been recently issued by the publisher, Robert E. Peterson, Fifth and Arch streets. These books, which carry with them the strongest commendations of Bishop Doane, and the warm advocacy of various religious periodicals of high character, have attained to great popularity, and very large numbers of them have been, and continue to be, sold. They are, indeed, beautiful and attractive little works, which cannot but long maintain their hold upon the public favor.

THE PASTOR'S WIFE.

A MEMOIR OF MRS. SHERMAN,

OF SURREY CHAPEL, LONDON.

EDITED BY HER HUSBAND, THE REV. JAMES SHERMAN,

PASTOR OF SURREY CHAPEL.

WITH PORTRAIT.

Second Edition—12mo., cloth, $1.

This work is admitted by all who have read it to be the best biography ever written; the following are a few of its many recommendations:

From the Philadelphia Christian Observer.

This is an interesting memoir of a Christian lady, whose life was a bright illustration of the hallowed influences of the gospel in the culture and development of all that is lovely and of good report in female character. In the words of the Christian Witness —It is "one of the most tender, beautiful, instructive, and edifying narratives, that for a long time has come under our notice."

From the Episcopal Recorder.

Few Christians will rise from the perusal of this interesting portrait of a Pastor's Wife without uttering the wish that such mothers in Israel were increased a thousand fold.

From the Presbyterian.

Her well sustained spirit in affliction and her triumph in death, illustrates the genuineness of the religious principles which were the main-spring of all her actions. We can commend the memoir as possessing more than usual interest, and as having intrinsic claims to the popularity it has already received.

From the New York Evangelist.

There is much instruction to be derived from the volume, and much powerful incentive to faith and religious zeal. Mrs. S. visited Gräfenberg and the water cure establishment there; and the record of her journeys and experience is very ably made and remarkably interesting. We can commend the work to Christian women as highly suggestive, pleasing and profitable.

From the Pennsylvania Inquirer.

It contains a memoir of Mrs. Sherman, of Surrey Chapel, by her husband, and is said to form one of the most tender, beautiful, instructive and edifying narratives that ever appeared from the press. It indicates and displays all the virtues and graces of the Christian character.

From the New York Literary World.

It exhibits a career of activity in the duties connected with an English Dissenting Chapel, and is varied by a tour on the Continent through Germany in search of health, with a residenc eat Gräfenberg. The details of the latter establishment, with Priesnitz at its head, with the traveling incidents in Prussia, are of considerable interest; a representation of the Continent from a point of view not taken by ordinary tourists.

THE NATIONAL COOK BOOK.

BY A LADY OF PHILADELPHIA,

A PRACTICAL HOUSEWIFE.

12mo., 75 cts.

This work contains almost exclusively American dishes. It is very rich in receipts for pastry, tea and sweet cakes and preserves. Great pains have been taken to make the receipts clear, concise and practical, and it is confidently believed that the National Cook Book will supersede all others—and prove an invaluable assistant to all housekeepers.

From the Philadelphia Inquirer, June 19, 1850.

THE NATIONAL COOK BOOK.—Mr. R. E. Peterson, N. W. corner of Fifth and Arch streets, has just published a volume with this title. It is by a Lady of Philadelphia, a practical housewife, and contains no less than 578 recipes for making and cooking soups, fish, vegetables, sauces, pastry, sweet dishes, cakes, preserves, medicines for the sick, and miscellaneous preparations. The work is the result of many years experience; and the author has endeavored to furnish the information in the most precise and simple form, and in all cases has sacrificed style to minute detail. This Cook Book is *decidedly one of the best publications of the class that has ever appeared*, and from its plain, practical and comprehensive character, it cannot but prove eminently successful. Every housekeeper should possess a copy.

From the Philadelphia Public Ledger, June 19, 1850.

COOKERY.—When Cooper, the novelist, denounced all cooks in America, he must have had reference only to the ordinary domestics employed in families, who, professing to understand the whole art of cookery, from an egg to a venison steak, manage to spoil more meat in a week than would go to supply the Irish nation in that kind of food for a month. He certainly did not intend to include all the intelligent housewives in this country, many of whom can roast, boil, stew or bake equal to the best European cook who ever handled a skewer, flourished a baster, or kneaded floury particles into dough. The experiences of many of these ladies have found their way into books, and the National Cook Book, by a Lady of Philadelphia, published by R. E. Peterson, will show all the inexperienced how they may profit by the knowledge of others. The authoress has perfect confidence in her work, and to show the excellence of its teachings, she sent with the volume a cake prepared according to one of her own receipts, which we can vouch is as good an article of the kind as can be manufactured out of flour and fruit.

From the Saturday Evening Post, July 6, 1850.

THE NATIONAL COOK BOOK, by a Lady of Philadelphia, a Practical Housewife. Published by Robert E. Peterson, N. W. corner of Fifth and Arch streets, Philadelphia.

Here is a book that we can confidently recommend to our lady readers as one that will give great satisfaction—as our female acquaintances who have examined into its merits, speak of it in the very highest terms. It is not, as so many of the receipt books are, filled with receipts that are entirely useless to nine-tenths of the American housekeepers; but is a book calculated for the American *taste*, and plain but substantial and generous mode of living. Great care has been used in the wording of the receipts; so that they may neither be too diffuse, nor too concise.

The receipts for the sick room, some sixty in number, have been prepared according to the directions of eminent physicians of this city, and are an exceedingly valuable portion of the book.

The book itself is got up in a plain, substantial, serviceable style, calculated for use rather than ornament—and we predict will soon become, in fact as well as in name, the *National* Cook Book.

From the Baltimore American, July 1, 1850.

The National Cook Book.—This valuable work, lately published by R. E. Peterson, of Philadelphia, deserves of housekeepers much consideration, the simplicity of its arrangements and the receipts for making all kinds of Pastry, Tea and Sweet Cakes, and Preserves, Baking, Boiling, Stewing and Roasting, and more especially cooking for the sick, are clear and concise, so much so in fact, that if housekeepers go strictly by its rules they may depend upon always having good and healthy food, easy of digestion, and admirably calculated for the promotion of health and strength.

From M'Makin's Model Courier, July 6, 1850.

The National Cook Book, 300 pages, of Family, Culinary and Miscellaneous Receipts.—We have no doubt about its value, from the simple style in which they are "cooked up," for simplicity is with us a cardinal virtue. It is taken for granted that a plain, sensible style in writing, indicate a similar quality in experimental cooking; and hence we are free to commend a volume which like the present, must prove a very useful one to those amiable housewives who always study economy and comfort, as well as high seasoning and rich delicacies; a capital book of its kind.

From the Pennsylvanian, July 15, 1850.

Our enterprising friend, R. E. Peterson, N. W. corner of Fifth and Arch Streets, has published the National Cook Book, by a Lady of Philadelphia—a practical housewife. It is a work of great merit, and those who ought to know, pronounce it to be far superior to any thing of the kind that has appeared in many years.

From the Morning Post, (Pittsburgh) July 9, 1850.

Here is a book for the ladies, worth a thousand magazines filled with fashion plates. Nothing makes home more happy and comfortable than a pleasant wife and a well cooked meal. Let husbands, who are fond of wholesome living, buy this book for their wives.

From the Christian Chronicle, July 31, 1850.

The National Cook Book. By a Lady of Philadelphia.—This is a book of about 300 pages, is neatly and firmly bound, and gives specific rules for cookery of all descriptions. It has the reputation of being the best book of the kind, and may be consulted with advantage by all our female friends who pride themselves on setting a rich and fashionable table. It is published by R. E. Peterson, Fifth and Arch streets.

From Scott's Weekly Paper, August 3. 1850.

The National Cook Book.—The ladies of our household have been testing the recipes in this book for the past month, and they agree in pronouncing it the very best practical cook book that ever came under their notice. They have tried many, but to the National Cook Book they award high praise for the economy and excellence of its recipes.

THE BOOK OF CAGE BIRDS,

BY HENRY B. HIRST.

4th edition—1 vol. 12mo. cloth, 75 cts.

The following Advertisement to the first edition, is from the pen of the late Bernard Duke, the favorably known seedsman:

"The following work the publisher presents to the public with feelings of considerable gratification. That the want of a good publication of this description has long been severely felt he is well aware from the many inquiries at his establishment. Upon discovering this, he immediately took measures to insure the production of a complete and practical treatise on the various birds which are to be found, singly and collectively in an American Aviary. The book is written by a gentleman well known as one of the best practical Ornithologists of the day. This fact must give to the directions in its pages the fullest credit and reliance. The portion devoted to the Canary Bird (Fringilla serinus) is the most perfect description of its character and habits ever published; while the remainder displays the most correct judgment and scientific knowledge.

From M'Makin's Model American Courier.

The third edition of this scarce and popular book has been issued by R. E. Peterson, corner of Arch and Fifth streets, who has purchased of the widow of the late Bernard Duke the whole work, including the valuable copyright. Our readers who take any interest in the sweet songsters, generally know that the author of "The Book of Cage Birds" is our well-known poet, Henry B. Hirst, Esq. That gentleman—a true sportsman, for all seasons—is perhaps the best bird fancier in the country, and abundantly able to treat of birds as birds deserve to be treated. It is a complete practical treatise on the various birds which are to be found, singly or collectively, in an American aviary. Particular attention is, we perceive, bestowed upon that general favorite, the Canary Bird, and every thing in relation to their habits, treatment, &c., is set down in detail. So also of the Java Sparrow, the Linnet, Gold-Finch, Sky and Wood Lark, Bull-Finch, Black-Winged Summer Red Bird, Blue Linnet, Painted Bunting, Song Sparrow, Yellow Bird, Starling, Rice Bird, Magpie, Robin, Thrush, Blue and Mocking Birds, Parrots, Doves, and Partridges. In short, every bird that delights the eye, charms the ear, or ministers to a dainty appetite, is here exhibited in the author's most simple, captivating style. The brief but beautifully written preface is in itself a delightful treat to one cooped, if not caged, in a city office room. Like the sick man, in reading it we almost fancy ourselves out once more among the green fields and pleasant valleys.

ROBERT E. PETERSON IS ALSO AGENT FOR

GREENLEAF'S SERIES OF ARITHMETICS,

CONSISTING OF—

1. Mental Arithmetic, upon the Inductive Plan, designed for beginners. By Benjamin Greenleaf, A. M., Principal of Bradford Teachers' Seminary.
2. Introduction to the National Arithmetic, designed for Common Schools. Improved Stereotype Edition. 324 pp. half bound.
3. The National Arithmetic, for advanced Scholars in Common Schools and Academies. Improved Stereotype Edition. 360 pp. full bound.

Complete Keys to the Introductory and National—for Teachers only.

The above works are now used as text books, in the State Normal Schools in Massachusetts, under the direction of the State Board of Education; the Normal Schools in New York City; Rutger's Female Institute, New York; Brooklyn (N. Y.) Female Academy; Abbott's Female Academy, and Phillip's Academy, Andover, Chauncey Hall School, Boston; Bradford Female Seminary; Philip's Academy, Exeter; Young Ladies' Institute, Pittsfield; Worcester County High School, Worcester; Williston Seminary, East Hampton, Mass; together with the best schools in Boston, New York, Philadelphia, Richmond, Charleston, Savannah, Mobile, New Orleans, and other cities; and wherever the work has been introduced, it is still used with great success.

The recommendations of the above books, from various Teachers, are so numerous that it would fill up too much space in this Catalogue to publish them. Teachers desirous of selecting the best works for their schools, and of examining the above, are desired to apply for copies, which will be gladly furnished them.

R. E. PETERSON IS ALSO AGENT FOR THE

"MANUAL OF MORALS" FOR COMMON SCHOOLS,

212 pp., 16mo.

"Some work on Morals," says the Hon. Horace Mann, "which shall excite the sympathies as well as inform the intellect; which shall make children love virtue, as well as understand what it is, is the greatest desideratum of our schools." The following pages are an attempt to supply this want. The work is designed to be placed in the hands of every scholar of our public schools as soon as they are able to understand it, and to be studied like any other book.—[*Extract from the Preface.*]

This book has recently been adopted by the "Public School Society," of the City of New York, to be put into all their public schools, and also by the School Board of the City of Brooklyn, N. Y.

A distinguished friend of education, in Connecticut, writes as follows:—"*I have read with great interest the 'Manual of Morals;' it is the best book which has been published for years. It ought to be introduced into all of our schools.*"

☞ A Catalogue of my new and second-hand Theological, Classical, &c., Books, sent to all who request it by letter pre-paid.

www.ingramcontent.com/pod-product-compliance
Lightning Source LLC
LaVergne TN
LVHW011150110826
845150LV00006B/1204
* 9 7 8 1 4 2 5 5 4 6 6 0 1 *